S

This book introduces the student and the general reader to Shakespeare's tragedies and to many of the problems, both old and new, of interpreting them. Traditional questions and answers regarding the texts, as well as their realization in performance, are freshly examined, and it is shown how the plays do not offer easy or final solutions to the tragic dilemmas presented, but engage the reader and spectator in a debate with more than one possible outcome.

Each of the tragedies (*Titus Andronicus, Romeo and Juliet, Hamlet, Othello, King Lear, Macbeth, Julius Caesar, Antony and Cleopatra, Coriolanus, Timon of Athens,* and *Troilus and Cressida*) is examined separately, with discussions of its provenance, its stage history and critical history, and of the problems associated with its categorization as part of the 'tragic' genre. The analyses do not pretend to lead up to a single authoritative thesis; Professor Mehl's intention is rather to point out conventions, difficulties, possible solutions, and beauties within the plays, and in the ways they have been treated by critics and theatre-goers alike. He refers widely to a representative body of Shakespearian criticism, and provides a useful bibliography which indicates the best, as well as the most up to date, sources for a reader wishing to pursue individual themes further.

The book is carefully written, and should serve as a valuable introduction for anyone wanting to gain a sense of the richness of the plays and the diversity of debate and interpretation that has surrounded them.

Shakespeare's Tragedies
An Introduction

DIETER MEHL

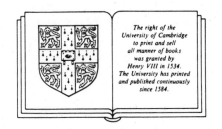

The right of the
University of Cambridge
to print and sell
all manner of books
was granted by
Henry VIII in 1534.
The University has printed
and published continuously
since 1584.

CAMBRIDGE UNIVERSITY PRESS

Cambridge

New York   Port Chester   Melbourne   Sydney

Published by the Press Syndicate of the University of Cambridge
The Pitt Building, Trumpington Street, Cambridge CB2 1RP
40 West 20th Street, New York, NY 1011-4211, USA
10 Stamford Road, Oakleigh, Victoria 3166, Australia

First published in German as *Die Tragödien Shakespeares: Eine Einführung* by
Erich Schmidt Verlag GmbH, 1983 and © Erich Schmidt Verlag GmnH, 1983

English translation © Cambridge University Press 1986

Published in English by Cambridge University Press 1986 as
Shakespeare's tragedies: an introduction
Reprinted 1987, 1988, 1991

Printed in Great Britain at
the Athenaeum Press Limited, Newcastle upon Tyne

British Library cataloguing in publication data
Mehl, Dieter
Shakespeare's tragedies: an introduction.
1. Shakespeare, William — Tragedies
I. Title   II. Die Tragödien Shakespeares.
English
822.3'3   PR2983

Library of Congress cataloguing in publication data
Mehl, Dieter
Shakespeare's tragedies.
Bibliography.
Includes index.
1. Shakespeare, William, 1564–1616 – Tragedies.
I. Title.
PR2983.M38   1986   822.3'3   86-9564

ISBN 0 521 30423 7 hardback
ISBN 0 521 31690 1 paperback

Contents

Preface

THE ORIGINAL VERSION OF THIS BOOK WAS WRITTEN AS AN
introduction to the study of Shakespeare's tragedies for German
students, and I can only hope that these interpretations will be of some
interest and use to English readers too. There is, of course, no lack of
critical aids of similar scope and it is not surprising that many books on
Shakespeare begin with an attempt to justify their existence. Yet it is
simply in the nature of great works of art that they refuse to be tied down
to any 'definitive' reading. Each generation has to discover its own
approach and even the most brilliant criticism, while it can make the task
a lot easier, tends to strike us as distinctly dated after some time.

It has not been my intention to offer a comprehensive guide to all
aspects of Shakespeare criticism or a handbook of facts and problems,
but to sharpen the reader's awareness of the undiminished vitality of
these plays. I have neither suppressed my own personal preferences nor, I
hope, presented an all too one-sided view of the texts. Above all I have
tried to encourage the kind of active collaboration of readers (and
spectators) that seems to me the chief end of good criticism. I have put
rather more emphasis on the dramatic characters than has been usual or
fashionable for some time because it is still through these characters that
most readers and theatre-goers begin to get interested in the plays. I have,
at the same time, tried to give a reasonably full account of previous
scholarship, of traditional problems and the more interesting controver-
sies. Again, this is bound to be selective and personal, but the sheer bulk
of Shakespearian criticism makes any other method equally questionable
and I hope, at least, that many of the most stimulating critics are
represented and that the reader is offered enough guidance to pursue his
own interests further if he wishes to.

It is hardly necessary these days to remind ourselves that Shakespeare's
tragedies were written first of all for performance, that they are the work
of a practitioner as much as of a poet. The theatre has, in fact, done more
to keep these plays, their poetry and their characters, alive than the

vii

scholars. But each new performance is, in the last resort, inspired by the same text, however freely it is treated, and the literary critic should not attempt to replace his explication of the text by an imaginary performance. Each production is, by its very nature, designed for a particular time and a particular audience, and even the most impressive performance is more transitory than what has survived of Shakespeare's words.

Of course, the student of Shakespeare should make himself familiar with the physical conditions and the practice of the Elizabethan theatre as well as with the history and the present state of Shakespearian production. The volumes of the new Oxford Shakespeare and the New Cambridge Shakespeare are particularly helpful in these matters. It is often astonishing to find how many problems of interpretation that have puzzled critics for centuries seem to vanish or appear in a new light when the printed text is transferred to the stage. I have tried to keep this in mind, even though I am primarily concerned with the words on the page and have only sporadically referred to questions of staging or to particular productions. At least, I am conscious that my appreciation of the tragedies owes as much to the theatre as it does to literary criticism.

The present book is a rather free translation, updated and revised in the light of discussions and impressions since the appearance of the German edition in 1983. Both the German and the English versions owe a great deal to the resources and to the hospitality of the Shakespeare Bibliothek in Munich, especially to Dr Ingeborg Boltz. This is, however, only a small part of my long association with Wolfgang Clemen and many of his pupils. Without his inspiring and generous scholarship this book would never have been written. It can only be a very modest and fragmentary expression of gratitude to a great scholar and teacher.

Marie-Theres Harst and Barbara Möller were reliable helpers when I was preparing the German edition. Throughout my work on the English adaptation I had the competent assistance of Christa Jansohn whose practical initiative and critical encouragement were a most valuable support. Jochen Meibrink did a very helpful amount of checking and compiled the index.

A note on the texts

AFTER SOME HESITATION, I HAVE DECIDED TO QUOTE THE TEXTS
not from one of the single-volume editions most frequently used, but
from what seemed to me the best and most up-to-date available edition of
each play. Thus, I have used either the Arden Shakespeare, the New
Penguin Shakespeare, the Oxford Shakespeare, or the New Cambridge
Shakespeare, with references to other editions, as the case may be.
The disadvantages of this procedure seem to me negligible: the line-
numbering hardly ever differs enough to cause real inconvenience. More
important is the advantage, to draw the reader's attention to the rich
choice of thorough and stimulating modern editions and to discourage
the illusion that there is such a thing as a definitive text.

I quote from the following editions:

Titus Andronicus, ed. Eugene M. Waith, The Oxford Shakespeare
(Oxford, 1984)

Romeo and Juliet, ed. G. Blakemore Evans, The New Cambridge
Shakespeare (Cambridge, 1984)

Hamlet, ed. Harold Jenkins, The Arden Shakespeare (London, 1982)

Othello, ed. Norman Sanders, The New Cambridge Shakespeare (Cambridge, 1984)

King Lear, ed. G. K. Hunter, The New Penguin Shakespeare (Harmondsworth, 1972)

Macbeth, ed. G. K. Hunter, The New Penguin Shakespeare (Harmondsworth, 1967)

Julius Caesar, ed. Arthur Humphreys, The Oxford Shakespeare (Oxford,
1984)

Antony and Cleopatra, ed. Emrys Jones, The New Penguin Shakespeare
(Harmondsworth, 1977)

Coriolanus, ed. Philip Brockbank, The Arden Shakespeare (London,
1976)

Timon of Athens, ed. G. R. Hibbard, The New Penguin Shakespeare
(Harmondsworth, 1970)

Troilus and Cressida, ed. Kenneth Palmer, The Arden Shakespeare
    (London, 1982)
Other editions are referred to in the notes.

1

Introduction:
Shakespeare and the idea of tragedy

WHEN THE EDITORS OF THE FIRST COLLECTED EDITION OF Shakespeare's plays (the First Folio of 1623) decided on a classification of the thirty-six plays they had assembled, they divided them into three groups, namely 'Comedies', 'Histories' and 'Tragedies'. In this they were making use of traditional generic terms that had hardly ever been seriously questioned and are still in use today, even though an exact definition or a clear distinction between them may not be possible in each particular case. The history play, to be sure, is largely a product of the Renaissance and has always occupied a rather special place, but comedy and tragedy have been firmly established types of drama almost from the beginnings of Western literature and theatre; they are among the most long-lived of all literary genres. Thus, tragedy, in spite of many variations in form and substance, has proved remarkably consistent, and this can hardly be explained by literary reasons alone. In common usage the word 'tragedy' denotes not just a form of drama, but a particular kind of event, a specific experience, or even a general view of our world-order. 'Tragedy' can mean some strikingly unhappy accident or a merciless, arbitrary destiny, a moral *exemplum* of just retribution or an unfathomable catastrophe, suggesting an essentially malevolent fate. As a rule, to be properly called tragedy, the disaster has to have an element of heroic pathos or some sensational and astounding quality. In the context of literature, tragic suffering implies an idea of dignity and of inevitability, of more than average stature, even though this may not be true of every single stage tragedy. The lasting impact of tragedy throughout the centuries can only be explained by the fact that its subject is more than some individual, regrettable misfortune. Any great tragedy touches on the fundamental questions of the ultimate cause of human suffering, the origin and nature of evil in man, and the existence of a destructive or benevolent fate. It is an expression of a universal desire to come to terms with these disturbing uncertainties.

In this connection, it is significant that in English, the word 'tragedy' appears for the first time in Chaucer's translation of Boethius' *Consolatio Philosophiae*, a work in which the experience of suffering and the feeling of utter helplessness produced by it are discussed with particular intensity. For Boethius and Chaucer, tragedy is an experience as universal as it is incomprehensible, an experience that makes the sufferer feel very much in need of explanation and consolation.

Chaucer explains the term for his readers as if it had been unfamiliar to them before:

Tragedye is to seyn a dite of a prosperite for a tyme, that endeth in wrecchidnesse.[1]

By his fall from a state of happiness and prosperity into misery, man is forced to face the problem of guilt, destiny and divine providence.

Shakespeare's tragedies, though shaped by very different literary conventions, have to be seen within this tradition. Lear's agonized question, 'Is there any cause in nature that makes these hard hearts?' (*King Lear*(III.6.76–7)), is repeated, in some form or other, in nearly all his tragedies. Man's bewildered attempt to come to terms with suffering, loss, or disillusionment is at the heart of almost every tragedy of his age. The problems of tragic guilt, catharsis and Christian redemption in Shakespearian tragedy that have been debated time and again in Shakespeare criticism, are all aspects of this impact.

It is much more difficult, however, to find a less general common denominator for Shakespeare's tragedies. Most critics are agreed that these plays do not follow a fixed literary pattern, though not all would go as far as Kenneth Muir, who begins his own survey with a warning that has often been quoted since:

There is no such thing as Shakespearian Tragedy: there are only Shakespearian tragedies.[2]

True enough, the twelve plays gathered under the heading 'Tragedies' in the First Folio are so different from each other – leaving aside the problem that they include *Troilus and Cressida* and *Cymbeline* – that so far there has been no successful and convincing attempt to formulate a definition applicable to all of them. Either a group is singled out, such as the 'great' tragedies, while others are ranked below them as deviations from the ideal type; or else the common features listed are so general that they could just as well apply to many other plays, either by contemporaries of Shakespeare or even from very different periods. This difficulty is to be attributed above all to the undogmatic delight in experiment that is so characteristic of many Elizabethan dramatists who, unworried by any fixed poetic precepts or narrowing conventions, produced a multiplicity of forms that resists any neat systematization. As to subject-matter, form, dramaturgy and language, the Elizabethan dramatist had so many options before him that the diversity of plays, even when composed almost simultaneously, is often astonishing. *Othello*, *Macbeth* and *King Lear* are so different from each other that it is very difficult to say anything useful that applies to them all. If we include Shakespeare's other tragedies, the diversity becomes so overwhelming that Kenneth Muir's pragmatic refusal to accept any abstract model is all too understandable.[3] He is, of course, aware of the fact that the historical and literary context imposes certain limits, wide and indistinct though they may be, and provides certain models not really valid for other periods in the history of drama, so that none of Shakespeare's tragedies, for all their diversity, could really be confused with a play by Sophocles, Racine, Schiller or Ibsen. The history of the reception of Shakespeare's plays suggests, moreover, that many generations of playgoers and readers have found his tragedies to be something very special and unmistakable. They are certainly more than just an arbitrary collection of individual plays and they keep challenging the critic to find some common elements even though it is, in the last resort, much more interesting and rewarding to study the specific shape and substance of each tragedy by itself.

Chaucer's definition of tragedy in the context of his translation of Boethius has already made clear that for him, 'tragedy' was not in any way related to drama or theatre, but referred to a particular type of story or rather story-pattern. Chaucer himself gave a demonstration of this in the monotonous series of sad stories contributed by the Monk to the *Canterbury Tales* and, more seriously, in his *Troilus and Criseyde*, an ambitious epic poem he himself calls a tragedy, which draws on some central ideas of Boethius, describing the 'double sorrow' of the hero in the context of a running debate about the causes of misery, the power of capricious fortune and the problems of free will. It is certainly the most moving tragic work of literature in English before Shakespeare. Other works that have been discussed as antecedents or models of Renaissance tragedy, such as Boccaccio's *De Casibus Virorum Illustrium* (1355–60) or the Elizabethan collection of 'tragedies' published and repeatedly augmented under the title *Mirror for Magistrates*, often reduce the tragic to a pathetic account of a 'fall': the lamentable descent of a formerly powerful and prosperous person becomes a tragedy in the narration.[4] This aspect is taken up in Shakespeare's *Richard II* (often described as a tragedy by critics) where the King presents his own pitiful situation as an occasion for retelling the tragedies of others:

> For God's sake let us sit upon the ground
> And tell sad stories of the death of kings,
> How some have been deposed, some slain in war,

> Some haunted by the ghosts they have deposed,
> Some poisoned by their wives, some sleeping killed,
> All murdered.   (III.2.155–60)[5]

This sounds like a brief summary of collections of 'tragedies' in the sense of Chaucer's Monk or the authors of the *Mirror for Magistrates*; later in the play, the King talks of his own story as 'the lamentable tale of me' (V.1.44) that will move later listeners to tears. Such utterances suggest that for the Elizabethans too, the subject and its application was more important as the essence of tragedy than any formal conventions. Seneca's tragedies, for instance, often discussed as important models for Elizabethan tragedy, were only one among many different influences and certainly did not determine either its form or its tragic themes.[6] It is true of Shakespeare, as of most of his contemporaries, that each of his tragedies tries out new ways, from the choice of subject to its scenic presentation, without being cramped by many abstract concepts, such as the classical unities of time, place and plot, or rigorous ideas of linguistic decorum.

The only thing that seems to be, at first sight, really indispensable for Elizabethan tragedy is a marked turn of fate, ending in the hero's destruction. In the simpler forms of the *de-casibus* tragedy the fall of the protagonist is a demonstration either of man's guiltless subjection to an unpredictable fate or capricious fortune or else of well-deserved punishment for criminal wickedness or overweening pride. In more subtle ways, these questions have been endlessly debated by Shakespeare critics over the last three centuries: the hero's downfall is explained by some 'tragic flaw', some recognizable weakness of character or fatal error. That the tragic ending is, if not a just retribution, then at least a kind of sacrificial atonement for an offence against the moral order, is the view of those critics in particular who try to understand the tragedies from the standpoint of Christian orthodoxy. It is only too easy, however, to overestimate the didactic definiteness of Shakespeare's plays. In this respect, there seems to be a fundamental difference between the medieval morality plays or many overtly didactic plays by contemporaries, and his own kind of drama, which leaves much of the moral evaluation and application to the individual member of his audience.

This explains, at least in part, the number of contradictory, even mutually exclusive interpretations of the tragedies, but at the same time it has contributed to the lasting impression the plays have made on the most diverse kinds of readers. It is, of course, a commonplace, often repeated, that each generation finds in Shakespeare what it is looking for, but this is not an invitation to arbitrary reading, rather a manifestation of a shared experience: Shakespeare does not impose on his audience a ready-made appraisal of the dramatic events and characters; rather he confronts us with surprises, incongruities and contradictions to provoke doubt and second thoughts. One only has to compare one of Shakespeare's tragedies with any of the countless smoothing or simplifying adaptations – from Dryden's *All for Love* to Edward Bond's *Lear* – to become aware of the difference between an undogmatic, continually stimulating work of art and one that seems quickly exhausted and will hardly ever spark off any creatively controversial debate. This is also why no interpretation should aim at relieving the reader of the effort to face the coexistence of conflicting points of view and to come to terms with undogmatic indefiniteness.

The question, certainly of central importance, of the relationship between tragedy and Christian beliefs provides an instructive example. It is, no doubt, a simplification to claim that tragedy and Christian orthodoxy are basically incompatible.[7] On the other hand, Elizabethan tragedy strikes us as most disturbing where it does not simply confirm traditional tenets or generally accepted moral principles, but presents without mitigation the experienced reality of evil, the unpredictability of human nature and man's helplessness in the face of a fate that seems indifferent if not hostile. Few readers will perceive an untroubled affirmation of a justly and reasonably ordered world in Shakespeare's tragic endings, and if they do, it must be their own assurance, not the play's. Kenneth Muir's comment on *King Lear* can be applied, though with differing emphasis, to nearly every tragedy by Shakespeare or one of his more interesting contemporaries:

The play could not have been written in the ages of faith, but neither could it have been written in an age of unbelief or an age of reason. At the beginning of the seventeenth century the right conditions existed: a universal Christian society, but with some of its basic tenets called in question by intellectuals; a realisation that the qualities which make for success are not the basic Christian virtues; and the beginnings of a conflict between science and faith.[8]

The unmistakable dynamic quality of Elizabethan tragedy comes from the discovery of the individual human character, from a burning interest in its potentialities for good or evil, its corruptibility as well as its exhilarating power to inspire and impress:

What piece of work is a man, how noble in reason, how infinite in faculties, in form and moving how express and admirable, in action how like an angel, in apprehension how like a god: the beauty of the world, the paragon of animals –

(*Hamlet* II.2.303–7)

Hamlet here describes one of the fundamental discoveries of the Renaissance, but his own attitude mirrors the dilemma on which this tragedy – and not just this one – is based:

5

and yet, to me, what is this quintessence of dust? (308)

The biblical allusion to man's transitory nature is a moving reminder of the precariousness and uncertainty of humanist optimism.

All this may help to explain why, from the beginning, problems of character, above all of the protagonist's character, have been at the centre of most discussions of Shakespearian tragedy; for the spectator, too, the impact of a Shakespeare play is produced most of all by the characters, even though Shakespeare criticism has from time to time appeared to deny this and concentrated on other aspects of the plays.

This does not at all mean that interpretation is reduced to psychological speculation or that we confuse the plays with the more realistic literature of later ages. Nor does the refusal to discuss the plays in narrowly theological or eschatological terms necessarily imply that we deny the presence of supernatural agencies or the reality of religious experience. However, in their painful struggle with destructive forces within themselves or from the world outside, Shakespeare's heroes receive no help from any power beyond. Providence and fate are hardly ever blamed for the hero's downfall, at least not alone. Even where the concept of tragic guilt can hardly be applied, as, for instance, in the early tragedy *Romeo and Juliet* or the late *Timon of Athens*, we are made to feel that tragedy is a matter of human responsibility and moral decisions rather than of an anonymous Fortune.

Thus, we can hardly describe Shakespearian tragedy in terms of external action and story-pattern alone. In nearly every case, the real tragedy is produced by the protagonist's experience, his realization that he himself or what is most dear to him has been destroyed and that he has to face this sense of utter and final loss.[9] As a rule, however, this is not only a question of the individual's disillusion, since the hero's hopes and disappointments are experienced within the context of a community whose peace and happiness are closely related to the fate of its most prominent members. Romeo and Juliet are agents and victims of the family feud that threatens the internal order of Verona; Hamlet is heir to the throne of Denmark and his life is most closely associated with the political health of the state; even Othello's downfall is by no means presented as a 'domestic tragedy' only, but is firmly set within a political and social context. The interdependence of conflict within the individual character and the claims of the community is crucial for Shakespeare's idea of tragedy. Thus, a much larger number of characters is usually involved in or at least vaguely connected with the protagonist's fate than, for instance, in Greek tragedy, and they are often quite different in social rank. The protagonists are surrounded by a more or less diversified group of minor figures some of whom are drawn into the catastrophe against their will or are deeply affected by it. In the histories, the moral and political foundations of society and the threats of its precarious order are the central concerns, but this aspect is never really lost sight of in the tragedies either.

As far as the hero's individual character is concerned, Shakespeare's tragedy is not confined to a narrow range of types. Although, in a very general sense, Aristotle's famous dictum that there should be no completely good nor any completely bad character in tragedy seems to be observed, it would be difficult to discover many character traits common to Hamlet, Othello and Macbeth that would be very helpful in understanding their tragedies. If in spite of this, most readers get the impression that Shakespeare's tragedies somehow belong together and are noticeably different from the tragedies of his contemporaries, this is due to the sheer power and wealth of his poetical language, his inventive dramaturgy, and his surprising range of insights into human character more than to any clearly definable common elements of plot or theme. The impact of his tragedy is so complex and changeable because it is not produced by one single character or one clear-cut conflict, but by the way the reader is confronted with a whole world in which an often rather mixed group of human beings are trying to find their way, even though the hero's dilemma often overshadows all other concerns. This is why many interpretations of the tragedies attempt to elucidate the interplay of character constellation, plot and thematic associations and these recurring questions alone tell us something about the literary form of Shakespearian tragedy.

The real substance of the tragic conflict – most critics seem to be in basic agreement on this – can only be understood in moral categories, by the experience that there is a fundamental opposition of good and evil determining all human intercourse but resisting any simple explanation and never smoothed over by unambiguous type-casting or an uncritical application of poetical justice. The spectator is not put at his ease by a comforting distribution of reward and punishment; he is confronted, without homiletic soft-soaping, with the reality of wickedness and its power to corrupt the good, to make the world poorer and more hopeless. The history of Shakespeare criticism shows how very differently whole generations of readers as well as individual readers have reacted to the dramatist's habit of disappointing conventional expectations, but wherever this has led to attributing to the plays either a depressing lack of firm orientation or else an emphatic affirmation of moral order and humanist (or Christian) optimism, essential aspects of the tragedies and often even their most original qualities were left out of account or completely lost sight of. The most helpful and stimulating interpretations, however, are those aware of the intensity of doubt and bewilderment as well as of the presence of a moral order wanting to be realized in human society, a common desire for goodness and stability. Bradley's classical definition of Shakespearian tragedy may sound a little too much like a semi-theological 'system' and does not quite speak in the language of our own generation and its literary criticism, but I do not think it has really been surpassed either in the force of pregnant expression or depth of insight:

Shakespeare was not attempting to justify the ways of God to men, or to show the universe as a Divine Comedy. He was writing tragedy, and tragedy would not be tragedy if it were not a painful mystery ...
We remain confronted with the inexplicable fact, or the no less inexplicable appearance, of a world travailing for perfection, but bringing to birth, together with glorious good, an evil which it is able to overcome only by self-torture and self-waste. And this fact or appearance is tragedy.[10]

Critics of a later generation who tell us that we come away from *King Lear*, for all the despair and suffering it so mercilessly presents, with the conviction that it is better to be Cordelia or Edgar than Goneril or Edmund obviously mean something very similar.[11] It is, of course, in the first place a description of individual subjective impressions, but these are supported by very clear statements and signals in the text which the reader has to become sensitive to, perhaps with the help of perceptive critics. Any reader who finds in the tragedies only despair and defeat is in danger of imposing his own convictions on the text just as, on the other side, the critic who is sure of his own Christian point of view believes he alone is able to 'reach the heart of tragedy'.[12] If we approach the texts with an open mind we will not be content with simple alternatives nor try to fix the dynamic movement of dramatic action by inflexible definitions which are all too often inappropriate for any work of creative fiction and for Shakespeare's tragedies in particular.[13]

A NOTE ON THE PROBLEM OF CLASSIFICATION

The heterogeneous nature of Shakespeare's tragedies, not ruled by any strict formal conventions, makes classification problematic and not particularly relevant. Any kind of grouping according to action or theme is based only on some partial common denominator and may be useful for the larger area of Elizabethan drama, but is not very satisfactory for Shakespeare's tragedies. To group *Romeo and Juliet*, *Othello* and *Antony and Cleopatra* together as 'love tragedies' can help us to become aware of important connections and developments.[14] Other labels, like 'revenge tragedy', 'tragedy of intrigue' or 'tragedy of power', are less useful when it comes to Shakespeare's plays. The bracketing of *Hamlet*, *Othello*, *King Lear* and *Macbeth* as Shakespeare's 'great' or 'mature' tragedies, largely due to Bradley's authority, has, for all its subjectiveness, been sanctioned by tradition. The same can be said of the Roman plays, evidently linked by their subject and Shakespeare's source. One should, perhaps, not attach too much importance to the problem of classification because any grouping can illuminate certain essential connections while at the same time drawing artificial dividing lines.

For the purposes of my own survey I have arranged the plays partly according to chronological aspects and partly according to their subject matter, not to replace familiar classifications by a new one, but to point out certain patterns and parallels and, above all, to stand as little in the way of an appreciation of each individual play as possible. It seems to me important to note, however, that Shakespeare's source and the nature of the plot he chose to dramatize are more important for the form of each tragedy than any formal models or conventions, even though, as in the case of the Roman plays, the source was very little help to the dramatist as far as scenic arrangement was concerned. *Troilus and Cressida* and *Timon of Athens* were, presumably, very much affected by particular stage conditions and by their transmission, but it is also worth noting that they are both dramatizations of classical stories. *Hamlet, King Lear* and *Macbeth* make use of legendary history and this links these plays together, as much as the fact that Shakespeare's art of tragedy seems to have reached its peak with these tragedies. *Othello* occupies something of a special place among the 'great' tragedies, which is partly explained by Shakespeare's use of an Italian *novella*; this in turn accounts for the love theme and, perhaps, for the prominence of comic elements in the play. Whether one considers similarities with *Hamlet* and *King Lear* to be more important than those with *Romeo and Juliet* and *Antony and Cleopatra*, or vice versa, largely depends on the way one looks at the plays and need not be decided here. Date and literary context provide good reasons for grouping the two early tragedies, *Titus Andronicus* and *Romeo and Juliet*, together; the traditional four 'great' tragedies can be seen as a series of attempts to widen the scope of the tragic hero's experience in various directions. Lastly, the Roman plays and the other two tragedies on classical subjects are usefully seen together. The arrangement is not, however, of crucial importance for this study, which is concerned primarily with the plays themselves, not with any all-embracing system, and makes no claim to present a general theory of Shakespearian tragedy.

2

The early tragedies

ALTHOUGH SEVERAL OF SHAKESPEARE'S EARLY PLAYS CANNOT BE dated with complete certainty, we can confidently assume that his first two tragedies, *Titus Andronicus* and *Romeo and Juliet*, along with two of the histories that come closest to tragedy, *Richard III* and *Richard II*, are separated from the later tragedies by an interval of a few years.[1] After that, it seems hardly possible to group the tragedies chronologically. At the beginning of his career as a dramatist, however, Shakespeare evidently experimented with various forms of tragedy available at the time, wrote his cycle of history plays and then turned to comedy. With *Julius Caesar* and *Hamlet* he returned to tragedy and these two plays show very clearly how much Shakespeare's own style and, presumably, the tastes of his audience had changed in that short space of time.

Both *Titus Andronicus* and *Romeo and Juliet* appeared in print fairly soon after their first performance and must have been very successful. *Romeo and Juliet* has always been one of the best-loved and most frequently performed of Shakespeare's plays while *Titus Andronicus* is, by and large, appreciated only by specialists and is rarely seen on stage. This is not necessarily an absolute indication of artistic inferiority, but, if anything, evidence of striking differences in the longevity of literary conventions and of unpredictable changes in taste.

TITUS ANDRONICUS

Shakespeare's first tragedy, it seems, is based on conventions that were out of fashion less than a generation after its first performance.[2] We may deduce this from the often quoted allusion to the play in the 'Induction' to Ben Jonson's comedy *Bartholomew Fair* of 1614, where the individual playgoers' judgements and tastes are satirically discussed. One particular type of playgoer, the sort who stubbornly refuses to adapt his opinion to changing tastes, is characterized as 'He that will swear *Jeronimo* or *Andronicus* are the best plays yet, shall pass unexcepted at, here, as a man whose judgement shows it is constant, and hath stood still, these five and twenty, or thirty years. Though it be an ignorance, it is a virtuous and staid ignorance.'[3] Such a jibe suggests that *Titus Andronicus*, here bracketed together with the even more obsolete *Spanish Tragedy*, was once far more popular than at the time of *Bartholomew Fair* and was considered rather *passé* by the more judicious in 1614. How far this also applies to *Romeo and Juliet* is difficult to say, but the conventions of love-poetry in general suffered much less radically from the changes in literary taste than the revenge tragedy.[4]

Titus Andronicus has never regained its popularity, though on the whole the stage has taken more kindly to it than the critics. An adapter of the late seventeenth century, trying to rescue the play for the Restoration stage, says in his preface: ''tis the most incorrect and indigested piece in all his Works; It seems rather a heap of Rubbish then a Structure' and he denies that Shakespeare gave more than 'some Master-touches to one or two of the Principal Parts or Characters'.[5] For a long time, this view reflected the general critical estimate of the play. Peter Brook's brilliant production at Stratford in 1955, with Laurence Olivier convinced many spectators that *Titus Andronicus* was a considerable play and could only be by Shakespeare, but in the long run neither the stage nor a majority of readers have really been able to warm to this tragedy. Shakespeare criticism of the last decade or two has, however, drawn our attention to some remarkable qualities of the play which closely relate it to pre-Shakespearian tragedy, but also to Shakespeare's later tragedies, and which had gone unrecognized for a long time. Unless one is content with the superficial impression that this is nothing but a gratuitously blood-thirsty and cruelly sensational potboiler, one has to take the trouble to look a little more closely at some of the conventions and assumptions behind the text. This will certainly not convince many readers that the play is a hitherto unappreciated masterpiece and I am not attempting to turn all its immaturities and incongruities into virtues, but I think that the beginnings of Elizabethan tragedy and many of its formal as well as thematic conventions can be much better appreciated if we start from *Titus Andronicus* and do not try to confine our attention to those tragedies that are more easily accessible to the modern reader.

Subject matter and dramatic technique suggest the influence of Senecan tragedy as it was received by the Elizabethan dramatists. As in comedy (see Shakespeare's adaptation of Plautus in *The Comedy of Errors*), Shakespeare seems to have been very much under the influence of classical models when he began writing tragedy, though even *Titus Andronicus* shows close affinities to the popular theatre, a very independent handling of the correct classical form and a concentration on themes that are very far from Seneca.[6] To be sure, the story is taken from legendary Roman history; there are many references to classical mythology, not all of them necessarily suggested by the dramatic events; the climax is reached in such literal parallels as the rape of Lavinia, a repetition and even outdoing of Ovid's story of Philomela, or the cannibalistic meal served by the revenger to his enemies, a new version of the myth of Atreus dramatized in Seneca's *Thyestes*. Moreover, the unmitigated presentation of extreme passions, in suffering as well as in inflicting pain hardly seems possible without the influence of Seneca, modified by the conventions of the Elizabethan popular theatre.[7] This close relationship to classical tradition, the learned rhetoric, and the most unrealistic stylization of the dramatic events make it more than likely that the play was by no means designed to appeal to crude audiences, eager for superficial sensationalism and unable to appreciate any more sophisticated effects, but aimed at a synthesis of bookish classical tradition and the dramatic representation of strong emotions and violent action. This is confirmed by the way Shakespeare adapted his source material which is not unlike his method in the later tragedies.

We are not quite certain about Shakespeare's immediate source. Apart from a ballad entered in the Stationers' Register in 1594, but only extant in a print of 1620, there is a prose history of Titus Andronicus published in an eighteenth-century chapbook which may well be a reprint of a much older pamphlet and is now assumed by many scholars to be Shakespeare's main source.[8] It is a sensational narrative about the last, barbarian phase of the Roman Empire, emphasizing the violence and horror of the events described and not concerned with any deeper motivation or rhetorical stylization. Comparison with the play shows how deliberately Shakespeare has selected, condensed and shaped the individual episodes and linked them so as to form a thematically unified chain of events. At the same time, he made skilful use of dramatic conventions, gleaned mainly from Thomas Kyd's *Spanish Tragedy* and Christopher Marlowe's *Jew of Malta* so that the prose narrative becomes a series of memorable stage tableaux, intensified by highly elaborated rhetoric and spectacle. The political context is more sharply articulated and the gruesome family history thus becomes a metaphor of the bloody mutilation of the commonwealth by unscrupulous ambition and selfish discord.

The beginning and the ending of the tragedy show surprising similarities with Shakespeare's histories. Rome's victory over the barbarians could be the beginning of a period of internal peace and prosperous harmony. However, reckless egotism among those called upon to provide responsible leadership produces latent hatred and, finally, an internecine holocaust until a new ruler emerges from the general bloodbath who proclaims to the survivors his noble intentions for a new beginning. The fatal crimes are recapitulated, the dead lamented, and the spectators, on stage and in the auditorium, are urged to mark the lessons taught by history and to value the blessings of unity. It is not very different from the endings of *Richard III*, *Hamlet*, *King Lear* or *Macbeth*:

> You sad-faced men, people and sons of Rome,
> By uproars severed, as a flight of fowl
> Scattered by winds and high tempestuous gusts,
> O, let me teach you how to knit again
> This scattered corn into one mutual sheaf,
> These broken limbs again into one body; (v.3.66–71)

It is obvious that Shakespeare added this frame to the story he found in his source, thus giving thematic coherence to the apparently arbitrary horror of the events described.

On the level of characterization, too, the dramatist has motivated the individual episodes more consistently so that they are not just entertaining fragments of a story, but reveal something about the actors involved. Thus, it is Titus' disastrous mistake in the first scene that sets in motion the fatal train of events. Like Lear in the later tragedy, he offends against elementary laws of the community, not from any criminal intention, but from lack of insight into the true situation as well as the foreseeable reaction of those he has hurt and estranged by his decision. By the revolting sacrifice of the young Prince of the Goths, Rome descends to the level of the defeated barbarians; the spectators can only agree with Tamora who, beseeching the victor to spare her son's life, speaks of 'cruel, irreligious piety' (1.1.130). In the further course of the action, too, Titus shows himself to be a ruthless representative of traditional Roman 'virtue' whose stubborn enforcement weakens his own authority and makes implacable enemies for himself. He creates the irresponsible Saturninus Emperor, kills his own son, and is unable to prevent his daughter becoming the object of a fierce fight for possession. Thus, after the very first scene, the glorious victory is practically given away and the imminence of deadly conflict seems inevitable.

The political aspects of the story fade into the background during the following scenes, yet the 'frame' determines the scope and the public character of the action and it is taken up again in the last scene when Titus' son accepts the rule and becomes Emperor by common consent.

The crimes Shakespeare found in his source are presented in such a way that they form dramatic scenes that would remind Elizabethan theatre-goers of Kyd and Marlowe and might thus become more easily intelligible: the vicious Aaron has been turned into the Machiavellian stage villain whose color and race are an emblem of his unprecedented wickedness and totally corrupted nature; the combination of prurient lecherousness, inventive cruelty and complete indifference to any moral appeal place him somewhere between Marlowe's Barrabas and Shakespeare's Iago. With both of them he shares elements of the diabolic Vice figure of the moralities who draws the audience into his confidence and reveals his devilish designs in extrovert soliloquies.[9] Even in his last moments he shows no signs of regret or repentance, but remains hardened in his proudly confessed and flaunted wickedness. The catalogue of his crimes, recited with triumphant gusto, can hardly be understood as realistic self-expression, but rather as an effective rhetorical aria by a consummate stage villain whom the audience has to accept as a conventional ingredient of tragedy.

Another feature of the play which is very characteristic of a certain type of revenge tragedy, fully developed in *The Spanish Tragedy* and still unmistakably present in *Hamlet*, is Titus' change from the self-assured ruler and victor to a shattered old man whom excessive grief has bereft of reason and whose mad raving is a pathetic expression of his impotent search for justice. He becomes the lonely victim of universal injustice and a social outcast, fruitlessly railing against society and increasingly incapable of any effective planning, like Kyd's Hieronymo, the often quoted and imitated model for all later revengers. The later 'Additions' to the *Spanish Tragedy* show that it was this aspect more than any other that tempted adapters to improve on the play by adding even more extreme manifestations of a deeply disturbed mind.[10] The banquet scene in *Titus Andronicus* (III.2), first printed in the Folio of 1623, might well be a similar kind of 'addition'; it does not contribute anything vital to the action, but presents the revenger's mental collapse by his grotesque fit of anger at the mere fate of a fly, revealing again his monomaniac obsession with justice and retribution. The weird trial scene in *King Lear* (III.6), hardly less bizarre, but much better integrated in the dramatic action, is part of the same tradition. Titus' madness begins as the mask of the revenger who, like Hamlet, tries to hide his grief and revulsion from those around him in order to plan his vengeance, but, overwhelmed by the experience of triumphant evil, loses all control over his own actions and descends to the same level of unbounded brutality as his adversaries. The repulsive atrocities themselves Shakespeare found in his source. Whether the story was really quite unsuitable for the stage in any form or whether he managed to make the gruesome tale somewhat more intelligible to the audience is the question we must try to answer if we want to evaluate the play.

The answer will certainly be negative if we look at the events from the point of view of familiar psychology, even though the extraordinary vitality of Aaron makes the revolting cruelties to Titus and his family more acceptable as part of the conventions of revenge tragedy, and Titus' hysterical longing for revenge prepares us for the unprecedented ghastliness of his vengeance. An audience whose expectations were formed by Seneca and classical accounts of crime and punishment would hardly be shocked by *Titus Andronicus*, especially as the play openly admits its indebtedness to classical tradition at every turn. The spectator who had seen the plays of Kyd and Marlowe would also understand without difficulty that the tragedy confronts us with characters larger than life, not to be judged by the standards of everyday experience. On the other hand, Shakespeare has modified the traditional form of tragedy in such a way that the gap between the dramatic characters and the audience's experience of human behavior and its motivation seems not quite as unbridgeable and a certain degree of identification becomes possible. By and large, however, the characters in *Titus Andronicus* remain in the distance, in a tragic world that seems to ask for a very different kind of response than *Hamlet* or *Othello*.

The dramatic language plays a very important part in this. It is more static and much less communicative than in the later tragedies. It makes much more extensive use of rhetorical set-pieces that rarely appear to be addressed to a particular partner, but rather betray the dramatist's ambition to impart to the more popular drama, addressed to a large and mixed audience, some of the verbal artistry and stylistic virtuosity usually confined to poetry or verse narrative. The early printed editions of *Titus Andronicus* and *Romeo and Juliet* not only testify to the popularity of the two plays on the stage; they may also be an indication of the literary ambitions of a writer who tried to bring drama and sophisticated poetry into closer contact and who had already made a name for himself as the author of two narrative poems that seem to have met the tastes of the judicious.

It has often been noticed how closely related *Titus Andronicus* is to Elizabethan poetry, especially to the brief verse epic.[11] It is quite instructive to look at Shakespeare's own poem *The Rape of Lucrece* in this connection, published in the same year (1594) as the first quarto of *Titus Andronicus*. The story of the violated wife who is not prepared to outlive her shame had already been told by Chaucer in his *Legend of Good Women*, where Shakespeare may well have read it; it is closely related to the tale of Virginius, also translated into English by Chaucer (the 'Physician's Tale') and by Gower (in his collection *Confessio Amantis*), who kills his own daughter to save her from dishonor and who is referred to approvingly in the last act of Shakespeare's tragedy (v,3.36–51).[12] *The Rape of Lucrece*, which evidently helped to establish his reputation as a poet, exhibits a very similar tendency as the play: to create static verbal images, to translate extreme emotions into stylized poetic arias, and to underline the universal significance of the tragic experience by elaborate references to classical myth. Ovid's narrative art, in particular his illustrations of perverted human behavior and its repercussions in the world of natural phenomena, served as important models for the Elizabethan verse epic as well as for *Titus Andronicus*.[13]

Shakespeare's use of the Philomela story is perhaps the most obvious example. It had already contributed some important motifs to the popular prose history of Titus; in the play, however, it is explicitly quoted and deliberately outdone in atrocious cruelty. Lavinia's ravishers try to avoid the fate of Tereus by cutting off not only the victim's tongue (as in Ovid), but also her hands so that she cannot, like Philomela, reveal the crime by means of ingenious embroidery. When Marcus finds his maimed niece, he refers to the classical model in a way intelligible even to those spectators who have not read Ovid's story:

> Fair Philomela, why she but lost her tongue,
> And in a tedious sampler sewed her mind;
> But, lovely niece, that mean is cut from thee.
> A craftier Tereus, cousin, hast thou met,
> And he hath cut those pretty fingers off,
> That could have better sewed than Philomel. (II.4.38–43)

Ovid also provides the means of discovering the crime and its authors when Lavinia uses her mutilated arms to point at the Philomela story in a copy of the *Metamorphoses* (IV.1). As the crime, so the vengeance is designed to outdo the classical model:

> For worse than Philomel you used my daughter,
> And worse than Procne I will be revenged. (V.2.194–5)[14]

If we look at Ovid's version we shall find that Shakespeare by no means tried to outdo his model in the presentation of gruesome details or their decorative stylization. The description of Lavinia's rape and mutilation reveals a very similar tendency to distance the horrifying events by rhetorical virtuosity and self-conscious artifice, to remove them from any idea of immediate personal experience.[15] If Shakespeare sometimes seems to go beyond Ovid in the excess of poetical bravura, this may be partly because of the peculiar nature of dramatic representation that might more easily suggest a realistic concreteness detrimental to the tragic effect. It is not very easy to imagine a really convincing realization of Shakespeare's stage direction:

Enter the Empress' sons, Chiron and Demetrius, with Lavinia, her hands cut off, and
her tongue cut out, and ravished   (II.4)

The problem is certainly more acute in the theatre than in a poetical
narrative. A certain degree of unrealistic detachment was perhaps
achieved by the mere fact that Lavinia was acted by a boy, but more
important is the way this awful spectacle is, by the elaborate rhetorical
display, frozen into an emblematic picture that provides an opportunity
for decorative lament and an inventive use of metaphor:

> Speak, gentle niece, what stern ungentle hands
> Hath lopped and hewed and made thy body bare
> Of her two branches, those sweet ornaments,
> Whose circling shadows kings have sought to sleep in,
> And might not gain so great a happiness
> As half thy love? Why dost not speak to me?
> Alas, a crimson river of warm blood,
> Like to a bubbling fountain stirred with wind,
> Doth rise and fall between thy rosèd lips,
> Coming and going with thy honey breath.   (II.4.16–25)

It almost sounds like a lover's complaint, with Lavinia as a symbol of
despoiled nature. The imagery links her fate with the hunting scenery of
the whole act and, at the same time, reminds us of the slaughtering of
Alarbus in the first scene which has really set in motion the whole revenge
plot.[16] Other scenes, too, could be used to illustrate this technique of
arresting the action from time to time to create static tableaux that are
then made the occasion for poetical elaboration and stylized emotional
outbursts.

Behind this poetisizing of horrifying events and extremes of passion
there is a concept of tragedy that does not want to appeal to our personal
sympathy so much as to impress us by the representation of human
suffering, and of a society threatened by chaos and barbarism. The
exceptional situation provokes the anguished question that might well
come to *King Lear*:

> When will this fearful slumber have an end?   (III.1.251)

Man is at a loss for an explanation of a natural order that appears to
tolerate and even enjoy the prospering of evil:

> O, why should nature build so foul a den,
> Unless the gods delight in tragedies?   (IV.1.58–9)

Titus again and again raises the question of why there is such suffering in
the world, but he is unable to find any reason:

> If there were reason for these miseries,
> Then into limits could I bind my woes;   (III.1.218–19)

Like other Elizabethan revengers, he discovers that 'Extremity of griefs would make men mad' (IV.1.19) and, as in *Hamlet*, it is Hecuba who is cited as the classical example of a mind deranged with excessive grief. The problem of divine justice becomes ever more urgent as the events take their terrifying course, but as there is no answer to it within human society it is addressed to the cosmos at large:

> O, heavens, can you hear a good man groan,
> And not relent, or not compassion him?   (IV.1.122–3)

In spite of everything, Titus is 'a good man', more sinned against than sinning. His pitifully perverse idea of sending arrows with messages to the gods above is a futile attempt to convey the universal cry for justice to the right address, to establish some contact with providence, since earth and hell have proved deaf to his agonized questioning.

By placing the narrowly moralistic action of the popular pamphlet in this wider context, Shakespeare associates the play with the theme of the *Spanish Tragedy*, showing, at the same time, the connection between personal vengeance which one should leave to Heaven (see IV.1.128) and the individual's responsibility for justice in human society. The reference to Coriolanus (IV.4.67) and the action of Lucius underline the political dimension of the events while Aaron represents evil in the form of personal hatred and indifference to any moral appeal. Even this unredeemable villain, however, gives evidence of Shakespeare's reluctance to present simple types of good or evil; although his monomaniac hatred and his delight in diabolic stratagems make him almost a personification of wickedness and remove him from any possible sympathy on the part of the audience, his emphatic concern for the life of his bastard son reveals a surprisingly 'natural' aspect in him which is not in any way motivated or developed in the play, but adds some modifying touch to the conventional Machiavellian stage villain (see V.1.53–86). On the whole, the attempts to free the classical tragedy of blood from the restrictions of formalized poetic traditions by more audience-oriented forms of characterization are rather half-hearted, but it is equally clear that Shakespeare's tragedy provides more than gruesome spectacle and rhetorical virtuosity; it raises some of the fundamental questions that have tormented all tragic protagonists from the beginning and places them in the context of individual suffering as well as of political disorder. Still, it probably takes a very powerful and imaginative production to move the audience to genuine emotional participation and to achieve the impact of great tragedy, the kind of impact described by Marcus in the last scene:

> My heart is not compact of flint nor steel,
> Nor can I utter all our bitter grief,

> But floods of tears will drown my oratory
> And break my utt'rance, even in the time
> When it should move ye to attend me most,
> And force you to commiseration.   (v.3.87–92)

As often in Shakespearian tragedy, the action is briefly recapitulated towards the end and the deep impression made by the tragic events on the survivors is insisted on. The unprecedented atrocities and the final catastrophe leave behind a little group of frightened spectators who will preserve the memory of the tragic events and help to build a more hopeful future. At least in the discovery, the punishment and the rehearsing of the crimes by deeply moved witnesses we can see the reflection of a more just moral and political order, 'a world travailing for perfection', to use Bradley's term. In this respect, *Titus Andronicus* is indeed very close to Shakespeare's later tragedies.[17]

ROMEO AND JULIET

At the end of *Romeo and Juliet*, as in *Titus Andronicus*, survivors and spectators listen once more to an account of the chief events that have led to the catastrophe and make up their minds to draw the appropriate lesson from them for the benefit of society and a brighter future. The tragedy we have witnessed is described as an instance of unprecedented suffering and grief:

> Go hence to have more talk of these sad things;
> Some shall be pardoned, and some punishèd:
> For never was a story of more woe
> Than this of Juliet and her Romeo.   (v.3.307–10)[18]

The nature of these events and their social context are completely different in the two tragedies, which makes the similarity of the reaction and of the intended effect all the more remarkable.[19] It is something nearly all Shakespeare's tragedies have in common however much they vary in subject, characters, and the nature of the tragic conflict.

Romeo and Juliet was not inspired by the tradition of classical tragedy; it is one of the first English love tragedies, dramatizing a story that came to England from the Italian novella by way of France. It does not try to impress the reader by a spectacle of murder, intrigue and violent fate, but presents very different emotions; the vulnerable nature of love and the disturbing capriciousness of Fortune are the chief roots of the tragic turn of events. Whatever we may think about the question of tragic guilt in this play, there is no doubt that the hero does not become a criminal; his death is not the result of villainous machinations and the problem of human suffering appears in a very different light.

The original choice of subject and theme shows that Shakespeare was casting about for new forms of tragedy that would allow for a greater variety of style and a closer relationship between play and audience. The Italian collections of novellas, obviously very popular in translation, became a rich fund of story material for the Elizabethan dramatists. Even the first love tragedy, *Gismond of Salerne*, acted between 1566 and 1568 at the Inner Temple, was based on a story from Boccaccio's *Decameron*, and the author of Shakespeare's chief source, Arthur Brooke (who also wrote plays for the Inner Temple) claims in the preface to his verse narrative *The Tragicall Historye of Romeus and Juliet* (1562) to have seen the story acted on the stage.[20] *Gismond of Salerne*, however, is a classical tragedy in the narrow sense, very limited in style and theme, and there is not much Shakespeare could learn from it; the great majority of plays that make use of Italian novellas are, in fact, comedies, like Shakespeare's own adaptations of such stories, *The Merchant of Venice, Much Ado About Nothing, All's Well That Ends Well* and *Measure for Measure*. As a distinctly lyrical tragedy of love which is at the same time strikingly close to comedy, *Romeo and Juliet* is without any real model.

Brooke's long narrative poem – it has 3020 lines of fourteen syllables and is thus much longer than the play – presents the story of the lovers as a warning example; at least, this is what the preface 'To the Reader' says:

And to this ende (good Reader) is this tragicall matter written, to describe unto thee a coople of unfortunate lovers, thralling themselves to unhonest desire, neglecting the authoritie and advise of parents and frendes, conferring their principall counsels with dronken gossyppes, and superstitious friers (the naturally fitte instrumentes of unchastitie) attemptyng all adventures of peryll, for thattaynyng of their wished lust, usyng auriculer confession (the kay of whoredome, and treason) for futheraunce of theyr purpose, abusyng the honorable name of lawefull mariage, the cloke the shame of stolne contractes, finallye, by all meanes of unhonest lyfe, hastyng to most unhappye deathe.[21]

This simple-minded moral interpretation, however, seems to reflect the author's honorable intentions or, perhaps, deference to the sensibilities of the audience rather than his own artistic temperament, because the narrative itself devotes far more space and poetical energy to the description of love, in particular the bliss and suffering of the lovers, than to their moral condemnation. The monument to be erected for the couple is intended to keep alive 'The memory of so perfect, sound, and so approved love' (l.3012) and the closing lines of the poem, with their superlative praise of this monument, are very similar in spirit to Shakespeare's tragedy:

> There is no monument more worthy of the sight,
> Then is the tombe of Juliet, and Romeus her knight. (ll.3019–20)

This does not sound like 'wished lust' and 'whoredome'; the author's personal disapproval is firmly kept outside the poem itself.

Structure and thematic concern of Brooke's poem are obviously to a considerable extent modelled on Chaucer's ambitious verse novel *Troilus and Criseyde*. Both poems call themselves tragedies and both lay particular stress on the hero's fall from the height of happiness, achieved by perfect fulfilment of love, into the depths of separation, despair and death. Both stories have a comic go-between and both devote a great deal of rhetorical art to the lovers' complaints. It is probable that Shakespeare knew Chaucer's famous poem at this early stage in his career and I feel that he is much closer to Chaucer in *Romeo and Juliet*, with its deeply moving picture of doomed love within a complex world governed by egotism and hatred, than he is in his later tragedy *Troilus and Cressida*, his own, much less romantic version of the classical love story. It also seems very likely to me that he went directly to Chaucer, rather than to Brooke, for some of the more subtle touches of characterization and for much of the comedy.[22]

The Prologue to the play, however, shows very clearly that Shakespeare's priorities are somewhat different from Brooke's or Chaucer's. It announces a tragical love story, but refrains from any moral evaluation. If there is any condemnation, it is directed not at the young lovers, but at the family feud between the two houses which can only be brought to an end by the children's death. Their love is characterized as 'star-crossed', i.e. it is threatened by some higher power, and its course is described as 'death-marked'. Thus, the inseparable connection between love and death is insisted on from the beginning; it is one of the central themes of the tragedy.[23]

Some of Shakespeare's intentions become even clearer if we compare the different versions of the story and look at the more conspicuous changes he introduced. A certain amount of pruning and condensing is, of course, inevitable whenever a circumstantial narrative text has to be translated into scenes and dialogue. The structural proportions, however, are revealing. In *Romeo and Juliet*, Tybalt's death and Romeo's banishment, that is, the decisive reversal of fate, occur almost exactly in the middle of the play. The lovers' first night together belongs already to the second half of the tragedy. In Brooke's poem, wooing, marriage and consummation, as well as Romeus' banishment, occupy only about a third of the text. The tragic working out of the disaster, futile planning, pathetic lament and the final catastrophe are extended to take up about 2000 lines. Even more important are the changes in the time-scheme: after the lovers' first night together there is, in Brooke's poem, an interval of 'a month or twayne' (l.949) during which the lovers enjoy the 'summer of their blisse' until, with the death of Juliet's kinsman and her husband's banishment, the sudden turn of fortune sets in. In Shakespeare's play all the action is concentrated into a space of a few days and the order of events is changed in such a way that Romeo's banishment falls between the wedding and the consummation. Thus, their love is 'death-marked' from the very beginning, and this is underscored by the fact that Tybalt has already sent off his written challenge to Romeo at the time of the marriage ceremony. The simple pattern of the tragedy of Fortune, with its unambiguous sequence of rise and fall, is replaced by a rather more complex development. Our attention is directed very firmly at the precarious and fragile nature of this love, since the lovers are not even granted a single moment of completely unclouded happiness. Shakespeare's play can, therefore, neither be adequately described as a tragedy of inconstant Fortune nor as a tragedy of sin and retribution.[24]

Form and style of *Romeo and Juliet* were, of course, not determined by Brooke's poem alone, but also by a number of other literary models which were, in fact, rather more important as far as characterization and language are concerned. Brooke's narrative is not at all remarkable for stylistic range or inventiveness. Its tone is rather uniform and there is not much attempt at dramatic variation and contrast. Shakespeare's play, in contrast, is quite unusual for the surprising prominence of comic elements and for the close relationship with Elizabethan love-poetry, its sophisticated reflection about the nature and the effects of love, its conventional imagery, rhetorical conceit and ingenious wordplay.[25] Several passages in Shakespeare's tragedy read like dramatized sonnets, metaphors translated into stage action, and poetic images turned into visual spectacle. The dialectic interrelation of love and death, consummation and dying, dance and grave, is one of the most widespread conventions of Elizabethan love-poetry and it reappears, as has often been noticed, in various forms throughout Shakespeare's play. *Romeo and Juliet* is richer in lyrical passages than any of the later tragedies and this evidently plays an important part in directing our response to the characters and the tragic action.

At the same time, comedy is a more prominent element in this play than in any other Shakespearian tragedy.[26] The very first scene introduces the family feud on the level of crude comedy; even the harmless and uninformed dependants are involved in the quarrel between their betters; for them, it is a welcome opportunity for coarse jokes and vigorous street-fighting. As the quarrel escalates and the highest representative of civil order appears on the scene, we begin to realize that the whole community is threatened by this kind of personal animosity, but the play soon returns to seemingly peaceful harmony and comic good humor, by introducing the illiterate servant (simply called Clown in the first editions) who is supposed to deliver invitations to Capulet's feast, and the more complex comic characters of Mercutio and the Nurse. Both are only vaguely sketched in Shakespeare's source and their vital presence seems to be out of proportion in relation to their actual significance for the plot.

It is true that by the time he wrote *Romeo and Juliet* Shakespeare was already a highly successful comic author whose brilliant parodies of various personal and social idioms and linguistic idiosyncrasies reveal his delight in stylistic experiment and variety; but this is not quite enough to explain the importance of comic elements in this early tragedy. More relevant is the observation that these comic characters and techniques help to create a fictional world in which tragedy is, at first, only one element among others, a possibility that only becomes real and inevitable fairly late in the play. There is, if we disregard the ominous Prologue, no sense of an unavoidable catastrophe during the first few scenes and this also modifies the concept of love implied in the story. The love experienced by Romeo and Juliet is but one section of a much larger area of experience that includes very different kinds of 'love' as well, and the lyrical intensity of their language is continually accompanied by a polyphonic chorus of quite contradictory stylistic attitudes. One possible (and traditional) explanation is that these contrasts only serve to bring into relief the youthful idealism, innocence and purity of these young lovers in the midst of an unsympathetic society, corrupted by internal strife; and this is certainly an important aspect of the play's effect on many readers and spectators. If we look at the text more closely, however, we soon discover that the comedy is by no means confined to the minor figures, but extends to the central characters and to their idea of love.

Romeo himself, when he first appears on the scene, seems to be the kind of romantic lover we know from Shakespeare's early comedies and have learned to view with a certain amount of amused detachment. He is not a contemptuous mocker of love, like Chaucer's Troilus, but the transition from a rather conventional and theatrical pose to a feeling of personal commitment and dedication is equally sudden in both cases. His worship of Rosaline reminds us of the bookish posturings in *Love's Labour's Lost* and of some of the less inspired clichés of Elizabethan love-poetry, and this makes the pragmatic realism of the Nurse and the more intellectual cynicism of Mercutio more convincing as a criticism of conventional concepts of love which is not altogether unjustified. On the other hand, Romeo's lovesickness appears in a more positive light after the street-fight we have just witnessed. At least his illusion does not in any way threaten the peace of the community and he has no part whatever in the family hatred:

Here's much to do with hate, but more with love: (1.1.166)

When, however, he falls headlong in love with Juliet at first sight only a few hours later it seems as if one illusion is driven out by a new one, a well-tried remedy recommended by Benvolio. Friar Lawrence, too, expresses his doubts as to whether the second love will be more permanent than the first – doubts that seem reasonable in the circumstances – and he only decides to offer his help because he hopes for a reconciliation between the families through this love-union.

None of the later tragedies leaves the spectator so uncertain about the kind of play he is watching, and for so long, if again we discount the Prologue (which the editors of the Folio did not take over from their copy, probably the Third Quarto of 1609). There, the tragic ending is announced in no uncertain terms, but for most readers and spectators it is the beginning of act three that marks the decisive turning-point: the deaths of Mercutio and Tybalt are irreversible acts of violence that no comic solution can gloss over. There is no Shakespearian comedy in which one of the major characters is murdered on stage; after that explosive scene, no conventional comedy-ending is thinkable. In spite of it, however, the lovers, with the aid of Friar Lawrence, try to find a way out of their dilemma and they make use of devices that often prove successful in comedy.[27] Simulating death is a favorite trick in Elizabethan comedy; in *Romeo and Juliet*, it helps to create a scene that hovers precariously and provocatively between comedy and tragedy. Juliet's pretended death, experienced by her with an intensity that foreshadows her suicide in the last scene (see IV.3), produces a situation in which the distracted grief of the parents, the Nurse, and the disappointed bridegroom is undercut by the superior knowledge of the audience. We know about the trick and this is why the sorrow of the bereaved to us is nothing but a necessary and transitory step in the great plan that will eventually lead to a happy outcome. It is, in many ways, a classical comedy scene, a mock tragedy whose essentially comic character is underlined by the entrance of the clownish musicians and by the trite lamentations of the Nurse. They are suspiciously similar to the parodistic rhetoric of the dying lovers Pyramus and Thisbe in the 'tragical mirth' acted by the craftsmen in *A Midsummer Night's Dream* written at about the same time:[28]

O woe! O woeful, woeful, woeful day!
Most lamentable day, most woeful day
That ever, ever, I did yet behold!

> O day, O day, O day, O hateful day!
> Never was seen so black a day as this.
> O woeful day, O woeful day!   (IV.5.49–54)

The defeat of parents who are led solely by family egotism and the thought of profit, by the determination and cunning of the young generation is a traditional motive in the Italian novella and in Renaissance comedy and it is clear that *Romeo and Juliet* is deliberately drawing on these traditions.

In the last act, however, unfortunate coincidence, misunderstanding, and some characters missing each other by a few minutes, precipitate the catastrophe, and many readers have concluded from this that *Romeo and Juliet* is a tragedy of coincidence and misfortune rather than of character and moral dilemma. Love, it seems, is not defeated by its own inadequacy or by some flaw in the lovers themselves; it is destroyed by an apparently arbitrary fate from outside. 'O, I am fortune's fool', Romeo cries out when he has killed Tybalt (III.1.127), and the Prologue too, announcing a pair of 'star-crossed lovers', seems to suggest a deterministic interpretation. Taken literally, however, this would reduce the message of the play to a rather banal formula which is effectively refuted by the diversity of stylistic attitudes and the controversial nature of the issues raised by the characters.

Many interpretations of Shakespeare's tragedy that concentrate on the lovers' shortcomings and guilt, just as Brooke does in the preface to his poem, are in danger of discussing problems Shakespeare deliberately passes over, such as disobedience to the will of the parents, selfish indulgence, abuse of the sacrament of matrimony, or the sinfulness of suicide. Even in Shakespeare's source, the author seems to pay lip-service only to orthodox morality and to be much more fascinated by the dramatic nature of the story. In the play, there is not even an attempt to impose a neat moral on the tragic conclusion.[29]

Still, the play is concerned with guilt as well as with impersonal fate, but not in the simple way of balancing sin and error against punishment or from any censorious point of view. What is insisted on, from the very first lines of the Prologue to the concluding speeches of the play, is the close connection between the young people's love and the hatred between their families. The children pay for the parents' inability to create a society in which there is room for a love such as theirs. Their death is the price to be laid down for a final reconciliation and in this sense they become 'Poor sacrifices of our enmity' (v.3.304).[30] The ending makes greater demands on the spectator than the conventional tragedy of Fortune. In spite of all coincidence and capricious stars there is a clear interdependence of human failing and tragic action. It is the older generation who lives to witness the end of its hopes, but none of the survivors try to deny their own responsibility by blaming fate or accident and none of them call the lovers' integrity in question. The words of the Prince, 'All are punished' (v.3.295), are evidently addressed to the living, not to the dead, and they express the conviction that even in this tragedy there is something like the justice of a Nemesis. The lovers are only lamented as victims; their death would not have been possible, let alone necessary without the failure of public order and adult authority.

The love story itself, which is at the play's centre, cannot be described as a case of guilt and punishment; rather it is an attempt to explore a wide range of love-experience, by presenting side by side many different attitudes, situations, and modes of expression. Romeo and Juliet represent the most attractive form of a mutual attachment that stakes everything on the total communion with the beloved, disregarding any worldly considerations. This may seem laughable from the point of view of the realistic cynic, like Mercutio, and it may result in complete blindness to the realities of hatred and violence, as in the instance of Tybalt's murderous antagonism. Shakespeare's early comedies provide many examples of conventional love-posturings held up for ridicule or criticism and confronted with a less idealistic reality. Romantic love becomes questionable and no longer quite trustworthy when it seems to be professed for its own sake, bypassing the complexities of genuine experience; but wholehearted dedication, prepared to risk everything and to ignore prudent respect for custom and self-interest, is valued much higher in the comedies than the uncommitted scepticism of the cynic. Within the world of Verona, the love of Romeo and Juliet appears like a utopian dream; it is not allowed the time to mature into true partnership, yet it is no mere romantic pose, like Romeo's lovesickness in the first act, because it is prepared to hazard life and prosperity for the sake of complete union with the beloved. This love can produce the kind of evidence of its sincerity for which Rosalind claims to look in vain among lovers in *As You Like It*:

The poor world is almost six thousand years old, and in all this time there was not any man died in his own person, videlicet, in a love-cause. (IV.1.89–92)[31]

She reminds Orlando of classical love stories, of Troilus and of Leander:

But these are all lies: men have died from time to time and worms have eaten them, but not for love. (IV.1.101.3)

Rosalind herself knows well enough, of course, that this is not the whole truth because in the end she is willing (as she, in fact, was from the very beginning) to share her whole life with Orlando by giving herself to him (v.4.116). *Romeo and Juliet* also leaves us in no doubt that romantic love can never be adequately understood from an attitude of pragmatism and cautious doubt. The lovers' death would be a meaningless farce, like the theatrical suicides of Pyramus and Thisbe in *A Midsummer Night's Dream*, if it were presented to us as the consequence of misled youthful illusion and error. It proves, on the contrary, the reality and value of a reckless commitment, prepared to sacrifice life and everything rather than be separated from the beloved. In the world of the play, this final and complete proof of love's power is rated much higher than rational wisdom and prudent self-interest.[32]

At the same time, however, the tragedy does not gloss over the fact that Romeo and Juliet represent but one aspect of the rich and complex variety of possible love-experience. The same can be said of the majority of Elizabethan love lyrics; but Shakespeare's own sonnets, possibly written around the same year, draw a far more complex picture and discuss aspects of love that are completely absent from the play. The young lovers neither give much thought to the individuality of the partner nor to a life together, beyond the ecstasy of their first union. Nor does the question of procreation, so prominent in the sonnets, at all arise.[33] This does not cast any doubt on the lovers' sincerity, but it should also make us realize that the play does not claim to present the totality of love and all its social functions. The love of Romeo and Juliet is incapable of coming to any arrangement with a hostile and unsympathetic world; it can only accept unconditional fulfilment or death and even the wise and by no means unrealistic counsel of Friar Lawrence proves quite ineffectual in dealing with the lovers' total and uncompromising dedication to each other.[34] It is part of the play's stature and certainly an aspect of its undiminishing impact through the centuries that it does not deny us such insights into the immaturities and limitations of conventional romantic love, but rather encourages them by allowing a surprising amount of room to very different concepts of love. Even the garrulous Nurse for whom love only exists within the narrow pale of physical enjoyment and for whom one lover is as good as the next one, clearly oversteps the normal bounds of a comic supporting character by her exuberant vitality. Like Chaucer's Pandarus, though not quite as active, she is an indispensable go-between and offers practical help where the lovers seem incapable of purposeful action.[35] Mercutio, who plays the part of the intellectual mocker, likewise sees love only in terms of sensual pleasure or as childish illusion, but he does not ever know Romeo's real love – his sarcasm is all the time directed at Romeo's original infatuation for Rosaline – and he is unable to pass beyond a negative detachment. His phantastical dream of Queen Mab (1.4.53–95) is deliberately opposed to

Romeo's visions of love and is meant to distract the melancholy friend, and again the weight and importance given to this minor character is remarkable. 'Thou talk'st of nothing', Romeo interrupts him, but, like the Nurse's long-winded reminiscing, Mercutio's rhetorical narrative provides a contrast that is much more than comic by-play and contributes to the impression of a much richer world outside from which the lovers are increasingly excluded.

The figure of Old Capulet combines traditional parental authority, wistful memories of former youth and levity (''tis gone, 'tis gone, 'tis gone' (1.5.23)), and a very pragmatic view of marriage, another deliberate contrast to the uncompromising idealism of the lovers, understood by no one else in the play. Friar Lawrence, too, disapproves of Romeo's heat and impatience and only lends his help in the hope of averting greater disaster. His often quoted lines on the dangers of 'violent delights' are neither discredited by the context as homiletic banality nor are they offered to us as a definitive evaluation of the young people's love:

> These violent delights have violent ends,
> And in their triumph die like fire and powder,
> Which as they kiss consume. (11.6.9–11)

This is the voice of experience and wisdom, not a confident verdict.

The very diversity of critical appraisals, often mutually exclusive, demonstrates that the text does not strictly take sides on the moral issues involved, but leaves the final assessment of this love to the reader and spectator. An attitude of superior moral censoriousness is certainly not sanctioned by the play and its poetical portrait of unselfish, totally committed love. On the other hand, it seems just as inadequate, in view of the complex vitality of Shakespeare's Verona, to see the play as a triumphant glorification of 'Liebestod'. Provocative inconclusiveness and an unresolved juxtaposition of divergent points of view make *Romeo and Juliet* a characteristic example of Shakespeare's tragic style, even though the tragic impact is not produced by complex character-conflict, but by the pathetic failure of sincere and absolutely inoffensive love to achieve the wished-for happiness within a society torn by internal strife and disunity. Whether the monument erected by the sorrowing, but reconciled parents, remains but a transient consolation prize or whether it really immortalizes the victory of love under discord and death, is a question the play does not decide for us. It is not assured confidence of moral judgement the tragedy wants to encourage, but compassionate sympathy and deeper insight into the concept of romantic love and its implications. As a brilliant poetic achievement, it is itself a lasting monument and can thus give permanence to short-lived youth and beauty. It is a theme further developed with impressive assurance in Shakespeare's sonnets.

Perhaps this is the deeper reason for the play's lasting appeal. The depressing finality of the ending seems largely outweighed by the lyrical high moments in the play in which traditional situations and emotions are celebrated and, as in *Titus Andronicus*, translated into stage images: the lovers' first meeting, the beginning of love and the reluctantly granted kiss are presented as a dramatized love-sonnet (1.5.92–105). Dialogue and lyrical conceit are blended in this playful exchange on the metaphor of the pilgrim worshipping at the holy shrine. The balcony scene, one of the most famous passages in the canon, uses the motif of wooing and of the lovers' vow to create a dramatic situation of unprecedented lyrical intensity and genuine emotion in spite of rhetorical stylization (II.2.). Similarly, the lovers' sad parting at dawn which had already been cast in dialogue form in many medieval lyrics, the 'aubade', is presented as a moving scene without losing any of its lyrical concentration (III.5.1–65).[36] Finally, Juliet's expectant soliloquy, expressing her impatient desire for night and the consummation of her marriage, is in the long tradition of the classial 'prothalamion'.

Such use of conventional lyrical forms gives a kind of stylized permanence to the dramatic moment which might appear untheatrical at first sight; but the very combination of formalized lyricism and scenic concreteness creates the impression of genuine individual experience and uniquely felt emotion. This applies to the stage even more than to the printed page. Any imaginative and well-acted production can convey to the audience what the play so powerfully expresses: the timeless and at the same time unique quality of love. Romeo and Juliet enact a traditional and often played drama, yet every fresh reading and every good performance can convince us that they are experiencing their love for the first time at this very moment.[37]

Romeo and Juliet is a love tragedy not only because it tells a story of 'death-marked love', as the Prologue announces, but in a much deeper sense: it is a play about the richness and the vulnerability of a particular kind of love, as movingly beautiful as it is exceptional in a world that is basically hostile and unsympathetic to it.

3

The 'great' tragedies

HAMLET

LIKE THE TWO EARLY TRAGEDIES, *THE TRAGICALL HISTORIE OF Hamlet, Prince of Denmarke*[1] ends with a glance back at the events we have just witnessed and with the express wish to make intelligible to the survivors the magnitude of the tragedy and to do justice to the memory of the dead. Hamlet himself prevents Horatio from following him into silence and asks him to protect his reputation by a faithful report of what he alone knows:

> O God, Horatio, what a wounded name,
> Things standing thus unknown, shall I leave behind me.
> If thou didst ever hold me in thy heart,
> Absent thee from felicity awhile,
> And in this harsh world draw thy breath in pain
> To tell my story. (V.2.349–54)

Horatio's first announcement of this public duty, however, surprises the spectator by a summary of the action which hardly agrees with our own impression of the play:

> And let me speak to th'yet unknowing world
> How these things came about. So shall you hear
> Of carnal, bloody, and unnatural acts,
> Of accidental judgments, casual slaughters,
> Of deaths put on by cunning and forc'd cause,
> And, in this upshot, purposes mistook
> Fall'n on th'inventors' heads. All this can I
> Truly deliver. (V.2.384–91)

This sounds like a catalogue of traditional revenge tragedy clichés that would fit the *Spanish Tragedy* or *Titus Andronicus* much better than *Hamlet*. It is, on the other hand, a reminder of how much the action of *Hamlet* really has in common with the early tragedies. Shakespeare has

30

taken over a remarkable amount of external detail from his models and it makes, I think, the approach to the play much easier if we recognize this close relationship to the still very popular and vital tradition of revenge tragedy.

Shakespeare's sources can only be determined in rough outline. There is no doubt that the story of Hamlet was not only known to Elizabethan readers, but had already been successful on the stage.[2] François de Belleforest's collection of *Histoires Tragiques*, frequently reprinted, was a welcome reservoir of alluring subjects for Elizabethan dramatists. The history of Hamlet, contained in volume five (1570, seven times reprinted before 1600), was apparently not translated into English until 1608, in a version that already reveals the influence of Shakespeare's tragedy; but it is evident that the playwright was fairly familiar with the French text. Whether he owed anything to a revenge tragedy on the subject which is alluded to as early as 1589 and from which Thomas Lodge, in 1596, quotes the Ghost's cry 'Hamlet, revenge', can only be a matter for speculation because the play itself, the so-called *Ur-Hamlet*, has not survived. It is often taken for granted that its author was Thomas Kyd, but there is no definitive proof. The only thing that is certain is that there was a ghost in it who does not appear in Belleforest, and this suggests that it belonged to the same type of revenge tragedy as *The Spanish Tragedy*, which it most likely preceded.[3]

The astonishingly long and continued popularity of the revenge tragedy cannot be accounted for by the specific moral problem of revenge. This is complex enough, of course: the unambiguous biblical commandment to leave revenge to the Lord is contradicted by the duty of loyalty towards family and friends. The revenger who wants to take up the cause of justice and to pay back injury, especially murder, inflicted on his nearest relations, usually has the audience's sympathy on his side, at least in the initial stages of the tragedy, because we would take silent acquiescence as a neglect of duty and as personal failure. Many documents show that for the Elizabethans this was a burning topic and by no means a foregone conclusion. The orthodox answer was not universally felt to be a satisfactory solution and a review of revenge tragedies, from Kyd's *Spanish Tragedy* to Tourneur's *The Atheist's Tragedy*, reveals that very different responses to injury received were discussed and their implications explored.[4]

Very often, however, the moral justification of revenge is not the central issue of revenge tragedy; even in *The Spanish Tragedy* and in *Titus Andronicus* the dramatist's interest is concentrated on the dilemma of the hero who finds himself surrounded by a world of injustice and begins a desperate search for some means of putting it right. In this endeavor he himself gets more and more infected by the methods and the mentality of his opponents; he outdoes them in ruthless brutality and perishes along with them. This general pattern offers enough opportunities for the kind of spectacular crime and intrigue summarized by Horatio at the end of *Hamlet*. Above all, however, it enables the dramatist to present a hero who is confronted with a task beyond his powers and who comes away from the conflict haunted by a sense of corruption and guilt, like Orestes in Aeschylus' *Oresteia*, the chief prototype of all later revengers. In the case of Kyd's Hieronymo and Shakespeare's Titus, the dilemma finds its expression mainly in grotesque fits of madness, uncontrolled despair, cunning deceit and bestial vengeance. These elements are still present in *Hamlet*, but they are subordinated to a wide-ranging discussion of the traditional situation of the revenger and its moral and philosophical implications. Theatrical raving and hysterical outbursts are largely replaced by agonizing self-doubt, endless reflection and sudden attempts at resolute action. The unusual length of the text, hardly actable in its entirety, suggests that this kind of play tempted authors and adaptors to add new scenes, with further illustrations of the hero's tragic dilemma in different character-constellations and stylistic attitudes; the 'Additions' to the *Spanish Tragedy* are another case in point. The revenge tragedy thus seems to have been particularly hospitable to various kinds of themes, emotions, and dramatic devices; such variety might well endanger the play's formal unity, but the figure of the revenger effectively works against any impression of diffuseness; he is, in fact, the most important unifying element and the very centre of the drama.

Hamlet, too, is completely dominated by one single character. The Danish Prince is not only one of the biggest parts in the canon as far as the number of lines is concerned, he is, above all, a most powerful presence in every scene of the play, even when he is actually absent from the stage. There is no part of the action without him and no dramatic suspense that is not directly related to his character. At the same time, the action is certainly not set in motion by him, but the play's characteristic effect is achieved by the striking contrast between the restless activity around the hero and immediately concerned with him, and his own evident incapacity for swift and unreflected action. This extraordinary contradiction directs the attention of the reader and the spectator firmly at the protagonist's character, and it is easy to see that character and action are far more closely interrelated here than in the earlier tragedies. This is also why for a long time, the character of Hamlet occupied critics to the exclusion of almost everything else in the play.

It is worth noting that the most fascinating and many-faceted character whom the Elizabethan theatre has produced comes from the tradition of the revenge tragedy. Here, Shakespeare found a dramatic situation particularly suitable for combining and further exploring a number of themes he had already been interested in when he wrote his early tragedies, histories, and comedies: the conflict between an individual and a society which in no way answers to his own aspirations and ideals; the poisoning of human intercourse by deception and hypocrisy; the replacing of an old order, felt to be reliable and humane, by a new kind of pragmatic opportunism.

The world of the Danish court, as it confronts us in the very first scenes of the play, casts a strange and unexpected light on the familiar conventions of Elizabethan revenge tragedy. The first scene, with the brief questions shouted out of the dark, the immediate atmosphere of uncertainty, tension and threat, and the sudden intrusion of a reality completely other than everyday experience, at once creates an impression of a world too complex for the book-learning of Horatio or the simple popular wisdom of Marcellus. The appearance of the Ghost, several times mentioned and discussed before it actually happens, is a particularly impressive demonstration of Shakespeare's remarkable ability to transform dramatic conventions into unique experience. The Ghost at first remains completely silent, thus raising more questions than he answers. Before we can learn any more about him, the reactions of those present create a context of mixed theories about ghosts, of political unrest and of sinister foreboding:

> This bodes some strange eruption to our state. (I.I.72)

The impression is intensified by Horatio's initial scepticism. His genuine shock at the Ghost's actual presence gives conviction to the reality of the experience and once and for all refutes the suspicion that it might be all imagination or hallucination. Another prospect of tragic possibilities is disclosed by Horatio's reference to Caesar's murder, dramatized by Shakespeare immediately before or even simultaneously with *Hamlet*, and also heralded by supernatural portents. The return of the deceased King awakens memories of a glorious past and hints at an unquiet present that will not let the dead sleep in peace. The discussion of Christian theories about ghosts prepares us for Hamlet's doubts about the nature and the trustworthiness of this appearance. Thus, even before the Ghost has spoken, the audience knows that it is much more than a traditional Senecan spirit of revenge (as, for instance, in the *Spanish Tragedy*) and that some far more disquieting disaster seems to be in the air than political murder or military invasion.

This exposition leaves the audience considerably more in the dark than the first scene of *Romeo and Juliet* (quite apart from the Prologue, which is lacking here), and yet it gives us a strong sense of imminent evil.[5] The court scene that follows is clearly overshadowed by the threat of 'some strange eruption to our state', and the demonstrative assurance of the new King appears in a somewhat dubious light. His glib rhetoric and untroubled competence are even less convincing when contrasted with the gloom of Prince Hamlet who evidently takes quite a different view of the whole situation and is unable to join in the general satisfaction. His grief for the dead father is seen by Claudius as a stubborn pose and the trite consolation offered by him to the bereaved nephew almost reminds us of Feste's mockery of Olivia's ostentatious dedication to the memory of her dead brother in *Twelfth Night* (1.5). Of course, the situation and the dramatic context are entirely different and Hamlet's sorrow is presented with far greater intensity and credibility. It remains completely untouched by the insincere comforting clichés declaimed by the diplomatic King. When he himself insists on the fundamental difference between a grief displayed merely for show, with attributes that can easily be simulated, and his real state of mind, he draws attention to the contrast between 'show' and reality which will be of crucial importance throughout the play and, at the same time, will become less and less clear-cut:

> I know not 'seems'.
> 'Tis not alone my inky cloak, good mother,
> Nor customary suits of solemn black,
> Nor windy suspiration of forc'd breath,
> No, nor the fruitful river in the eye,
> Nor the dejected haviour of the visage,
> Together with all forms, moods, shapes of grief,
> That can denote me truly. These indeed seem,
> For they are actions that a man might play;
> But I have that within which passes show,
> These but the trappings and the suits of woe. (1.2.76–86)

In comedy, it is usually easy enough to distinguish between an adopted role and the real person behind it. In *Hamlet*, however, it becomes increasingly clear during the course of the action how futile the search for a completely undisguised reality becomes and how 'real', on the other hand, deceitful masks and play-acting can appear. This is, of course, a question very closely related to the theatre's claim to be able to assist us in understanding and improving reality through a feigned reality, and there is no doubt that *Hamlet* is in many ways Shakespeare's most theatre-conscious play.[6]

The transition from the public court-scene to Hamlet's anguished soliloquy makes finally explicit the hero's complete isolation within the world of Denmark. At the very outset of the tragedy, its hero has already been stripped of all his untroubled confidence and assurance by a most deeply disturbing experience: life is but a depressing burden to him. His mother's hasty re-marriage has shattered his belief in human loyalty and truth, and with it the whole of society for him has grown into an 'unweeded garden' (1.2.135). In contrast to Romeo, Hamlet does not appear to us as one who has assumed some fashionable pose, soon to be replaced by the shock of genuine experience. Though his hopelessness and death-wish agree with conventional symptoms of Elizabethan melancholy and seem, to the rest of the court, quite inappropriate to the real situation, there is no doubt whatever as to the sincerity of his disillusion; it is, we suspect, even deeper and more soul-destroying than he can possibly express in words and gesture. It is, moreover, directly related to the appeal of the Ghost and to all the further action of the play, as the audience will presently discover.

Hamlet's encounter with the Ghost, then, hits him when he is already in a state of extreme excitement and in a situation when heart-broken silence seems to him the only choice left. This accounts for the mood of feverish expectation at the end of the second scene and for Hamlet's obsessed eagerness to throw himself headlong into the uncertain adventure in the fourth scene. No other Elizabethan ghost is introduced with so much suspense and genuine sensation. The melodramatic stage convention has been turned into a personal crisis, an experience that will change the Prince's whole life by confronting him with a task that will from now on be the sole concern of his existence. This element of complete dedication to a duty, whose magnitude seems to become increasingly overwhelming, is much more important for an adequate understanding of the Ghost scene than the traditional controversy about the theological significance of the supernatural command.

The text does not tell us explicitly and unambiguously with what kind of authority the deceased King speaks to Hamlet and what exactly he asks him to do.[7] A number of conventional explanations are offered in the course of the play, but so much is left unsaid that we can easily sympathize with Hamlet's bewildered uncertainty throughout the following scenes. All neat definitions of this Ghost – as hallucination, as an instrument of diabolic temptation, as the voice of natural filial duty – reduce the dramatic intensity of the scene, with its most original variation of the revenge-ghost motif, to a mere commonplace. It seems to me that at this point in the play it is neither possible nor necessary to decide whether this is an evil or a benevolent spirit, a deceitful apparition or 'an honest ghost', as Hamlet tells his comrades (1.5.144). The dramatic purpose of the scene is Hamlet's 'call' to revenge, but his reaction makes very clear that it is not just the traditional duty to avenge your next of kin, but a command which is far more difficult to define and to fulfil. The Prince himself sees his task as something far beyond the present occasion and beyond the simple demand of vengeance:

> The time is out of joint. O cursed spite,
> That ever I was born to set it right.   (1.5.196–7)

This statement, underscored by its position at the end of the scene, prepares the audience for what the play makes more and more obvious: Hamlet cannot possibly do justice to the Ghost's message by a swift and simple stratagem of revenge, and this may be a provisional answer to questions discussed endlessly by earlier critics, as to the reasons for Hamlet's alleged oversensitive procrastination.

What is much more important is to see the connection between the Ghost scene and Hamlet's first soliloquy. His experience of a society that is 'weary, stale, flat, and unprofitable' (1.2.133) has made him extremely susceptible to the revelation forced on him by the murdered father. The history behind the sudden change of government and his mother's remarriage not only confirms Hamlet's hitherto unarticulated pre-monitions and suspicions ('O my prophetic soul! My uncle!' (1.5.41)), but it also gives a name to the evil, felt so far only as a general impression, and suggests the possibility of restoring justice by one's own activity. Thus, the text establishes a very close association between the Ghost's appear-ance and Hamlet's emotional state at this point in the play. The Prince is the only person to whom the Ghost speaks, the only one able to receive his message. Shakespeare here gives dramatic expression to the tradi-tional theory that good and evil spirits often exploit for their own purposes a particular emotional crisis in the person they have chosen to visit. It is an idea that begins to trouble Hamlet himself later in the play, though in a rather restricted sense:

> The spirit that I have seen
> May be a devil, and the devil hath power
> T'assume a pleasing shape, yea, and perhaps,
> Out of my weakness and my melancholy,
> As he is very potent with such spirits,
> Abuses me to damn me.   (II.2.594–9)

As the witches' prophecies in *Macbeth* evidently stir up some latent spark of ambition in the hero, so old Hamlet's Ghost gives utterance to some voice from within, persuading the son that it is his duty to avenge his father and convincing him that his vague suspicions are justified. This is not to reduce the supernatural apparition to a psychological phenomenon, but it is a very characteristic feature of Shakespeare's art of portraying complex states of mind that he combines conventional devices of theatrical representation with a precise analysis of conscious or unconscious mental processes. It is also worth noting that in any reasonably successful production the question of the Ghost's real nature hardly arises for the audience because it is Hamlet's reaction that demands our full attention and the Ghost speaks so directly to him that we immediately believe in the reality of this decisive experience. No objective and reliable details are given either to Hamlet or to the spectator, but instead an account of the events that have led up to the present situation, obviously colored by the speaker and by the whole dramatic situation. Above all, there is a strongly emotional appeal to the listener's pity for the dead and love for his father's memory. When the Ghost, on the one hand, asks Hamlet to avenge his murder and on the other, to spare his mother and preserve his own moral integrity, he at once gives a very clear description of the tragic dilemma and reveals his own ambiguous nature. He cries for revenge where there seems an undeniable case of criminal murder, but at the same time refers to Heaven's prerogative and to the authority of a guilty conscience as an instrument of retribution. The Ghost's injunction, 'Taint not thy mind' (1.5.85), seems hardly compatible with the call for revenge and strongly suggests that Shakespeare wanted to make us aware of the moral dilemma implicit in the situation of the revenger from the start, thus excluding such simple solutions as in the *Spanish Tragedy* and many later revenge tragedies. The Ghost does not provide any clear guidance and has no easy recipe for swift action, but he confronts the hero with an imperative duty he cannot possibly fulfil without a fundamental moral conflict.

The first result of this decisive encounter, as far as the play's action is concerned, is Hamlet's complete isolation. Not even his closest friend, Horatio, can be taken into his confidence. The play at first follows the traditional model of revenge tragedy insofar as the hero tries to hide his knowledge and his intentions behind the protective mask of insanity: Hamlet himself announces his 'antic disposition' (1.5.180) as a deliberate means of disguise, but the whole scene suggests at the same time such an extreme state of emotional tension and hysteria induced by the Ghost that we already begin to doubt whether Hamlet is still quite master of his own words and actions. Such doubts have played a prominent part in critical discussions about the play, but I am convinced they belong with all those questions to which the text only supplies rather indefinite and tentative answers. It is, indeed, an indication of the intensity of Hamlet's dilemma that it makes him incapable of perfectly deliberate action and rational planning, and yet it is impossible to state precisely, at any given moment, how far he is still in control of his reactions.

This element of uncertainty is effectively underlined by a change in dramatic perspective. Before Hamlet himself reappears on the stage we see him through the eyes of other characters. After the encounter with the Ghost, the first thing the audience hears about him is Ophelia's frightened account of his visit to her closet. The text does not tell us whether the scene is supposed to be an immediate consequence of the Ghost's revelation or a reaction to her obedient refusal to receive any further communications from the Prince; it would probably weaken the dramatic impact of Ophelia's description if we knew more about Hamlet's motives at this point. His profoundly disturbed state of mind is presented as an appeal and a challenge. The impression, already present in the previous scene, is confirmed that Hamlet has not, by the Ghost's command, been filled with an invigorating sense of a worthwhile task or with the active certainty of a great mission, but has, above all, gained a terrifying insight into the diabolic potentialities of human nature, perverting all his former familiar relationships. His disordered dress evidently betrays to the audience the assumed mask of madness, but his expression reveals much more than cunning disguise or play-acting. Ophelia is as shocked by it as Hamlet himself was by the Ghost:

> As if he had been loosed out of hell
> To speak of horrors, (II.1.83–4)

This hardly invites the conclusion that Hamlet intended this visit only as a first demonstration of his 'antic disposition'; at least, the spectators know much more about the 'horrors' than Ophelia, and they will hardly fail to see a direct connection between Hamlet's state and the previous scene, although some time must have elapsed in-between and Polonius accounts for the Prince's behavior by Ophelia's dutiful inaccessibility. His own explanation, 'This is the very ecstasy of love' (II.1.102), is, for the audience, a rather comical if understandable mistake and Bradley thought that it was the deliberate purpose of Hamlet's visit to encourage this kind of mistake.[8] It is clear, however, that there are two conflicting time-schemes in the play: simple calculation reveals that several weeks must have gone by since the end of the first act, but this interval remains empty for the audience and thus somehow unreal. We are not told anything about Hamlet's development since his encounter with the Ghost. It turns out, in the following scene (II.2), that Hamlet's 'transformation' has become a matter of concern for Claudius, which he is very anxious to clear up; but within the play, Polonius obviously hears about it for the first time from Ophelia, and this creates the strong impression that the reported visit to Ophelia is Hamlet's first reaction to the revelations of the Ghost. The technique of dramatic narration, used here with particular virtuosity, makes it possible for the playwright to be his own producer for a crucial scene and to describe the impact of Hamlet's apparition very precisely without being dependent on an actor's individual interpretation. This prepares the audience for Hamlet's entrance during the following scene and corrects, for us, the theories of the King and his counsellors about the Prince's malady. At the same time, however, the dramatist does not put an end to all this uncertainty by an unambiguous signal, e.g. a soliloquy, and we are left to form our own impression during the following events.

The general uncertainty – helpless apprehension on the part of the Danish court, sympathy and a sense of foreboding on the part of the audience – gives rise to all kinds of speculations about Hamlet's state of mind and its deeper cause: This takes up the greater part of the second act and also sets in motion various intrigues and stratagems, directed mostly against the Prince. The discrepancy between Polonius' simple explanations and Hamlet's complex and impenetrable mental state is an effective dramatic device to alert the audience to the tragic impasse. Polonius thinks of cunning strategies to spy on his own son, and Hamlet likewise finds himself watched and sounded from all sides. All these crude attempts to draw him out prove ineffective, however, and are more important as a means of characterizing the Prince than as parts of the dramatic action, although, at first, all the initiative seems to come from the opponents rather than from the protagonist.

Hamlet has this in common with many other tragedies of revenge that the lonely hero, excluded from any real communication by his disguise or by an actual derangement, is opposed by an unsympathetic and hostile court who wants to assess him and to render him harmless. Most of the second act is devoted to the dramatic representation of the court in its relation to the Prince whom, for the most part, we see only from the outside, though in varying roles, until, at the end of the extraordinarily long scene II.2, all the forcefully pent-up emotion erupts without any disguise in a passionate soliloquy: 'Now I am alone' (II.2.543). The very length of the scene creates an impression of time wasted inactively and without any definite purpose. Hamlet is only reacting to the advances and stratagems of those around him and no action comes from him. On the other hand, it is his mental state, his striking 'transformation', which provokes the busy intriguing zeal of Polonius and the servile obsequiousness of Rosencrantz and Guildenstern and which even attracts most of our interest during the encounter with the actors.

Polonius' presence at the beginning of the scene introduces a brief intrusion of the political action that will prove decisive for the fate of the Danish kingdom, but is practically ignored by Hamlet himself. When, however, the obviously much esteemed counsellor proceeds to expound this theory of the Prince's madness, he is comically discredited by his wordy and meaningless rhetoric: it tries to turn Hamlet into a conventional lover whom the coldness and disdain of his adored has bereft of reason. This picture might be appropriate for a romantic comedy or for the Romeo of the first act of Shakespeare's early tragedy, but in view of the nature of the Danish court and of the Ghost's revelation it must appear to the audience as a grotesque misjudgement. Ophelia's situation, too, is related to comic conventions; however, in comedy, the daughter who is secretly wooed by a desirable suitor is usually much less obedient and has no intention of severing the connection with him merely because he is disapproved of by her parents; but Ophelia is no comedy-heroine and the play does not encourage us to speculate about how Hamlet's love might have developed under different circumstances.[9] She makes no determined attempt to stand up for Hamlet and allows herself to be used as a willing object in Polonius' clumsy plan: 'I'll loose my daughter to him' (II.2.162). Whatever we are told about Hamlet's wooing only permits the conclusion that his love, whether it was quite sincere or not, belongs to that period of his life he is trying to forget completely. On this point, however, the play only provides rather fragmentary and partly contradictory information, not any unambiguous statement. Ophelia speaks of Hamlet's solicitings almost as of a genuine proposal of marriage, but without any emotional commitment of her own (see her 'In honourable fashion' 1.3.111); for Polonius and for Laertes, it is only the superficial toying of a Prince that is bound to end in Ophelia's ruin. The Queen, on the other hand, seems to hope for a permanent connection that might have a beneficial influence on her son (III.1.38–42). Hamlet's letter to Ophelia, quoted by Polonius (II.2.115–23), is another example of Shakespeare's provokingly indirect dramatic method. Its conventional style is in clear contrast to the rest of the dialogue and might make us suspect that it is meant as an ironic play with courtly clichés, but this suspicion is not really confirmed by the text, and the whole scene is so obviously designed to illustrate Polonius' mistaken diagnosis that any speculations about the date or the precise intention of the letter are likely to miss the particular technique of characterization or they are founded on the wrong kind of expectation as to psychological consistency and verisimilitude in every detail.[10]

The further development of the play makes clear that Ophelia and her relationship with Hamlet are relevant only as aspects of the revenge plot. In his present tragic dilemma, Hamlet's love is no more to him than a memory from his past. When he makes use of Ophelia or suspects that he is made use of by her, it is only in connection with his new duty which occupies all his faculties. On the other hand, the Ophelia plot underlines the important fact that this total commitment cannot be separated from any other areas of experience. Hamlet's complete disillusion with his mother's behavior has a profound influence on his attitude towards Ophelia, and his hatred of Claudius affects her whole life most fatally.

The conventional love-comedy motifs are soon perverted by the course of events as well as by the realities of the Danish court. Polonius only uses the conventions of courtly love to show his loyalty to the new King. Similarly, as Hamlet soon realizes, the friendship of his former associates Rosencrantz and Guildenstern is cunningly exploited to pry into his secret. During his talk with them, before he begins to suspect them, and, above all, in his dealings with the actors, the audience is allowed a glimpse of a carefree and confident Prince, of the witty and well-read courtier he once was and still might be. This helps to give to the play that intellectual depth and the range of experience which is Shakespeare's most important addition to the revenge story.

The chief dramatic purpose of the long scene with the travelling actors is the introduction of the play within the play, another device that recurs in many revenge tragedies. What is particularly interesting here is the way Shakespeare, by means of this episode, provides a particular fitting opportunity for discussing the themes of play-acting, disguise, imitation of reality and the function of the mimetic arts. During the court scene of the first act, Hamlet had already reflected on the way external gesture and true state of mind can often be in conflict (see 1.2.76–86, quoted above). From the professional actors, however, he learns that the acting or imitating of emotions can produce an effect as powerful and as 'real' as the thing itself; indeed, it can be even more convincing in its impact than genuine reality. This unique faculty of true art, especially the art of the actor, makes Hamlet ask himself how he can use this new discovery for his own purposes, as a means of getting at the truth without giving himself away. The famous 'Pyrrhus-speech' recited by the actor, not only makes a most disturbing impression on Hamlet who can hardly fail to recognize the parallels between himself and the son of Achilles avenging his father, it also moves the actor himself to tears – be they genuine or artificial – and thus gives a moving reality to the far-off murder of Priam and the grief of his widow, a reality as potent and effective as many actual events. This is an idea frequently remarked and meditated on in Elizabethan poetry. One of Sidney's sonnets from *Astrophil and Stella* is particularly interesting in this connection; in it, the lover complains about the fact that his beloved actually sheds tears about some fictional love story, but is completely unmoved by his own real sorrow. This makes him propose that the lady should receive his anguished protestations as if it were a merely poetical tragedy and grant her pity to the fiction if not to the reality:

> Alas, if fancy drawn by imag'd things,
> Though false, yet with free scope more grace doth breed
> Than servant's wrack, where new doubts honour brings;
> Then think, my dear, that you in me do read
> Of lover's ruin some sad tragedy:
> I am not I, pity the tale of me.[11]

Similarly, Hamlet contrasts his own inactivity (in spite of actual crime) with the real tears of an actor, untouched by any genuine emotion. Hecuba means nothing to him, and yet he can make her the subject of a truly moving lament. To Hamlet, this is a reason for self-reproach because, instead of effective action, he can only hurl insults into the air, hurting no one: his soliloquy is an eloquent example of it. At the same time, this experience of the powerful impact of the actor's art suddenly puts the idea into his head that he might take advantage of the players to further his revenge. As in other scenes of the tragedy, we have here a characteristic example of Shakespeare's skills as a producer: Hamlet gives a vivid description of a theatrical performance, fusing the actor's art with the Prince's actual grievance:

> What would he do
> Had he the motive and the cue for passion
> That I have? He would drown the stage with tears,
> And cleave the general ear with horrid speech,
> Make mad the guilty and appal the free,
> Confound the ignorant, and amaze indeed
> The very faculties of eyes and ears.   (II.2.554–60)

It is the wishful ideal of a performance that produces visible moral effects such as many Elizabethan dramatists claimed to work for. It was an accepted theory that good tragedy (and comedy, for that matter) would indeed 'Make mad the guilty and appal the free'.[12]

In the course of his soliloquy, Hamlet forms the plan to put the King's conscience to the test by a stage performance, thus making sure that the Ghost has spoken the truth. I do not think that we are meant to speculate too much about the logic of Hamlet's reasoning at this point or about the sincerity of his doubts. Critics have suggested that he is only looking for an excuse to postpone his revenge, but this is a rather superficial explanation, quite irrelevant to the dramatic purpose of this soliloquy. It is not so much a subtle psychological process that is the issue here, but the evident contrast between Hamlet's whole personality and the part he is demanded to play. He knows well enough what an uncomplicated and unscrupulous revenger would have done in his position:

> I should ha' fatted all the region kites
> With this slave's offal. (II.2.575–6)

Everything the audience has seen of Hamlet so far must have convinced them that this is no realistic alternative for the hero and that he must achieve his revenge in a very different way. The idea of a play and its moral impact is much more in tune with his own concept of guilt and retribution than swift murder because for him this is not just a matter of simple revenge, but a fundamental ethical conflict in which he feels himself called upon to combat all the evils infecting society. Claudius must not just be removed, he must be made to recognize his guilt. Thus the soliloquy combines the hero's helplessness in the face of a corrupt society with the problem of the moral function and the efficiency of art. Of course, Hamlet's doubts about the Ghost's trustworthiness would hardly have surprised Shakespeare's contemporaries and in our century, many critics have taken up the debate. The text of the play is not very explicit on this point, however, but firmly directs our attention to Hamlet's tragic dilemma. He knows so much about the delusive nature of outward appearances and simple actions that it would be surprising indeed if he accepted the authority of the Ghost as unquestioningly as any conventional revenger.[13]

The whole soliloquy demonstrates again the distance between this play and the tradition of revenge tragedy, with its despairing, mentally deranged, and often aimlessly raving hero. In contrast, Hamlet's self-reproaches combine a sense of personal failure with a knowledge of the very limited scope of all human activity and hope in the superior authority of the actor's art. The soliloquy is not just a piece of rhetorical declamation; it is hardly even a monologue in the traditional sense, but, by its passionate language and the absence of patterned stylization, it gives the impression of a spontaneous outburst of long repressed emotions and of an intellectual process whose result is by no means certain from the beginning.[14] The hero gives vent to his frustration in unreflected execrations, recognizing at the same time the futility of such uncontrolled raging. The idea of the play seems to offer a solution and a way out of this feeling of useless failure.

The third act consists of a series of intrigues and counter-intrigues. The King is still trying to get to the bottom of Hamlet's secret, and the Prince wants to penetrate Claudius' public mask. Both of them succeed only to a very limited extent, but each of them is soon persuaded of his opponent's dangerous nature. At first Claudius acts much more purposefully and effectively. Hamlet's treatment of Ophelia is enough to convince him that his nephew is not a lovesick melancholic, but that a far more disturbing and threatening change of personality has taken place; the audience knows from the previous scene that he has thus arrived at a much truer assessment of Hamlet's mental state than Polonius. Again, we see the Prince from different points of view, none of them really objective or reliable; they supplement each other, but do not add up to a consistent portrait or an authoritative interpretation as yet.

Hamlet's third soliloquy is hardly integrated in the surrounding scene, either thematically or dramaturgically; it reflects a train of thought that seems quite independent of the actual situation and does not directly refer to the events happening around the hero. Most critics today would no longer accept the older interpretation of this famous passage, suggesting that Hamlet is contemplating suicide at this point; this is true only in a very general sense.[15] Hamlet has learnt for himself that the experience of the injustices, sufferings, and disappointments of our mortal existence forces on us the fundamental question why man decides to stay alive at all, since he can choose to abandon this life of his own free will. What are the chances if we want to alter this disillusioning state of things, either by acting or by suffering? Death, as the obvious way out, only presents the prospect of even worse, because unknown terrors, but this knowledge of unbounded and unpredictable threats lurking behind every possible decision will always sap our will-power and prevent any determined action; it is what Hamlet calls 'conscience':

> Thus conscience does make cowards of us all,
> And thus the native hue of resolution
> Is sicklied o'er with the pale cast of thought,
> And enterprises of great pitch and moment
> With this regard their currents turn awry
> And lose the name of action.   (III.1.83–8)

Many interpretations of *Hamlet* have read these lines as the most exact description of Hamlet's real dilemma and I think they are right to do so, although the passage can be paraphrased in many different senses: psychologically, philosophically, historically, or with a religious bias. It is obvious that Hamlet's intellectual disposition is averse to any simplifying and unpremeditated decision; any spontaneous action becomes for him problematic, not because of cowardice, feeble will-power, or an over-developed sensibility, but because of a most sensitive consciousness of omnipresent danger, deception and infectious corruption. Hamlet knows that it is hardly possible to commit oneself to any determined action without becoming guilty of rashness, injustice, or self-deception. This kind of summary hardly does justice to the soliloquy's wonderful wealth of associations and mature experience. It can only hint at the way a conventional revenge plot has provided an opportunity for wide-ranging moral reflection and the popular device of the dramatic monologue has been put to quite novel and unexpected uses.

The scene with Ophelia immediately following the soliloquy, again shows Hamlet from a very different point of view and leaves her with the impression of a pitifully shattered personality. Since she is here being used as a kind of decoy,[16] or at least does not meet him of her own initiative, her reproachful complaint about Hamlet's change of mind is somewhat surprising:

> for to the noble mind
> Rich gifts wax poor when givers prove unkind. (III.1.100–1)

As we have, so far, only been told about her own obedience in refusing any love-tokens from him, we have reason to doubt her complete sincerity here, and Hamlet's reaction shows that for him the whole affair is a thing of the past.[17] His more and more passionate outbursts are often explained – in criticism as well as on the stage – by the idea that at some point during the scene he gets wind of the eavesdroppers and begins to see through the whole deceptive maneuver.[18] Since he has already unmasked Rosencrantz and Guildenstern as the King's spies, his suspicion would not be surprising. His deep disturbance on account of his mother's behavior would also explain why Ophelia's role, as the instrument of the corrupt court, provokes him to such venomous attacks against her chastity, against procreation, birth and the truth of women in general. To Hamlet's 'antic disposition' is added the violence of spontaneous rage about her treachery which, in the context of the whole action, must seem far more vicious to him than to the audience because it confirms for him the experience of general moral corruption. Whether he actually sees the King and Polonius in the course of the scene or whether his excitement only comes from a general sense of human perfidy and deception does not materially affect the interpretation of the scene, and I am sure the text leaves the producer considerable freedom in this respect. I have seen the scene 'work' in very different productions.

Ophelia's own inner conflict is not dramatized by Shakespeare; all her behavior suggests weakness and helplessness rather than active falsehood, and the sincerity of her shocked grief at Hamlet's transformation is in no way called in question by the style of her moving lament. The portrait of Hamlet implied in her pathetic outburst is that of an ideal courtier; it hardly gives an idea of the Prince's individuality, but at this point in the play it is important in reminding us of the radical change in Hamlet and of his former stature:

O, what a noble mind is here o'erthrown!
The courtier's, soldier's, scholar's, eye, tongue, sword,
Th' expectancy and rose of the fair state,
The glass of fashion and the mould of form,
Th'observ'd of all observers, quite, quite down!   (III.1.152-6)

Since the audience sees only the various masks of Hamlet, except for his soliloquies, this reminder of what he once appeared to be, is particularly necessary to keep us aware of what has been destroyed.

The whole of the following scene, apart from the brief conversation with Horatio (III.2.52–90) shows Hamlet predominantly in his adopted role as madman until, after the play, there is an outburst of hysterical triumph. His manner of speech is, most of the time, that of the unpredictable and largely irresponsible court fool and satirist whom nobody calls to account, even where he is plainly offensive. By this strange behavior, however, he spoils the effect of his own plan because the court is more convinced of his rebellious and aggressive nature than of Claudius' guilt. At the end of the play-scene, Hamlet is quite certain that his suspicion is justified and that the Ghost's revelation was true, but he is no nearer to the execution of his revenge; on the contrary, he has betrayed his knowledge to the King who is now in a much better position to take precautions.[19]

For a long time, critics have argued about the question why the King interrupts the play at this particular point, and I think there are several equally 'right' ways of acting the scene without falsifying the text. What the text does make clear is that Claudius leaves the performance, thus breaking it up, and that there is a general impression of Hamlet having given offence. On the other hand, Hamlet glories in his success, without being contradicted by Horatio. Immediately afterwards, the King makes the most unambiguous confession of his crime we have yet heard, although Shakespeare has informed the audience even before the play-scene by an unmistakable aside of Claudius' guilt (III.1.49–54). We have known all the time that Hamlet's doubts are unjustified.

The play within the play dramatizes several possible effects of a stage performance in a particularly original manner. The court appears in the role of the audience, and the spectator in the theatre is able to observe different degrees of illusion.[20] The sensational playlet is clearly contrasted with the rest of *Hamlet* by its formalized language which gives it an antiquated and in many ways primitive character. It reduces the complex action of *Hamlet* to a simple murder story again and it presents at the same time, if indirectly, the events that took place before the play began, which we know only from the Ghost's report, but have not yet seen acted on the stage. The preliminary dumb show, too, belongs more with the primitive technique of popular drama and shows us the murder as a crude piece of pantomimic action. This makes it all the more memorable and leaves the spectator free to concentrate on the play as well as on the reaction of the stage-audience. That this prologue-like anticipation of the plot does not shock the King enough to make him leave the play, should not really be a matter for surprise. The whole play has already shown him to be a 'practised hypocrite';[21] it seems, above all, clear that it is the combination of play, dialogue and Hamlet's tell-tale comments that really persuade him to stop the performance. Its moral effect is only very limited, however, because it has not driven Claudius to a public confession of his crime, as Hamlet had obviously hoped. His confident announcement, 'If a do blench, / I know my course' (II.2.593–4), remains unfulfilled. The initiative still remains largely with Claudius whose public position is hardly affected by the play, although in the prayer-scene he betrays his grave uncertainty and sense of guilt.

This scene, at last, puts Hamlet in the position of Pyrrhus. With raised sword he stands above the defenceless King, but, unlike Pyrrhus, he is unable to kill his victim. The reasons he gives for his strange scruples are confusing rather than really consistent and may serve as an illustration of the way 'conscience does make cowards of us all'. Trying to anticipate all the consequences of his act, he arrives at the conclusion that to kill Claudius at this moment would be a reward, not a punishment. This is neither morally nor theologically convincing, but it demonstrates that Hamlet is incapable of deliberate and decisive action because he lacks the stupidity and ruthless determination of the traditional revenger as well as the untroubled confidence that such a simple act would really be the adequate answer to the Ghost's disturbing command. Apart from Hamlet's somewhat tortuous reasoning, however, the play does not give the impression that the Prince has failed in his moral obligation or that he has wrongfully ignored the Ghost's demand. In other revenge tragedies of the period, the hero does indeed feel that his vengeance must be as cruel and as original as possible and that his victim, even in the hour of death, must be tortured by the revelation of all his crimes;[22] but this is hardly the reason why we sympathize with Hamlet's hesitation in the prayer scene and find his decision entirely justified. The whole play has made sufficiently clear by now that simple retribution, according to the pattern of conventional revenge tragedy, would not remove any of the fundamental evils that corrupt the court and its head. The killing of Claudius, so obviously suggested by the situation, would not restore Hamlet's confidence in a just universe and would neither undo his father's death nor his mother's adultery. The play presents a world in which Hamlet's incapacity for spontaneous and decisive action seems the natural consequence of being fully alive and conscious and it convinces the audience that Hamlet's tragic dilemma cannot be sorted out by a conventional catastrophe. Claudius, on the other hand, is more like the traditional political criminal who is haunted by his sins, but who is unwilling to do practical penance. He remains a hardened sinner trying, above everything, to secure his gains and to protect himself from any possible retribution. Thus, he has already arranged for Hamlet to be shipped to England and given his assent to Polonius' plan, immediately after the 'nunnery scene', to have his mother talk to him (III.1.183–90).

The 'closet scene' (III.4) that follows begins as another eavesdropping scene, but soon takes a very different turning. The spontaneous killing of Polonius is Hamlet's first really decisive and unpremeditated action of any consequence; it is done so swiftly that there is no time for 'conscience', but it is as wrong as it is disastrous. Instead of the King, Hamlet has dispatched the overzealous, but by no means malicious or evil counsellor and he has thus become the murderer of another dearly loved father. After the murder of old Hamlet, reported by the Ghost and re-enacted by proxy in *The Murder of Gonzago*, this is the first real killing in the world of the tragedy; after this, there can only be a tragic outcome. Hamlet still has not come any nearer to the fulfilling of his great task; there is no indication in the text that he has ever thought of Polonius as the King's accomplice. He has now forfeited the mask of the harmless melancholic and his crime will set in motion another revenge plot, very different from his own procrastination, with himself as the object of an avenger's hatred and almost on a level with Claudius. The swift deed stands in pointed contrast to the previous scene. Moved by sudden passion, Hamlet is indeed capable of a decisive and fatal act, but to commit a murder while fully conscious of all the implications and consequences, is quite impossible for him.[23]

The contrasts within the scene itself, however, are just as striking as the contrast to the prayer scene. Hamlet has come with the intention of being 'cruel, not unnatural' (III.2.386) and of impressing on her the magnitude of her sin, while she, on her side, at the instigation of her husband and Polonius, wants to get to the bottom of his secret. The dialogue between mother and son stands almost exactly in the middle of the play and it is particularly characteristic of Shakespeare's effort to broaden the theme of revenge and to present the hero's tragic dilemma as a moral problem of fundamental relevance. In a way, the scene is a variation of the traditional persuasion scene, but comparison with similar situations in other plays shows how much more unpredictable and wide-ranging Shakespeare's version is.[24]

Hamlet does not threaten his mother, as she thinks at first, but tries to make her understand her guilt and its impact on himself. This is almost Hamlet's first determined initiative which the audience sees acted on the stage and, after *The Murder of Gonzago*, his first deliberate attempt to live up to his task as he sees it. The intensity of the scene makes clear that, for the first time in the play, Hamlet is putting all his soul into his speech and action. The desire to bring his mother to a recognition of the moral issues involved is evidently even more important to him than conventional ideas of revenge, just as his mother's adultery was more fundamentally disillusioning for him than his father's murder.

The unexpected reappearance of the Ghost also underscores the central significance of this scene, but it is no less ambiguous than the first apparition. Again, it is 'the very witching time of night' (III.2.379), and we realize how little has really happened, in terms of a revenge plot, since that first night on the battlements. Hamlet feels the return of the murdered father to be a reproachful reminder of his neglected duty and the Ghost confirms it, though with tantalizing brevity. More urgent for him, as for the Prince, seems to be the concern for Gertrude's soul: again, the play suggests a remarkable congruence between the apparition and Hamlet's state of mind. The Ghost is visible only to him and it is not some supernatural command from outside that he delivers, but an admonition that closely agrees with what Hamlet's own conscience tells him.[25] It is also the Ghost's last appearance in the play; there is no hint as to whether this unquiet spirit finds his eternal rest at the end of the tragedy. This ambiguous role shows once more that he is only partially modelled on the traditional spirit of revenge who is only concerned with cruel vengeance and who can therefore express his satisfaction at the final holocaust, as the Ghost of murdered Andrugio in Marston's *Antonio's Revenge*, written at the same time:

> 'Tis done; and now my soul shall sleep in rest.
> Sons that revenge their father's blood are blest.   (v.3.114–15)[26]

This is hardly the sort of comment we would expect from Old Hamlet's Ghost.

The surprising appearance of the Ghost has put Hamlet in a state of extreme tension and excitement, very similar to that in the first act, and it confirms his total obsession with the task laid upon him, even though this task is so vaguely defined and so difficult to fulfil.

What also remains rather vague is the result of Hamlet's confrontation with his mother. He has extracted from her a promise of silence and a profession of regret for what she has done (as in Shakespeare's source), but the text does not make quite clear whether true repentance and a genuine recognition of the moral situation has been achieved. The chief effect of the scene is a deeper exploration of Hamlet's character: again it is made quite clear to the audience that the delaying of his revenge is not at all due to a general weakness of purpose and will-power, but to a strong sense of what the Ghost's demand really involves. For Hamlet, it can only be satisfied by moral insight and a change of heart. He feels himself chosen as an instrument of Heaven, scourged and punished, but also destined to be a scourge and a punishment for others:

> heaven hath pleas'd it so,
> To punish me with this and this with me,
> That I must be their scourge and minister.   (III.4.175–7)

Hamlet's dilemma and the revenge theme are thus again combined with a penetrating diagnosis of the poisoned court society and the evils of our mortal existence. The end of the scene, however, brings us back to a world of political intrigue and deceitful stratagems.[27] Hamlet reasserts his intention to outwit his opponents from behind his mask of madness and to defeat them with their own weapons:

> For 'tis the sport to have the enginer
> Hoist with his own petard, and't shall go hard
> But I will delve one yard below their mines
> And blow them at the moon. O, 'tis most sweet
> When in one line two crafts directly meet.   (III.4.208–12)

This sounds more like the traditional revenger than the philosophical and procrastinating Prince and reveals an aspect of Hamlet we have hardly been prepared for. It introduces a phase in the play which is dominated by Claudius' defensive strategies and Laertes' passionate thirst for revenge, but only serves to illustrate, in the last resort, the questionable nature of such unscrupulous activity in which Hamlet takes no part at all, except as the passive victim. He hardly appears during the whole of the fourth act, and up to the very end of the tragedy we only see him in the role of one who waits and reacts, with none of his opponents' inventive business. The general pattern is similar to that after Hamlet's first encounter with the Ghost, though with significant variations and more sinister purpose. The brief appearance of Fortinbras is a characteristic example. His theatrical military adventure is another instance of noisy activity, without convincing motivation, and Hamlet is disturbed by it, just as he was by the actor's impressive tirade and the story of Pyrrhus. Again, he finds himself confronted with a spirit of effective and unreflected action which stands in pointed contrast to his own 'conscience'; the contrast is visually underlined by the simultaneous presence of the two young princes and heirs on the stage with no direct contact between them. Hamlet's soliloquy, left out in the First Folio, at first sight seems a little unnecessary here. The Prince, who once more reproaches himself for his own inactivity and tries to whip himself into a mood of murderous passion, is more impotent than ever before and a long way from the realization of his revenge because he is practically a prisoner and, according to the King's plan, on the way to his death. It is the only scene of the play which is clearly set away from the Danish court and the only scene in which he is not recognized as the Danish Prince. In this hopeless situation, his simple resolution,

> from this time forth
> My thoughts be bloody or be nothing worth.   (IV.4.65–6)

strikes us as a desperate attempt to play the part of the traditional revenger, but it remains a mere gesture without practical consequences, except for the not very impressive counter-intrigue against Rosencrantz and Guildenstern, and the soliloquy itself suggests quite a different attitude. Though he feels ashamed, he really has nothing but scorn for Fortinbras' theatrical expedition; his motive is an 'eggshell' (IV.4.53), even more trivial than the grief of Hecuba that moved the actor to tears. The monologue as a whole does not give the impression that this is a real alternative to Hamlet's own inactivity; most spectators will sympathize and identify with Hamlet's kind of activity, such as he showed in the 'closet scene' rather than with the martial gestures of Fortinbras. Hamlet's 'bloody thoughts', however, are no more than a desperate intention, and when we see the Prince again at the beginning of the last act, after a long absence from the stage, nothing seems to be left of this revengeful and ruthless mood.

Most of the fourth act, with its very lively and swift-moving action, can be seen as an indirect commentary to Hamlet's violent self-reproaches. Everything we have seen of him in the first three acts has demonstrated that even a much graver cause than an 'eggshell' or a 'straw' cannot move him to swift action although his right, his honor and his filial duty are far more directly involved than in the case of Fortinbras. Yet for the audience none of the examples of quick determination presented by the play will appear as a convincing alternative to Hamlet's disabling conscience, and even during his long absence from the stage the spectator will increasingly appreciate his moral scruples. Laertes' impetuous, but quickly diverted rebellion against the King is a superficially heroic reaction to the death of a father, just like the noisy expedition of Fortinbras. He turns into action what Hamlet only talks and thinks about, and his impulsive and at the same time undignified stratagems strongly remind us of the fact that these are exactly the courses Hamlet does not choose to adopt although he is quite capable of equally spontaneous phantasies. His first violent reaction to the Ghost's revelation is just like Laertes' actual behavior, but it is only a verbal gesture:

> Haste me to know't, that I with wings as swift
> As meditation or the thoughts of love
> May sweep to my revenge.   (I.5.29–31)

The audience knows what has become of this protestation, and Laertes' hysterical threat, 'To cut his throat i'th' church' (IV.7.125), strikes us as a brutal and not very impressive outburst in comparison, in spite of our sympathy with his grief at his father's death and his sister's mental collapse and in spite of Hamlet's wistful admiration for this kind of unscrupulous impetuosity.

In the context of the whole play, the Laertes plot is, of course, another variation on the theme of revenge.[28] For Laertes, Ophelia unwittingly fulfils the function of the Ghost, urging him to avenge his father:

> Hadst thou thy wits and didst persuade revenge,
> It could not move thus.   (IV.5.167–8)

His desire for revenge makes him ignore all those considerations and obligations that for Hamlet are insurmountable obstacles:

> To hell, allegiance! Vows to the blackest devil!
> Conscience and grace, to the profoundest pit!
> I dare damnation. To this point I stand,
> That both the worlds I give to negligence,
> Let come what comes, only I'll be reveng'd
> Most throughly for my father.   (IV.5.131–6)

He is prepared to risk 'both the worlds' for his revenge, thus making light of the crucial question reflected in Hamlet's 'To-be-or-not-to-be' soliloquy where it was the very uncertainty of our knowledge about the other world that prevented, to Hamlet's mind, any determined action. Almost for the first time in the play, the orthodox condemnation of revenge is tacitly taken for granted; Laertes knows that revenge has something to do with 'damnation' and 'grace'. This theological debate is apparently ignored by Hamlet; at least he does not use the same terminology. On the other hand, it is the Christian arguments against revenge, an awareness of its temporal as well as eschatological consequences, and the conviction that injury cannot be atoned by injury, which are, in the last resort, decisive for Hamlet's inactivity, even though they are not analysed, but mentally experienced.

At the end of the fourth act, an elaborate intrigue has been worked out against the absent hero; the initiative is now all on the side of his enemies and no scheme of revenge is remotely in sight. The conventions of revenge tragedy have been completely reversed since in most traditional revenge tragedies it is at this point that the vengeance approaches its execution and the revenger has succeeded in gathering about him a group of like-minded associates.

The graveyard scene, therefore, comes as a surprise to the audience after all the activities of the last act and directs our attention to very different aspects of the revenge theme. The grave-digger and his fellow – in the early editions they are simply called 'Clowns' – begin a comedy dialogue that makes Ophelia's death the subject of pseudo-learned hair-splitting and macabre witticism. The conventional technique of comic word-play and repartee is applied to a tragic event; it is hardly appropriate to speak of 'comic relief' here, because death and decay are little less real and disturbing when discussed at this stylistic level. In fact, it is one of the particularly significant achievements of Elizabethan tragedy that it admits such popular elements which are diametrically opposed to stylized pathos, even in moments of the greatest tragic intensity.

It is characteristic of Hamlet's astonishing versatility, demonstrated already in the first half of the play, that he can adapt to this new tone with complete ease and show a real interest in the clown's profession. In this unusual encounter, death confronts him with an immediacy that adds a new, urgent directness to all his previous reflections and even makes the corrupt Danish court appear in a different light. The tradition of the Dance of Death, an insistent *memento mori*, reappears again and again in the tragedy of the period, with particular aggressiveness, for instance, in Tourneur's *The Revenger's Tragedy* and the *The Atheist's Tragedy* where skulls become a rather macabre and over-emphatic stage-property and even part of the action.[29] In *Hamlet*, however, it is not a matter of sensational effect, but of the intensely felt experience of mortality and impermanence. In his witty exchange with the clown Hamlet, who has himself played the fool on other occasions, by no means gets the better and even finds himself indirectly mocked in the grave-digger's account of young Prince Hamlet. His own grotesque enlarging on the theme of decay, mildly criticized by Horatio, combines pseudo-logic with the terrifying realization of general corruption. Even the duty to revenge suddenly takes second place in view of this powerful impression of mortality, and many readers have wondered why Hamlet seems to waste his time with these clowns in such seemingly unconcerned and relaxed manner, without even mentioning the task that has occupied him so exclusively up to now. More helpful than attempts at psychological explanations is the recognition of thematic links. Hamlet's questioning has assumed a new urgency and the radical nature of his reflections must have its bearing on his former conviction that he was born to set right the times that are out of joint. The text strongly suggests that Hamlet has reached a new degree of wisdom and maturity; but this is not presented as a continuous and consistent development, rather like a sudden leap onto a different level of discourse.[30]

The following scene, with Hamlet's account of his adventures at sea, makes even more evident that he seems to have adopted a different attitude to the problems of human initiative and divine providence. Even 'rashness' and 'indiscretion' are, for him, no longer aspects of personal responsibility, but subordinated to a higher will:

> Our indiscretion sometime serves us well
> When our deep plots do pall; and that should learn us
> There's a divinity that shapes our ends,
> Rough-hew them how we will – (v.2.8–11)

The questions that have troubled Hamlet are no longer, as in the central soliloquy, answered by an admission of our incapacity for spontaneous action, but rather by retreat into a kind of relaxed wisdom that seems to see no reason for self-reproach, but puts his trust into 'a divinity' beyond our human planning. Whether the spectator interprets this as resignation, irresponsibility, or confident reliance on God's providence depends largely on his own convictions. There is no doubt, however, that this gives a completely new direction to the traditional revenge tragedy. To be sure, Hamlet has, as he announced in the 'closet scene', crossed Claudius' murderous stratagem by an equally unscrupulous counter-intrigue, posting his old school-fellows to their certain death, but he does not see this as a personal success, but as the inevitable side-result of a larger confrontation. He explicitly refuses to accept moral responsibility for their death: 'They are not near my conscience' (v.2.58). For him they are only instruments of the King whom it is 'perfect conscience' to quit in his own manner (v.2.67). Hamlet's attitude to this second murder is quite different from his sincere regret after the killing of Polonius and his quarrel with Laertes in whom he sees a mirror of his own tragic case.[31]

In terms of the plot, however, Hamlet has become guilty of new murder and has furnished his opponents with another good reason for proceeding against him. This also means that his revenge must now be a race against time, which greatly adds to the dramatic suspense. Yet in spite of Hamlet's awareness that 'The interim is mine' (v.2.73), the initiative remains entirely on the side of the King and Laertes; in fact, the last act is the very opposite of the conventional finale of a revenge tragedy in which the revengers execute their deadly scheme, usually in the course of a ceremonial entertainment or 'show', such as the performance in

Kyd's *Spanish Tragedy*. In *Hamlet*, the pageant of the public duel is staged by the revenger's enemies and he is killed, according to plan. In a way, Laertes has now taken over the role of the traditional revenger. The plotters themselves, of course, perish as well, as victims of their own ingenuity, and Hamlet is finally avenged, though hardly by his own activity, but by a form of providence that agrees with his own idea of 'divinity'. He does kill Claudius in the brief moments still left to him, but this is a 'rashness' beyond all planning and foresight. The idea of some higher justice, whose instrument Hamlet has become, is also underlined by Laertes' comment 'He is justly serv'd' (v.2.332). Although he himself has struck the fatal blow, there is a strong impression that, in a deeper sense, the revenge has been taken out of his hands, and the end of the tragedy, demonstrating the self-destructive forces of evil, can be seen as a confirmation of Hamlet's belief, obviously derived from the New Testament, that 'There is a special providence in the fall of a sparrow' (v.2.215–6). For an Elizabethan audience at least, this would have been a reminder of the Christian concept of a just providence to whom man may confidently leave the initiative (and the revenge).

This concept does not stand alone in the play, however, but is held up against other attitudes and ideas of how man's fate is determined. Hamlet himself refers to 'providence' while stressing his personal independence of discouraging premonitions: 'We defy augury' (v.2.215). He evidently means some inner voice, warning him against the duel, and he ignores sensible objections which might also be the work of providence and could well have saved his life. The final ending does not endorse any simple theory. It satisfies the audience's desire for justice in a technical sense, but it is not a triumph for Hamlet. Old Hamlet's death is avenged at last, but the son has fulfilled his father's demand only in a rather indirect manner and at the cost of his own life.

In view of this ending it is pointless to ask whether Hamlet has, in the last resort, failed or whether the play is a vindication of his scruples and his trust in providence.[32] No other tragic hero in Western literature reflects so deeply and intensely upon the possibilities and dangers of his situation, and none is so painfully aware of the disabling complexity of moral dilemmas. This deadly struggle with a task he feels to be beyond his powers, yet can neither reject nor fulfil by some precisely defined action seems to me at the heart of this fascinatingly inconclusive tragedy, and an audience who, after all this, still has the assurance to give moral marks to the protagonists, has really failed to face up to these most distinctive qualities of the play.[33]

Readers and spectators will probably give very different answers to the questions whether Hamlet in the end has come any nearer the fulfilment of his self-assigned task to set right a corrupt society. Neither impetuous determination nor inactive waiting for providence appeared to him really practicable alternatives. In the end, it is the uncomplicated warrior Fortinbras, obviously untroubled by any disabling reflection, who suddenly finds himself King of Denmark and orders Hamlet to be buried with military honors:

> For he was likely, had he been put on,
> To have prov'd most royal;   (v.2.402–3)

As at the end of *Romeo and Juliet*, it is, above all, the glorifying memory of the dead and of their brave fight against hostile odds that is the last message to the survivors. This is evidently more important to the dramatist than the prospect of an uncertain future. In most of Shakespeare's tragedies, this prospect is rather muted and at best mildly hopeful. The tragedy turns our attention from the exceptional heroic situation to a much less intense and glamorous, sobering reality.[34] The unreflecting competence of Fortinbras will set very different standards from those of Hamlet's intellectual and moral restlessness. The poison corrupting all the Danish court has been removed with the death of Claudius, but this court will have become much emptier without the insistently questioning and challenging presence of the Prince, and the audience will leave the play without being particularly interested in the further fate of the Danish kingdom. Hamlet's changed attitude in the last act and the fundamental relevance of the questions raised by his situation has the effect that our emotional involvement has already been to some extent turned away from the dramatic action, and the actual execution of the revenge has already been displaced as the real centre of tragic suspense by other issues before the final scene, since Hamlet himself has increasingly recognized the futility of passionate action and confident planning. The deeper and more lasting suspense is created by Hamlet's mental agony, by the wide range of political, moral and philosophical themes, as well as by the rich stylistic diversity. This may explain why generations of readers and spectators have been able to identify with a Prince whose situation at first hardly seems to differ from that of many conventional revengers, but who embodies such an energy of intellectual honesty and moral responsibility that all the psychological riddles and the unsolved problems of the text seem to be of comparatively little moment.

OTHELLO

Shakespeare's second 'great' tragedy is so different from *Hamlet* that there is much to be said against treating the two plays under the same heading. On the other hand, any classification becomes dubious if too much significance is attached to it. *The Tragedy of Othello, the Moor of Venice*[35] may be described as the tragedy of a fundamental disillusion that destroys the hero's life, and as such we may usefully associate it with *Hamlet*; though other links are equally illuminating. As a tragedy of love, *Othello* suggests comparison with *Romeo and Juliet* and, even more, with *Troilus and Cressida*, written shortly before (between 1601 and 1603), where the protagonist suffers an experience very similar to that of Othello. *His* jealousy and disillusion, to be sure, are entirely justified by the actual events and are not the result of deceitful slander, but they hit him with equally destructive force. Even more striking are the affinities with Shakespeare's comedy *Measure for Measure* (1604), written, it seems likely, almost simultaneously with *Othello*, in which the theme of temptation also plays a crucial part.[36] Both plays are based on Shakespeare's reading of Giraldi Cinthio's *Hecatommithi* (about 1564–5), a collection of novellas in the tradition of Boccaccio's *Decameron*, which Shakespeare seems to have used either in the original or in a French translation of 1583. Even at the level of the sources, then, there are surprising parallels between *Othello* and Shakespeare's romantic comedies: all his other tragedies, with the exception of *Romeo and Juliet*, are based on historical or legendary story material.[37]

In the frame of Cinthio's story collection, specific problems of love are illustrated by different tales, as in Boccaccio's *Decameron*. After the story of an unfaithful wife, justly punished by her husband, a different tale is announced as a rejoinder: it is to be the case of a loving and faithful wife, guiltlessly murdered by a weak husband who is deceived by malicious slander. As always, it is most instructive to trace the changes introduced by Shakespeare in relation to his source. The similarities between the two versions are quite striking, but it is even more remarkable how the dramatist has condensed the action, remodelled the character of the tempter and completely altered the ending.

As in the case of *Romeo and Juliet*, the time of the action – weeks and months in the source – is compressed into a few days. A long and apparently untroubled marriage is changed into a very brief moment of blissful ecstasy, a single, repeatedly interrupted wedding-night and a catastrophe whose irresistible swiftness leaves no time for rational reflection. There is hardly any room for sober meditation and deliberate planning in the rushed sequence of events, whereas in the novella, it is only after the wedding that the slanderer makes his appearance. He has tried to win the lady's favor for some time without success and this is why he devises his scheme of revenge which is then carefully prepared by the two men and executed with great circumspection; the discovery and punishment of the murderers come later: 'God, the just observer of men's hearts, did not intend such vile wickedness to go without proper punishment.'[38]

Shakespeare combines this concentration of the temporal sequence with a dramatic tightening of cause and effect. Iago becomes the omnipresent manipulator, working out intrigues from the very beginning. He has already given some proof of his inventive and deceitful cunning before he starts to goad Othello into a jealous rage that is as blind as it is groundless. Here the dramatist has obviously been influenced by the popular convention of the hypocritical stage-villain and tempter, and indeed, it is clear that the dramatic tradition, the use of dialogue and soliloquy, the arrangement of scenes, and the rhetoric of characterization were much more important for the final shape of the play than the mere story outline.

Still, the nature of the action is to a large extent determined by the Italian novella tradition. As in *Romeo and Juliet*, we are introduced to one of the Italian city-states of the Renaissance, where public politics and domestic intrigue often merge and the children's idealistic expectations of love clash with the parents' concept of dynastic family arrangements. Here too, the play begins almost like a comedy. Othello is no youthful Romeo, but, in league with the daughter, he deceives the old father, and the conclusion of the first act is almost like the happy ending of a romantic comedy of love. The helplessly protesting father whom the young people have outwitted, is a traditional character of comedy and the whole situation reminds us of other Shakespearian comedies derived from Italian novellas, such as *The Taming of the Shrew*, *A Midsummer Night's Dream*, *The Merchant of Venice* and *All's Well That Ends Well*.[39] The tone, however, is rather more sinister from the very beginning, due to a number of threatening elements that darken the impression of a harmless comedy-world. Neither Iago the intriguer nor, perhaps, the obtuse Roderigo are pure comedy-figures: the nocturnal encounters and the political crisis overshadow the apparent triumph of the lovers who soon find themselves entirely on the defensive. Above all, Othello's race and color are unmistakable pointers to the fact that this is not the conventional union of two lovers destined for each other, but a partnership far more exceptional and beyond the limits of romantic comedy. This is another reason why the father's opposition cannot be ignored quite as light-heartedly, although the sympathy of the audience is firmly on the side of the lovers.

As in the earlier love tragedy, the first scene creates the atmosphere of a society divided by personal animosity. Iago introduces himself as the slighted honest man who finds that it is impossible to rise in this world without hypocrisy and deception, and he stirs up public disorder to vent his hatred of Othello. His coarse diction, brutally emphasizing the animal nature of love, reminds us of the role of Mercutio and seems to class him as a comic character, just as Brabantio's eloquent accusation echoes the loud lamentations of Shylock after Jessica's elopement. In this world, Othello's love offends against established rules and makes for a complete change of tone as well as a new quality of human relationships. When the lovers first appear in the play, wooing, mutual vows, and the decision to marry are already behind them. The tragedy focusses on a very different stage in the development of love from that presented in *Romeo and Juliet* and most romantic comedies. This couple confronts an unsympathetic society with the same uncompromising assurance and determination to belong to each other. Their love, however, is not just threatened from without, but by its own exceptional quality which is repeatedly stressed during the first scenes of the play. It is not his family or social status that makes Othello unacceptable as a son-in-law for Brabantio, but his very individuality and otherness, symbolized by his color, and unlike Romeo, he cannot offer, even rhetorically, to change his name.

Othello's great speech before the Senate in defence of his love recapitulates for the audience the events preceding the first act, and this narrative does not confirm any idea of a comic elopement we might have formed, but gives particular emphasis to the fundamental difference between this love and the clichés of romantic passion.[40] It is not love at first sight, but a love that is fully aware of the partner's individuality formed by his past, of his unique quality, and a love, furthermore, that has not been aroused by enchanting appearance and courtly wooing, but by undisguised self-revelation. For both of them, their love has opened up completely new areas of experience. Before his encounter with Desdemona, Othello has lived only in a world of military exploit and exotic adventure, and through him Desdemona catches her first direct glimpse of this glamorous form of life, so different from all her familiar environment. Her amazed fascination by his impressive account turns into worship of the man, and this in turn awakens his equally unconditional love:

> She loved me for the dangers I had passed,
> And I loved her that she did pity them.   (1.3.166–7)

Desdemona's love seems like the fulfilment of the desire Sidney's Astrophil addresses to Stella: 'pity the tale of me.'[41] Speech, as the expression of the whole person, calls forth sympathy and pity, the chief reaction expected by the courtly lover of his lady; in traditional love poetry, it is always pity that is the first step towards full acceptance.[42]

The quality of this exceptional union comes out even more emphatically in Desdemona's confession of a love that is not based on superficial desire, but on a recognition of the other's personality; it cannot possibly be changed for a different partner, like so many couplings in Shakespeare's romantic comedy:

> My heart's subdued
> Even to the very quality of my lord.
> I saw Othello's visage in his mind
> And to his honours and his valiant parts
> Did I my soul and fortunes consecrate.   (1.3.246–50)

In retrospect, the modern reader may well ask whether this kind of fascination by the unknown can really be a reliable basis for a lasting marriage and whether the partners really know what they commit themselves to. The text does not give the least hint of any doubt or misgiving, but confirms the impression of an unconventional and unconditional love that is completely sure of itself: 'My life upon her faith!' (I.3.290).[43]

The claim of such love to the whole person of the beloved is made concrete in Desdemona's expressed wish to accompany her husband on his military expedition to Cyprus. Soldier and lover are to be united in his person, and he accepts this part with the emphatic assurance that his love is not to be mistaken for youthful passion and therefore will by no means prevent him from fulfilling his military obligations. This motif is already in Shakespeare's source, where it is expressly stated that the lady is 'impelled not by female appetite but by the Moor's good qualitites'.[44] Shakespeare underlines this aspect of their love in a way that leaves open the question of possible dangers to this exceptional union. It is a union, at any rate, hardly appreciated by society, even though it is tolerated in view of the political emergency and even though the Duke obviously does not share Brabantio's revulsion, but advises him to accept the inevitable (I.3.200–7). The triteness of these sententious couplets adds to the impression of thoughtless unconcern and, consequently, of the couple's complete isolation. Othello is accepted and needed by the Venetians only in his capacity as an expert military leader. In his role as lover and husband he is left entirely to himself, pursued by the curses of Brabantio and the scheming hatred of Iago whose soliloquy concludes the scene; it gives further weight to the forebodings of imminent dangers gathering around the unsuspecting lovers.

The prose dialogue between Iago and Roderigo, too, returns to the level of envious intrigue and deliberate disparagement of idealistic love. Roderigo's jealousy and stupidity is skilfully exploited by Iago for his own purposes and Othello's love dragged down to his own level of speech. Iago deliberately suggests that these lovers are no different from all those who are ruled by the lowest instincts of selfishness and sexual lust, in a world without lasting affection and faith. Iago's own actions, however, show that he himself does not believe in this view and the audience is even less likely to be convinced by it; but the dialogue gives some indication as to the vulnerable side of Othello's love and of the kind of test to which he will be submitted.

In his soliloquy Iago finally reveals himself as a consummate practitioner of deception and as a resolute intriguer. Like Hamlet, he presents to the audience a very different face from that seen by the other characters and comments to the audience on his role-playing. Disguise and stratagem, in contrast to Hamlet, only serve his own selfish ends and are instruments of his deadly hatred, though the reasons he offers for this hatred seem hardly sufficient to account for its violence. From what we have seen of Othello so far, it is difficult to take Iago's jealousy of him very seriously and, as critics have pointed out, Iago himself does not state in so many words that the vague rumors of Othello's sexual escapades are really the chief justification for his malicious activity. He is far more concerned with the practical consequences of his hatred than with its motivation. Coleridge's famous description of the soliloquy as 'the motive-hunting of motiveless malignity' is still a more adequate account of most readers' and spectators' first impression than many later speculations about Iago's personality and the reasons for his villainy.[45] The text also suggests, of course, that Iago feels slighted by Cassio's promotion, and he is obviously less worried by his wife's possible infidelity than by the idea of public humiliation; but Shakespeare's rhetoric and the whole character of Iago persuade us that all these reasons are insignificant in comparison with the relentless energy of his malevolence. His function in the play and the technique of his soliloquies obviously characterize him as a descendant of the diabolic tempter and Vice, who appears in many morality plays of the sixteenth century.[46] Even without this historical reminiscence he demonstrates the disturbing possibilities of an intellect determined to corrupt, to deceive, and to ignore all moral considerations; even the trusting generosity and idealism of his opponent is exploited as a means to manipulate and to destroy him. The soliloquy takes the audience into the speaker's confidence and almost makes us accomplices of his sinister scheming, but the result appears to express the dramatist's verdict rather than genuine self-knowledge on Iago's part:

> I have't. It is engendered. Hell and night
> Must bring this monstrous birth to the world's light.　(1.3.385–6)

Here, as elsewhere in the play, the terminology suggests associations between Iago's activities and the Christian concept of the satanic tempter, which is another reason why his hatred needs as little psychological justification as Desdemona's unselfish love.

The first act looks like the prologue to the real tragedy. The break is emphasized by an unspecified time interval and a striking change of scenery, the only one in the whole play. The transition from the public affairs of the community to the more restricted area of personal relationships is particularly noticeable in this tragedy.[47] The presence of the Venetian envoys in the last scene refers us back to the beginning and reminds us once more of Othello's public responsibilities. Even though the play's central conflict comes close to the genre of domestic tragedy and the hero's fate is not as closely identified with that of the state as in *Hamlet*, *King Lear*, or *Macbeth*, his downfall affects the whole community of Venice, whose concept of order and civilization is threatened by it; the political background is unmistakably present even in the 'domestic' scenes of the play. As Othello's trust in Desdemona's faith is gradually undermined, his competence as the preserver of law and order declines, and the Venetian outpost is seriously endangered. Without making such parallels too obvious, the tragedy suggests an inner connection between the Christian war of defence against the Turks and Othello's tragic struggle against chaos; a contemporary audience, still under the impression of a very real danger of the Turkish aggressors to Europe, would have felt these associations much more immediately than a twentieth-century spectator.[48]

In Cyprus, the lovers are outside the social frame of reference that, for Desdemona at least, has so far been the only norm she has known, and they are, in a way, completely dependent on each other. Neither full integration into society nor determined revolt against its sanctions are possible here. Love, as the mutual partnership of two individuals, is put to the test and this turns into a conflict between order and chaos, Christian self-control and uncontrolled passion.

The arrival of Othello once more combines the private and the public themes. The Turkish danger seems to have been averted for the time being, the tempestuous sea has safely been crossed, and the island welcomes the victorious governor who represents their hope of lasting peace. The dramatist creates the impression that the lovers' reunion after a separation full of dangers for each of them is the very climax of their love's fulfilment and at the same time an act of public recognition. Like Romeo, Othello gives expression to this ecstatic happiness by a death wish that suggests an unconscious awareness of the precarious nature of such bliss:

> If it were now to die,
> 'Twere now to be most happy; for I fear

My soul hath her content so absolute
That not another comfort like to this
Succeeds in unknown fate.   (II.1.181–5)[49]

Desdemona's love does not express itself in this kind of rhetorical profession, but in a simple sentence stating her hope that their mutual affection will go on growing and maturing. The dramatist's stylistic means of characterizing her are very different from those used in the case of Juliet, whose far more lyrical speeches rather emphasize the almost symmetrical mutuality of their love. Desdemona is much less declamatory in her utterances than Othello, but the very simplicity and unsophisticated precision of her declarations of love contradict any interpretation – on stage or on paper – that hints at some insincerity or superficiality of her affection. For the dramatist, a less emphatic form of characterization evidently seemed sufficient in her case because the whole action shows her to be the victim of unfounded slander, and less determination or independent decision are demanded of her by the plot than of Juliet. The fact that her unrestrained and completely unsuspicious behavior seems to offer a foothold for Iago's intrigue can certainly not be held against her, but helps to make the following developments more credible. The first scene of the second act ends, very much like the preceding one, with a dialogue between Iago and his first victim Roderigo followed by another soliloquy in which the villain explains his intentions to the audience. This gives further prominence to the schemes prepared against the lovers and to the imminence of dangers gathering around them, while they themselves are completely unaware of any threat to their happiness.

One of the most important of Shakespeare's additions to his source is the early introduction of the intriguer, who makes his appearance even before the hero (not, as in Cinthio, after the wedding) and whose consummate art of deception and scheming occupies far more room in the tragedy than in the novella. In Cinthio's story, he makes use of his suspected rival's demotion to slander him; in Shakespeare, the demotion is his own work, the first intrigue successfully planned and carried out by him. It is an impressive demonstration of his dangerous intelligence and of Othello's trusting nature which makes his later corruption by Iago far more credible. Iago deceives everybody, not just Othello, and it shows a complete misunderstanding of dramatic convention as well as of the play's moral premises to accept Iago's portrait of Othello as an ass, easily led about by the nose (1.3.383–4), as some critics have done.[50] The whole tragedy is based on the traditional idea that it is above all the honest characters, incapable of deception themselves, who fail to see through the mask of the diabolic hypocrite. Thus, Fielding's aside to the critical reader about Squire Allworthy's apparent gullibility applies equally to Shakespeare's characterization of Iago and his victims: 'Mr Allworthy must have had the insight of the devil (or perhaps some of his worse qualities) to have entertained the least suspicion of what was going forward.'[51] Like Fielding's reader, the spectator is in a privileged position because he is the only one who knows Iago's real intentions, and he is guilty of a psychological error (or indeed, for Fielding at least, a moral error) if he lets his superior knowledge direct his judgement of the characters deceived. In an actual performance, of course, a lot depends on the way Iago is acted, but it would be a serious distortion of the text if he were played in such a manner that only a credulous fool could be taken in by him. His manipulation of the carousing soldiers and the drunken Cassio is so skilful and generally convincing that even the publicly dishonored lieutenant thinks of him as his only reliable friend, and Othello only accuses him of an excess of naive good nature. It is true that Iago can only succeed so quickly because Cassio really does not show much self-command and cannot carry strong drink; Othello's reaction suggests that his self-control, too, has its limits. His authority restores order and he himself insists emphatically on the contrast between the Venetian Christians and Turks, heathens or barbarians. But even Montano's diplomatic half-truths nearly put him out of countenance and his quick dismissal of Cassio, without any serious attempt to get to the bottom of the whole incident, makes us rather doubtful of his real strength under emotional stress. At the end of the scene, Iago appears as the triumphant winner. His handling of Cassio and Roderigo gives further evidence of his supreme ability to adapt his speech to the occasion and to the particular partner. Thus, in his conversation with Cassio, he uses arguments he would not accept from Roderigo; he talks of Desdemona as having 'so blest a disposition' (II.3.291) and extols her virtues, whereas earlier on he has spoken of her rather slightingly and has scornfully dismissed Rogerigo's praise of her 'most blest condition' (II.1.236–7).

In his great soliloquy at the end of the scene he parades his satisfaction at the astonishing success of his stratagem and uses older stage conventions in the way he directly addresses the audience.[52] His ironical defence against imaginary critics suggests exuberant pleasure in his own resourceful cunning:

> And what's he then that says I play the villain,
> When this advice is free I give, and honest,
> Probal to thinking, and indeed the course
> To win the Moor again?...
>   How am I then a villain
> To counsel Cassio to this parallel course
> Directly to his good?   (II.3.303–6,315–17)

His characterization of himself is equally unreserved:

> Divinity of hell!
> When devils will the blackest sins put on,
> They do suggest at first with heavenly shows
> As I do now.   (II.3.317–20)

Here, too, deliberate play-acting and 'authorial' comment seem to merge in the conventions of the villain's solo performance which treats the spectator as confidant, almost as an accomplice. It can hardly be understood in terms of realistic character-portrayal, but as a traditional means of audience information. When Iago refers to 'Divinity of hell' and to 'heavenly shows', he once more directs our attention to the theological aspect of his strategy, as well as to its efficiency proved by long experience.[53] Equally significant is his declared intention to work the victims' destruction by exploiting their most admirable qualities: 'out of her own goodness make the net/That shall enmesh them all' (II.3.328–9). Again, the conflict is explicitly presented as the confrontation of Good and Evil, and that, for all sophistication in detail, is what it basically amounts to. This makes any interpretation seem anachronistic that attempts to blur this fundamental moral constellation, e.g. by making Iago a personification of Othello's own worse qualities.

This question seems to be crucial for an adequate understanding of the central situation: Othello's 'temptation' and fall. The history of *Othello* criticism shows that it is an issue that has produced very controversial responses.[54] In the case of this tragedy, it is particularly clear that the contradictory readings are really due to a basic disagreement about the moral premises of the play. Of course, a moral assessment of the characters is hardly possible without considering the nature of dramatic conventions and the kind of realism to be expected from a poetical tragedy. Thus, it is completely inappropriate to see Othello as an easily corruptible character only because he undergoes a radical change within a single scene. The suddenness of the transformation is, without doubt, an important aspect of Shakespeare's technique of characterization and certainly not a simple proof of stupid credulity, as has been suggested.[55] It is necessary to insist on this because *Othello* criticism has often been devalued by moralizing arguments that tend to trivialize the moving pathos of this tragedy.

Up to the beginning of this century there seems to have been general agreement among the best and most influential Shakespeare critics, with very few exceptions, that the description of Othello as 'noble', repeated several times in the play, is an accurate assessment of his character as he appears to the reader and to most audiences; he is the pitiful victim of

Iago's diabolic cunning.[56] Different degrees of this view are possible, but they all have in common that we accept Othello's self-characterization as 'one not easily jealous' (v.2.341) and are fully convinced of the sincerity of his first love. Bradley's first lecture on *Othello* is a particularly impressive, if occasionally too idealizing, instance of this interpretation. His Othello is a truly admirable character, of heroic stature, exemplary self-control, and wonderful imagination, for whom we should only feel respect and compassion. When the play turns into the tragedy of his corruption, there must be an end to any moral evaluation: 'from this point we may abandon the ungrateful and undramatic task of awarding praise and blame'.[57] Many later critics have ignored this warning, which is inspired by a very deep understanding of Shakespeare's art, and have allowed themselves to be provoked by Bradley's unfamiliar pathos to fierce dissent. The most famous statement of such protest against the traditional reading is F. R. Leavis' spirited essay, 'Diabolic Intellect and the Noble Hero: or The Sentimentalist's Othello', charging Bradley with 'sentimental perversity', 'comical solemnity', and 'obtuseness to the tragic significance of Shakespeare's play'. In opposition to Bradley's 'noble hero', he presents an Othello who, from the start, has no real confidence in Desdemona, reacts with astonishing promptitude to Iago's insinuations, and idealizes himself in the end as a heroic martyr.[58] Iago represents something in Othello himself: 'the essential traitor is within the gates.'[59] According to Leavis, Bradley and many other critics have been taken in by Othello's sentimental rhetoric and blindly accepted his idealizing portrait of himself. Such a reading, repeatedly modified by later critics, really boils down to reducing the play to a tragedy of jealousy, a jealousy that can only be provoked to this extraordinary pitch because Othello's love has always been too selfish to survive any serious test.

Modern variants of this interpretation see the play as the tragedy of a marriage based on the spouses' complete ignorance of each other and lacking the mutual, unselfish trust of a genuine partnership.[60]

It is evidence of its teasing ambiguities that it appears to encourage such pyschological readings, more appropriate to the nineteenth-century novel than to Elizabethan drama, and there is no doubt that these aspects can be made quite prominent in a particular production. Important areas of the text are left out of account in this way, however, and it is interesting to note that some of the best more recent interpretations are marked by a partial return to Bradley's view. His reaction to the play is more attentive to Shakespeare's words as well as more generous and humane than the superficial psychological realism and moral censoriousness of the Leavis-kind of criticism. In Shakespeare's tragedy, even Iago himself never questions Othello's sincerity and greatness, and the general admiration and respect enjoyed by him also make him stand out as the exemplary leader and warrior. Nor would the heroic ideal of the soldier have presented the same kind of problem to an Elizabethan audience as it certainly does for many twentieth-century spectators.[61] If the Moor were intended to be 'easily jealous', the play would be dangerously near to a comedy of the cuckolded husband and Iago be reduced to a resourceful intriguer who exposes the hero's weakness to ridicule and devises an appropriate punishment.[62] Such a reading is, of course, contradicted by the whole tone of the play. I am convinced that the majority of readers instinctively experience something many critics seem to find impossible to imagine or to put into words: namely, that Othello's love is as sincere as it is vulnerable, that he is corrupted into a state of perverse and brutal jealousy, and yet the impression of genuine affection, integrity and dignity is not quite wiped out. If we read Othello's final speech only as an attempt to justify himself, based on an absurd delusion, then the temptation was indeed a revelation of his real character. It is quite obvious, however, that the dramatist meant it to be a diabolic act of poisoning and corruption, even though there is, as in every serious temptation, a kind of sinister interaction between the tempter and his victim. Iago's slanders are purposely aimed at Othello's most personal experience of love and they find the weak spot in his emotional make-up of which we had a glimpse earlier in the play. The dramatist does not, however, invite us to speculate on the psychological basis of Othello's love and its corruptibility; he is far more interested in the tragic experience of the man who believes himself to be fundamentally deceived in this wholehearted love. Othello's affection may well be founded on an insufficient knowledge of Desdemona, but it is above all, even more so than Romeo's love, a sincere, basically unselfish and humane decision, an act of faith, trust and dedication. Iago's intrigue does not, by any means, unmask an exaggerated claim or an unrealistic pose, but it deliberately destroys an ideal on which Othello has staked his entire existence.[63]

The decisive turning-point in the third act occurs in the long scene of dialogue between Othello and Iago. Desdemona only makes some brief appearances. Her insistent pleading for Cassio may seem imprudent to the spectator who knows Iago's plan, and it can create the impression that she is interfering in affairs that for Othello are not within the sphere of domestic and matrimonial discussion.[64] The audience must know, on the other hand, that Cassio is not as guilty as Othello assumes and therefore deserves her good will. What will be fatal for her is her completely unsuspecting solidarity with her husband's tried confidant and it is an important part of the dramatic motivation that her perfectly unambiguous and open behavior can be maliciously misinterpreted in the context of the whole episode with some semblance of plausibility. In referring to Cassio's 'honest face' (III.3.50) she shows a much clearer judgement than Othello, even though a little earlier she has revealed that she also thinks of Iago as 'honest' (III.3.5). The word keeps recurring throughout this part of the play with constantly changing implications. It is applied to Cassio as well as to Desdemona, but most often to Iago, a forceful reminder of the effectiveness of his mask and the thoroughness of the deception practised on everyone around him.[65]

It is unnecessary to retrace for the reader every step of Othello's painful corruption. Iago's consummate art of provocative hint, of pitying concern confessed with apparent reluctance, and of carefully selected half-truths, will be evident to any attentive reader. Never before in Elizabethan drama has the thorough disturbance and poisonous destruction of a human being by another, merely through insinuating speech, been portrayed so movingly and with such a wealth of stylistic nuance. Iago builds his strategy upon Othello's unsuspicious trust in his ensign's 'honesty', but above all upon the Moor's own awareness of his love's unusual qualities and his position as an outsider within an unfamiliar society, as well as on his uncompromising temper. To Othello, his love for Desdemona is like a new lease of life that saves him from relapsing into chaos and lawless passion. This is mentioned as an unreal possibility at a time when he is still absolutely sure of his love and has not the faintest suspicion of imminent danger:

> Excellent wretch! Perdition catch my soul
> But I do love thee; and when I love thee not,
> Chaos is come again. (III.3.90–2)

This is precisely what happens in the following scene: it is one extended dialogue between Othello and Iago, except for a brief interlude which helps to give the illusion of a longer development and illustrates Desdemona's loving care by a simple gesture. At the same time, the loss of the handkerchief provides Iago with the unforeseen opportunity of another intrigue.

The confrontation between Othello and Iago powerfully suggests the idea of barbarian animal forces, temporarily brought under control by the Moor's integration into the Christian community, but ready to erupt again at any time, like the Turks. They are not merely destructive, but exist side by side with genuine and elementary human virtues, like simple trust and an inability to practise deceitful cunning or to disguise one's own emotions. For Othello, the slightest doubt about Desdemona's faith must be doubt about everything that gives meaning to life and preserves it from utter chaos. He is completely incapable of imagining a world in which one might take infidelity and untruth – in marriage or friendship – for granted, and Iago's insinuation that this is exactly the kind of world Othello has allied himself to, is one of his most effective arguments because it makes Desdemona's behavior suddenly appear in an entirely new light. Against this view, Othello can only set his instinctive trust, but no firm knowledge of Venetian society based on familiar experience.

The more Iago succeeds in undermining the security of an irrational trust by insinuating doubt as to the validity of Othello's own experience, the more Othello feels the urge to gain a new kind of certainty by ocular proof. He surrenders to Iago's manipulated evidence as unconditionally as he had surrendered to Desdemona's love. He believes in the possibility of the most sophisticated deception and yet he is unable to enter imaginatively into the mentality of a hypocrite and to suspect the slanderer's most flimsy chain of evidence.[66] This obsessive inability to be satisfied with half-certainties and to brush aside vague suspicions makes him virtually greedy for tangible proof of Desdemona's infidelity:

> I swear 'tis better to be much abused
> Than but to know't a little.   (III.3.337–8)

In contrast, Iago has the perfect ability to analyse his opposite from a cold distance at any moment, and he takes careful note of the effect of his slanders which he describes most accurately to the audience:

> The Moor already changes with my poison:
> Dangerous conceits are in their natures poisons,
> Which at the first are scarce found to distaste
> But, with a little act upon the blood,
> Burn like the mines of sulphur.   (III.3.326–30)

The loss of confidence and trust is like a poison, changing for Othello all the world around him, making worthless all the familiar heroic and military ideals: 'Othello's occupation's gone' (III.3.358).[67] In this state of mind, 'Trifles light as air' assume for him the authority of biblical evidence (see III.3.323–5), and the dreadful vows in which he asks Iago to join him show him pursuing the thought of revenge with the same dedicated determination that had characterized his first love for Desdemona. He welcomes Iago's 'love' with 'acceptance bounteous' (III.3.471) and the significant gesture of joint kneeling deliberately suggests associations with a perverted marriage ritual by which Othello binds himself to Iago, divorcing himself from Desdemona. This is underlined by Iago's concluding statement, 'I am your own for ever' (III.3.480).

Imprisoned in his tragic error, Othello, subjectively, goes through a very similar experience to that of Hamlet. The woman who was to him symbol and living proof of a meaningful world has turned out to be a 'fair devil' (III.3.479), and the thought of revenge soon gives rise to the illusion that justice must be re-established by him. Personal insult is seen as a crime against human society and its values in general that can only be cured by a most cruel vengeance. But, as the whole scene makes clear, Othello has allowed himself to be dragged down to Iago's level; this becomes apparent above all in his language: he takes over Iago's cynical diction, and the loss of all self-command is revealed in the absence of that heroic rhetoric and imagery that had marked his introduction into the play from the first.[68] Of course, his pose as the revenger, inspired by just moral indignation, is at best a sinister parody of Hamlet's tragic dilemma; but the comparison can make Othello's genuine suffering more understandable. His pain is as real and sincere as his blindness is grotesque, and this should make him an object of moving compassion for the audience rather than of moral detestation; at least I am convinced that such is the dramatist's intention.

From this point, Othello sees himself in the role of the traditional revenger, one with which Hamlet can never quite identify; but in the later tragedy revenge is presented quite unambiguously as the infernal opposite of trusting love, and there is not the slightest moral ambivalence. Language and gesture emphasize the fact that Othello has come to an existential decision. By severing his bond with Desdemona and binding himself to Iago he chooses, in Christian terms, damnation instead of salvation, and it is by no means inappropriate to compare him to Marlowe's Doctor Faustus who turns his back on Heaven and vows allegiance to the Devil:

> Look here, Iago,
> All my fond love thus do I blow to heaven;
> 'Tis gone.
> Arise, black vengeance, from thy hollow cell!
> Yield up, O love, thy crown and hearted throne
> To tyrannous hate! Swell, bosom, with thy fraught,
> For 'tis of aspics' tongues. (III.3.445-51)

The passage combines the bloodthirsty rhetoric of Senecan revenge tragedy with the motif of moral choice familiar to Elizabethan audiences from the early moralities. From this point, Othello becomes more and more obsessed by his error, until in the end he himself recognizes the full extent of its perversity and, like Doctor Faustus, realizes all too late what he has lost. The tragedy of this fatal blindness is reduced to a rather trivial problem play if we read it like a modern debate on marriage, in which Desdemona has to share in the blame because she is not sufficiently considerate of Othello's violent temper, pleads too warmly for Cassio, and denies having lost the handkerchief.

However much modern productions may succeed in making the play's basic assumptions acceptable to a sceptical audience, the dramatist leaves us in no doubt that Desdemona is completely innocent of Othello's terrible transformation, even though her ignorance and her genuine concern for Cassio's reinstatement inevitably add fuel to his blind obsession. Since she is quite incapable of even imagining a state of mind such as his, it is also impossible for her to use diplomatic arts, to answer his suspicions directly, or to justify herself. Only the spectator who makes an effort to enter imaginatively into Othello's poisoned and feverish mind will be able to understand the provoking effect of some of her remarks, but the play makes it absolutely clear that Iago's slanders are without any foundation whatever, and that Desdemona fulfils the part of the true and loving wife without any qualification, as the slanderer himself knows as well as anybody. It is because she is so perfectly sure of their unchanging love and mutual trust that she can intercede for Cassio with such serene insistence, though her tactics may not be very skilful, or cover her embarrassment about the loss of the handkerchief (of which she is entirely innocent) with a lie.

For Desdemona, jealousy is 'baseness' (III.4.23), and the dramatist pointedly contrasts her unqualified trust not only with Othello's tortured agony, but also with Bianca's vulgar jealousy: it is to this level Othello and Iago descend in the eavesdropping scene (IV.1). The more obsessed and repulsive Othello's suspicions of Desdemona become, the firmer and purer her unshakeable love appears. This love is no illusion and it is not a subtle form of self-regard; it needs no superficial confirmation, but accepts the very otherness of the partner. Even to the most humiliating insults Desdemona responds with sadness and grief, not with resentment or a desire for revenge:

> Unkindness may do much,
> And his unkindness may defeat my life,
> But never taint my love. (IV.2.158–60)

She reaffirms this even more emphatically at a time when he has already laid plans for her death:

> my love doth so approve him
> That even his stubbornness, his checks, his frowns –
> Prithee, unpin me – have grace and favour in them. (IV.3.18–20)

The touchingly trivial little gesture underlines the unheroic simplicity of her profession. There is no trace of subversive irony here, in the sense that her naive unworldliness or childlike ignorance of the true situation are to be exposed to ridicule. That this is not the case may be supported by Shakespeare's own definition of true love in one of his best-known sonnets, where 'the marriage of true minds' and its blissful independence of time, age and mortality are celebrated:

> Love is not love
> Which alters when it alteration finds,
> Or bends with the remover to remove. (Sonnet 116)[69]

This describes with great precision the difference between Othello's and Desdemona's idea of love. His love is perverted into pitiful despair, but also malignant hate as soon as he believes himself deceived in the object of his affection. Desdemona's love, in contrast, is (in the words of the same sonnet):

> an ever-fixèd mark
> That looks on tempests and is never shaken;

She is indeed completely unshaken in her devotion to her husband, in spite of the frightening alteration that becomes increasingly apparent in the scenes following the temptation. His behavior towards her is governed by the same disillusioned revulsion as Hamlet's attitude towards his mother and Ophelia. In both plays, love turns to violent nausea under the impression of general sexual corruption in which the beloved is transformed into a common prostitute. In the context of the whole play, of course, Desdemona is not only the motive for revenge, but also its object: for Othello she is, as it were, Claudius, Gertrude and Ophelia all in one. In both plays, the hero's tragic perversion is lamented with regretful reference to his most promising past and his true potential. We are reminded of Ophelia's 'O, what a noble mind is here o'erthrown!' (*Hamlet* III.1.152), when Lodovico comments sadly on Othello's decline:

> Is this the noble Moor whom our full senate
> Call all-in-all sufficient? Is this the nature
> Whom passion could not shake? Whose solid virtue
> The shot of accident nor dart of chance
> Could neither graze nor pierce?...
> Are his wits safe? Is he not light of brain? (IV.1.255–60)

There is obviously a fundamental difference between Othello's tragic experience and Hamlet's 'antic disposition': Othello's fatal disillusion is only the product of the slanderer's art and the Moor's own imagination. There is no sinister prologue, with a history of crime and villainy to this play, as in the case of *Hamlet*. Othello is the object of a most unselfish love and fails to recognize it. He is confronted by evil, not in the shape of a corrupt court, but in the much more unpredictable form of an envious, dissimulating hypocrite and the barbarian passions within himself. Othello is not Hamlet: it was Bradley who began his first lecture on *Othello* with this commonplace; tragic disillusion does not move him to frustrating reflection, but to determined action; yet there are evident similarities in the kind of tragic experience Shakespeare portrays in the two plays, and they may help to a deeper understanding of what is at stake.

The fourth act, showing Othello's jealousy in its most repulsive brutality, also brings Emilia somewhat nearer to the centre of the stage who has, so far, only played a minor and rather unremarkable part. Like Juliet's nurse and Mercutio, she represents an attitude of complete obtuseness to the lovers' unconditional idealism, but she is the first to guess the cause of Othello's sudden alteration and the first to stand up unreservedly for Desdemona's innocence:

> For if she be not honest, chaste, and true,
> There's no man happy. (IV.2.16–17)

Her immediate reaction to Othello's treatment of his wife is the spontaneous anger of an unbiased observer who sees the tragedy from outside and instinctively grasps part of the truth. There is a brilliant moment, combining intelligent diagnosis and dramatic irony, when she describes to Iago, without any rhetorical soft-pedalling, the character of the slanderer as he appears to her:

> I will be hanged if some eternal villain,
> Some busy and insinuating rogue,
> Some cogging, cozening slave, to get some office,
> Have not devised this slander; I'll be hanged else. (IV.2.129–32)

This unambiguous portrait of Iago is more than a hint to the spectator; it is a precise moral verdict, leaving the villain without any heroic glamor and putting the blame firmly where it belongs. Though Emilia is unable to understand the real emotional drama behind the outward events, she is in no doubt about the moral significance. Her unsentimental realism is a comment on Desdemona's innocence who believes that there is no such thing as infidelity among married couples, and her garrulous defence of female revenge suggests associations with the world of burlesque comedy where the war between the sexes, as Emilia describes it, is taken for granted (IV.3.57–99). This comic simplification of the tragic conflict intensifies rather than weakens our impression of Desdemona's suffering as well as of her unselfish devotion and it is characteristic of Shakespeare's dramatic style that he gives such prominence to a very incongruous point of view. Neither Othello's agonizing pain, demanding our pity, nor his descent into a bestial desire for revenge are in the least softened by the tragedy as they often are in interpretations of it. On the one side, there is his hysterical threat, 'I will chop her into messes' (IV.1.188), which prevents any romantic stylization of the catastrophe and confirms the radical transformation of the 'noble Moor' with stark directness; on the other side, the text, especially in some of the brief scenes with Desdemona, evokes the tragic portrait of a man deeply wounded in the most sensitive part of his soul, whose shattering disillusion is not unlike Hamlet's:

> But there where I have garnered up my heart,
> Where either I must live or bear no life,
> The fountain from the which my current runs
> Or else dries up – to be discarded thence... (IV.2.56–9)

Neither moral disapproval nor forgiving idealization are adequate responses to such genuine, but largely self-inflicted misery.

The same kind of provocative contrast can be observed in the dramatic style and the rhetoric of the last two acts. Intrigues that are almost comic, like the eavesdropping scene, are juxtaposed with moments of tragic intensity and heroic declamation. To these is added the lyrical scene in which Desdemona unknowingly prepares herself for death, creating by her pathetic song a powerful impression of innocence sacrificed, like Ophelia, of whose fate we are reminded by the story of Barbaby.[70]

The last act begins with a scene that shows Iago as the cunningly ruthless disturber of public order again, as at the beginning of the play and in the second act; but this time Othello is his accomplice. In Shakespeare's source, some time elapses between the abortive attempt to kill the alleged rival and the cruel dispatching of the wife; in Othello, it all happens in one night, and the crime is executed in a very different way. Whereas in Cinthio's story, Disdemona is brutally slaughtered by the Moor, with his Ensign's active assistance, and the two murderers succeed for a while in hiding the traces of their deed, Shakespeare creates a significant contrast between the primitive brutality of the street-fight and the murder in which Othello is the only actor. The contrast is heightened by Othello's vicious threat against the absent Desdemona as he leaves the scene of the brawl for her bed-chamber:

> O brave Iago, honest and just,
> That hast such noble sense of thy friend's wrong!
> Thou teachest me. Minion, your dear lies dead,
> And your unblest fate hies. Strumpet, I come! (V.1.31–4)

Othello's perversion has reached its lowest point, but, as the following scene shows, the murder itself is not executed in this vindictive spirit.

Something of his former dignity returns in the deadly seriousness of his delusion and the sincere conviction that he is fulfilling the office of a judge and executioner; murder appears to him not as vengeance, but as a sacred duty.[71] No less impressively, the text suggests the reawakening of his former love as he looks at the sleeping Desdemona. His kisses before she wakes up recall Romeo's similar gesture in the tomb of the Capulets. The love-union is once more reaffirmed, in the hope that it will have permanence beyond death. Othello's hatred seems forgotten. The closeness of the scene to the idea of mutual 'Liebestod' distinguishes Othello's tragic fall from Iago's criminal activity and from the brutal Moor of the source. Unlike Claudius and Hamlet, he does not want to send his victim to damnation without due preparation and allows her time for a last prayer, but her lament for Cassio again rouses his primitive jealousy, and he kills her not as a judge, but as a murderer:

> O perjured woman! Thou dost stone my heart,
> And mak'st me call what I intend to do
> A murder, which I thought a sacrifice. (v.2.63–5)[72]

The pose of the impartial executioner collapses before the deed is done. The tragedy by no means glorifies murder, and the bond with Iago is endorsed by his 'Down, strumpet!' (v.2.80). Othello's 'great revenge' (v.2.75) links him with the deranged protagonists of earlier revenge tragedies; only that the injustice he feels it his duty to avenge has never been actually committed, but is all a malignant fiction.

.It is understandable that after such a revolting crime, many readers refuse to be convinced by Othello's heroic rhetoric, and his last speeches have been interpreted as blind self-justification by critics like T. S. Eliot and F. R. Leavis. The point of the last scene is not, however, to either condemn or defend Othello. The dramatist presents different views of the catastrophe side by side and each of them draws attention to an important aspect of the play's total effect. Thus, in contrast to the source, the murder is discovered by Emilia immediately after the deed, and her spontaneous revulsion expresses something of our own response, no less than the more complicated emotions provoked by other parts of the final scene:

> This deed of thine is no more worthy heaven
> Than thou wast worthy her...
>   O gull! O dolt!
> As ignorant as dirt. (v.2.159–60,162–3)

In view of this by no means unjust invective, it seems very difficult to re-establish Othello's heroic dignity, but this is exactly what the play is doing. Emilia is the one who clears up the slander and exposes the villain, but she does not have the last word.

Othello's suffering reaches a new degree of tragic intensity when he begins to realize how deeply he was loved and how blindly he has destroyed what was the most beautiful achievement of his life. The anguish of this recognition, shared by no other character in the play, goes much deeper than frustrated desire for revenge because it is not only his reputation among the Venetians that is involved, but his own sense of personal integrity and a life worth living. He sees himself as one of the damned, forever excluded from the sight of Heaven at the last judgement:

> When we shall meet at compt
> This look of thine will hurl my soul from heaven
> And fiends will snatch at it. (v.2.271–3)

This despair of one irredeemably cast off is again reminiscent of Doctor Faustus, who realizes too late what he has forfeited, though the Christian implications are not as explicitly spelt out.[73]

Othello's death is, on the other hand, obviously indebted to the heroic tradition of tragedy in that the hero passes judgement on himself and executes it at the same time, after he has drawn a portrait of himself such as he wants to leave to posterity. To see this as unrepentant arrogance or vain idealization of a repellent crime is to misunderstand the long established convention of the dying protagonist's self-vindication. There is no shirking of personal responsibility when the heaviest blame is allotted to the tempter, as is quite in harmony with the Christian concept of sin and diabolic seduction. Lodovico's question accurately defines the tone of awed compassion that should also inform the spectator's reaction to the tragic outcome:

> O, thou Othello, that wert once so good,
> Fallen in the practice of a damnèd slave,
> What shall be said to thee? (v.2.288–90)

Othello describes himself as one who has been cruelly misled ('ensnared my soul and body?' v.2.299), and I do not think he is speaking as a braggart, but with the authority of the dying who has the final say, when he calls himself 'one that loved not wisely, but too well' (v.2.340); and 'one not easily jealous' (v.2.341). It is not Shakespeare's method to let the protagonist die deluded or as a deliberate hypocrite. It is, in nearly all cases, a reliable insight that is gained at the moment of death, to guide our final judgement of the hero at the end of the tragedy, just as in Cassio's unambiguous obituary: 'he was great of heart' (v.2.357).

If we accept this emphatic judgement of the actors in the tragedy we join all those readers whom Leavis criticizes for being sentimental; but this criticism, even if it were justified, would be directed at the dramatist rather than at his audience because he leaves us in no doubt whatever that Othello's unbounded love was the expression of a wholly admirable trust in the possibility of unselfish faith and devotion. Iago's view of life is proved to be wrong in spite of his temporary 'success'. Desdemona's 'goodness' is the ultimate demonstration of a love that cannot be shaken by any evil insinuations or even lovelessness itself, a love that 'bears it out ev'n to the edge of doom' (Sonnet 116). The 'tragic loading of this bed' (v.2.359) once more reminds us of the two lovers united in death at the end of *Romeo and Juliet*. The play's conclusion does not decide for us whether we are to feel joy at the triumphant affirmation of love or horror at such a radical corruption of a noble mind, but it certainly does not encourage us to feel superior and to offer detached criticism of Othello's delusion or to speculate about his fate in a world beyond.[74]

In its final effect, the ending of *Othello* is more intimate than that of the earlier tragedy. The murder is justly punished and outward order is restored, but there is no public gesture of reconciliation equivalent to the mutual exchange of remorse and forgiveness between the heads of the two houses in Verona and the promised monument. Far from the scene of the tragedy, the Venetian community will hear of 'This heavy act' (v.2.367), but the chief person interested in it, Desdemona's father, is already dead, and the fact that Cassio will succeed Othello as governor of the island is hardly relevant to the final impact of the play. The contrast between the lovers' complete devotion to each other and the standards of an unsympathetic society, which seemed to be quite important in the first part, has receded more and more into the background towards the end and is subordinated to the hero's personal tragedy, even though at the moment of death he proudly remembers his services to the Venetian state and his military exploits. It is not love's victory over family feud and civil disorder that is the play's main concern, but rather the absolute value of a love and a trust ('My life upon her faith!' 1.3.290) that are triumphantly vindicated in the last scene in spite of the hero's fatal blindness and his tragic repudiation of that love.

KING LEAR

A glance at the critical history as well as the stage history of Shakespeare's third major tragedy shows that readers and theatre-goers of the last three centuries have responded differently to this play than to *Hamlet* or *Othello*. When Nahum Tate brought out his sentimental adaptation in 1681, he referred to the intractable shape of the text, 'a heap of jewels, unstrung and unpolished', as the chief justification for his new version.[75] Its success lasted for more than a century and a half, longer than that of Shakespeare's original play, and it seemed to confirm his claim that the text as it stood was unactable. But even this flattened and bowdlerized *King Lear*, tamed and indeed distorted by a happy ending, appears to have made a profound tragic impact. The greatest actors of the eighteenth and nineteenth centuries impressed their audiences in the part of the ageing King, and several critics, from Dr Samuel Johnson to A. C. Bradley, wondered whether, in the theatre at least, Tate's version might not have something to be said for it.

There is a particularly vivid and instructive description of a famous Viennese production in Adalbert Stifter's novel *Der Nachsommer (Indian Summer)*, published in 1857. For the hero of this classic *Bildungsroman*, it is the first formative experience of the theatre and of Shakespeare's tragedy. What he saw was obviously not Tate's version, but a rather less radical adaptation, although the tragic ending was still omitted. Still, the impression of a most moving tragedy was hardly softened by the suppression of Shakespeare's ruthless finale. The narrator's excitement reaches its climax when Lear kneels before Cordelia:

My heart was at this moment, as it were, crushed; I was almost beside myself with pain. I had never expected anything like this; there was no question of a stage-play any more, this was the most real reality before me. The fortunate ending which, in those days was attached to the play to soften the terrible emotions which the action arouses, made no impression on me any more, my heart said that this was impossible, and I almost lost consciousness of what was going on around me.[76]

Like Stifter's young Heinrich Drendorf, a majority of readers and spectators have felt that in *King Lear* Shakespeare presents extremes of human suffering and cruelty that touch the very confines of dramatic art and may well tempt one to try and escape into falsifying harmonization. Bradley, who probably never saw any but heavily truncated versions in the theatre, gives an account of the play's tragic impact that still seems to me unsurpassed in its pregnant and undogmatic wisdom:

Its final and total result is one in which pity and terror, carried perhaps to the extreme limits of art, are so blended with a sense of law and beauty that we feel at last, not depression and much less despair, but a consciousness of greatness in pain, and of solemnity in the mystery we cannot fathom.[77]

Many modern readers may disagree with the tone and the confident idealism of this interpretation; but to me, Bradley's insight into the play's elemental power and its radical consistency defines a central aspect of its unique effect from which any further analysis can proceed.

A few observations on Shakespeare's sources can already reveal some particularly original features of this play that distinguish it noticeably from his earlier tragedies. The dramatist took his material from quite heterogeneous sources and he adapted it with unusual freedom.

The history of the legendary King Lear appears as early as in Geoffrey of Monmouth's *Historia Regum Britanniae* (about 1135) and in several later accounts of English history based on Geoffrey's influential work, such as the compilations of the Tudor historians Shakespeare had extensively used for his English history plays, especially Raphael Holinshed's *Chronicles of England, Scotland and Ireland* (second edition, 1587). His most important source, however, was the anonymous play *The True Chronicle Historie of King Leir and his three daughters*, printed 1605, but written presumably in the early nineties.[78] It was evidently a successful play which can hardly be called a history, but rather a romantic and at the same time didactic dramatization of legendary material, with comic, pathetic and edifying episodes. The action is placed within a Christian society and is mainly presented as an *exemplum*, illustrating good and sinful behavior between parents and children. At the end, Leir is reinstated in all his former dignities and powers and he has learnt his lesson:

> Ah, my *Cordella*, now I call to mind,
> The modest answere, which I tooke unkind:
> But now I see, I am no whit beguild,
> Thou lovedst me dearely, and as ought a child. (2649–52)

What Shakespeare has added to this story is more interesting than what he has kept: the parts of Kent and the Fool, as well as Lear's madness are his own contributions to the plot, quite apart from the fact that the rich and complex texture of the play's language – surprising even in comparison with *Hamlet* – owes nothing to the much more trite and undistinguished style of the older play which lacks any tragic intensity or rhetorical brilliance. Most of Shakespeare's alterations have to be seen in relation to his basic decision not to adopt the optimistic solution found in all previous versions of Lear's story. The fundamental human and philosophical conflicts raised by his dramatization cannot possibly be glossed over by repentance and the willingness to make a new start – though there are interpretations of *King Lear* that sound no less edifying than the ending of the old play.

Shakespeare's most striking contribution, however, is the insertion of a second plot, lifted bodily from an entirely different source. In Sir Philip Sidney's pastoral novel *Arcadia* (about 1590) he found an episode that bore an unmistakable resemblance to King Lear's story, not only in plot outline, but, above all, in its moral implications. It is, in fact, much closer to the spirit of Shakespeare's tragedy than the chronicle play. In it, the

blind King dies after putting the crown on the head of the son he has
found faithful at last: 'his hart broken with unkindnes and affliction,
stretched so farre beyond his limits with this excesse of comfort, as it was
able no longer to keep safe his roial spirits'.[79] Like King Lear, he
discovers that the child he has disinherited and cast off has stood by him
in the hour of extreme physical and mental desolation and has requited
the father's fatal error with filial loyalty and loving care. The high moral
claims of Sidney's *Arcadia* and the discussion of fundamental philosophical and ethical issues, such as the challenge presented to Christian virtue
by paganism and superstition, has, most probably, exercised a profound
influence on Shakespeare's play. The addition of a second plot was
obviously meant to enrich the moral implications of the play, just as the
numerous digressions and side-episodes woven into the structure of
Sidney's novel do. No other Shakespearian tragedy has a subplot of
comparable importance.[80]

The thematic parallels as well as the differences between the two plots
are easy enough to recognize. Their chief effect is to direct our attention
to the universal moral laws common to both plots and to the exemplary
relevance of the tragic events rather than to the fate of the individual
actors. This does not by any means turn the play into a morality, but it
certainly explores a wider range of general social and philosophical issues
than *Othello*. Not Lear and Gloucester only, but several of the other
characters are forced by their experience to reconsider their traditional
ideas of human nature and divine providence. More radically even than
Hamlet, this tragedy inquires into the ultimate roots of human behavior
and of society, bypassing anything that seems merely ephemeral, arbitrary, or conventional. It is also remarkable that, in contrast to the earlier
tragedies, there is a consistent avoidance of Christian terminology. The
play is set in a pagan world and its characters are excluded from the
possible solace of Christian answers to their tragic dilemma, though this
does not mean that the tragedy can be understood without the context of
an intense theological debate, such as it is conducted in Sidney's *Arcadia*
as well as in many other fictional and discursive texts of the period.[81] To
what extent the interpretation of *King Lear* should be guided by such
considerations has been one of the more controversial issues of *Lear*
criticism, but it is certainly an issue raised by the play's insistent
discussion of moral and philosophical problems.

Both plots describe a process of suffering and painful experience; the
protagonist is reduced to a state of complete isolation by his moral
blindness, but this cruel disillusion brings him to an awareness of his
folly. The metaphor of sight, of perception and blindness, is to be found
in Shakespeare's two most important sources, and this may well have

given him the idea of linking the two stories.[82] In the old play of *Leir*, it is the King's faithful counsellor who moralizes:

> Ah, who so blind, as they that will not see
> The neere approch of their owne misery? (577–8)

In Sidney's *Arcadia*, the King who has also been deceived in his favorite child, learns to see his own error when his eyes have been put out: 'his kindnes is a glasse even to my blind eyes, of my naughtines' (p.405). What here still appears as a moral commonplace and a rhetorical conceit has, in Shakespeare's text, become a rich and complex pattern of metaphors, scenic images, and themes that link the different strands of the action, which are more important in determining our response to the tragedy than the dramatic events and the fate of the individual figures.[83]

A comparison between the opening scenes of *King Lear* and the old *Leir* play reveals how consistently Shakespeare has neglected psychological motivation for the sake of a more complex presentation of human relationships and ethical issues. In the older play, the division of the Kingdom is preceded by two scenes in which the ruler himself explains his intentions and, on the other side, the two elder sisters plan their own tactics in order to lower Cordella in their father's esteem. We learn straightaway why Leir wants to stage this love-contest and how the daughters intend to flatter him, so that the great state scene, when it comes, only confirms what we have already been led to expect.

In *King Lear*, the imminent division of the realm is only mentioned by an outsider and barely commented on. The sharing out of dowries is talked of as an indication of the King's relative affection for the two sons-in-law, and the subject is discussed in the context of a humorous conversation about Gloucester's sexual escapade. As in most of Shakespeare's earlier tragedies, central themes are first introduced from the play's periphery, often in a light-hearted or cynical tone. Gloucester seems to make as little distinction between his two sons in his love as King Lear; but for a contemporary audience Edmund's illegitimacy could not be glossed over by flippant jokes about the attractions of his mother. Gloucester's harmless levity soon turns out to be a disastrous misjudgement of filial loyalties and parental duties.

The division of the Kingdom is, at best, indirectly foreshadowed by this brief introduction and thus comes as a much greater surprise for the audience than in Shakespeare's source. Lear's 'darker purpose' (I.1.36) is announced without clear reasons given, just as the daughters' reaction to it seems to arise spontaneously from the actual situation, as an unpremeditated expression of their calculating natures. The actors' motives remain largely unexplained and the events that took place before the play's beginning are far less significant than in the other tragedies. The King's determination to divide his realm is presented as a fact, and the love-contest only seems to be a rather pointless whim to give some additional color to the whole ceremony. Lear's announcement is an expression of his own sense of power and dignity, whereas in the old *Leir* play, as in *Gorboduc*, which is thematically quite close to it, the King is accompanied by a good and an evil counsellor.[84] This is another reason why Lear's decision to retire from the throne seems much more arbitrary and ill-advised. For Elizabethan and Jacobean audiences, who had been incessantly warned against the evils of disunity and divided rule by preachers, historians and poets, there would have been no doubt at all as to the seriousness of the King's error. The impression of an irresponsible neglect of political and parental obligations is further underlined by the introduction of a map and the idea of the division as a distribution of rewards for dutiful behavior. The dismembered parts of the Kingdom are given away like an heirloom and Cordelia is asked by her father to earn a particularly rich share for herself by even more fulsome professions of love than those of her sisters:

> what can you say to draw
> A third more opulent than your sisters'?   (1.1.85–6)

She instinctively feels unable to accept this kind of mechanism. Like Hamlet, she points out – and these are almost her first words in the play – that our deepest emotions cannot possibly be expressed by outward gestures or profuse rhetoric, and like the Danish Prince, she is immediately isolated by her protest within a court where show and empty words count for everything.

Cordelia has often been charged by critical readers with unnecessary stubbornness and lack of accommodating diplomacy, though in the context of the scene, there is not the slightest uncertainty about the sincerity of her affection and the rightness of her silence in the face of so much artificial verbosity. Lear has turned the momentous question of political unity, of such vital importance for the continuation of a peaceful community, into an undignified contest of hollow flatteries, merely to gratify his own vanity. The excessive oath he hurls at Cordelia, repudiating every natural bond between them, underscores his completely perverted sense of what constitutes a family or any human community – especially in the ominous image of the barbarian devouring his own offspring; it grimly foreshadows the dissolution of all human loyalties and civilized values ultimately caused by Lear's abdication:

> The barbarous Scythian,
> Or he that makes his generation messes

> To gorge his appetite, shall to my bosom
> Be as well neighboured, pitied, and relieved
> As thou my sometime daughter.   (1.1.116 – 20)[85]

Like Desdemona's undiplomatic intercession for Cassio, Cordelia's uncompromising sincerity is by no means presented as a moral flaw that can in any way justify the reaction produced by it, but it is a dramatic device to give more credibility to the clash of two opposing principles on the level of personal temperament and spontaneous reactions. Such dramatization of the individual moment not only adds to the tragic suspense, it also involves the spectator more directly in the process of moral reflection and evaluation than more explicit forms of preparation. Thus, the hypocrisy of the elder sisters is not announced in so many words, but experienced in action. Cordelia is not the innocent victim of an insidious stratagem; rather she becomes a martyr to her own convictions, of whose justice the whole scene leaves us in no doubt. Lastly, Kent, who obviously fulfils the traditional role of the good counsellor, is not the static representative of orthodox wisdom: he bursts out into spontaneous anger when he sees the King's fatal perversity and gives his well-meant warning in an offensive tone. A conventional situation is dramatized and turned into an unpremeditated protest against political and personal folly which excludes the faithful warner from the King's favor along with Cordelia.

Shakespeare's Lear banishes his most loyal counsellor as well as his most affectionate daughter. Thus, his stubborn error is deliberately magnified in comparison with the source. Cordelia's role is also made more prominent by the presence of two suitors whose reactions mirror the contrast between flattery, calculating policy, and genuine love. By this time most spectators will have understood that this is not a world of political realities and that they are not watching a history play, but rather a cautionary legend. The King of France, who is prepared to accept Cordelia as his wife without any dowry, only for her personal qualities, is not a serious politician, but a romantic lover whose noble declaration on behalf of ideal and disinterested love reminds us of Shakespeare's sonnets rather than of the old chronicle play:

> Love's not love
> When it is mingled with regards that stands
> Aloof from th' entire point.   (1.1.238–40)

Lear's fond belief that he can keep 'The name and all th'addition to a king' (1.1.136) when he has given away all his power and responsibility, flies in the face of the most elementary principles of political theory and experience, and this not only for a seventeenth-century audience. His complete blindness to his daughters' true natures reveals the same kind of dangerous illusion.

The conclusion of the scene, with the brief exchange between the two wicked sisters, replaces a similar dialogue *before* the state scene in the old play and gives some indication of future developments. It confirms our suspicion that Lear is even despised by those who flattered him most and on whom he means to build his future comfort. It is quite characteristic of Shakespeare's dramatic art that the motives of the chief actors are not explained before the end of the scene, after the audience has first been left to form its own judgement, and that the most clear-sighted appraisal of the hero comes from his antagonists. The sisters know as well as Kent that Lear's banishment of Cordelia was unjust:

He always loved our sister most; and with what poor judgement he hath now cast her off appears too grossly.   (1.1.289–91)

They also know that this is not merely 'the infirmity of his age' because 'he hath ever but slenderly known himself' (1.1.292–3).

Coming after the great state scene, the brief dialogue has an important function in manipulating our sympathies, making us reconsider our first reaction to Lear's disastrous folly. His error was gross enough and his behavior towards Cordelia and Kent clearly repulsive, but he now appears as the victim of merciless and unnatural deception that strikes us as morally more despicable than Lear's anger. In retrospect, this now seems deplorably imprudent and over-emotional rather than selfishly calculating because he will hurt himself more than anybody else. Shakespeare makes Lear's blindness more complete and obsessive than the *Leir* play, as we have seen, but at the same time he makes it more difficult to form a simple and unambiguous judgement by the context and the change of viewpoint.

The second scene continues this technique by a variation of similar patterns of human behavior on a more domestic level. Edmund's soliloquy immediately characterizes him as a scheming and calculating play-actor, like Iago, with whom he shares his outspoken scorn of traditional pieties and the bluntness of his self-revelation that establishes a direct contact with the audience. As in the previous scene, the father's fond love and, with it, the inheritance, are made the object of a sinister intrigue and deceitful avarice. Edmund's illegitimate birth raises the question of family loyalties in a more literal manner than the flatteries of Lear's daughters. What Edmund apostrophizes as 'nature' in this context, placing it above the accepted principle of legitimacy, is really nothing more than primitive energy denying abstract norms. For the majority of Shakespeare's contemporaries, these could only be ignored at the expense of social order and stability. The ridiculing of 'honest madam's issue' (1.2.9) and the frivolous idea that the bastard was really begot with more enthusiasm and vitality than the legitimate offspring are the expressions of a cynical wit that dares to put the paradoxical and heretical into shocking words;[86] as a principle of individual or political action this can only lead to chaos and inhuman strife.

If Lear is deceived by hyprocritical rhetoric, Gloucester falls a victim to calculated intrigue and insidious slander. Edmund, charging the absent Edgar with unnatural behavior, employs the same technique of seemingly well-meaning honesty as Iago. Dramatic ironies point at significant associations with the first scene of the play and make Gloucester's short-sighted delusion even more poignant. He sees well enough that Lear has sinned against nature, but he completely fails to notice the obvious parallels between the King and himself. He takes these ominous events as confirmation of his own superstitious forebodings of approaching doom which make him all the more susceptible to Edmund's lies and he comes to the conclusion that Edgar follows Lear's example in offending against sanctified family loyalties, the sin he himself is just about to commit. The nervous prose of his lament about a world out of joint strongly suggests that this is a hysterical scenario, intended to strike us as somewhat naive pessimism at this point, but already foreshadowing the tragic dissolution of all familiar order, to which Gloucester himself contributes by equating Edmund's 'loyalty' with Kent's 'honesty'.

Edmund is, however, different from the brilliant schemer Iago: his scorn of Gloucester's primitive faith in the significance of the stars and vague fears of general disaster reveal him as an instance of a new kind of heretical humanism that acknowledges only the individual self as moral standard and authority. Any belief in supernatural destiny or respect for traditional order are for him only signs of weakness and resignation:

> All with me's meet that I can fashion fit. (1.2.180)

The moral issues are more sharply outlined here than in the main plot. Edmund's villainy is more agressive and more obvious than that of the wicked sisters, but the constellation is quite similar: Edgar is despised by him – as Cordelia is by her sisters – because of his very incapacity for deception and he is (for the benefit of the audience) characterized as a thoroughly honest and unsuspecting person:

> a brother noble,
> Whose nature is so far from doing harms
> That he suspects none; on whose foolish honesty
> My practices ride easy – (1.2.175–8)

For Shakespeare and the dramatists of his period, this is the key to the success of a hypocritical schemer.

The main plot of the tragedy, in contrast, is rather more complex because there is no one-sided intrigue, but a clash of determined personalities. Lear's fond notion that he can exercise royal authority without royal power and responsibility makes Gonerill's annoyance at his overbearing behavior as a guest more understandable at least, although all we hear about it comes from herself.[87] Her description of the King as

> Idle old man,
> That still would manage those authorities
> That he hath given away! (1.3.17–19)

puts the finger on the very essence of his political failure and makes it much more difficult for us to side with Lear unconditionally than in the source play, where we are told by the good counsellor:

> But he, the myrrour of mild patience,
> Puts up all wrongs, and never gives reply: (755–6)

This is a very clear manipulation of our sympathies, whereas Shakespeare's Lear learns this kind of 'patience' only towards the end and is, at first, by no means prepared to suffer wrongs silently. The lamentations of the wise counsellor in the *Leir* play are more like Gloucester's wholesale pessimism:

> Oh yron age! O times! O monstrous, vilde,
> When parents are contemned of the child! (761–2)

Again, Shakespeare has transferred the undifferentiated simplicity of the play to his supporting plot. The loyalty practised by Kent is much less sententious: despite his unjust banishment, he risks his life to serve his lord, still loved and honored by him. His love is even more unselfish than that of his model in the sources, since Shakespeare's Lear is, at this point, not very lovable and has publicly dismissed his most faithful servant.

Kent's unquestioning loyalty in fact contributes more to our sympathy for the King than Lear's own behavior. He recognizes the royal authority in spite of his abdication and he is prepared to persist in honoring him as King, i.e. he refuses to take note of his abdication and thus shows more true regard for the royal title than its bearer has done himself. At the same time, the humiliating treatment of Lear by Gonerill and her subordinates is not just reported as a fact (as it is in the old play), but presented on the stage in all its perverse cruelty and deliberate offensiveness. Kent's drastic dealing with Oswald, remains a rather impotent, though honest and spontaneous gesture of solidarity with the insulted King.

The figure of the court fool represents another form of devoted loyalty. In Shakespeare's comedy *As You Like It*, written about 1599, the role of the fool had already been surprisingly prominent and different from earlier clowns. Many critics have seen this change in direct connection with the actor Robert Armin who joined Shakespeare's company at about this time and may well have helped to inspire a new type of stage fool, whose instinctive wisdom, intellectual wit, and pointed disregard of polite forms or cautious diplomacy are used to unmask pretentious attitudes and hollow authority of all kind. These fools are more than incidental characters; they are closely woven into the plot and they deliberately take sides.[88] Touchstone, out of affection and loyalty for the Duke's daughter, suffers the discomforts of banishment, and Feste takes an active part in the humiliation of the sour puritan Malvolio in *Twelfth Night*. In the tragedies, fools had, so far, only appeared in peripheral scenes and had hardly made a significant contribution either to characterization or to the thematic structure. In *King Lear*, the Fool is, next to Kent, the King's most faithful companion on his way into powerlessness and isolation and he has an important share in the gradual awakening of his self-awareness. Like Feste, who exposes Olivia's excessive mourning as unrealistic folly, he calls Lear's obtuseness by its real name without being banished for it. The close association of Lear and the Fool is a memorable dramatic device to make the King's folly and loss of authority even visually explicit, but it also demonstrates that there is still some loyalty left and that the King is more and more prepared to listen to the voice of foolish wisdom. In contrast, Gonerill, Regan and Edmund are not even able to communicate with the Fool.

The comments of the Fool accompany the whole scene in which Lear begins to see his unnatural error. These fragments of disillusioned experience, well-tried popular wisdom, and impertinent song form a brilliant counterpoint to the shattering collapse of Lear's traditional certainties. Between him and Gonerill, no real dialogue is possible and there is no genuine attempt to reach an understanding, but from her spiteful behavior towards him Lear comes to realize the radical finality of the breach and the complete dissolution of filial ties. By the Fool's barbed jibes he is forced to see that it was the King himself who first began to turn family order and political hierarchy upside down; the father has degraded himself to become a child asking for punishment:

...e'er since thou madest thy daughters thy mothers; for when thou gavest them the
rod and puttest down thine own breeches... (1.4.168–70)[89]

Even more drastically, Lear is addressed by his Fool as a figure O, a nothing, representing even less than the Fool himself who at least is aware of his own folly and knows his place in society. His sharp analysis of the true situation is not enough, however, to make Lear realize the full extent of his mistake and its consequences because, unlike the Fool, he still believes that Regan will act differently and join him in his hatred of Gonerill. His prayer to 'Nature', asking for divine vengeance (272–86), shows that he, too, intends to dissolve all natural ties and answers Gonerill's treatment of him in her own spirit, without stopping to reflect on his paternal responsibility.[90] This radical denial of all natural obligations and hopes (like fertility) proclaimed by Lear, as against Cordelia in the first scene, links him to the world of Edmund and Gonerill. His illusion that the abdication might yet be revoked betrays a pathetic ignorance of his daughters' true nature and the real distribution of power, clearly visible to the spectator by Gonerill's emotionless calculation. At the same time, the dramatic context ensures that we do not see Lear with Gonerill's eyes alone, as a stubborn old man whose brain is softened by 'dotage' (1.4.290), but are made to experience the tragic collapse of a person who finds himself deceived in everything that gave meaning to his life. Any production that turns Lear into a senile choleric is sure to miss the rich suggestiveness of the text and the tragic depth of his angry despair. Paradoxically, it is Kent and the Fool more than anybody else who insist on the dignity of the ruler whose royal authority is in no way diminished by his wilful abdication. Even at this early point in the play it is clear that his tragic experience cannot be reduced to the concept of just punishment or wisdom gained through suffering. Like Othello's jealousy, Lear's disillusion calls in question his own identity and the possibility of a meaningful existence: 'Chaos is come again' (*Othello*, III.3.92). The fact that he has already reached this abyss in the first act of the play, is an indication of how deliberately Shakespeare has accelerated the hero's fall to present his madness – only hinted at in *Othello* – in all its terrifying stages. Even after Gonerill's first words he asks himself whether he is awake or dreaming. His helpless question, 'Who is it that can tell me who I am?' (1.4.226), is not a general reflection on seeming and being, but reveals the deep insecurity of a man to whom even his own identity no longer seems reliable.[91]

Lear's violent departure in the direction of Regan appears as a last attempt to make sure of the old familiar order in one place at least, but even the brief transitional scene, practically all dialogue between Lear and his Fool, adds to the strong impression of a deeply disturbed personality. Lear takes note of the Fool's jokes and replies to some of his riddling questions, but the events have set in motion a process of reflection in him that is hardly dependent on any other presence and makes most of his own utterances seem like fragments of a soliloquy.

Thus, his sudden realization, 'I did her wrong' (1.5.24) has no direct logical connection with the context, and only the spectator, who is familiar with the play he has seen so far, knows to whom Lear is referring.[92] He appears to drift away from the real situation and hardly seems to register the bitter truths uttered by the Fool. This form of dialogue, used very occasionally in *Othello*, conveys a strong sense of a complete breakdown of communication caused by the intensity of lonely suffering and mental preoccupation. At first, Lear's insight is a disquieting awareness of possibilities rather than a full realization of his true state. He himself begins to see the danger of mental derangement as a consequence of his overwhelming experience, an experience too radical to be absorbed by the usual process of mental adjustment:

> O let me not be mad, not mad, sweet heaven!
> Keep me in temper; I would not be mad! (1.5.43–4)

Unlike Othello, Lear is so completely uprooted by his disillusioning experience that the possibility of one final, purifying act of revenge is out of the question. Nothing is left but a complete collapse of all rational thinking and planning. Nor is the satirical resignation of the Fool an attitude he can possibly adopt; his popular wisdom provides contrast and provocation rather than a model that can be directly applied on a higher level of responsibility and knowledge. Departing, the Fool reminds the audience of the natural course of things that changes everything and should stifle our laughter, but it would be a rather sentimental overinterpretation to suggest that he has a really adequate idea of Lear's tragic experience.

The second act escalates the intrigues and finally destroys the last remains of Lear's hopeful belief in a reliable natural order. The spectator is prepared for another inhuman denial of all family loyalty by Edmund's new scheme against Edgar. Though Lear knows nothing about it, it clearly demonstrates that his tragic disillusion is justified not only by the exceptional wickedness of his two daughters, but must be seen in the context of other manifestations of human perversity and unnatural disloyalty. Like Iago, Edmund successfully stages a scene in which someone completely innocent (Cassio, Edgar) appears to threaten the peace of the community. Inflicting on himself a wound which he claims to have received from Edgar, he unknowingly anticipates his own later fate and, at the same time, begins the family conflict which Gloucester turns into a deadly pursuit of the legitimate son. While Lear has already realized that he has been cruelly deceived and has cast off his eldest daughter, Gloucester still thinks of Edmund as his only loyal son who honors natural family ties and will replace his legitimate brother as the only heir: 'Loyal and natural boy,...' (II.1.83).

For the spectator, his blindness becomes more disturbing by the obvious parallel with Lear, even though the bold impudence of Edmund's scheme makes it more plausible than Lear's deception. Gloucester's sigh, 'my old heart is cracked; it's cracked' (II.1.89) is a rather more shallow, but in a sense more realistic version of Lear's approaching madness. The connections between the two plots are further underlined by the meeting of Edmund and Cornwall and by Regan immediately taking sides against Edgar. The fact that Regan and Cornwall ally themselves with the slanderer without any further investigation, only confirms our impression that this is a society deeply divided into Good and Evil, although Shakespeare does not, by any means, reduce the tragic conflict to the clear-cut contrasts of a morality play. Edmund is praised for his 'child-like office' (II.1.105) and taken into Cornwall's service, while, in the very next scene, the King's only truly faithful servant is punished in a deliberately humiliating manner because he has stuck up for his master with somewhat undiplomatic heat. The noisy quarrel between Kent and Oswald, which has an element of comedy in it, dramatizes the conflict between Lear and his daughters on the level of the subordinates. Kent's unrestrained barrage of insults is surely meant to strike the audience as a rather endearing zeal on behalf of a just cause ('anger hath a privilege' (II.2.68)), an extreme form of honest directness in a world of hypocrisy and deception. It is also a subtle way of manipulating our sympathies towards Lear on whose behalf this unselfish demonstration of loyalty is given and whose lack of wise restraint is, perhaps, seen in a more human light after Kent's eruption. The tempers of these two men are obviously very similar. Oswald, in contrast, is the opportunist time-server who supports the stronger side and is prepared to stoop to any baseness in their service. The fight provoked by Kent disturbs the public peace too, but, in contrast to Edmund's calculating mock-duel, it has the effect of a refreshing outburst of just wrath and a deserved punishment.

Kent's humiliation is, of course, an indirect insult to the King before he has even arrived. Regan's treatment of her father thus seems even more insidious and repulsive than Gonerill's behavior which for the audience was more closely related to Lear's rash dealings in the state scene. Since then, however, we have witnessed such repellent instances of ruthless egotism and falsehood that Lear's disastrous error appears, in comparison, less reprehensible. We see him more and more as a victim of unnatural wickedness, not as morally corrupt, like his antagonists. Kent's firm belief in a restoration of just order and Cordelia's letter, quoted by him, are the first clear hints of a positive counter-movement and a reminder of the fact that the two people most injured by the King will be faithful to him to the last (II.2.158–68). Kent trying to cheer himself up in his 'shameful lodging', is the first instance in the play of indignity suffered patiently and undeservedly, made bearable by the hope of a turn for the better. Gloucester's compassion for the outcast King adds further weight to this impression of beneficial forces rallying in Lear's defence and of human integrity reasserting itself. For the time being, however, the tragic structure of the action gives more scope to the agents of hatred and brutality, leaving the King's supporters powerless.

Again, the subplot takes up the same motifs, suggesting an atmosphere of universal suffering. The parallels are impressed on us by visual means as well, because the sleeping Kent is obviously meant to remain on stage during Edgar's soliloquy.[93] Edgar is not only banished and cast off, like Kent and Cordelia, but is threatened with immediate execution. His mask of madness and his utter helplessness foreshadow Lear's experience, but Edgar's mental derangement is never more than an adopted role, an 'antic disposition', and his extreme exposure to the elements is a disguise to save his life. Only as a mad, begging outcast is he still existent, as Edgar he is 'nothing' (II.3.21). It is here that the play's radical questioning begins: to what state can a human being be actually reduced? How much can you take away from him? Edgar rids himself of everything he ever possessed in the way of outward protection and civilization. He voluntarily descends to the level of the very lowest and worst-off members of Elizabethan society, a society where the most acute misery and destitution was probably found away from the cities, in the open nature, unmitigated by any romantic idealization. Though (as the exiles in *As You Like It* sing) rain and wind are not man's most cruel enemies, they are, like hunger and cold, manifestations of all those life-destroying powers against whom man has always tried to protect himself by material possessions and social order. The naked beggar marks the very lowest stage of humanity and the one nearest to the inarticulate animal; the alms such a creature can hope for are usually not given out of a genuine feeling of human solidarity, but are rather forced out of the luckier members of society by the abnormal behavior of the outcast whom everyone wants to keep at a safe distance.[94] The play thus provides a telling context for Lear's path into extreme isolation and suffering; the action covers the full span of human civilization, from the artificial splendor and ceremony of the court to the lonely hovel on the heath far from the shelter of convention where all the usual means of subsistence have ceased to exist.

The following scene ends with the King being thrust into the same unprotected isolation. His royal *entourage*, for him an indispensable attribute of his former authority, is first halved and then, in brutal scorn, whittled down to nothing at all. Lear's inability to grasp the full extent of his isolation is satirized by the Fool as obtuse lack of simple wisdom and common experience. It comes out in the pathetic bartering about the number of his followers and his futile appeal to his daughters' love and sense of duty. As in the great state scene, he is forced to recognize that love and affection, like royal dignity, cannot be quantified. When he tells his daughters that even the beggar has more than he needs if you examine his case closely enough, this is for him a paradoxical idea, meant to support his own sense of 'need' (11.4.259–65), but, as it turns out, the life of a beggar is an experience he himself is destined to go through. It had already been hinted at in the Fool's poignant allusions to the hardships of winter and the need to provide against them. Lear, for his part, is completely incapable of coming to terms with a world in which loyalties are denied; any reconciliation with the daughters that would imply a recognition of his state as a powerless old man is quite unthinkable for him, but his vow to be avenged becomes a childish and ineffective threat and, like a child, he is allowed to let his impotent rage run its full course.

It has often been felt that no other Shakespearian play and very few works of literature in general describe the all but total collapse of a powerful personality with such unalleviated consistency and present us with such extremes of suffering. The third and fourth act of *King Lear* extend the expressive potential of the Elizabethan stage in an unprecedented manner and confront the spectator with an intensity of stark isolation and inhuman bestiality that seems hardly bearable. Many readers have wondered whether it is at all possible for the stage to achieve an adequate representation of these scenes, but I think quite a number of very different productions might be quoted as convincing answers to this question.[95] Of course, the style of representation in Shakespeare's theatre was designed to appeal to the imagination of the audience and to stimulate mental cooperation rather than give an illusion of reality, and it is in the storm scenes more than anywhere else that one should keep in mind the emblematic quality of the platform stage. Neither realistic stage thunder nor electronic sound effects or operatic music can equal the characteristic combination of dramatic poetry and basic human situation that is Shakespeare's most astonishing achievement in this part of the play. The storm, made so vividly present to the spectator by rhetorical means, is continually related to the destructive power and the disorder of human passions by the characters themselves and, at the same time, experienced as demonstration of nature's complete indifference to man's suffering. For Lear, the raging of the elements is an indication of the breakdown of cosmic order, reflecting the loss of his own bearings and welcomed as a divine judgement, while the Fool can see only those effects of the storm that are common to everybody. His pathetic stanza, quoting

Feste's song at the end of *Twelfth Night*, sharply reminds us of the contrast between the world of comedy and the unmitigated experience of indifferent and unfeeling nature (III.2.74–7). Kent has to find a shelter for Lear almost by force, as Edgar has to beg for alms, but the servant's loving care for the King suddenly makes Lear aware of the poor Fool's helpless suffering. His prayers for revenge give way to a concern for another human being such as we have not seen in him before:

> Come on, my boy. How dost my boy? Art cold?
> I am cold myself...
> Poor fool and knave, I have one part in my heart
> That's sorry yet for thee.   (III.2.68–9,72–3)

The simple gesture of human solidarity suggests to us the possibility that Lear in his extreme humiliation has understood something his self-absorption and his office had so far hidden from him. This is made more explicit in the next scene but one, in which the King gives precedence to the Fool, thus deliberately brushing aside all outward differences and expressing his deep compassion for all outcasts. In the context of the play, this is a complete reversal of social rank and conventional notions of priority:

> Poor naked wretches, wheresoe'er you are,
> That bide the pelting of this pitiless storm,
> How shall your houseless heads and unfed sides,
> Your looped and windowed raggedness, defend you
> From seasons such as these? O, I have ta'en
> Too little care of this! Take physic, pomp;
> Expose thyself to feel what wretches feel,
> That thou mayst shake the superflux to them
> And show the heavens more just.   (III.4.28–36)

'I need not quote more', Bradley says about the first line of this passage, 'This is one of those passages which make one worship Shakespeare.'[96]

There is, however, a danger of reading too much of our modern sensibilities into these lines if we take them out of their context. To be sure, Lear's soliloquy reveals an awareness of social injustice particularly sympathetic to the twentieth-century reader, suggesting a remarkable maturity; yet in the context of the whole tragedy it is just as important to remember that Lear is here speaking not as a king, but as one who is, in Chaucer's phrase, 'fallen out of high degree'. He has become one with his servant and his Fool, and in this situation he is able to voice some radical social criticism such as Shakespeare only puts in the mouths of fools, madmen, and those without any responsibilities. Lear's growth to this new degree of insight and wisdom – if growth is indeed the right word for it – cannot be separated from this terrifying downfall, with the loss of all authority and dignities. The paradox 'reason in madness' has become a critical commonplace in this connection, and it certainly describes an important aspect of Lear's 'progress'; but it should not be understood as something in the nature of an edifying consolation prize. What is so disturbing is that in the world of this play, most profound and humane insights are granted only to the very lowliest and least influential and have no visible effect on society. Lear is not an example of Christian wisdom won by suffering, nor can his collapse be seen as a just punishment for his error, but the audience is made to feel that, in view of such painful humiliation and exposure any simply moralizing expla-nation falls far short of the magnitude of anguished sorrow endured by the protagonist and can satisfy only the most superficial beholder.

Lear's 'growth', then, is only one aspect of his outward and inward collapse. He is never given an opportunity to put his hard-won com-passion for the houseless into practice, to act as King according to this new sense of social responsibility. Within the context of the storm scene, Lear's solidarity with the poor naked wretches seems only a passing mood which soon reverts to impotent hatred and threats of revenge against the ungrateful daughters. There is another flash of radical wisdom when Lear meets the disguised Edgar and suddenly becomes aware of how utterly destitute human existence can become:

Is man no more than this?   (III.4.99–100)

This question, too, belongs to those unorthodox sentiments that men dare put into words only in extreme situations; they are, as a rule, reserved to fools, madmen and satirists, and generally indicate that the speaker has reached a turning-point in his life.

Shakespeare here, as has often been noted, brings together very different forms of madness, folly and obsession to suggest the frightening dissolution of all human order. It is achieved without any spectacular stage effects, almost exclusively by means of a dramatic language in which the breakdown of familiar structures of syntax and thought is rendered with a stylistic resourcefulness quite unprecedented in the drama of Shakespeare or his contemporaries. Each speaker has his own idiom; the hectic irrationality of Edgar is contrasted with the inventive freedom of the Fool, whose professional wit becomes more and more subdued in view of the physical suffering and the crumbling assurance of the King, manifested, for instance, in the transition from verse to prose.

The lowest point of Lear's descent from the ceremonial power of the first scene is reached when he tears off his clothes to rid himself of the last attributes of civilized humanity, and it is characteristic of the play's tragic structure that at this moment Gloucester appears to save him from the worst exposure to the vicious elements. Again, this demonstration of active loyalty and resistance against the inhuman hatred of the daughters hints at the possibility of a happy outcome, although the King's complete mental collapse makes it rather likely that all external help will come too late.

The complex effect of this scene (III.4) is intensified by comic and grotesque elements accompanying the tragic action.[97] Not only are folly and madness traditionally associated with comedy rather than tragedy, at least for Shakespeare's contemporaries, the poignant role of dramatic irony and of disguise also reminds the spectator of comedy and its conventions. Thus Gloucester talks of the 'poor banished man' in the presence of the disguised Kent, and he laments the wickedness of the son he has cast off while Edgar, too, is on stage (see III.4.156–63). In this instance, he is himself still blinded by his unjust suspicion and his own shattering disillusion is still to come; at the same time, he has a vague inkling of the similarities between his fate and that of Lear: 'I am almost mad myself', and 'The grief hath crazed my wits.' This form of a parallel subplot commenting on the main plot is another device that was familiar to Shakespeare's audience more from comedy than from tragedy.

Such unexpected comic associations in moments of the highest tragic intensity are certainly not meant to soften the seriousness of the tragic suffering, but rather to prevent any false harmonization by uniformity of tone. Neither Lear nor Gloucester are invested with the blameless dignity of the martyr. Guilt and suffering are not neatly weighed against each other and an impression of incomprehensible strangeness remains. The spectator can neither comfort himself with his own moral superiority nor feel undivided sympathy with the tortured victims because the ironies and unpredictabilities cast doubt on any simple reaction.

This applies more to the plot centred on Lear than to Gloucester's story. Lear is increasingly lapsing into a state where reality and illusion begin to merge. The fictitious trial of the unnatural daughters – 'the most complex lyric structure in modern drama'[98] – once more dramatizes Lear's pitiful disillusion which has turned into a monomaniac obsession. His powerless accusation, hurled into the empty space of an indifferent nature, can only awaken compassion in the audience because it reveals the complete loss of any predictable touch with reality and a degree of misery even worse than the physical destitution. Edgar's 'aside' underlines the pathos of Lear's humiliation, which even detracts from his own suffering:

> My tears begin to take his part so much
> They mar my counterfeiting. (III.6.59–60)

In his madness, Lear again raises the question of what makes nature so irrational and incomprehensible, this time with an almost unbearable literalness:

let them anatomize Regan, see what breeds about her heart. Is there any cause in nature that makes these hard hearts? (III.6.75–7)

It is a question which, in the context of this play, only the madman can put and to which there is no simple answer. But again, Kent's loyalty and Gloucester's active desire to help are strongly emphasized at the moment of extreme tragic gloom and thus modify the impression of hopeless despair. Lear's progress through agony and loneliness is not acted in an empty space or in front of a deaf cosmos, but remains in the context of natural human relationships and spontaneous reactions. This is made explicit in Edgar's soliloquy, which concludes the scene and, by its position and sententiousness, assumes the authority of an objective statement. Next to Kent and to Cordelia, Edgar is the most reliable commentator, the one least compromised by disguise and deception, and his reactions are a guide for the audience. For him, the King is an overwhelming demonstration of human misery, not only a fellow-sufferer:

> How light and portable my pain seems now,
> When that which makes me bend makes the King bow (III.6.106–7)

This clearly recalls the traditional idea of tragedy which defines the intensity of suffering by the social position of the sufferer. The King's misery is more moving than the pain of lowlier characters who may, like Edgar (and the audience), take comfort from this reflection and forget their own pain in feeling pity for their betters.

Gloucester's downfall, when it comes, is swifter, more brutal and more definite than Lear's. Edmund does not just cast his father out, like Gonerill and Regan, but hands him over to a barbaric revenge that can hardly be explained in terms of punishment for his blind credulity. It must appear to the spectator as the immediate consequence of Gloucester's humane intercession for the outcast King, or almost like a cynical answer to Kent's grateful blessing: 'The gods reward your kindness!' (III.6.5). Reward and punishment evidently do not follow predictable or rational laws in this play, and they resist any comfortable explanation.

For the audience, however, there is a deeper, if more complex connection between Gloucester's misjudgement and the savage punishment inflicted on him. Edgar's banishment and Edmund's rise to power are, in the last resort, his own work and cannot be undone by his loyalty towards the King. Thus, Edgar, at the end of the play, when Edmund's villainy has become manifest and he himself has been publicly vindicated, can point at his father's fate as evidence of divine justice. He does this at a time when a happy outcome still seems to be in sight and justice seems to be fully restored:

> The gods are just, and of our pleasant vices
> Make instruments to plague us:
> The dark and vicious place where thee he got
> Cost him his eyes. (V.3.168–71)

Whether this neat explanation is entirely convincing in view of the final catastrophe will be discussed later. During the actual scene of the blinding, however, hardly any spectator will think of justice or punishment: Gloucester is the tragic victim of inhuman cruelty, of the same forces that have struck down Lear, and he suffers as a loyal subject of his legitimate King.

Again, as earlier in the play, the horror of relentless hatred is softened by a simple human gesture of compassion and a feeling of what is right, and again it is the subordinate servants who preserve their integrity where all familiar loyalties are despised. At the very moment when Gloucester learns that Edmund, to whom, in the name of nature, he calls for revenge, has betrayed him, a servant sacrifices his own life to protect him and becomes an instrument of retribution. Two others look after the blinded master and voice their idea of justice, which, in the midst of all this anarchic bestiality, insists on the clear difference between right and wrong:

> I'll never care what wickedness I do
> If this man come to good.
>   If she live long,
> And in the end meet the old course of death,
> Women will all turn monsters. (III.7.98–101)

The voice of the common people carries particular weight in this play since they repeatedly express an awareness of basic human values like decency, solidarity and compassion, that seem all but forgotten by the majority of the powerful and the influential. What is even more significant for the final impact of this tragedy is that those representatives of the lower social orders are mostly proved right by the course of the action. At the end of the scene, Cornwall has already received his death-wound, and Regan, too, will soon die an unnatural death. The servant's unsophisticated confidence that the wicked cannot possibly thrive is certainly not refuted by the play as a whole.[99] These supporting characters are, therefore, just as important for a full understanding of *King Lear* as the more spectacular scenes.

The fourth act deepens the impression of painful misery and endurance, though there are also repeated hints of various counter-movements. When Edgar meets his father, he painfully discovers that he has still not experienced the full extent of suffering and misery; there seems to be no limit to the agony that can be inflicted on a human being. Yet, this encounter also marks the restoration of the disjoined family bond and the beginning of chastened reconciliation. Gloucester's often quoted cry of despair,

> As flies to wanton boys are we to the gods;
> They kill us for their sport. (IV.1.36–7)

is more than understandable in view of his present situation. For the audience, however, it is qualified by the visual presence of the outcast son on stage, supporting the helpless father. Thus, Gloucester's misery is not quite as desperately hopeless as he himself thinks. In addition, Edgar's disguise and the way he deceives his father introduce an element of comedy and may remind us of related situations in very different contexts.[100] Grotesque comedy and relentless tragedy are sometimes hardly distinguishable in this play.

Gloucester's despair, underscored by his attempted suicide, is clearly contrasted with Lear's doubts about his own identity and his insistence on his right, pursued to the point of madness. In the context of the play, Gloucester represents an attitude of simple superstition collapsing completely under such extreme stress.[101] Yet, in his utter destitution, he also discovers in himself a new degree of pity for the poor and the homeless, and he asks the servant to provide some clothing for Edgar. Like Lear, he suddenly becomes aware of the unjust distribution of worldly goods and prays for a society in which everybody has enough (IV.1.64–70). The stark extremes of pain and unprotected helplessness are somewhat domesticated here and appear in a more familiar form so as to present tragic suffering as well as the possibility of loyalty and hope from a slightly different perspective.

Three brief scenes and changing localities give glimpses of friends and adversaries before we see Gloucester and Lear on stage again. Albany, by dissociating himself from Gonerill and emphatically taking the part of the outlaws, raises hopes of final defeat of the evil forces. The beginning rivalry between the two sisters for Edmund's favors also confirms the view that this is a world in which evil is self-destructive:

> Humanity must perforce prey on itself
> Like monsters of the deep. (IV.2.49–50)

This apocalyptic vision obviously does not mean indiscriminate and wholesale slaughter, but a kind of final judgement that ends in mutual destruction of the wicked.

At the same time, the return of Cordelia to the action makes clear that Lear is not without powerful friends and that the most active help comes from the disinherited children. Shakespeare presents the Anglo-French war without any topical implications whatever; it is only a fight for Lear's right and a fulfilment of filial duty:

> No blown ambition doth our arms incite
> But love, dear love, and our aged father's right.   (IV.4.27–8)

At this point, *King Lear* departs markedly from the old *Leir* play, where Leir and Cordella are described invading England together and gloriously defeating their English opponents. Shakespeare leaves the political aspect deliberately vague: Anglo-French relations are not the issue here, only Cordelia's determination to help her outlawed father. Nothing but Lear's 'sovereign shame' (IV.3.42) seems to stand in the way of a final reconciliation.

Against this background of rallying supporters, Gloucester's situation, too, seems more hopeful. Edgar leads him towards Dover and, what is more important, prevents him from taking his own life. He dies in the end, not in sinful despair (as a Christian audience would see it), but in joyful surprise and finally reconciled with the child he had cast off.

The scene in which Edgar exploits his father's blindness to turn his attempted suicide into a grotesque farce, again makes use of comic conventions, evidently to give added force to his beneficial design:

> Why I do trifle thus with his despair
> Is done to cure it.   (IV.6.33–4)[102]

Gloucester is saved and, like Lear, learns patience. The encounter between the two old men, chastened and humbled by their suffering, also hovers precariously between comedy and tragedy. More even than the utter destitution and exposure to the elements in the storm scenes, it is Lear's madness that demonstrates the full measure of his downfall, and we are again reminded that this is the tragedy of a King whose pathos lies in the very magnitude of his fall:

> A sight most pitiful in the meanest wretch,
> Past speaking of in a king.   (IV.6.204–5)

The whole scene insists on the paradox of tragedy, illustrated by the experience of the sufferer. The traditional notion that children and madmen are often wiser and nearer to the truth than the untroubled and seemingly 'normal', is restated here in the conceit of 'Reason in madness' (IV.6.176) and visually impressed on the spectator, just as Gloucester is a moving illustration of Lear's dictum, 'A man may see how this world goes with no eyes' (IV.6.151–2).[103] The unconventional and complex effect of the scene cannot be reduced to a simple generic term, like 'tragic' or 'grotesque', and it prevents such paradoxical wisdom from sounding like a glib epigram. Any neat rephrasing out of context tends to simplify the extraordinary sweep of this encounter that contains Lear's disillusioned description of human existence as 'this great stage of fools' (IV.6.184) as well as the Gentleman's confident assertion that Cordelia 'redeems nature from the general curse' (IV.6.205–7) brought on her by the two elder sisters. At the end of the scene, Lear is in the hands of well-wishing friends and Gloucester has been saved by Edgar's effective intervention from the murderous threats of the opportunist Oswald. For the time being, the representatives of loyalty and legitimate order seem to be gaining the upper hand.

When, in the last scene of the fourth act, Cordelia and Lear come together again for the first time, the action has reached the point where, in the source play, a general reconciliation and Leir's reinstatement in all his former dignities begin. It is here, however, that Shakespeare has departed most radically from all earlier versions of the story, giving it an entirely new meaning and creating one of the most disturbing problems of interpretation in the whole canon. It has worried and divided critics for three centuries.

The conventional ending of the old *Leir* play combines outward military triumph and untroubled reconciliation. Shakespeare's Lear, in contrast, has gone through depths of suffering and a change of personality that would make such a harmonizing conclusion utterly incredible. For him, the reunion with Cordelia is no happy surprise, but at first seems like a new torment. Shakespeare's play portrays most impressively a tragic experience so overwhelming that it cannot be smoothed over by a simple turn of the plot. Cordelia's unconditional loyalty and loving care are, for the audience, comforting signs of natural behavior, all the more so for being hardly appreciated by Lear. It needs, however, the physician's art as well to bring him back to full consciousness. The traditional formulas of poetic justice are inadequate to balance the excess of tragic suffering, but in the world of this play, the winding up of the plot seems, fundamentally, less relevant than the way each character behaves in situations of moral conflict. Cordelia's unquestioning readiness to forgive and her filial love, demonstrated by every word and action, without any rhetorical show, are manifestations of a moral integrity that is a more effective answer to the helpless despair of the suffering than any happy ending could be, and the same can be said of Kent's loyalty, Edgar's protective care for his blind father, and Albany's rejection of Gonerill. None of Shakespeare's earlier tragedies puts so much emphasis on the idea of reconciliation and spent vitality, most memorably supported by the stage image of the royal father kneeling in front of the daughter he once so peremptorily dismissed from his sight. Lear's 'great rage' is, according to the physician, 'killed in him' (IV.7.78–9), yet his state can be described neither as resignation nor new-won wisdom, and any interpretation that insists too confidently on Lear's redemption and new insight is in danger of idealizing the pathetic impotence of the King's broken resistance, the merely passive acceptance of his own failing: 'Pray you now, forget and forgive. I am old and foolish' (IV.7.83–4).

But this is still not the end of the tragedy whose structure is in important ways different from Shakespeare's other tragedies. It is the only play in which he has altered a plot that in all earlier versions ended with a happy dénouement and brought it to a conclusion many readers and spectators have felt to be unbearably painful, so that Tate's most successful adaptation and several others after it re-introduced the happy ending. If the last scene of *King Lear* strikes us as even more disturbing than the deaths of Hamlet, or Othello, or even of Desdemona, then this is not so much because Lear never regains his kingdom, but because of Cordelia's death, nearly prevented but for an unlucky accident and offending against all traditional notions of poetic justice. The defeat of the tragic protagonists might be explained as an atonement for some fatal error or flaw, but the hanging of Cordelia seems arbitrary, unnecessary, and the work of a completely indifferent fate.[104]

To be sure, in the earlier tragedies there are also innocent victims who are crushed between opposing forces without bearing any responsibility whatever for the tragic clash, such as Mercutio, Ophelia, Desdemona and Emilia. Insofar as the action of *King Lear* can be understood in terms of guilt and punishment at all, Cordelia's death is, in the last resort, the consequence of Lear's disastrous misjudgement in the first scene, which gave scope to the powers of evil and effectively encouraged those who wished to destroy Cordelia and all who stood up for her. The banishment of the only truly loving daughter is a sin that may be forgiven, but its consequences are beyond human control. The betrayal of paternal duties by Lear and Gloucester brings greater misery on themselves and on the community than is at first apparent, and the death of Cordelia is the most disturbing demonstration of the irredeemable loss caused by unnatural guilt and blindness. It is this that makes *King Lear* a true tragedy, even though the sequence of events seems at first less consistent and less easily intelligible than in *Othello*.

This alone, however, would be a rather cheap justification for Cordelia's death, and one can only repeat that the play does not offer a neat balance of crime and punishment. This has already been recognized by Bradley whom later critics have charged with offering a rather too harmonizing view of Shakespearian tragedy. The end of the play, he says, 'flashes on us the conviction that our whole attitude in asking or expecting that goodness should be prosperous is wrong'.[105] He combines this with a more general observation on tragedy whose substance seems to be passed over all too lightly in many interpretations: 'it is necessary to tragedy that we should feel that suffering and death do matter greatly, and that happiness and life are not to be renounced as worthless'.[106] Where suffering and death are balanced too neatly by reconciliation and poetic justice, the intensity of tragic experience, so pointedly described by Bradley, is discredited and made harmless.

Still, the conclusion of this tragedy is more disquieting than that of *Hamlet, Othello,* or *Macbeth* because time and again, hope is raised and consolation offered which turn out to be illusory.[107] On the battlefield, contrary to the source, it is to Lear's enemies, not to his friends, that victory is granted. Gloucester's despair is reproved by Edgar with a rather too sententious assertion that seems to do less than full justice to the terrible catastrophe:

> Men must endure
> Their going hence even as their coming hither;
> Ripeness is all.
> (v.2.9–11)

The wording is reminiscent of Hamlet's 'The readiness is all' (v.2.218) and suggests stoic indifference rather than positive consolation, but behind it, there are Edgar's integrity and loyalty which we have witnessed throughout the play and this must have the weight of a more substantial commentary. Taken out of context, the word 'ripeness' allows of different interpretations.[108] As an answer to Gloucester's 'a man may rot even here' (v.2.8), it asks for a more considered readiness to meet death as well as to accept the challenge of a full life, and it is thus a preparation for the death scenes that follow almost immediately.

The last great scene of the play consists of a series of surprising turns of the action and is quite different from the conventional and straightforward tragic finale. With the unmasking of Edmund and the mutual destruction of the two wicked sisters, the adversaries of Lear and Gloucester seem to be eliminated and justice restored. Even Edmund tries, 'Despite of mine own nature' (v.3.242), to do some good and to prevent the crime he has already commanded. He is one of the very few truly repentant tragic villains in Shakespeare. But, as earlier in the play, the action does not conform to the characters' good intentions and pious hopes: Albany's 'The gods defend her' (254) is answered by the entry of Lear with the corpse of Cordelia. Subjective reactions to this moving stage image of cruelty and despair will, inevitably, differ, yet the majority of readers and spectators will probably agree that 'no other ending would have been imaginatively right.'[109] The world this tragedy has presented hardly allows any other outcome of evil design and practice. The justice of the gods, repeatedly called upon in the last part of the play, becomes manifest in the relentless self-destruction of injustice and wickedness which achieve only short-lived successes, but it cannot altogether put a stop to the destructive power of hatred and inhumanity.

There have been long and intense debates about the ultimate significance of the play's ending: is it meant to endorse Christian hopes of salvation, or does it leave nothing but mute despair or at best resignation? I think this kind of question arises from rather one-sided and inappropriate expectations and tends to isolate aspects of the play that can only be understood in the context of the whole structure. A confident description of *King Lear* as 'a genuinely Christian tragedy of redemption'[110] appears to pass over the really disquieting demonstration of human cruelty somewhat too lightly and presents Lear's terrifying experience in a rather too orthodox light. Yet, when Bradley proposes the title *The Redemption of King Lear* for Shakespeare's poem, as he calls the play in this connection, it becomes very clear from his interpretation that he is not thinking of a Christian morality or losing sight of the painful price to be paid for this 'redemption', as some critics have done who took up his term.[111]

Equally reductive is, to my mind, an interpretation that questions any kind of moral orientation and guidance for the spectator; Nicholas Brooke has expressed this view most poignantly: 'We are, in short, forced by the remorseless process of *King Lear* to face the fact of its ending without any support from systems of moral or artistic belief at all.'[112]It is interesting to see that Brooke, like Bradley, puts the emphasis on the reaction of the audience which is, inevitably, conditoned by its own moral convictions. To be sure, the play does not offer any ready-made explanations, but presents without any illusions an image of human society that forces each individual spectator to reflect on his own ethical standards and beliefs. The absence of any unequivocal moral lesson is not, however, the same as arbitrariness or lack of orientation. There is a general idea of humane behavior implied in the tragedy as a whole and insisted on with unconventional intensity, and this is by no means despairing or indifferent: 'we know it is a greater thing to suffer than to lack the feelings and the virtues that make it possible to suffer...we know it is better to have been Cordelia than to have been her sisters'.[113] How much weight we attach to this kind of observation depends to a large extent on our own experience and expectations, but it is very clear from Shakespeare's text that in the world of *King Lear* there are fundamental alternatives of moral behavior that demand each individual's personal decision.

Though Lear's development within this polyphonic drama is very central, it is not the only aspect of the tragedy determining our reaction, which is very much influenced by the attitudes and actions of the other characters as well; this is why our experience is more complex than that of the protagonist alone, and the question of his personal redemption is not the only criterion by which to judge the play's ending.[114] There is no doubt that King Lear gradually becomes aware of his fatal error, that he is reconciled with the daughter he has cast off and does not remain fixed in his stubborn attitude of hurt majesty and revengeful wrath; but how much he has actually learnt about the duties of a ruler, the office of a king and his social responsibilities, cannot really be estimated because he never regains his former power and the play does not give him any opportunity to prove his changed personality by responsible political actions. The reinstatement in his old dignities as King remains a symbolic act of piety, without any practical consequences for the state. Even the most loyal friends do not wish to prolong his life. The text suggests that at the moment of death, Lear still has hopes of Cordelia's reawakening, and this impression is not made invalid by the fact that these hopes are unfounded, as the audience knows. The King does not die in hopeless despair since up to the very end he retains some of his majestic vitality and even potential optimism, even though, admittedly, the play leaves much open and makes no final pronouncements.[115]

Unlike the earlier tragedies, *King Lear* does not end with a message to posterity; Lear is no longer interested in the name he will leave behind, like Hamlet and Othello, and the survivors are faced with a world less threatened by the powers of evil, yet painfully reduced. The last words do not express hopeful confidence in a brighter future, but rather a consciousness of irredeemable loss and the necessity of a completely new beginning. Albany's conventional announcement of reward and punishment (v.3.300–2) is interrupted by Lear's death and the actual ending is merely a tentative attempt to put the general feeling of grief and awe into words, to place it in some relation to one's own life. Edgar is not yet prepared to assume the authority of the new ruler, like Fortinbras, and he explicitly refuses to make any official statement such as we normally expect at this point of the tragedy. It is only in keeping with the design of the whole play that it does not end with a sententious epigram, but with a reminder of the magnitude and the dignity of suffering and the modest role of the surviving beholders who can only take note of the tragic experience lived through by the protagonists, not really claim to share it:

> The oldest hath borne most; we that are young
> Shall never see so much nor live so long. (V.3.323–4)

Several themes of the play are briefly alluded to in these last lines, but more important is the impression that what we have seen cannot be neatly rounded off by a rhetorical formula. The words of the survivors will have less permanence and less authority than Lear's tragic experience.[116]

MACBETH

Compared with *King Lear*, *Macbeth* appears much more simply constructed and easier to understand. Its structure is tight, almost classical in its compelling consistency and there is only one plot. The tragic action, at first sight, is equally transparent. One may, if one is fond of crisp formulas, like V. K. Whitaker reduce it to 'simply the yielding of a great and good man to temptation and the degeneration of his moral nature resulting from his first deed of sin'.[117] But this glib description is hardly adequate to account for the play's unusual fascination and makes it sound like an edifying morality. It is more appropriate to try and understand it in relation to the other three major tragedies and to its historical context.

Although plot and subject are quite different from *Hamlet*, *Othello* and *King Lear*, there are close thematic links between these three plays and *Macbeth*. The burning question of how evil comes into society and why it has such power over individual characters is only touched on in the earlier tragedies, usually in connection with the protagonist's tragic experience; in *Macbeth*, it is right at the heart of the play. Claudius, Iago and Edmund are presented as the very incarnation of hatred and corruption, but the dramatist tells us very little about their motives and he never makes them objects of our sympathy. Their well-deserved exposure and punishment is not a central aspect of the tragic impact, but the confirmation of moral order and poetic justice. In *Macbeth*, however, as has often been remarked, the villain and criminal has become the tragic hero, not in the sense of a cautionary history, but as a disquieting study of human corruptibility and ruthless lust for political power. Lear's agonized question, 'Is there any cause in nature that makes these hard hearts?' (III.6.76–7), is not answered, yet in *Macbeth* Shakespeare has made it the central theme of his tragedy, mainly by a change of perspective. It is not the victims of wickedness and sin that the play is concerned with, but wickedness and sin itself, yet not from an attitude of orthodox certainty, but from a dramatic point of view so close to the protagonist that any superior detachment is made impossible.[118]

The problem of evil is made spectacularly concrete by the introduction of the Elizabethan mythology of witchcraft, including elements of popular superstition as well as theological speculation. It was well known that the new King James I was deeply interested in all kinds of supernatural phenomena and witch-lore, and it seems reasonable enough to assume that, with this play, Shakespeare deliberately touched on a theme that could not fail to fascinate his monarch and the patron of his company, the King's Men, just as the actual subject, early Scottish history and the descent of the Stuarts from Banquo, seems an obvious compliment to James. Thus, visiting Oxford in 1605, the King was greatly pleased when, in the course of an allegorical pageant, he was hailed as Banquo's heir by the same three Fates who had once promised the crown to his ancestor and his progeny for all eternity.[119] This topical significance of the tragedy had, without doubt, consequences for the presentation of the story.

It probably explains why Shakespeare's Banquo, in contrast to the dramatist's most important source, Holinshed's chronicle, is not implicated in the murder of Duncan as Macbeth's fellow-conspirator, but serves as a positive moral contrast. There were, however, perfectly good dramatic reasons for this change, as for several other alterations of the historical material. Most of them are due to Shakespeare's most original conception of his tragic hero.

If one compares *Macbeth* with Holinshed's account, the first thing to be noticed is again the skilful concentration of the action. The Macbeth of the chronicles has ruled justly and with obvious success for some ten years before he turns into a tyrant and his enemies begin to unite against him. The murder of Duncan is more conventionally motivated by the King's weakness, to which Macbeth objects, and by his apparent exclusion from the succession: contrary to established Scottish practice, Duncan declares his son to be his heir, which Macbeth takes as an affront. The murder is the work of a conspiracy, not the brutal crime of an individual. The particularly repulsive circumstances of the act Shakespeare took over from another case of regicide reported by Holinshed: about a century before Macbeth, Donwald vented some private hatred against King Duff and murdered him, at the instigation of his wife, while entertaining him as a guest in his own home. The crime was followed by supernatural portents: for six months there was neither sun by day nor moon by night, and there were several other frightening signs of divine wrath until the deed was avenged, all the murderers cruelly executed and the body of the King properly buried according to his rank. Macbeth's crime, in comparison, is much more political and less spectacular. It is also morally less revolting and of less consequence for the whole realm. The dramatist has transferred some of the supernatural and cosmic phenomena accompanying the murder of Duff to Macbeth's story. He has also condensed the time of the action into a few months and has particularly emphasized the aspect of 'pricke of conscience'[120] by the apparition of Banquo's Ghost and the sleep-walking scene, neither of which are mentioned in the sources. The comic solo of the porter, too, is his own addition.

Shakespeare's source clearly links this tragedy to his history plays and the similarities with *Richard III*, including even verbal parallels, have often been noticed.[121] Tillyard calls *Macbeth* 'the epilogue to the histories' and rightly calls attention to the fact that state and community are more important aspects of the tragic action here than in the other tragedies.[122] It is not only the party of Macbeth's opponents that is victorious at the end, but the whole kingdom, a community whose welfare is dependent on order and law. Malcolm stands for the principle of a good monarch in a much more concrete and meaningful sense than Fortinbras or Albany. *Macbeth* is in many ways an eminently political play; it demonstrates, very similarly to *Richard III*, the law of crime and punishment or sin and retribution in history, a law insisted on again and again by Elizabethan historians as well as by the authors of *The Mirror for Magistrates*. Prophecy and tragic irony as well as the close relationship between individual guilt and cosmic order had already been important issues in Shakespeare's histories and had often even determined their dramatic structure. These plays were, however, less concerned with the individual's struggle against temptation or with private morality. Richard III is in many ways a most fascinating character, but we can hardly say that he undergoes a genuinely tragic experience or that there is any marked personal development. His villainy and his dynamic inhumanity are a part of his nature that is taken for granted; they are not explored in any depths or taken as a central problem in the play, although they can be made more prominent and disturbing in performance.

At the end of the play, Richard, who is confronted by imminent destruction and revenge, talks of his conscience and, in a long soliloquy, sees himself as one of the damned. This is a rather conventional form of self-recognition at the moment of death, and the stylized rhetoric as well as the rather schematic scenic form of the last act makes it difficult for us to see him as a tormented human being with whom we can really identify.[123] At least, the possibility of tragic conflict is not pursued much further in the rest of the play and it is obvious that the play wants us to side with Richard's enemies, most of all the victorious Tudor Richmond.

All this does not mean that it is easy to draw the line between history and tragedy, either in Elizabethan theory and practice or by a general abstract definition; yet most critics agree that the traditional grouping of *Richard III* with the histories and *Macbeth* with the tragedies is justified by the character and the subject of the two plays. In spite of its topical interest for Shakespeare's audience and its politcal aspect, *Macbeth* is not a historical play. What really absorbs the spectator is not so much the fate of Scotland, but the protagonist's agonizing mental conflict, his far-reaching moral decision, and his total collapse under its consequences.[124] It was even Bradley who spoke of our 'sympathy' for Macbeth[125] and though the reactions of individual spectators are bound to differ, the play's undiminished popularity throughout the centuries, in the study as well as on stage, is evidence that Shakespeare has dramatized Macbeth's criminal career in such a way that it does not merely arouse indignation and revulsion, but also a sense of personal involvement and sympathy in the literal sense of our suffering with the hero, which could hardly be said of Richard III. Macbeth's tragic experience is, of course, very different from that of Lear, but it is of the same intensity and energy of imagination and it is no less directly related to fundamental ethical issues. There is a very similar view of human existence as a series of moral decisions beyond the reach of comfortably orthodox definitions.

This is in no way qualified, but rather highlighted by the presence of the witches. Like the Ghost in *Hamlet*, they are not to be explained as a phenomenon by itself, but are inseparably related to the protagonist and his tragic dilemma. Their first appearance is, above all, designed to create a striking atmosphere of suspense and foreboding. The spectator finds himself transported into a world where human beings are closely observed by supernatural spirits eager to create confusion and to take advantage of man's infirmities. The witches are a rather more sinister version of the elves and fairies in the *Midsummer Night's Dream* who make fun of the mortals and are amused by their folly. For the 'weird sisters', the political quarrels and bloodshed among men are no more than 'hurly-burly' (I.I.3) where it is all the same who wins and who loses. All the familiar standards of everyday experience are irrelevant to them and thus there is, from the start, a clear opposition between man-made order and this dimension of the unreliable and deceptive, acting as a threat and a challenge: 'Fair is foul, and foul is fair' (I.I.9). Here it is already evident that these apparitions are neither benign spirits of order nor agents of an inescapable fate, but, in a way that is particularly characteristic of Shakespeare's dramatic art, combine elements of popular belief and a syncretistic mythology. It is a combination that is possible only in a theatre that is at the same time popular and learned, as only the Elizabethan and early Jacobean theatre was.[126]

Against this background, the second scene is bound to seem rather less impressive despite its martial rhetoric and talk of heroic exploits. The epic pathos of the blood-smeared eye-witness – obviously modelled on the classical messenger-speech – is clearly marked as something of a declamatory pose by the completely different style of the previous scene. The slightly false grandeur of the diction makes Macbeth's celebrated victory sound like a bloody slaughter as much as a glorious success. The action that is to follow is not anticipated in any detail, but some important themes are sounded and, in retrospect at least, most spectators will notice the ominous equation of 'that most disloyal traitor,/The Thane of Cawdor' (1.2.54–5) and Macbeth who inherits that 'former title'. The protagonist is introduced rather indirectly at first, similar to Hamlet, Othello and (very briefly) Lear. Loyalty and a soldier's toughness are the chief virtues ascribed to him from the first, and both are a kind of starting-point for the conflicts that are to follow. With Macbeth's help the King has overcome all his external and internal enemies and he can now, it appears, rely on the new Thane of Cawdor for loyalty and protection.

In the following scene, the two worlds to which we have been introduced confront one another directly, and it is immediately clear from the dramatic style and the language that this is not a normal encounter of partners in a dialogue, but an apparition arranged by the supernatural beings in the course of which the mortals are told as much and no more as lies within the will and the power of the spirits. Like Hamlet, Macbeth and Banquo are directly addressed by the apparition, but they are by no means granted any reliable information. They try to extract some firm instruction, teased by the possibility of obtaining some usually hidden knowledge; the witches, however, create confusion, not certainty and this is perfectly in keeping with Elizabethan ideas of such ghosts and their influence on humans.

In contrast to his source, Shakespeare lays great stress on the different reactions of Banquo and Macbeth and this alone should make perfectly clear that the 'weird sisters'' power over human will is very limited; they can suggest, not direct, and they do not directly circumscribe the freedom of their chosen victim. Macbeth's reaction, effectively described by Banquo for the spectator's benefit, is one of immediate terror and shock. The annunciation of royal dignity fills him with cold fear and this strongly suggests that it hits him in a particularly sensitive spot, that he, like Hamlet, has somehow been prepared for a revelation of this kind, even though this need not be something of which he is himself aware. The spectator knows, however, that the witches who address him as 'Thane of Cawdor' have the advantage of Macbeth who is still ignorant of his new title, and this must give him an idea of their superior knowledge. Banquo, on the other side, is completely unimpressed and sees the witches as a curiosity or a strange deception of the senses. Their announcement is for him no more than a surprising incident, not to be taken too seriously, and he watches its powerful effect on Macbeth with genuine astonishment.

The immediate arrival of Duncan's messengers who greet Macbeth officially as 'Thane of Cawdor' gives to the witches an appearance of prophetic authority and again Shakespeare emphasizes the different effect of this revelation on Banquo and on Macbeth. Banquo's first reaction is amazement at the deceptive power of evil ('What! Can the devil speak true?' (1.3.106)). For him, the obvious explanation is provided by the Christian commonplace that the Fiend often puts on the mask of truth and trustworthiness to deceive us all the more effectively, and he pronounces it with the certainty of an orthodox doctrine:

> And oftentimes, to win us to our harm,
> The instruments of darkness tell us truths;
> Win us with honest trifles, to betray's
> In deepest consequence. (1.3.122–5)

There is no doubt that for many Elizabethans this was the only possible answer to the question of the origin and the authority of supernatural forebodings, and Shakespeare's plays are full of similar statements. Attractive half-truths and pleasant flattery ('honest trifles') are well-tried means of temptation and corruption; but it is only for those who are unaffected and uncorruptible that they are as transparent as they are for Banquo and for the spectator enlightened by him.

Remarkably, both Banquo and Macbeth understand the witches' prophecy as an invitation to act, although this is not explicitly spelt out, and therefore needs the active cooperation of the listener. Banquo uses traditional terms to describe the Devil, and Macbeth, too, speaks of 'supernatural soliciting' (1.3.129). This may be an accurate description of the effect on him of the witches' address and of their secret intention, but it cannot be said that there is any 'soliciting' in their actual words; it is Macbeth's own mind that does the soliciting.[127] It will not be lost on any reader that his reaction provides a terrifying confirmation of Banquo's confident explanation. The witches' prophecies have activated his brain with an irresistible intensity, as Shakespeare makes clear by a most original form of dramatic soliloquy. The conventional 'aside', which usually serves as a device to inform the spectator directly or to draw our attention to deliberate deception on the speaker's part, is here used in a novel way: it indicates a state of intense mental preoccupation and a temporary withdrawal from the dialogue in which he takes part only with a few meaningless phrases. What has really taken possession of his whole mind is reflected in an 'aside' that more and more turns into a monologue audible only to the audience. Temptation is not, as in the moralities, an act of persuasion by a seducer, but a mental process within the individual consciousness. Shakespeare here leaves behind him the more conventional dramatic method he himself used in *Othello*, where Iago still plays the part of Vice and the wicked counsellor. Macbeth, however, is tempter and tempted at the same time, and only the spectator is able to witness his internal struggle. All the other characters on stage can merely see what Banquo describes for them:

> Look how our partner's rapt. (1.3.142)

In the case of more conventional villains, the complicity of the reader or spectator can produce a feeling of amused superiority, perhaps even sneaking admiration. In *Macbeth*, the technique is obviously a means of manipulating our sympathy.[128] The intensity of the inner conflict qualifies, for us, Banquo's unambiguous, but rather abstract explanation; it is invested with a disturbing concreteness by Macbeth's agony, and this makes it impossible to remain in a state of detached superiority. The driving force behind this tragic conflict is his irrepressible imagination which many critics, before and since Bradley, have described as the hero's most distinct and fatal quality.[129] It compels him to pursue relentlessly the ideas suggested to him by the witches and it prevents him from resisting their destructive consequences. This is what makes the whole scene so characteristic and crucial for what follows. Macbeth does not make a clear-cut, conscious decision to take the evil course, unlike Richard III, whose 'I am determined to prove a villain' (1.1.30) suggests a very different conception of tragedy and may illustrate the fundamental contrast between the two plays. For Macbeth, evil seems to be anything but an attractive alternative to his previous innocence; rather it is a terrifying possibility, and the effect of these imaginings on his whole being is unmistakable:

> why do I yield to that suggestion
> Whose horrid image doth unfix my hair,
> And make my seated heart knock at my ribs
> Against the use of nature? (1.3.133–6)

This is a completely new tone in Shakespearian tragedy. Macbeth's description reminds us of the Ghost's account in *Hamlet*, hinting at the horrors and torments of Hell, of whom he 'could a tale unfold' (1.5.15). Here it is, however, the sudden and frightening discovery of one's own hellish thoughts that is the most disturbing experience.[130] Man's extra-ordinary capacity for completely immobilizing himself by visions of infernal pain and punishment, so powerfully expressed in Hamlet's famous soliloquy, is presented *in actu*:

> Present fears
> Are less than horrible imaginings.
> My thought, whose murder yet is but fantastical,
> Shakes so my single state of man
> That function is smothered in surmise,
> And nothing is but what is not. (1.3.136–41)

The border-line between reality and imagination becomes increasingly blurred. Macbeth's soliloquy is a demonstration of the experience that the products of our imagination can assume a presence as powerful and active as reality itself. For the first time, the word 'murder' appears in this connection, not introduced by any tempter from without, but entering Macbeth's thoughts of its own accord, as it were, and smothering all normal impulses. None of Shakespeare's tragic heroes before Macbeth has undergone the same experience. Marlowe's Doctor Faustus, perhaps, comes nearest to it. Knowingly he chooses Hell rather than salvation; but then, the terms of his temptation are very different and it is not his imagination as much as his insatiable desire for knowledge and intel-lectual power that leads him to damnation.

Macbeth does not make a definite decision, but leaves it all to 'chance' and 'time' (1.3.143 and 147), yet the intensity of his temptation and his complete isolation, emphasized by the dramatic technique, prepare the spectator for the sinister development which in the following scene already becomes more clearly foreseeable. The contrast between the outwardly loyal Macbeth, in whom the King puts all the trust dis-appointed by the previous Thane of Cawdor, and his 'black and deep desires' (1.4.52), is again underlined by an 'aside' that shows his deeply divided mind. The crime now appears as a real possibility that wants to shut out the light of day. He has obviously almost succumbed to the temptation before his wife drives him to the actual committal of the murder, and it is the prophecy of the witches acting on his imagination rather than any more clearly defined political consideration that brings about his fall. The text does not give us all the precise psychological steps that lead to the final decision, but it is clear that Malcolm's proclamation as Duncan's heir – which is not, as in the sources, a clear rejection of Macbeth's own just claim – as well as the announcement of the royal visit make him draw closer to his purpose which even his own eye must not see

(1.4.52). Not even his different senses are in harmony with each other, and Macbeth's rhetorical division of eye and hand seems to express an illusory hope that one can commit a crime without being accountable for it with one's complete person.

The whole scene is informed with the contrast between Macbeth's outward behavior and the internal conflict known only to the audience. It is further emphasized by the rhetoric of his professions of loyalty and the unsuspecting trust of the King. The description of the traitor's exemplary death and Duncan's comparison of Macbeth's loyalty with a banquet also contribute to the tragic irony of the scene.

The preparation of the crime stretches over several scenes and this creates the impression of a long and painful temptation which does not happen with the inexorable speed and concentration of Othello's corruption, but needs various different influences and succeeds only after a series of agonizing struggles and strong inner resistance. In this process Lady Macbeth does not, by any means, play the part of a Iago. Before her first appearance, Macbeth has already considered the crime as an actual possibility and he has been changed by the witches' prophecy more than his wife can be aware. Her own, much less scrupulous determination and rejection of any moral doubts rather act as a contrast to the world of his much more complex imagination and direct our sympathies towards Macbeth into whose ear she intends to pour her own poisonous spirit. The progress of his corruption is, in a way, retarded by the presence of his wife because it seems as if it is not the witches alone who set him on his way to damnation. At the same time, this progress is now, in terms of the dramatic situation, cast in the form of persuasion and personal influence, whereas before it was only presented as a lonely struggle of the hero with his own phantasies.

In *Othello*, as we have seen, the most genuine appreciation of the hero's qualities (as well as of Cassio's) come from the mouth of the slanderer. Similarly, in Lady Macbeth's first speech we get a portrait of her husband whose most humane features seem all the more reliable as they have obviously impressed someone who knows him well and are not, as in the case of Duncan's praise, the result of hypocritical flattery. What Lady Macbeth fears as the chief obstacle to her husband's advancement, 'the milk of human-kindness' (1.5.15), is the very reason why, for the spectator, he becomes a tragic hero and one with whom we can, to some extent, identify because he does not give in to wicked temptation without an agonizing struggle. Lady Macbeth knows nothing of such painful conflict with one's own 'horrible imaginings' (1.3.137) and sees only indecision and weakness where there are genuine scruples. Bradley thought that her lack of imagination was indeed the chief difference between the two.[131] The witches hardly mean anything to her, and her determination to commit the crime is as radical as it is unreflected. Her emphatic dedication of herself to the spirits of evil, coupled with an explicit denial of her sex (1.5.38–49), has much more in common with Lear's curse against his eldest daughter (*King Lear* 1.4.272–86), and the wording clearly indicates that she is invoking powers that are against nature, that she is, in fact, repudiating her own human nature by asking to be barren. She deliberately chooses to be one with the witches, and her whole speech reveals that she is already possessed by the spirits to whom she prays. At least, this is how an Elizabethan audience would most probably have understood the scene.[132]

In spite of all the dramatic energy of her character, which has made her part one of the most famous and most effective actress's roles in all the tragedies, she is, in comparison with the protagonist, not a very complex character. What makes her so fascinating to the audience is chiefly her fatal impact on Macbeth, not her own character problems or any tragic conflict within her. Her language, too, is much less imaginative, not as rich in associations, but unambiguous in the simplicity and inflexibility of her will-to-power. Still, her dynamic speeches and her powerful impression on other characters in the play provide an ample potential for any great actress, and the impact she can make in a good production is much stronger than her comparatively simple characterization in the text might suggest.

The structure of the first act, with its seven relatively brief scenes, mirrors Macbeth's inner conflict and portrays a world of very contradictory values. Lady Macbeth's threatening expectation of the 'fatal entrance of Duncan' (1.5.37) is followed by Duncan's actual arrival which combines in a particularly impressive way tragic irony and the poetical evocation of untroubled harmony between man and nature. The hoarse raven mentioned by Lady Macbeth is contrasted with the 'temple-haunting martlet' whose trustful nesting in Macbeth's castle make Duncan and Banquo feel all the more secure and welcome within its walls. Critics have noticed that Shakespeare's imagery creates for us a world of natural harmony and peace that makes the violation of all human loyalties and traditional ties by Macbeth and his wife all the more repulsive.[133] The same nature that is completely perverted in Lady Macbeth is presented to us in these images as a power that is fruitful and constructive. But the popular superstition proves to be deceptive and the trusting bird has as little intuitive foreknowledge of the unnatural treason prepared within these seemingly hospitable walls as Duncan who is taken in by the hypocritically fulsome rhetoric of his hosts. The vision of a natural order based on harmony and trust is crucial for our own orientation within a play whose action is shaped by murder and blood. What is all-important, however, is the fact that Macbeth is most conscious of this order and has not, like his wife, once and for all rejected it.

His first great soliloquy, following immediately on his reception of Duncan, once more reviews the possible consequences of the projected deed, but especially its inhuman character. Like Hamlet, who is deeply worried by 'the dread of something after death', Macbeth recognizes man's uncertain fear of a life beyond and of being asked to account for his actions as a powerful impediment when it comes to making moral decisions. He himself describes the unnatural ugliness of the murder he is about to commit in no uncertain terms as well as its inevitable consequences. The image of the 'angels, trumpet-tongued against/The deep damnation of his taking-off' (1.7.19–20) obviously suggest eschatological associations, while 'Pity, like a naked new-born babe' (1.7.21) once again reminds the audience of the unprotected helplessness of an innocent life that can only be shielded by pity from destruction. Divine punishment and retribution, not human revenge are what really frightens Macbeth and they direct the further course of the action. The soliloquy does not announce a decision already made, but it reveals a clarity of vision and a painful awareness of the true situation that again remind us of Hamlet. Lady Macbeth does not add anything to this insight. Her function is rather to cloud his imagination than to oppose his fears and forebodings with a positive vision or an inspiring aim. From the very beginning, it is striking to see how much Macbeth's language and thought are pre-occupied with the bloody nature and consequences of the murder and how little there is in his speeches of the real allurements and the hoped-for gain. This obsession with the terrors and the sinister consequences of crime rather than with its glorious rewards marks a characteristic difference between Macbeth and Marlowe's tragic heroes whose dynamic ambition, even where it becomes plainly criminal in execution, is always informed with an alluring vision of the wonderful prize to be reaped in the end. Macbeth and his wife know what they want to gain, but the play's rhetoric hardly ever suggests that the honor they hope to win is worth the terrible price to be paid for it. They seem almost more fascinated by this price than by their original ambition.

The final persuasion is more the result of Lady Macbeth's dynamic and unscrupulous will than of clever arguments or inventive eloquence. She does not really take any notice of his genuine scruples or try to refute them. His intention to abandon further thought of the deed, announced at the beginning of their decisive encounter, is apparently rather superficial and easily dispelled. Nor is her reminder of his oath – of which the audience knows nothing – a carefully prepared argument, but rather a demonstration of her ruthless determination, whose firmness impresses him, just as Hamlet is impressed by the unreflecting impetuosity of Fortinbras and Laertes. All that really frightens him is brushed aside by her insistence on an idea of simple manliness whose most important quality is a fearless readiness to act. To this he can only oppose half-hearted caution, 'If we should fail?' (1.7.59), which she has no difficulty in overruling. For a brief moment, near the end of the scene, he seems to have adopted her firm determination, overwhelmed by her show of masculinity which is only an expression of her obsessed denial of all that is woman in her. When Macbeth himself now decides to combine all the energies of his body in the service of this crime, 'bend up/Each corporal agent to this terrible feat' (1.7.79–80), he acts in opposition to what he himself has experienced and what is more characteristic of his own nature: the agonizing conflict between different senses that makes a really determined and concentrated effort all but impossible for him. This side of himself will soon gain the upper hand again.

The second soliloquy, immediately before the murder, is again the expression of a deeply divided personality and it reveals to the audience the power of an uncontrollable imagination that will always be beyond Lady Macbeth's grasp.[134] The imaginary dagger (II.1.33) symbolizes the unreal nature of the prize Macbeth is aiming at, a 'fatal vision', like the apparition of the witches and just as illusory and elusive. This again raises the question of how reliable our senses are since eyes and hands seem to perceive different things. Macbeth experiences the particular nocturnal hour with an intense awareness of the brutality he is about to commit. This awareness does not in any way diminish the criminal sinfulness of the act, but it brings the hero much closer to the audience because he himself describes the horrors of his crime with such clarity of vision and such intense moral consciousness.[135] The deed is undertaken without any of the enthusiastic determination and enjoyment of his own villainy that is so characteristic of Richard III. There is no cheerful expectation of a glorious reward. Terror and anguish are the prevailing emotions, and the murderer goes off to his victim like one doomed. No murder in the tragedies is committed with so little conviction, and not even a short-lived, liberating triumph is gained by it.

The soliloquy again contributes to a vivid emotional engagement on the part of the spectator, mainly because it does not, like the traditional soliloquies of the villain, try to establish a secret understanding between the speaker and the audience. It need not be spoken right at the front of the stage, in close contact to the auditorium, but rather serves to express the hero's complete isolation. His vision of the fatal weapon, dramatized in a most effective and original manner, cuts him off from everything around him. Again, a comparison with the soliloquies of Marlowe's Doctor Faustus is instructive: there, too, we have solo scenes whose main purpose is neither reflection nor planning, but the portrayal of a deep emotional and intellectual crisis. Shakespeare departs from his previous practice in the use of soliloquy in order to present Macbeth's fundamentally divided character by this disturbing vision. He is obviously making a moral decision of a most far-reaching nature, but he is clearly beyond rational reflection and a conscious weighing of the issues involved. Without any self-justification or any illusion he really believes in, yet fully conscious of the 'present horror' (II.1.59) he leaves the stage to commit the murder that has already taken place in his (and in our) imagination. When, only twelve lines later, he re-appears, the irrevocable has happened, and all the rest of the play describes the mental and political convulsions set in motion by this crime. As in classical drama, the actual murder is executed off stage, but *Macbeth* is perhaps the best example of the way in which the terrifying inhumanity of the crime is impressed on us all the more powerfully by this indirect form of presentation. Poetry and dramatic rhetoric are more effective here than visual representation.

Lady Macbeth herself appears to experience the unnatural atrocity of the murder:

> Had he not resembled
> My father as he slept, I had done't. (II.2.12–13)

Even she is unable to commit parricide, yet as King, Duncan is no less sacred, and her hesitation at this point underscores the magnitude of the crime, the violation of natural order and loyalty. 'My father as he slept' also reminds the audience of the familiar world of blood-relationship and domestic harmony that is brutally negated here.

Macbeth's own disturbed state of mind demonstrates the fatal consequences of the crime, following immediately on its execution, even more impressively. As before the deed, his imagination now proves to be completely beyond his control and it becomes the most dangerous instrument of divine revenge. Lady Macbeth's sensible advice, 'Consider it not so deeply' (II.2.30), is totally ineffective and only underlines the intellectual as well as the moral distance between the two; this will continue to widen as the play goes on, in spite of their complicity.

Macbeth's language, with its disjointed and, in places, fragmentary syntax, especially its memorable images, suggests a deeply disturbed consciousness in which the idea of violated order and a peaceful existence never to be recovered has taken root once and for all. The knocking at the gate immediately makes clear that from now on even the most harmless incident turns into a reminder of his guilt. The contrast between his own conviction that his hands will never be clean again and Lady Macbeth's practical advice, 'A little water clears us of this deed' (II.2.67), may explain why, in spite of the repulsive gravity of Macbeth's guilt, the audience is not indifferent or simply hostile towards him, because, for all the progressive hardening of his mind, what Bradley calls 'a gleam of his native love of goodness' is left with him and distinguishes him from her.[136] The ultimate superiority of order and human integrity is made credible in this play not so much by any contrast with positive characters as by Macbeth's own lucid consciousness of moral values, by his continuous references to norms against which he has offended.

The discovery of the crime, the reports of the spectacular and frightening side-effects, and the seemingly successful play-acting of the criminals strike us, after what has gone before, as dramatically brilliant but comparatively conventional, as a diminishing of moral intensity. A certain easing of the dramatic tension before the actual reversal of the tragic development is not, however, a fault of the play's construction, but an important element of the dramatic rhythm which brings out the real significance of the crime all the more effectively. After Macbeth's horrifying visions before the deed, any of the usual consequences of such a murder must seem comparatively trivial and in the nature of an anticlimax.

Between the scenes of lonely anguish and the return to practical politics, there is a scene which earlier critics suspected to be an un-Shakespearian interpolation, but no modern reader will have any doubts as to its genuineness and its essential function for the total tragic effect of the play. This is the comic solo of the porter whom the knocking at the gate, so terrifying to Macbeth, has roused from his drunken stupor, immediately after Macbeth has expressed the futile hope that the sound might re-awaken Duncan.[137]

This kind of sharp contrast between two completely different stylistic registers is not unusual in Elizabethan drama or, indeed, in Shakespearian tragedy, even though the descent from tragic pathos to irresponsible clowning seems particularly abrupt here. It does not, however, appear to be out of place in a theatre which, like the Elizabethan public stage, does not aim at creating an illusion of realistic experience and does not attempt to disguise its role as popular entertainment, its eagerness to please. The audience is unashamedly reminded of the human actor behind the stage costume: 'I pray you remember the porter' (II.3.19). The clown, asking for his tip, stands for a world of unconcerned vitality; to him, even Hell is only a subject for good-humored joking. It has often been remarked that the scene is closely related to the traditional representation of the Gates of Hell in the moralities,[138] and this observation can help us to see the thematic significance of this interlude. In a comic manner it suggests religious associations and transforms Macbeth's castle into a place of the damned, if only as an imaginative game played by a drunken servant. The audience will hardly miss the ironic equation between the fictitious sinner greeted by the porter and the real criminals who are already within the gates. The pseudo-learned lecture on the effects of alcohol, too, plays on themes from other parts of the tragedy, especially the dangers of equivocation, of deceptive prophecy that can tempt man into futile efforts. The porter's mock-serious definition is a parody of the forces that have defeated Macbeth. What he says about drink is just as true of his fatal ambition: 'it makes him and it mars him; it sets him on and it takes him off; it persuades him and disheartens him' (II.3.30–1).

Whether we can call this 'comic relief' is a question of the effect of the scene on the individual spectator. Critics have argued about whether this comic interlude actually softens the horrors of the murder scene or makes it even more ghastly by contrast, but this can hardly be decided from the text alone: it depends very much on the disposition of the beholder. The juxtaposition of sublime rhetoric, tragic intensity and a realism without illusions or pretensions is, at any rate, very characteristic of Shakespearian tragedy, and the porter has often been compared with the gravediggers in *Hamlet* for his very similar function. Tragic experience never loses its vital connection with the world of trivial everyday experience. Even those characters who have yet to undergo shattering trials are usually shown, immediately before the catastrophe, in relaxed dialogue with socially much inferior representatives of unblinkered realism and simple wisdom (e.g. Hamlet, Desdemona, Juliet, Lear, Cleopatra). Shakespeare's drama never loses sight of the essential link between comedy and tragedy, their common roots in stylized role-playing.

Macbeth's own shocked horror at the deed he has committed is presented with such dramatic intensity, that the discovery and the frightened reactions of those around him at first only seem like a comparatively harmless epilogue. The spectator does not share the terrified surprise of the unprepared because he has witnessed the planning of the crime. He is thus able to concentrate his attention on the two murderers who successfully pass their first test in hypocritical dissembling and are, for the time being, able to avoid all suspicion, although the immediate flight of Duncan's sons anticipates later developments and clearly diminishes Macbeth's success. The official version of the murder is not accepted by those who are most nearly concerned and the brief transitional scene (II.4), in which we learn about Macbeth's imminent coronation, puts this outward triumph in a context that once more emphasizes the inhumanity of the murder. The figure of the Old Man who is completely separate from the play's action and obviously represents the point of view of simple humanity, further adds to the impression of unnatural violence and offence against sacred pieties. His blessing at the end of the scene answers the sinister events with a simple definition of humane integrity:

> God's benison go with you, and with those
> That would make good of bad, and friends of foes!   (II.4.40–1)

It is a pointed rejoinder to the witches' 'Fair is foul, and foul is fair' (I.1.9) that seems to have directed the dramatic action so far. Without these brief but insistent reminders of a natural sense of justice and human community *Macbeth* might easily have become a melodramatic presentation of meaningless horror and inescapable nightmare.[139]

Macbeth soon finds that one crime is not enough to win and to secure the crown for him. It is only by further murder that he can keep what he has gained by the first murder. The dramatist underlines this by making Banquo the first to suspect him and by reminding the audience, through Banquo, of the witches' prophecy of which only the first half has so far become true. By his first murder, Macbeth has tried to prove the truth of what the weird sisters foretold; by the murder of Banquo he wants to prove them liars, but their prophecy is confirmed even in that sense that is most fatal for him. 'fruitless crown' and 'barren sceptre' (III.1.60–1) are, ultimately, the prize for which he has given away his humanity and sold himself to the inexorable mechanism of crime.

There is a clear contrast between the agonized decision to kill Duncan and the calculating chill of the arrangements to rid himself of Banquo. Neither supernatural visions nor the energy of Lady Macbeth are needed, and no moral scruples seem to weaken his determination although he is fully aware of Banquo's 'royalty of nature' (III.1.49). As in other tragedies by Shakespeare, the special virtues of the villain's opponent are most eloquently and reliably praised by him who is provoked by them into destructive hatred:

> to that dauntless temper of his mind
> He hath a wisdom that doth guide his valour
> To act in safety. There is none but he
> Whose being I do fear; and under him
> My genius is rebuked as, it is said,
> Mark Antony's was by Caesar.   (III.1.51–6)[140]

Banquo is characterized almost more impressively by Macbeth's fears than by his own actions.

It is only for one brief scene that the audience witnesses a protagonist who is fully in command, who is capable of efficient planning and who confronts the murderers with the same ruthless determination as that shown by Lady Macbeth in the first act. Like her, he now presents to them a primitive ideal of undaunted manliness in order to persuade them to undertake the murder. It is one of the few scenes in which the initiative is all with Macbeth, but the audience already knows enough about the witches' prophecies to doubt the possibility of lasting success for him, and even the very next scene (III.2) reveals that, in contrast to Richard III, the part of the accomplished intriguer and murderer is only a mask, kept up with great effort. Even more striking and characteristic of Macbeth's tragic isolation is the increasing distance between him and his wife. His behavior makes her, too, gradually realize the questionable and elusive nature of what they have gained and she voices something like a superficial moral of the tragedy:

> Naught's had, all's spent,
> Where our desire is got without content.
> 'Tis safer to be that which we destroy
> Than by destruction dwell in doubtful joy. (III.2.4–7)

The rhyming simplicity of this orthodox commonplace would be more fitting for a pathetic murder story like the anonymous play *Arden of Feversham*, where the sinning lovers, immediately after the murder of the husband who has stood in their way, find that all the joy has gone out of their union and the fruits of the crime prove to be illusory.[141] Something of this simple Christian experience is also taken for granted in *Macbeth*, but this does by no means 'explain' the play, because the intensity and complexity of Macbeth's struggle cannot be reduced to a simple morality even though, in the last resort, the play endorses, for the Christian spectator, the self-destructive sterility of evil.

Macbeth's anguished fears are beyond the reach of Lady Macbeth's comforting words and it is essential to notice that he does not take her into his confidence regarding his further murderous plans. In fact, their roles have temporarily been exchanged: it is he who appears to be concerned about her peace of mind ('Be innocent of the knowledge, dearest chuck' (III.2.45)) and who invokes the night to blind 'the tender eye of pitiful day' and to 'Cancel and tear to pieces' all moral law (III.2.46–50). It is no surprise to the spectator that the attempt fails completely. Banquo's son escapes and most contemporary spectators must have known that they were ruled by a supposed descendant of his.

The return of Banquo's Ghost, like so many similar apparitions in

Elizabethan and Jacobean drama, is a visual reminder of unrevenged crime and imminent retribution. It is one of the most original and dramatically effective variations of conventional ghost scenes. Macbeth's attempt to celebrate reconciliation, hierarchic order and peaceful community by a banquet is thwarted not by those around him nor by any suspicion against him from outside, but by his own inability to shake off the crime. Whether one interprets the Ghost as a kind of hallucination, which seems to be a rather too psychological and superficial explanation, or as reality, the work of a diabolic or a benign fate, it is certainly a powerful expression of the fact that even the murder he has delegated to others begins to haunt Macbeth and that his mental disturbance is now apparent to others besides himself.[142] He is unable to perform his duties as host and thus unable to justify his usurped power by domestic order and internal peace, as the Macbeth of the chronicles managed to do for a period of some ten years:

> You have displaced the mirth, broke the good meeting
> With most admired disorder.   (III.4.108–9)

The terror aroused by the Ghost within Macbeth is not so much a sign of moral compunction or fear of discovery, but rather the result of the sudden realization that nothing whatever has been gained by the murder and that the crime is not a thing of the past. All further action is determined by this violation of the social order. The façade of self-assurance can only be preserved by new guilt and by deliberate hardening against any human impulse. At the end of the scene, Macbeth is determined to proceed along this fatal path. From now on he lives only for his own safety and explicitly rejects any thought of a return:

> For mine own good
> All causes shall give way. I am in blood
> Stepped in so far, that, should I wade no more,
> Returning were as tedious as go o'er.   (III.4.134–7)

The idea of blood, which keeps reappearing in this tragedy with unusual insistence, is extended into a memorable image that anticipates Macbeth's further course for the spectator and expresses his frightening hardness of heart more powerfully than any theological treatise.

His decision to seek out the witches shows what power they have gained over his will and to what extent he is now prepared to submit to their fatal influence. His deterioration into a tyrant who has no other aim than to secure his throne, is complete and the following part of the play is mostly concerned with the opposing forces gathering against him. It is only towards the end that his own personality takes the centre of the stage again.

The scenes with Hecat (III.5 and part of IV.1) are of somewhat doubtful authenticity and it is quite possible that these spectacular incidents are later additions to satisfy the audience's interest in such stage-effects and in historical prophecy.[143] Hecat's speeches are rather out of tune with the style and the content of the other witch-scenes and they do not quite agree with the character of these creatures earlier in the play. Their function as instruments of hellish corruption is spelt out in too simple terms whereas in the first scenes, the witches only announced a few general prophecies that so deeply impressed Macbeth and made him commit double murder. By the time of this new meeting he has already become so dependent on them that there is little left for them to do. There is no question of actual temptation or corruption; Macbeth is only confirmed in his vicious course and encouraged with doubtful hopes. Hecat's words, though, suggest a more active function:

> raise such artificial sprites
> As by the strength of their illusion
> Shall draw him on to his confusion.
> He shall spurn fate, scorn death, and bear
> His hopes 'bove wisdom, grace, and fear.   (III.5.27–31)

This is a fairly exact description of Macbeth's further career, but the illusion that destroys him is no outward compulsion overruling man's free will; it activates Macbeth's determination to the point of a mono-maniac obsession with the securing of his power and the elimination of all possible enemies. At the same time, he is strengthened by a sense of false security founded on most ambiguous prophecies. The oracular promises are as deceptive as Macbeth's self-confidence, inspired by the witches' black magic. It is certainly their intention to deceive him, but, as before the murder of Duncan, his own cooperation is needed to make the deception effective. In this instance, he is evidently willing to interpret the riddling message rather hastily in a sense most favorable to him.

The vision of the long line of Banquo's descendants as future Kings may be a theatrical homage to the first Stuart King. It also dramatizes Macbeth's terror at the idea of his own short-lived glory. 'Sweet bodements' are succeeded by 'Horrible sight' (IV.1.95 and 121) and Macbeth is quite unable to preserve the detached integrity of his moral responsibility, as Banquo did. He realizes that his intercourse with the witches is for him a 'pernicious hour' (IV.1.132), limiting his personal freedom, and yet he allows himself to be deceived by the false authority of the magic spectacle and his future actions to be determined by it.[144] Will and imagination are finally corrupted when, at the end of the scene, he decides to exterminate Macduff's family. This exceeds even the brutality he has committed so far. At this point he has become most like the monster Richard III.

Although Shakespeare places the personality of his tragic hero, poisoned by his perverted imagination, firmly in the centre of the play (in contrast to the earlier history play), he also, especially in the second half, makes him part of the larger community of the state, not so much by political discussion or crowd scenes, but by the idea of a country suffering under tyrannous rule and by the contrast to the blessed government of Edward the Confessor in England. Between the two Hecat scenes, we hear of the generous reception of Malcolm at the English Court in the conversation between Lennox and 'another Lord' who has no further part in the action. There are strong hopes of liberation from crippling suppression and twice the word 'tyrant' is used within the brief dialogue. From now on, it frequently takes the place of Macbeth's name. The vision of a brighter future implies the collapse of all familiar order and all natural forms of community under Macbeth's tyranny:

> we may again
> Give to our tables meat, sleep to our nights,
> Free from our feasts and banquets bloody knives,
> Do faithful homage and receive free honours –
> All which we pine for now.   (III.6.33–7)

Even the most elementary forms of life have been threatened by Macbeth's crimes.

The pathetic family in Macduff's castle illustrates this kind of harmless and harmonious order, destroyed by the brutal will of the tyrant. The murder of these completely innocent and in no way dangerous blood-relations of Macduff cannot be justified by any political calculation, but is rather the manifestation of a blindly destructive bestiality to which Macbeth has sunk.

To this, the long scene at the English Court opposes a completely different form of rule and a demonstration of human integrity. It serves as a reminder of Macbeth's isolation and imminent defeat. Malcolm's royal nature, inaccessible to any corruption, proves that it is possible to resist the powers of evil that have been so successful up to now. There is no necessary and inevitable conflict between a man's appearance and his true nature; at least goodness must never make use of an evil mask, as Malcolm explains:

> Angels are bright still though the brightest fell.
> Though all things foul would wear the brows of grace,
> Yet grace must still look so.   (IV.3.22–4)

The biblical associations and the reference to the witches ('all things foul') are obvious. Malcolm lives in a world that is already outside

Macbeth's experience and the length of the scene is a sign of how important the contrast is for the dramatist. The testing of Macduff by Malcolm takes up a surprising amount of room in Holinshed's chronicle; it is obviously meant to show that Malcolm has all the qualities of the perfect king and that Macduff's integrity is above temptation. The dialogue unfolds the picture of an ideal king almost in the manner of a didactic debate. The impression of a world completely corrupted by the tyrant's murderous ambition is thus modified; in *Richard III*, this only happens very near the end, by the idealizing presentation of Richmond. Here, the principle of goodness and of beneficial rule is embodied not only in Macbeth's opponents, but in the English King, gifted with divine powers of healing, who makes England a haven of peace outside the 'poor country', tormented by tyrannous oppression and several times lamented in the course of the scene.[145] We are left with the vivid impression that Macbeth's personal tragedy has involved all the people of Scotland who are groaning under his yoke and longing for liberation. This idea is conveyed to the audience not so much in political terms as by the image of a living organism, personified as the bleeding victim of the murderer from whose clutches it must be saved. Macduff's own suffering is part of this general sorrow. Where wives and children can no longer live in safety, the commonwealth has broken down and there must be a completely new beginning. This duel between two opposing principles is clearly seen as the decisive confrontation of Good and Evil, Day and Night, legitimate rule and arbitrary tyranny, and in this respect *Macbeth* is closer to the traditional morality pattern than the other tragedies.

The contrast is underlined by the dramatic switch back to Macbeth's castle where the physician, presumably played by the same actor who represented the physician at the English Court,[146] confesses his powerlessness in the face of Lady Macbeth's illness. The sleep-walking scene recapitulates, in fragmented prose, important motifs from the first part of the play, in particular the ineradicable traces of the blood shed by the murderers. The fact that Macbeth's most hardened and determined accomplice breaks down even before him is an important aspect of the play's manipulation of our sympathies. His isolation becomes more and more complete and the presence of a vengeful fate is felt more and more acutely. The physician, too, points out that Lady Macbeth's disturbed state of mind falls outside the competence of medical advice:

> More needs she the divine than the physician. (V.1.70)

We are clearly reminded of the previous scene, with its account of the English King's healing gift.

Shakespeare has inserted yet another scene before the protagonist reappears on stage. As in *Hamlet* and *King Lear*, the hero is absent for some time during the fourth or the first part of the fifth act and the dramatic suspense is kept up by concentration on other aspects of the action as well as by indirect characterization. In *Macbeth*, this technique mainly strengthens the impression that the number of Macbeth's opponents is continually growing. Even his enemies, Angus and Menteth, regard him not just as a tyrant that has to be exterminated, but as a thoroughly 'distempered' and despairing murderer who can defend his position only with the greatest effort and whose royal dignity sits uneasily on him, like an ill-fitting garment (v.2.20–2). The comparison of his title with a 'giant's robe' that is far too large for this despicable moral stature harks back to earlier uses of the clothes metaphor and it makes very clear that Macbeth can no longer impress his subjects with his usurped authority.[147] The image of blood sticking to the murderer's hands is also brought up again (v.2.17) and it is thus evident that Macbeth's guilt is no longer a matter of his personal tragic experience, but a public affair that has set armies in motion and affected the whole nation.

When Macbeth himself comes back to the stage, he seems, on the one hand, completely obsessed by his belief in the witches' ambiguous prophecies, on the other, he describes himself as 'sick at heart' (v.3.19) and he is fully conscious of what he has forfeited. Again it is the contrast between his haunted life and the simple expectations of a 'normal' everyday existence that serves to show how utterly he has excluded himself from all human intercourse:

> And that which should accompany old age,
> As honour, love, obedience, troops of friends,
> I must not look to have;   (v.3.24–6)[148]

The brief dialogue with the physician once more draws attention to the poisonous infection that has spread from the guilty individual to the whole nation. Though Macbeth is, consciously, merely referring to the threat to his country from the invading troops, his metaphor has a much deeper resonance for the spectator, especially since the image of disease has been used in the play before with similar implications:

> If thou couldst, doctor, cast
> The water of my land, find her disease
> And purge it to a sound and pristine health,
> I would applaud thee...   (v.3.50–3)

The perversion of all human instincts by guilt has seized the individual ('a mind diseased' (v.3.40)) as well as the social structure and for both the physician's advice that the patient must 'minister to himself' (v.3.45–6) is, in the context of the play, equally valid. For the country it means casting out Macbeth in whom the disease seems to be personified, but he himself and his wife have passed the point where return and health are still a possibility. Unlike Marlowe's Doctor Faustus, Macbeth is not reminded of the divine grace that is still within reach until the last by any voice from within or without. Repentance and forgiveness of sins are no subjects for this tragedy. The tyrant must be exterminated if the country is to recover peace and lawful order.

And yet, even to the end, there is more than just horrified revulsion or untroubled satisfaction at Macbeth's death. The Aristotelian rule that the tragic hero must be neither all good nor totally evil is not altogether neglected in this case, even though the reaction of the audience is not likely to be entirely uniform. I think that Bradley's impression, 'To the end he never totally loses our sympathy', is shared by most readers of the play, as long as 'sympathy' is not interpreted in a narrow sense.[149] There is no question that the whole tragedy means us to side with Macbeth's opponents and that nobody can seriously wish him longer success, but it is equally clear that the play's ending is very different from the triumph at Bosworth, even though the political situation is not unlike that at the close of *Richard III* (as far as Malcolm's right of succession is concerned it is, in fact, even less open to debate) and Macbeth is not allowed any heroic gesture of self-recognition, like Othello.

What is crucial for our reaction, however, is that up to the end we never see Macbeth as a 'born criminal', but always remember the painful process of his corruption by illusion and blind ambition. Of Othello it is said, 'that wert once so good' (v.2.288), which would be hardly thinkable in the case of Macbeth because the play begins immediately with his temptation and fall. Yet the whole action of the play seems to be based on the assumption that his career, too, is, morally speaking, a fall from great height and that there was once a 'good' Macbeth whose corruption is the real centre of the tragedy.[150] The fact that at the end he has reached such an extreme degree of hardening that only his extermination can be hoped for, is no more than a disturbing consequence of his decision to listen to the voices of evil. The play shows us a different stage in the hero's tragic experience and a different kind of moral deterioration than *Othello*, but the two plays are based on a very similar concept of evil and its effects on human relationships.

At the very end, the hero does not suddenly come to realize what he has lost, because he has known that all along and, unlike Othello, he did not commit his crimes in the fond belief that his cause was just. He himself has experienced and described the reality of evil in such unambiguous terms that there is no need for any moral dénouement. The only thing that surprises him, as well as the spectator, about his defeat is the way in which the prophecy of the weird sisters, that had lulled him with a false sense of security, comes true. Once this is realized all hope and courage leave him, though this hardly seems to affect his deeper despair which makes him unable to think of anything but his own misery and fearful decline. He himself suggests that this hardening against the most basic human impulses and values is not something he was born to, but the result of a painful process that has changed his whole personality:

> I have almost forgot the taste of fears.
> The time has been my senses would have cooled
> To hear a night-shriek, and my fell of hair
> Would at a dismal treatise rouse and stir
> As life were in't.
>
> (V.5.9–13)

This is to remind us of a Macbeth we have only had very brief glimpses of, a Macbeth as the whole play assumes him to have existed before the beginning of his tragedy. When, however, he goes on to confess, 'I have supped full with horrors' (V.5.13), he takes up the image of the banquet, recalling the disrupted ritual of the third act as well as suggesting associations of an unholy alliance with the powers of evil, a communion that effectively excludes him from the community of man. In this state, the news of his wife's death seems to affect him very little because all human existence has become meaningless for him. If the passage in question were not so often quoted out of its context, it would hardly be necessary to point out that his frightening description of an absurd life is by no means an account of Shakespeare's personal convictions but is meant to characterize the agony of the protagonist:

> Life's but a walking shadow, a poor player
> That struts and frets his hour upon the stage
> And then is heard no more. It is a tale
> Told by an idiot, full of sound and fury,
> Signifying nothing.
>
> (V.5.24–8)

Biblical associations are combined with the traditional image of life as a stage-play. What for Jaques, in *As You Like It*, was no more than the expression of self-conscious melancholy ('All the world's a stage' (II.7.139)), is for Macbeth the painful experience of a tragic illusion. It is immediately followed by the report of the messenger who has witnessed the unnatural movement of Birnam Wood. This is the beginning of Macbeth's final defeat and the fulfilment of the witches' riddling prophecy. Macbeth himself begins to realize that he has been the victim of 'the equivocation of the fiend/That lies like truth' (V.5.43–4).

As in *Hamlet*, references to the language of the Bible and to Christian concepts of damnation and salvation appear more frequently towards the end of the play. For those readers and spectators who are familiar with this traditional background, Macbeth is one of the damned, and the pains of Hell he has to suffer consist mainly in his inability to forget or suppress what he has lost by his own free choice. Already Coleridge, and Bradley after him, felt that Macbeth reminded him of Milton's Satan who realizes with anguish that he is forever barred from any community with goodness, when he has sneakingly entered Paradise, and it seems to me quite probable that Milton was partly inspired by Shakespeare's tragedy when he made Satan reflect on his fallen state in *Paradise Lost*:

> For onely in destroying I finde ease
> To my relentless thoughts... (IX.129–30)

> But what will not Ambition and Revenge
> Descend to? who aspires must down as low
> As high he soard, obnoxious first or last
> To basest things. Revenge, at first though sweet,
> Bitter ere long back on it self recoiles; (IX.168–72)[151]

The parallel is instructive, though it only applies to one aspect of *Macbeth* and should not be generalized. Milton's openly stated intention to 'justifie the wayes of God to men' (I.26) is hardly the central concern of Shakespeare's play, but the intensity with which Macbeth's moral hardening is presented as a relentless process of deterioration and suffering at the same time, can explain why *Macbeth* has repeatedly inspired Christian interpretations, though these have often rather reduced than illuminated the tragic impact of the text.[152] Macbeth's decision and his gradual perversion are placed in a world of political and heroic values and are not primarily assessed in dogmatic categories, though the imagery suggests associations with a fallen angel as well as with Marlowe's Faustus. These biblical and religious associations, together with our insight into the moral and spiritual corruption of an individual meant by his creator to be good, are important elements of this particular tragedy and they prevent us from experiencing Macbeth's death only as the well-deserved end of a political criminal. The vitality of the dramatic rhetoric, the rich images and precise metaphors contribute to the impression of an intense questioning and seeking to discover coherence and meaning in a world of challenging opportunities. Macbeth is determined to act, not to wait patiently for the gifts of fortune, and he does not try to escape from the consequences of his own actions. All this does not in the least detract from his moral responsibility, but it may help to account for the fact that his fate affects most readers and spectators as more tragic (in the traditional sense) than the defeat of Richard III.

The ending confirms the presence of a benign providence that means to grant Scotland a period of stable peace and lawful order; yet the author of the disturbance and chaos is not denied all human greatness and potential integrity. Both points of view have to be recognized for an adequate understanding of the play.[153]

The patriotic optimism of the closing tableau is not likely to convince us, after all that has gone before, as a true and complete summary of the play's tragic vision. The country can breathe freely and 'the days are near at hand/That chambers will be safe' (v.4.1–2). 'The time is free' (v.6.94), but reader and spectator cannot merely rejoice at the liberation from the tyrant's rule because they have been witnesses to a dimension of the action of which the surviving actors themselves are unaware. None of the survivors knows anything about the supernatural influences embodied in the witches and none has any true idea of Macbeth's temptation and anguish of conscience.[154] For them it is enough to look at 'The usurper's cursèd head' (v.6.94) and to hear the promises of the new King. But it is partly this muted and only outwardly cheerful quality of the ending that makes it so different from the proclamation of Henry Tudor at the conclusion of *Richard III*. Our interest in the history of the community and the future of Scotland cannot quite suppress our sympathy with the fall of the protagonist and his lonely agonies. If critics insist on the play's more confident optimism in comparison with the ending of *King Lear* they often seem to me to take insufficient account of this ambivalence at the close. It is the result of the unusual combination of history and tragedy as well as the evocative poetry and the dramatist's manipulation of our sympathy which makes any simple moral interpretation totally inadequate. Bradley quite rightly includes *Macbeth* in his still very impressive description of Shakespearian tragedy or rather what he considers our reaction to it:

moral order ... has lost a part of its own substance, – a part more dangerous and unquiet, but far more valuable and nearer to its heart, than that which remains, – a Fortinbras, a Malcolm, an Octavius. There is no tragedy in its expulsion of evil: the tragedy is that this involves the waste of good.[155]

In this fundamental respect, *Macbeth* is not as different from the other great tragedies as it may seem at first sight, even though the emphasis is different and the process of moral perversion is explored with greater dramatic intensity than the experience of tragic suffering. This is why at the end there is not the customary obituary, paying due respect to the greatness of the departed hero. Only the audience knows that there is more that ought to be remembered than the survivors of the tragedy have witnessed and that much more has perished than 'this dead butcher' (v.6.108).[156]

4

Romans and Greeks in Shakespeare's tragedies

ABOUT HALF OF SHAKESPEARE'S TRAGEDIES TAKE THEIR SUB-jects from Graeco-Roman antiquity and this is not merely a question of sources or of the characters' names. It used to be said by critics that Shakespeare had transformed all his Romans and Greeks into Elizabethans, but such a general statement ignores important elements shared by these plays as well as the weight of common ideas about Roman virtues and the nature of the Greeks. To be sure, there is a great deal of intentional or unintentional anachronism and the plots have been adapted to Elizabethan dramatic conventions and native rhetoric. But for Shakespeare and the better read of his contemporaries the world of Rome and, chiefly filtered through it, the world of the Greeks, constituted a very precisely located historical epoch, remote in time, yet quite well known and more familiar than any other foreign history of the past. It was made more accessible even than early English history, at least more impressively so, by the Roman historians and it seemed particularly suitable as a model of political stability and the dangers to which it is exposed. Roman virtues and Roman patriotism suggested ideas that stimulated critical description and poetic exploration.[1]

Shakespeare's Romans combine Elizabethan character traits with an unmistakable individuality and foreignness that make the Rome of these tragedies a particularly impressive fictitious place. Leaving aside the earliest tragedy *Titus Andronicus* and the brief verse epic *The Rape of Lucrece* – though they are both important in this context – the three tragedies *Julius Caesar*, *Antony and Cleopatra* and *Coriolanus* form a coherent or at least consistent account of Republican Rome which has influenced the popular idea of classical Rome more deeply and more permanently than either the classical authors or modern historians.[2]

Comparison with the much more learned but, in this respect, more pedantic and less inspired Ben Jonson and his Roman tragedies shows that this is not a question of historical accuracy in every detail, but of the overall atmosphere and a memorable concept of what 'Romanness' really means.[3] *Sejanus His Fall* (1603) and *Catiline His Conspiracy* (1611) were both staged by Shakespeare's company, but though minutely researched, they seem to have failed to catch the audience's imagination from the very beginning and have always been among the least popular of Jonson's plays.

The precise differences between Shakespeare's Roman plays and the other tragedies can only be defined by detailed interpretation. They are a matter of style as well as of characterization: instances can be found in the plays' formal rhetoric that often approaches the declamatory diction of public speech, or the dramatic representation of suicide as a heroic gesture.[4] Patriotism in a particularly rigorous and demanding form is a recurrent theme in these tragedies. It can frequently clash with other loyalties, such as family, friends and love, and this leads to a kind of tragic conflict we rarely find in the English histories. Romantic and comic traditions play a very minor part in the Roman plays. Where love gets in the way of the individual's duty towards the state and the community, as in *Antony and Cleopatra*, it appears as something strange, suspicious, not Roman. The reader will also discover interesting differences in the way family relationships are presented: fathers like Polonius and wives like Emilia are hardly imaginable in Shakespeare's Rome.

These and other common features are the chief reason why the Roman plays have usually been treated as a group, especially by critics, but occasionally also in the theatre, even though productions that treat the plays as a cycle create their own problems.[5] The Roman plays are obviously related to each other in similar ways to Shakespeare's histories, more nearly related, at any rate, than they are related to any of the other tragedies. On the other hand, they evidently belong to the tragedies and it is important to keep the 'great' tragedies in mind when we read the Roman plays.

The Greeks were known to the Elizabethans mainly by way of the Latin classics and they were probably felt to be much less congenial than the Romans. They had certainly not yet been idealized by the concept of classical maturity and harmony discovered by Winckelmann and the German classicists of the eighteenth century or the enthusiasm of the Victorians. These later developments have changed the traditional view of ancient Greece considerably: Athens was seen as the model for many later city-states. But even in the Latin comedies which were probably most important in forming Elizabethan ideas of Greek mentality, Athens and the Hellenic world are peopled by cheaters and parasites, by epicures given to drinking and lust and by unpredictable charlatans. In contrast to Roman discipline, self-control and public order, Greece is often portrayed as a weird and suspicious place where the social and political climate is largely governed by magic, deceit and libertinism and where you can only survive by wary caution and suspicious cunning. It is more than likely that the epistles of Saint Paul in the New Testament also contributed to this idea, as well as Roman satire. At any rate, the word 'Greek', often used in conjunction with the adjective 'merry', had become a synonym for 'cheat', 'madman', or 'lecher'.[6] It is, therefore, hardly surprising that in Shakespeare's works the world of the Greeks appears mainly in comic or satiric contexts.[7] The two tragedies that are set in Greece or deal with the Greeks are very different from the Roman plays and cannot be classed with any other group of plays. It is certainly not a sign of Shakespeare's personal disillusionment or his scant regard for classical traditions that we find no Iphigenia or Antigone among his works, no Orestes and no Oedipus. If we read and discuss the two 'Greek' tragedies together with the Roman plays, this is mainly justified by the common origin of the plots in Roman literature or classical tradition in general; they are all set in a remote pagan world, clearly distinguished for the Elizabethans from Christian romance, legend, or English history, even though in style, theme and tone, *Timon of Athens* and *Troilus and Cressida* seem to have little in common with the three Roman tragedies.

JULIUS CAESAR

It is not only the setting which *Julius Caesar* and the other two Roman tragedies have in common, but also their chief source, Plutarch's parallel *Lives* of famous Greeks and Romans. By its date, however, the play belongs rather to a period just before the 'great' tragedies. Although one must be careful not to reconstruct in one's mind the fiction of an ideal artistic development, it still seems clear that *Julius Caesar* has a certain transitional quality, linking the history plays with the group of tragedies beginning with *Hamlet* and ending with *Antony and Cleopatra* or *Coriolanus*.

At the time of writing *Julius Caesar* (about 1599), Shakespeare had just finished the two historical tetralogies on the reigns of the English Kings from Richard II to the first Tudor, Henry VII, using Raphael Holinshed's *Chronicles of England, Scotland, and Ireland* (2nd edn 1587) as his main source. In Sir Thomas North's translation of *Plutarch's Lives of the Noble Grecians and Romans* (1579) he found a very successful work of vivid historiography that presents the historical events with more consummate literary art, bringing back to life an epoch familiar to Shakespeare's contemporaries from several other accounts, historical and fictional. Plutarch's biographies create a memorable impression of the fascinating interplay between dynamic personalities and political change, more consistently than the English historians and without their obvious didactic application to the present. There is no divine providence governing and patterning the events, and no national interest, like the 'Tudor-myth', serves as a general focus. On the other hand, a number of political issues are touched on that are also among the central themes of the histories, so that the transition from one period to another hardly meant a completely new beginning for the dramatist nor even a radical change of genre.[8]

As in the histories, the action of *Julius Caesar* is practically all concerned with public events and affairs of state. The characters have to make political decisions, and the republican state, represented by the most respected citizens, but also by the less individualized plebeians, is the life-giving organism whose welfare and stability are as important as the fate of the individual. The same might be said of *Hamlet*, but in its persistent emphasis on the close connection between personal action and the health of the community *Julius Caesar* is closer to the histories than to *Hamlet*, *Othello*, or even *King Lear*, whereas there are striking similarities to *Macbeth*.

The close affinity between *Julius Caesar* and the histories could be demonstrated by a study of the battle scenes, the presentation of the populace and the function of foreboding, but this still does not make this Roman tragedy a history play. It might be more helpful to approach it as the first of the mature tragedies. Several themes and human situations we find in *Hamlet* and the other 'great' tragedies can already be found in *Julius Caesar*, in particular the hero's tragic dilemma which, in the last resort, claims more of our attention and sympathy than the political fate of Rome, even though the two can hardly be separated. Indeed, it is the inescapable interrelationship between individual choice of action and its consequences for the whole community that is brought out so forcefully here for the first time in Shakespearian tragedy.[9]

When Shakespeare decided to write a tragedy about Julius Caesar, Brutus and Mark Antony he chose three characters who had been the subject of controversy for centuries. Earlier critics were divided into those who thought that Shakespeare shared the republican admiration for Brutus and those who felt that he was on the side of the monarchists and Caesar-worshippers, while more recent criticism tends to see the play as perhaps the most influential contribution to a long debate that was not concerned so much with party spirit or clear evaluation as with an argumentative assessment of complex, contradictory, and seemingly incompatible characters. There were, to be sure, some definite traditions, such as the image of Caesar as an overweening tyrant who was rightly assassinated, or the cautionary picture of the sacrilegious regicide Brutus, tormented, along with Judas Ischariot, in Dante's Inferno, but the more important aspect of the whole tradition of Caesar's murder was the idea of memorable and controversial men in whom admirable greatness and fatal error were so inextricably mixed that a conflict of historical dimensions was inevitable. 'The reassessment and reconsideration of such famous historical figures was a common literary activity in the Renaissance, not merely in poetry and drama (where licence is acceptable), but in plain prose, the writing of history.'[10] This, I think, is more helpful for an understanding of Shakespeare's characters than a minutely detailed comparison of the play with every possible source. In view of the highly sophisticated efforts of so many classical or Renaissance authors to weigh all the personal and political aspects of Caesar's murder it is altogether unlikely that Shakespeare should have been content with simple glorification or indictment. The two central characters in particular, Caesar and Brutus, are dramatically presented in such a way that the spectator is not encouraged to pass confident judgement or to take sides. Rather he is confronted with conflicting impressions, suggesting agonizing uncertainty and tragic tension, not a morality in which Good and Evil are opposed.

Shakespeare's Caesar is even less simple and predictable than Plutarch's, largely due to the form of the tragedy and the dramatist's techniques of characterization. From the very first scene, Julius Caesar is powerfully present, even though he does not enter the stage before the second scene. The way the other characters speak about him is as important for his overall portrait as his personal appearances.

The first scene, contrasting the relaxed holiday mood of the opportunist plebeians with the republican zeal and indignation of the Tribunes of the People, presents the demonstrative personality cult of Caesar side by side with the political fears and apprehensions it arouses, thus introducing the crucial phenomenon that Caesar's impact, throughout the play, is more powerful, indeed more real, than his physical presence. At first, when he himself enters the stage, he seems little more than a monarch surrounded by fawning courtiers and flatterers, who commands respect. His authority is taken for granted and does not have to be demonstrated by impressive rhetoric or despotic gestures. The dramatic structure of the long second scene is worth noticing as an effective means of characterization: Caesar himself only makes two comparatively brief appearances, closely observed by Brutus and Cassius, but it is especially during his absence that the dialogue is concerned with him. His personal presence seems comparatively undramatic. We can hardly tell from his short assertions of majestic self-confidence whether arrogant pride or natural dignity is the more characteristic trait. At any rate, he hardly strikes us as a dangerous tyrant or a villain consumed by ambition. His very precise estimate of the threat posed by the cramped Cassius is proved absolutely correct by the development of the action; by the same token, there is a strong element of tragic irony in his claim to be above fear and caution. His real personality comes out much more impressively through Cassius' attempts to influence Brutus and Brutus' tragic dilemma, as well as Casca's satirical account of what happened off stage. The fact that he is deaf in one ear – a handicap added by Shakespeare – and troubled with the 'falling sickness' does not mean that the dramatist deliberately reduced his heroic stature, but rather underlines the extraordinary force of his presence which is not even impaired by these physical defects. Nor will Cassius' tales about Caesar's weakness convince us that his authority is mere sham because they are so obviously dictated by hatred and envy and say more about the speaker himself than about the man he wants to belittle. It rather confirms the impression suggested by Plutarch's account that Caesar succeeded in overcoming such corporal odds. His public image of unmatched glory is not affected by it and will, of course, survive his assassination.

As the play proceeds Caesar still remains a figure seen from the distance rather than in close-up and we learn more about his impact on others than about the actual individual. Whenever he appears in person he seems more anxious to create an impression of superhuman stature and commanding presence than to allow us any revealing insight into his real thoughts and emotions. Even in his own home he talks like a public orator. The rhetorical device of speaking about oneself in the third person, used with particular frequency in this tragedy, contributes to this distancing effect, as if the speaker himself were of much less importance than the part he is playing and the legend attached to his name:

> Caesar should be a beast without a heart
> If he should stay at home today for fear.
> No, Caesar shall not. Danger knows full well
> That Caesar is more dangerous than he.
> We are two lions littered in one day,
> And I the elder and more terrible,
> And Caesar shall go forth.   (II.2.42 – 8)[11]

There is a hint here of the overweening pride of someone who will presently fall from the height of his power and prosperity, and Calpurnia's retort, 'Your wisdom is consumed in confidence' (II.2.49) is amply justified in view of what follows. More important in the context of the whole play is the way this sort of rhetoric turns our attention from the individual character in order to establish a personal myth. The name of Caesar and his power over other people is more interesting for the reader and spectator than the personal fate of the man behind the name, and this is how we have to understand the play's title. In spite of some more individual traits, made even more prominent by Shakespeare as compared with Plutarch, Julius Caesar is not really a tragic hero in a more than formal sense. His fall is, of course, quite in accordance with the classical pattern of tragedy, but it does not move us like the death of King Lear or even the murder of Duncan.

The real tragic conflict, to which all the audience's sympathy is directed, concerns Brutus and his decision to join the conspiracy. This rather unusual dramatic constellation is partly due to the story material and the sources, but even more to Shakespeare's evident intention to present Caesar's fall and his revenge from the murderer's point of view.

In Plutarch, the events that constitute the play's action form the basis of three different biographies: Julius Caesar, Brutus and Mark Antony. For each of the three eminent Romans the Ides of March mean something different and each of them might well have been the hero of a separate tragedy, depending on the choice of episodes and of the dramatic perspective. It was obviously in the person of Brutus that the dramatist saw the most promising elements of the kind of tragic dilemma that recurs, with variations, in the later tragedies. In *Othello* as well as in *Macbeth*, a man highly esteemed as 'noble' by all around him is corrupted and becomes a brutal murderer. Like Othello, Brutus falls victim to the illusion that a bestial killing may be stylized into a ritual act of higher justice or even a necessary sacrifice, and like Macbeth he finds that the blood shed by the murderer cannot be buried together with the corpse, but poisons all the hoped-for achievement.

As in *Othello*, the actual instigation to the murder is the work of skilful and calculated persuasion, yet even more the work of the murderer's own imagination which produces arguments and motives for the final decision where genuine justification is lacking. Cassius makes unscrupulous use of Brutus' momentary melancholic mood and of his not in all respects discriminating idealism to make him an accomplice in a scheme that is clearly foreign to Brutus' noble nature, as Cassius knows well enough. He is not, to be sure, the diabolic tempter of the moralities, nor is he, like Iago, presented as a villainous intriguer, but his part in the tragedy as a most fatal influence on the protagonist is not so different from the traditional motif of temptation. Shakespeare's evident desire to suggest a characteristically Roman climate is presumably the main reason why, in contrast to the later tragedies, moral categories or Christian ethical concepts play only a very minor part in *Julius Caesar*. 'Good' and 'Evil' bear the names of 'virtue', 'honor', 'nobility' and their opposites. Cassius appeals to Brutus' sense of honor and to his patriotism, and it is clear from the reaction of his partner that his words coincide with a process of reflection that had already begun before their meeting. Brutus himself feels that he is about to be pushed into a very dangerous decision and he is unwilling to commit himself on the spot.

The dramatic technique in this first temptation scene (1.2.) is quite similar to that employed in *Othello* and reads almost like a preparation for it: the temptation is briefly interrupted by the entrance of the victim, followed here by Casca's scornful account, but in fact it is, indirectly, continued all the time because Brutus' view of the events has been profoundly influenced by Cassius' insinuations and he is likely to interpret everything in a new light. There is another possible link with Iago in Cassius' concluding soliloquy in which he reflects on his success and clearly implies that what is at issue is the perversion of a noble mind, a mind which Cassius deliberately intends to turn into a direction quite uncongenial to it.[12] Cassius does not by any means hate Brutus, but he is prepared to sacrifice him to his own hatred of Caesar and to drag him down to his own level to this purpose. As in the case of Othello, it is Brutus' very nobleness that makes the corruption possible:

> Well, Brutus, thou art noble, yet I see
> Thy honourable mettle may be wrought
> From that it is disposed. Therefore it is meet
> That noble minds keep ever with their likes;
> For who so firm that cannot be seduced? (1.2.305–9)

This is clearly in the tradition of the villain's soliloquy by which the audience is informed about the schemer's designs and is, at the same time, presented with a particularly complimentary characterization of the hero which strikes us as especially reliable coming from the mouth of his opponent. Of course the situation is rather more complex here because of the political context. After what we have seen, the fear of tyranny does not seem to be entirely unfounded even though there are no very substantial grounds for assuming that a cruel reign of terror is imminent. Nor would an Elizabethan audience feel – as many twentieth-century spectators would – that the defence of a republican constitution was really a matter of life and death. Cassius' whole argumentation seems largely motivated by envious hatred of a man whom he cannot admit to be superior to himself and he insists on an abstract concept of honor which is not necessarily identical with the good of the whole community. On the other hand, the text does not rule out the possibility that, as suggested by Plutarch, there is some genuine political conviction behind his violent opposition to tyranny.[13] Cassius is considerably more than an envious hypocrite, as the rest of the tragedy will show.

As in some of the later tragedies, the threat to human order and harmony is accompanied by an uproar of nature. Destructive thunderstorms, often followed by supernatural apparitions, announce some monstrous crime or underscore the outbreak of uncontrolled human passions. The storm in the third scene, following immediately on Cassius' soliloquy, is in the tradition of theatrical foreboding and mirrors the character of the conspiracy and its fatal consequences. It is, however, explained in a variety of ways within the play itself and it is only in retrospect that we can really be sure of its ominous significance. Cicero rightly points out that interpretations of such phenomena are often quite subjective and thus touches on a theme that will return in *Macbeth*:

> But men may construe things after their fashion,
> Clean from the purpose of the things themselves.   (1.3.34–5)

Cassius provides a good example when he relates nature's upheaval to Caesar's tyrannical behavior, which is hardly supported by the play itself, whereas Casca is shaken by natural fear until Cassius succeeds in securing his support, more quickly and more thoroughly than in the case of Brutus. Later, however, Cassius himself equates the thunderstorm with the deed they are about to plan and thus casts some doubt on his own earlier interpretation:

> And the complexion of the element
> In favour's like the work we have in hand,
> Most bloody-fiery, and most terrible.   (1.3.128–30)

Cassius' choice of words already prepares the reader for Brutus' view of the conspiracy which more and more impresses itself on him during his nocturnal vigil. The first part of this impressive scene (II.1) can be seen as one long soliloquy, interrupted three times by Lucius' brief appearances. It is through this monologue that Brutus' central position as the real tragic protagonist of the play is established.[14] Shakespeare's most inventive adaptation of traditional forms of soliloquy can already be studied in *Romeo and Juliet* and in the histories, but it is only in the mature tragedies that we find the agony of a personality torn by conflicting impulses portrayed with such dramatic intensity as it is here. Outward impressions and deep reflection go hand in hand. Two aspects are worth singling out: soliloquy is no longer used as a kind of solo performance or aria, a recital of emotions or an unfolding of intentions for the benefit of the audience, but tries to render a continuous process of reflection, uncontrolled associations and worrying uncertainty. Equally significant for Shakespeare's interpretation of his material is the fact that Brutus experiences the whole problem of his part in the conspiracy as a moral conflict. Though his thoughts, banishing sleep, are concerned mainly with the political aspects of Caesar's ambition and the reasons that finally persuade him to join the conspirators have more to do with the well-being of the whole community than with individual morals, the intensity of the conflict sets Brutus apart from all the other enemies of Caesar and convinces the audience that this is not a decision arrived at by rational weighing of arguments, but a fundamental choice, involving the whole personality and determining all his future life. Brutus will never be the same again as he was before he had to face this agonizing decision. In this sense, though the whole context is quite different, Brutus is in a similar situation to Macbeth or, indeed, Hamlet.

The language of the soliloquy also points towards Hamlet and his lonely reflections, in particular his 'To-be-or-not-to-be' soliloquy whose syntax and occasionally even exact wording are anticipated here.[15] A number of particular considerations and fears seem to occur to the speaker and he tries to weigh their implications and consequences against each other. This is not addressed to the audience nor are we presented with a carefully considered statement, but rather with a mental process. Like Hamlet, Brutus appears to be thinking aloud:

> Crown him that,
> And then, I grant, we put a sting in him
> That at his will he may do danger with.
> Th'abuse of greatness is when it disjoins
> Remorse from power,　　　　　　　　　(II.1.15–19)

This form of arguing with oneself, not by consistent reasoning but rather by unpredictable association, makes it difficult to decide at what precise point Brutus actually makes up his mind, if there is such a point.[16] More important for our impression of him is the fact that Cassius' insinuations have robbed him of his sleep and have changed his whole personality. Like Hamlet, he finds himself confronted with a moral demand whose implications fill him with terror, but whose hold on him is inescapable. Cassius' additional device of sending anonymous letters of admonition strengthens Brutus' conviction that the Roman people expect him to liberate them from oppressive tyranny; at the same time it casts a somewhat dubious light on the whole enterprise and makes it look like a sinister intrigue that has need of such dishonest means.

Once conspiracy and murder are faced as a reality, the future begins to look like a horrifying nightmare, just as it does for Macbeth before the murder of Duncan. The tone of Brutus' imaginings is very like that of Macbeth's visions when he is haunted by the prospect of the deed:

> Between the acting of a dreadful thing
> And the first motion, all the interim is
> Like a phantasma or a hideous dream.

> The genius and the mortal instruments
> Are then in council, and the state of man,
> Like to a little kingdom, suffers then
> The nature of an insurrection. (II.1.63–9)

The way crucial moral experiences are dramatized is very similar to that in the 'great' tragedies, especially in the corruption of a potentially noble character by influences whose nature he but dimly recognizes. Brutus is not deceived by any illusion about the gravity of the crime he is envisaging, for which even the night is not dark enough (II.1.77–81). 'Conspiracy' is seen as something wicked, whose 'monstrous visage' must be disguised by a mask. The arrival of the fellow-conspirators is certainly not greeted with joyful conviction, but with a grim and sinister determination.[17]

It is also worth noting that Shakespeare has not made use of the best arguments for Caesar's removal he might have found in his sources, and Brutus himself seems unable to quote any actual tyrannical deeds committed by Caesar; he only talks himself into a righteous indignation about the likelihood of future acts of despotism. There is nothing really incriminating that can be said about Caesar as he is at present. Brutus even gives one of the most complimentary accounts of him to be found in the whole play, which again must raise grave doubts about the justification of the murder:

> and, to speak truth of Caesar,
> I have not known when his affections swayed
> More than his reason. (II.1.19–21)

This is a very different Caesar from the one Cassius describes as an overweening demi-god who must be removed in the common interest. More important than the question whether Brutus here gives a true account of the hero is the observation that he admits Caesar's admirable qualities and his essential integrity at the very moment when he has decided to kill him. Shakespeare evidently wants to make clear that Brutus does not act from any personal animosity, but is moved by genuine political concern, though it is equally clear that this concern is largely an illusion with very little foundation in reality. Brutus is about to commit a crime horrifying to himself and, like Othello, he is ruled by motives that arouse respect as well as revulsion. 'Noble Roman' and 'noble moor' are in a very similar manner characteristic of Shakespeare's concept of a tragic hero.

In his discussions with the conspirators, too, criminal intentions and gestures of genuine human greatness are presented side by side and their basic incompatibility seems to be apparent to the spectator alone. Brutus is led into grave tactical mistakes and into demonstrative declamation by his almost pathetic determination to turn the assassination into a disinterested sacrifice. The authority of his person makes him carry all before him even where he is palpably in the wrong. Thus, the decision to spare Mark Antony soon proves to be a fatal blunder. Even more disastrous is the erroneous notion that Caesar's spirit can be extinguished by the removal of the man. The whole play demonstrates that Brutus is unconsciously describing his own tragedy when he proclaims his illusion of a righteous and unbloody murder:

> Let us be sacrificers, but not butchers, Caius.
> We all stand up against the spirit of Caesar,
> And in the spirit of men there is no blood.
> O that we then could come by Caesar's spirit
> And not dismember Caesar! (II.1.167–71)

This separation of body and spirit soon turns out to be a fond illusion, sharply refuted by the political realities. Caesar's spirit, on the contrary, is untouched by the murder and in the end triumphs over the conspirators. Brutus' pose is discredited even by the fulsomeness of his rhetoric as well as by his complete isolation among the conspirators. None of them shares his heroic idealism, and the contradictions between the actual business of the conspiracy whose outcome the majority of the audience must know or are able to guess, and Brutus' euphoric enthusiasm – 'Let's carve him as a dish fit for the gods' (II.1.174) – are so obvious as to make him a lonely and tragic figure. In addition, his dialogue with Portia, following immediately on the departure of the conspirators suggests very strongly that Brutus himself is not really convinced of the worthiness and integrity of his purpose. To his wife, at least, he appears to be deeply disturbed and their marriage union is gravely affected by his mental struggle. The drama shows the effects of his heroic pose on the most intimate personal relationship and this brings us much closer to him because we see him not only as the domineering idealist, but as a man shaken and suddenly stripped of all familiar ties, a man, moreover, who has by no means lightly made up his mind to the murder and expects neither the gratification of personal ambition nor certain fame. The last part of the scene, too, the 'healing' of Ligarius, directs our sympathy more towards Brutus whose integrity inspires such unlimited confidence and whose heroic view of the murderous project no longer stands quite alone.

The whole exposition puts Brutus and his confrontation with Caesar's spirit firmly in the centre of the action. He is presented on his own as well as in conversation with a variety of characters, from Cassius to his boy

Lucius whose innocent sleep appears to him as the image of a mind untroubled by any conflict or worrying reflections, making him all the more conscious of his own dilemma. Like the King in *Henry IV*, Part II, or like Macbeth, Brutus finds that loss of sleep is perhaps the most disturbing consequence of the utter isolation produced by the agonizing moral decision he has to face.[18] His almost fatherly regard for the boy and his natural need for sleep – repeated before the final battle (IV.2.289–322) – is an important aspect of Shakespeare's characterization of him. His fatal blindness in matters of state by no means excludes admirable tenderness in his relations with others and this is obviously meant to secure him some of our sympathy in a situation where he might otherwise appear completely misguided and repulsive. The weight and pressure of the task he considers a political duty have indeed changed his personality, yet they have not perverted his selfless sensibility for the individual needs of those near to him. This clearly distinguishes him from some of the later tragic heroes who often seem to lose sight of this unheroic human context.[19]

In deliberate contrast to Brutus, Julius Caesar is presented without such personal ties. The interventions of the two wives, for instance, following almost immediately upon each other, are quite different in style and dramatic impact. Calpurnia's apprehensions are more general and far less personal than Portia's, caused by external forebodings and warnings rather than by her own observation of her husband, and Caesar's tone towards her is hardly different from his usual public manner, showing little personal concern or genuine affection. In view of what follows, his demonstrative equanimity appears rather like arrogant blindness, not true stoic courage. Whereas Brutus thinks of the outward impression made by his actions, if at all, only for tactical reasons, everything Caesar says seems calculated to produce a particular effect for the benefit of his public image. His rhetoric hardly ever gives to his replies the touch of a spontaneous reaction. Even where there are clear signs of wavering uncertainty, as in his first refusal to go to the Senate, it is quickly covered by high-sounding gestures.

In this case, however, the conspirators have included Caesar's excessive concern for his reputation in their plans, which is why Decius' not very subtle strategy succeeds in swaying his resolution. All this clearly contributes to a certain detachment in our attitude towards Caesar and Brutus, preventing any too personal involvement in the murder, since we have never actually seen Caesar without his public mask. It is 'the spirit of Caesar' that determines all the action of the play, not the inner life of an individual with whom we are asked to identify and of which the dramatist allows us barely a glimpse.

The assassination itself is staged as a pantomimic pageant rather than a scene of dialogue. Apart from Caesar's brief exclamation, '*Et tu, Brute?*' (III.1.77), taken straight from the source and made to sound like an impersonal quotation by the language alone, the victim is not given an opportunity for a dying speech or some last words to the murderers. He dies at the moment of supreme belief in his own power, proudly claiming invulnerability. The proclamation of an exceptional, super-human status is rhetorically impressive, but it is swiftly and visibly refuted by his downfall, which makes the scene almost an exemplary morality, showing us the punishment due to the sin of *superbia*, though the remainder of the action shows that this only applies to Caesar the man, not to his fame or his political impact. His far-reaching influence as well as the whole idea of glamorous monarchy associated with his name make his confident comparison of himself to the northern star that is above petty change in retrospect seem much less presumptious and absurd than it might do at first. In contrast to Duncan or old Hamlet, Caesar is not buried quietly and soon replaced. Not even the conspirators appear to count on an easy success because they immediately see themselves as defendants and victims of imminent persecution before they have time to make concrete plans for a better government. Shakespeare emphasizes the unrealistic euphoria of the murderers who are intoxicated with the historic magnitude of the moment and completely misjudge the actual political situation; Brutus even more than the rest. The fame of their deed, outliving many generations, is impressed on the audience by the prophetic glimpse of theatrical performances, such as the one we are witnessing while hearing these lines spoken. Like other Shakespearian characters, Brutus and Cassius know they will live on, immortalized by poetry:

CASSIUS
              How many ages hence
Shall this our lofty scene be acted over
In states unborn and accents yet unknown!
BRUTUS
How many times shall Caesar bleed in sport,
That now on Pompey's basis lies along,
No worthier than the dust!   (III.1.111–16)

These lines state the claim of Shakespeare's stage to contribute to the handing down and to the glorification of great human achievements, but they are also to be understood as an indirect commentary on the action because all poetic transmission is at the same time something of an illusion and has its share of the unpredictable nature of all human fate.[20] The audience is reminded of this by Cassius' continuation of the prophetic account:

> So oft as that shall be,
> So often shall the knot of us be called
> The men that gave their country liberty. (III.1.116–18)

This confident hope is justified neither by the historical events nor by the literary tradition, and even within the play itself it is soon disappointed.

The entrance of Mark Antony's servant, following almost immediately upon these lines, already marks a first turning-point in the action because his ambiguous profession of loyalty to the conspirators gives us a hint of the tactical superiority and the pragmatic calculation that are more than a match for Brutus. His sense of honor is as unrealistic as it is inappropriate on that political level to which he has now descended. Caesar's assassination, celebrated by Brutus as a glorious theatrical moment, is at the same time a very ugly political fact whose consequences cannot be glossed over by idealizing rhetoric. The ritual of bathing the conspirators' arms in the blood of the victim, staged by Brutus, remains a showy gesture, a last and ineffective attempt at presenting the murder as something of a religious ceremony. Antony's reaction, however, soon makes plain enough that Caesar's friends are not to be convinced by this kind of language. Brutus is outwitted in one decisive matter and Antony's soliloquy over Caesar's body draws a very different picture of the situation, one that, in the context of the whole play, appears no more biased or distorted than Brutus' idealizing image of a disinterested sacrifice:

> O, pardon me, thou bleeding piece of earth,
> That I am meek and gentle with these butchers!
> Thou art the ruins of the noblest man
> That ever livèd in the tide of times.
> Woe to the hand that shed this costly blood! (III.1.254–8)

After the calculated diplomacy of the dialogue, the soliloquy shows us the undisguised emotions of the speaker. His personal grief and his unqualified praise of the dead are a pointed means of manipulating our sympathy. Brutus' noble motives are neither known to Antony nor are they explicitly cast in doubt; in view of the bloody corpse, however, they seem rather irrelevant and Antony is not prepared to make any distinction between the individual murderers. For him they are all 'butchers' and this, to the spectator, must appear as a clear repudiation of Brutus' high-minded claim: 'Let us be sacrificers, but not butchers' (II.1.167).[21] Antony's own prophecy of internecine civil war turns out to be much more accurate and his metaphor of a revenge tragedy describes at least one important aspect of the following acts:

> And Caesar's spirit, ranging for revenge,
> With Ate by his side, come hot from hell,

> Shall in these confines, with a monarch's voice,
> Cry 'Havoc!' and let slip the dogs of war,   (III.1.270–3)

The terminology associates the following events with revenge plays in the Senecan manner, where personified revenge or classical revenge deities introduce and observe the action.[22] The parallels are quite unmistakable, in the inevitability of retribution and its fateful course and even more striking in the apparition of Caesar's Ghost. The whole action demonstrates that Caesar's spirit, of all things, was not destroyed by the assassins, but survives them all and is fearfully avenged.

To be sure, the revenge is not as straightforward as in many pre-Shakespearian tragedies. The complex historical background prevents an impression of personal vendetta and the contrasted characters of Brutus and Antony make it difficult if not impossible to take sides without qualification. If, immediately after the murder, Brutus appears as a rather blind idealist, who is unable to see the criminality of the deed, the following scenes continually emphasize his disinterested sincerity, his inspiring impact on others and his courageous readiness to face the consequences of his decisions while, on the other side, we are soon made to doubt whether his opponents are really above all concerned with avenging the murder and re-establishing a stable political order or whether there are less admirable motives at work as well.

The famous Forum scene is a good instance of the close interrelation of personal tragedy and political intrigue. The contrast between Brutus and Antony makes this particularly clear; both of them have to translate personal emotions and considerations into political action. Brutus can justify the murder to himself as well as to the state only if the people are prepared to go along with him and if the stability of the republic is not upset. His speech to this purpose is finally made ineffectual by Antony's brilliant performance, but it would be wrong to call it naive or to say that Brutus does not know how to handle an audience.[23] The change from verse to prose and the skilful use of syntactic symmetry emphasize the complete contrast to the rest of the scene. The speech is a consummate demonstration of mass-manipulation by an ostensible appeal to reason and a sense of public responsibility. The spectator in the theatre knows that Brutus is really unable to produce rationally convincing grounds for his action because for him the murder was only a preventive measure, though his speech pretends to a logic that almost compels the listener to admit the inevitability of the assassination if he does not want to appear as a friend of tyranny. Yet, since Brutus has not so much his own personal advantage at heart as the preservation of the liberty won by Caesar's death, his speech, in spite of all tactical shrewdness, gives an impression of sincerity and integrity. Paradoxically, the fact that it fails to achieve its object also makes us admire the speaker's honesty more than blame his lack of political judgement.

Brutus' crucial blunder lies in his failure to see Antony's supreme talent as a demagogue and its possible effect on the Roman plebeians. His own apparent (and very short-lived) success, above all the citizens' cry, 'Let him be Caesar' (III.2.50), make clear that the people have not understood the true political motives behind the assassination and are hardly able to follow a rational argument, but he is obviously unable to recognize the thoroughly unreliable nature of public opinion, and the play leaves us in no doubt that he commits a fatal error when he leaves Antony alone with his audience. The fact that Antony turns out to be a much more effective virtuoso in manipulating the masses does not make Brutus an inept rhetorician, but it does show his limited political foresight. Though the romantic notion of a Hamlet-like Brutus, too reflective and bookish for the harsh world of political realities, was plainly mistaken,[24] it is quite obvious that his illusion of a ritual sacrifice, a disinterested murder for the sake of Rome's liberty, is inadequate when it comes to dealing with the political situation after Caesar's death and this is the reason why the possible fruits of the crime are soon handed over to the enemy. It is Brutus' heroic pose as his country's liberator more than anything that makes him vulnerable against the unscrupulously plotted revenge of his opponents, much as it commands our respect for its noble sincerity.

Apart from Plutarch's brief hint to the effect that Brutus had a more Spartan, Mark Antony a more Asiatic and emotional rhetorical style there is nothing in the sources that could have given Shakespeare the idea of the two Forum speeches. The rhetorical contrast and the dramatic tension produced by these two efforts to sway an unpredictable audience are among the most brilliant and memorable moments in the entire canon. It is not a case of an inferior speaker being succeeded by a good one, but rather of two completely different temperaments and, accordingly, two different forms of demagogism presented side by side. Antony's triumph is by no means a victory for the better cause or for the more substantial arguments; it throws light on the irresponsibility of the people who are so easily betrayed into a complete dissolution of public order and are evidently in need of judicious and disinterested political guidance. It is not, however, critical satire of the unreliable and fickle mob that is the point of the scene, but the question of political stability and those responsible for it. As in the history plays, Shakespeare here seems particularly interested in the necessary qualities of true authority and leadership. In this respect, Antony is hardly superior to Brutus, as is brought home to the spectator in the subsequent scene where the utterly harmless and innocent poet Cinna is butchered in the street by the excited and totally irrational plebeians only because he happens to have the same name as one of the conspirators. Nothing illustrates better the threat of political chaos than his desperate and unsuccessful attempt to save his skin by explaining the mistake. The aimless rage of the mob, especially its blind hatred of civilized values, is strongly reminiscent of Jack Cade's popular rebellion in *Henry VI, Part II*: there the popular cry is 'Away with him! away with him! he speaks Latin!' (IV.7.55); here it is 'Tear him for his bad verses, tear him for his bad verses!' (III.3.30–1), which is hardly meant as an expression of practical literary criticism, but as a frightening outburst of inhuman brutality and political disorder of the kind most feared by the Elizabethans.

The destructive rage of the mob is the direct result of Antony's celebrated speech whose brilliant rhetoric, supported by well-timed gestures, pauses and visual effects, deliberately plays on the audience's emotions and stirs up the popular fury to an uncontrollable pitch. Brutus' point of view is ironically deflated rather than refuted by any argument and Antony's own grief, which is genuine enough and not merely put on, is made part of his rhetoric. Next to the deftly manipulated about-face in the reaction of the popular audience, the most important achievement of the speech consists in the impressive glorification of the dead, in the creation of a larger-than-life, idealized image of Caesar. It takes over Caesar's own idea of himself, continuing it beyond death. It is the first major demonstration of this great person's immortality and its power to direct all the following events. The scene also shows that the murder has unleashed forces not anticipated by the conspirators and certainly beyond their control.

The last part of the play presents the inexorable course of retribution, but it adds little that is new to our assessment of the characters. Brutus accepts his defeat and destruction with heroic dignity, but he also hastens them by tactical blunders and lack of self-criticism. As before with the conspirators, he now takes over, as a matter of course, the part of the authoritative leader and, here again, the catastrophe is an immediate consequence of his arrogant dismissal of Cassius' acute objections.

The long confrontation between Brutus and Cassius (IV.3) once more juxtaposes Brutus' integrity and his lack of superior foresight. His just wrath at the discrediting of the common cause by the soldier's iniquities is an expression of the tragic experience he has to undergo: he finds that the moral justification of the murder becomes more and more questionable. More shattering for him than outward defeat is the inescapable recognition that the effect to wipe out injustice has only produced new injustice. Once again he tries to present his own version of the events as actual fact:

> Remember March, the Ides of March remember.
> Did not great Julius bleed for justice' sake?
> What villain touched his body, that did stab
> And not for justice? What, shall one of us,
> That struck the foremost man of all this world
> But for supporting robbers, shall we now
> Contaminate our fingers with base bribes,   (IV.2.70–6)

This desperate clinging to an illusion, which the play has already exposed as hollow, throws light on Brutus' tragedy but also on his admirable sincerity, and this seems to be more important to the dramatist than the arrogance felt so deeply by Cassius. In principle, Brutus is in the right, and when we learn afterwards that all the time he must have been suffering under the fresh knowledge of his wife's death, it is again evident that the text wants to emphasize Brutus' essential nobility.[25] The whole scene presents the clash between two powerful and very different temperaments without putting all the blame on one of the two opponents. The quarrel and the reconciliation underline the importance of true friendship and affection in politics as well as in personal intercourse, just as Brutus' fatherly concern for the over-tired boy Lucius introduces an element of personal warmth and loyalty which makes us feel closer to the heroic Roman. On the enemy's side, the bartering about human lives and the open contempt of the triumvir Lepidus shown by his partners are a demonstration of a cynical attitude towards humane values (IV.1) that greatly diminishes our sympathy for the avengers. Brutus is loved by Portia, by Cassius and by Lucius, and this is in the last resort more important for our final assessment of him than his rather high-handed rhetoric, which is rather to be seen as Shakespeare's means of characterizing him as the representative of aristocratic Romanness. In contrast, Antony and Octavius seem only united by transitory common interest. Just as Antony plans to rid himself of Lepidus as soon as he has served his purpose, he himself will, not long afterwards, be thrown over by Octavius, as many of Shakespeare's early spectators would surely have known. Both of them are shown to be without that sense of human loyalty and integrity that is so characteristic of Brutus.

Though Brutus is the chief tragic protagonist in this play, he somewhat recedes into the background during the last scenes and we are not given much insight into his deepest thoughts and feelings. There is a certain distancing even in the last scene of the fourth act when the Ghost of Caesar appears to Brutus while he is watching out the night. The brief conversation with Lucius underlines the impression of an approaching crisis because it is made to sound like a final parting. The boy is unable to stay awake with his master who is then left on his own, just like Marlowe's Doctor Faustus during his last night alive or Christ in his agony in the Garden of Gethsemane. These associations are not explicitly suggested by the text, but they will be present for many readers familiar with the literary tradition, if only as a vague atmospheric reminiscence. In this situation, the apparition, which Shakespeare found in his source, could have been presented as the moment of tragic recognition, either by a sudden pang of conscience or a final hardening of heart. The dramatist, however, does not intensify the scene in this way. Brutus' surprise and terror seem to last only a very short while and the disturbed sleep of his attendants remains a rather vague gesture of dramatic foreboding without any deeper moral significance.

In some of Shakespeare's histories, too, the last night before the decisive battle is the time when the hero receives a last warning or encouragement, but Brutus is neither the murderous tyrant visited by his victims, like Richard III, nor God's own soldier who stands for justice and victory, like Richmond and Henry V. As an 'Elizabethan Roman' he is not particularly susceptible to spiritual impressions and he faces his impending fate with stoical equanimity:

> Why, I will see thee at Philippi then. (IV.2.336)

Shakespeare neither makes him conscious of his own guilt and defeat nor does he give him any opportunity for a final justification of his course of action. This may, perhaps, be explained by the dramatist's idea of the spirit of Rome or by his not completely developed concept of the tragic hero. There is, at any rate, no doubt that in the last act the dramatic tension appears to relax and the external action becomes predominant. To some extent, though, the same might be said of some later tragedies, such as *Hamlet* and *Macbeth*.

The battle that occupies all the fifth act, is presented mainly in terms of revenge for Caesar, whose spirit appears as the true victor at the end, not so much as a duel between two opposing moral principles or political concepts. The verbal sparring before the fight once more recapitulates the conflicting views of Caesar's assassination, though Brutus is not given the time for a reasoned account of his view. The whole sequence of scenes underlines the impression of an inescapable fate met by Brutus and Cassius with Roman fortitude. Brutus himself describes his philosophy in terms of 'patience' and 'providence', concepts which any Christian audience would be familiar with and which return in the later tragedies:

> – arming myself with patience
> To stay the providence of some high powers
> That govern us below. (V.1.106-8)

Up to the very end, Brutus insists on the dignity and integrity of his life
and he never views himself, as Othello does, as one who is guilty and has
deserved his destruction, but as a Roman who proves his virtue even in
death. His dying words, like those of Cassius, are concerned with Caesar
and his death, but his own fame means more to him than outward
success:

> I shall have glory by this losing day
> More than Octavius and Mark Antony
> By this vile conquest shall attain unto. (v.5.36–8)

This verdict is largely confirmed by the play and it certainly deserves our
respect. The audience will hardly take it as the author's last word,
though, since the total impression of the tragedy and its chief actors is
more complex than that.

There is hardly another Shakespearian tragedy in which right and
wrong seem to be so evenly distributed among the two opposing parties.
At least, the dramatist's manipulation of our sympathies is less clear and
more ambivalent than in the 'great' tragedies that follow *Julius Caesar*.[26]
Brutus' self-confidence is not often quite free from arrogance and
self-righteousness and the whole play, as well as the historical facts, can
be said to refute his illusion that the assassination of Caesar was a
necessary and beneficial act. On the other hand, neither are his enemies
guided by nobler motives nor is their final victory presented as a moment
of liberation or a triumph of justice. Though the concluding couplet has a
more cheerful and confident ring than the last words of *Hamlet*, *Othello*
or *King Lear*, the impression of great human loss, more definite than in
Macbeth, detracts from the glory of the victory and even those spectators
who are less familiar with the further course of Roman history, will
hardly fail to notice the threat of future conflict in Octavius' appeal:

> So call the field to rest, and let's away
> To part the glories of this happy day. (v.5.81–2)

More significant and decisive for our assessment of the victors and the
defeated is the unqualified tribute paid by Antony and Octavius to the
dead Brutus. Dramatic convention lends an authority to Antony's last
words, as a kind of final appreciation for posterity, which is clearly
intended to put less favorable aspects in perspective and leaves us with an
impression of heroic nobility:

> This was the noblest Roman of them all.
> All the conspirators save only he
> Did that they did in envy of great Caesar.
> He only, in a general honest thought
> And common good to all, made one of them.

His life was gentle, and the elements
So mixed in him that Nature might stand up
And say to all the world 'This was a man!'   (v.5.69–76)

It may be difficult to reconcile this ideal portrait with all that has gone before, but, as in the case of Othello, we are not asked to admire a criminal or to forget right and wrong, but to pay respect to human sincerity, greatness and tragic suffering. This last gesture, celebrating the dead with an obituary that seems to cast a glance at future historians and poets, links *Julius Caesar* with the 'great' tragedies and it also makes clear that it is Brutus who is the tragic protagonist.

Even in the last act the play has continually suggested contradictory views and has presented the hero as well as his opponents in turn as the champions of a just cause and as self-centred criminals, but this does not mean that we are offered no more than mutually exclusive alternatives that leave us alone to make our choice. The tragedy of *Julius Caesar* is not a 'problem play' in the sense that the dramatist deliberately withholds a solution to present the audience with an open question,[27] but a classical story is retold in such a way as to make again plausible why so many generations were fascinated by it and were provoked into a fundamental debate on political and human values, complex characters and controversial decisions. The audience is clearly invited to join in this debate, not just to accept a ready-made version of the events. The fact that the text does not allow a simple interpretation or a comfortable identification with one particular point of view does not make *Julius Caesar* radically different from the other tragedies, because in hardly any of them is it possible to divide the characters into good and evil according to unmistakable authorial signals. It seems clear, on the other hand, that for Shakespeare the world of the Romans, in contrast to the early history of Denmark, Britain, or Scotland, was not ruled and ordered by Christian values and the individual character is left with a secular morality as his standard of behavior, guided at best by a tradition of Roman virtues, unprotected and unrestrained by an ethical code shared with the audience. This may well be the reason why the Roman tragedies have often provoked particularly controversial interpretations.[28]

ANTONY AND CLEOPATRA

No other Shakespearian tragedy has divided critics as much as *Antony and Cleopatra* and there is probably none of which there are such contradictory interpretations regarding Shakespeare's dramatic mode and his supposed evaluation of the chief characters. The critical history of the play is a history of highly controversial and not seldom very personal reactions to the text and there is the danger that each new account of the play only adds another subjective version to this most colorful body of criticism.[29] It may be more useful to ask what are the qualities that have provoked such conflicting opinions because it is obvious that in this respect *Antony and Cleopatra* is different from the earlier tragedies, where the common basis on which most critics and readers would agree is somewhat wider.

Many influential critics have felt that *Antony and Cleopatra* shows a noticeable decline in dramatic intensity from the four major tragedies and the play's reception, especially in the theatre, partly confirms this. It is due less to the rather loose and episodic structure of the play, often criticized by earlier critics, than to Shakespeare's rather detached presentation of the human and political conflicts. The impressive range of localities, the exotic glamor of Egypt and the domestic rivalries in Rome, hardly convey the impression of a crisis in which fundamental issues, political survival or the ethics of public life, are at stake, at least not with the same urgency and immediate significance as in the case of *Julius Caesar*, but also in *Macbeth* and *King Lear*. Neither is the fate of the two protagonists presented as the kind of existential dilemma faced by Hamlet and Othello, as agonizing moral conflict, spiritual impasse or shattering disillusion, but rather as a series of abruptly changing attitudes and impressions, whose problematic nature is often more clearly seen by distanced observers than by the chief actors themselves. It is only in the last two acts that they experience the consequences of their decisions in terms of tragic loss and disillusionment, and even then one might feel that their histrionics are, as Eliot said of Hamlet's emotions 'in *excess* of the facts as they appear'.[30]

The unusual combination of a vast historical panorama and a romantic love story also makes the play rather different from the major tragedies. There are good reasons why it is usually grouped with the Roman plays, but also, especially in recent times, often seen in close connection with other tragedies of love. This double aspect, classical history and exotic passion, has probably been responsible for the particular appeal of this story from the beginning: as part of Rome's history, the defeat of Antony marks the final victory of Caesarism over the republican ideals of men like Brutus; as lovers, Antony and Cleopatra are the most famous couple in classical history, rivalled only by Aeneas and Dido, with whom they were often compared.[31] More even than Caesar's fall, the ruin of Antony by Cleopatra's fatal charms had been retold and variously interpreted by poets and playwrights. Plutarch and many after him portrayed Antony as the brilliant triumvir and general deflected from his heroic duties by his own weakness and the allurements of a seductress. Others, such as

Chaucer in his *Legend of Good Women* and the Countess of Pembroke in her translation of Garnier's *Marc Antoine* (1578), the *Tragedie of Antonie* of about 1590, presented Cleopatra as a pitiable martyr of love, as a faithful wife and victim of her own trusting credulity.[32]

Shakespeare's chief source, Plutarch's life of Antony, whom he follows fairly closely even to the details of particular phrases, anecdotes and little scenes, already gives an intriguingly complex account of the two main characters and does not force its verdict on the reader even though there is no mistaking its emphatic condemnation of the love affair. Plutarch is really more interested in the fascinating appeal of two unusual and unpredictable characters than in moral censure, and his biography of Antony is a splendid portrait, recreating the career of two unique personalities in a most impressive manner and with all the traditional devices of narrative rhetoric. No other Shakespearian tragedy keeps so closely to its source even though it is in other ways very independent of it. The rich and resourceful dramatic poetry which is perhaps the play's most astonishing achievement, owes very little to Plutarch's circumstantial prose.

Unlike the two neoclassical tragedies *Antonie* and Samuel Daniel's *Cleopatra*, which only select one or two crucial moments and strictly preserve the unity of place, it is the very diversity and the geographical sweep of the story that Shakespeare has attempted to recapture in his tragedy, which he has turned into a sequence of more than forty scenes. This loose dramatic structure has often been criticized, but for the Elizabethan stage, such rapid change of scene and locality was not unusual and presented few problems.[33] The modern theatre, of course, feels much more akin to this freedom from restricting classical precepts than the picture-frame stage of Bradley's day.

The structure of *Antony and Cleopatra*, as has often been observed, mirrors the fundamental contrast between Rome as the centre of an emerging world empire and Egypt which represents a completely different way of life. Between these two mutually exclusive worlds Antony finds himself torn by conflicting loyalties and impulses. He is bound to Rome by birth, nature, ambition and many duties, but he is fascinated and disorientated by Egypt. The continual 'oscillation' between the two contrasting worlds is a reflection of Antony's dilemma and provides a visual image of his inner conflict.[34] There is no other tragedy in which the antagonism between characters and attitudes is translated into dramatic structure in such a spectacular way. This was, of course, partly suggested by the nature of the story and by Plutarch's account, but it still needed the deliberate decision of the dramatist who could have found very different means to present a tragic conflict. It is worth noting that other forms of characterization which are quite typical of the major tragedies, are largely absent here, such as the soliloquy which, in comparison with *Hamlet, Othello* and *Macbeth*, plays a very insignificant part in this play and never conveys to the audience any of the intensity of the dilemma expressed by other means elsewhere. The hero's development is not presented in terms of pyschological introspection and insight into his lonely meditations, but rather by changing point of view, surprising action, and detached comment. This has probably in large part contributed to the controversial nature of critical assessments many of which have supplied by personal conviction and confident simplification what the text appears to be lacking in explicitness.

Plutarch leaves the reader in no doubt as to his general verdict on the story and his censure is probably representative of the predominant view with which Shakespeare had to reckon. Thus, the decisive phase of Antony's career is introduced in no uncertain terms:

> the last and extreamest mischiefe of all other (to wit, the love of Cleopatra) lighted on him, who did waken and stirre up many vices yet hidden in him, and were never seene to any: and if any sparke of goodnesse or hope of rising were left him, Cleopatra quenched it straight, and made it worse then before.[35]

Not many spectators would accept this statement as an adequate description of Shakespeare's tragedy; yet the question of how far *Antony and Cleopatra* actually departs from this evaluation has, for several generations, been the most debated problem of interpretation.

Shakespeare, too, begins his tragedy with an uncompromising condemnation of Antony's love:

> Nay, but this dotage of our general's
> O'erflows the measure. Those his goodly eyes,
> That o'er the files and musters of the war
> Have glowed like plated Mars, now bend, now turn
> The office and devotion of their view
> Upon a tawny front. His captain's heart,
> Which in the scuffles of great fights hath burst
> The buckles on his breast, reneges all temper,
> And is become the bellows and the fan
> To cool a gypsy's lust.   (I.I.I–I0)

With the stylized intensity of 'Roman' rhetoric, Antony's past greatness is contrasted to the present aberration, and it is important to note that this negative portrait is not, like Iago's insidious characterization of Othello, prompted by envious hate, but rather by sincere regret and uncomprehending anger. For the Roman soldier, anything that deflects the tried general from his glorious military career can only be evil and contemptible, but the particular dramatic technique of this scene leaves us guessing whether this is an authorial, chorus-like comment or a one-sided, at best limited voice of an individual observer. It largely depends on the subjective disposition of the spectator as well as (in the theatre) on the particular production how far the first scene is felt to be a confirmation, a qualification, or a refutation of this initial statement. What the scene does confirm is Antony's determination to turn his back on his former identity as a representative of Rome and his public commitment to a new loyalty, in particular, his new conception of 'nobleness' and of a meaningful life:

> Let Rome in Tiber melt, and the wide arch
> Of the ranged empire fall! Here is my space.
> Kingdoms are clay. Our dungy earth alike
> Feeds beast as man. The nobleness of life
> Is to do thus – when such a mutual pair
> And such a twain can do't, in which I bind,
> On pain of punishment, the world to weet
> We stand up peerless. (I.I.33–40)

This declamation, combining love-poetry conventions and political rhetoric, seems to oscillate between irresponsible bragging and heroic claim to an exceptional stature. The conviction it carries is largely determined by the context. Cleopatra's words alone hardly justify his idealized image of her; they rather suggest that it is the fancy of one blinded by passion, not informed by objective judgement:

> Fie, wrangling queen!
> Whom everything becomes – to chide, to laugh,
> To weep; whose every passion fully strives
> To make itself, in thee, fair and admired. (I.I.48–51)

Some of the lovers in Shakespeare's comedies use similarly hyperbolic languages and they are ridiculed for it by their rather more sober ladies, nor is Antony taken quite seriously by Cleopatra in this instance: 'Excellent falsehood!' (I.I.40).

The scene does not really make clear what Antony's newly defined 'nobleness' consists in and whether it really has any positive value. Nor does he present any general alternative to the traditional Roman virtues; rather he celebrates his personal decision, without any regard for the general fate of Rome or his own reputation. Bradley's classic comment describes most accurately and perceptively the ambivalent effect of this scene and indeed of the whole play:

Neither the phrase 'a strumpet's fool,' nor the assertion 'the nobleness of life is to do thus,' answers to the total effect of the play. But the truths they exaggerate are equally essential; and the commoner mistake in criticism is to understate the second.[36]

It is unlikely that readers and audiences will ever agree on whether 'equally essential' really does justice to the dramatist's intention nor am I convinced that he wished to produce such general agreement, if we look at the tragedy as a whole.

In the course of the exposition, Rome's opinion about the general's infatuation is made plausible enough. It is repeated by two observers at the end of the first scene and taken up by Antony himself in the following scene. The message from home has brought him to an estimation of himself that is not unlike the 'official' view, as the dramatist makes clear to us in an 'aside'. It is by its nature rather more reliable than Antony's public professions:

> These strong Egyptian fetters I must break,
> Or lose myself in dotage.   (1.2.117–18)

A few lines later, this determination is confirmed in a soliloquy:

> I must from this enchanting queen break off.
> Ten thousand harms, more than the ills I know,
> My idleness doth hatch.   (1.2.129–31)

Cleopatra is seen in these reflections only as harmful seductress, not as a person beloved, and her brief appearances as well as Enobarbus' outspoken comments produce the impression of a brilliant role-player rather than of a dedicated romantic lover. The function of Enobarbus in these scenes is very much like that of the fool or the disillusioned mocker who enjoys complete freedom of speech and undercuts the high-flown rhetoric of the lovers by the uninhibited directness of his rather limited realism. For him, as for Mercutio and Iago, passion is primarily a sexual experience and, unlike Romeo or Othello, Antony at first offers very little that could be set against this debased view of love. His parting from Cleopatra (1.3) seems to be the final conclusion to this aberration even though his somewhat glib conceit is meant to suggest a purely outward and passing separation.[37] The departure under the pressure of a sense of Roman duty is an obvious reminiscence of Aeneas' flight from Dido's Carthage, but in contrast to Virgil's hero, Antony is unable to tear himself from his love once and for all.[38] His real tragedy begins when it turns out that the separation has failed to put an end to his bondage, but has made him even more conscious of the indissoluble ties that bind him to Cleopatra.

The first three scenes, all set in Egypt, make the contrast between irresponsible indulgence and the soldier's duties appear comparatively simple and unambiguous. Egypt is a place of levity and thoughtless present whereas Rome stands for the appeal to a sense of responsibility and loyalty towards family and state. Cleopatra herself is aware of the limits of her influence in these terms:

> He was disposed to mirth; but on the sudden
> A Roman thought hath struck him. (1.2.83–4)

This simple contrast becomes rather more problematic as soon as our first impressions are qualified in surprising ways by the swift changes of perspective between the worlds of Rome and of Egypt. In a way, Caesar's first appearance on stage confirms what we have seen of Antony so far, his heroic past, his irresponsible infatuation and the hopes still placed in him, but Caesar's cool and self-righteous condemnation of the 'great competitor' (1.4.3) gives a rather personal slant to the political confrontation. There is a clash of two irreconcilable temperaments as well as a contrast of political convictions. Antony's greatness and the undisguised spontaneity of his Egyptian 'dissipations', so free from any shrewd political calculation or intrigue, are brought home to the audience more forcefully by Caesar's disapproving analysis than by Antony's own behavior and professions, especially since we know that Antony has already severed himself from the Egyptian allurements and has made his decision in favor of Rome.

On the other hand, the scene which follows makes the intensity of the love union more credible and convincing than the lovers' meetings at the beginning have done. The bond that unites them becomes even more real through the separation and it is made very clear that Antony means much more to Cleopatra than a political pawn or a lover who merely flatters her vanity. She evidently sees in him, and he in her, the exceptional personality who justifies all the conflicts arising out of their love. Her proud memories of the two other great Romans who lay at her feet, Julius Caesar and Pompey, also suggest a concept of love that has left behind it romantic indefiniteness and is founded on more stable as well as rational qualities. Here too, Shakespeare's source provided him with very precise hints. Thus, Plutarch introduces his account of this epoch in Antony's life with a reference to his predecessors:

For Caesar and Pompey knew her when she was but a young thing, and knew not then what the worlde ment: but nowe she went to Antonius at the age when a womans beawtie is at the prime, and she also of best judgement. (Bullough,v,273)

In Shakespeare's play, it is Cleopatra herself who makes this comparison with her 'salad days, / When I was green in judgement, cold in blood' (1.5.73–4), but it is characteristic of Shakespeare's dramatic presentation of his protagonists that this happens only after the exposition in which the Roman point of view seems to be taken for granted. The exceptional vitality of their mutual love is gradually unfolded after their first and, for all we know, final parting, by memories, imagination and irrational action, whereas Plutarch recounts in chronological order Antony's seduction, the wild joy of their dissipations and the conclusion of the episode with the reconciliation between Antony and Octavius Caesar. His colorful description of a fascinating partnership that is much more than either romantic worship or sexual passion, but a mutual attraction of two exceptional personalities, a reckless communion of extravagant enjoyment, is taken up by Shakespeare only in a number of retrospective sketches. This not only provokes the spectator into ambivalent and vacillating assessment of the characters, it also has the consequence that the lovers' separation and Antony's peace with Rome, which in Plutarch mark hopeful interludes before Antony's final relapse, appear as a futile attempt to solve an impossible dilemma. Cleopatra's behavior in the Egyptian scenes, skilfully interspersed between the Roman episodes (I.5, II.5, III.3), shows very clearly that she has not for a moment accepted the separation as a definite fact and still feels absolutely bound to Antony. On the other side, Antony as well as the audience are most conscious of the irresistible attraction of far-off Egypt during the Roman scenes.

All this makes for a noticeable concentration of the action in comparison with the dramatist's source and this applies to the external action as well as to the highly dynamic and often puzzling presentation of the characters, which is particularly evident in the first three scenes of act two. The brief introduction of Pompey serves to show us Antony's position in yet another light: for his ambitious rival, his Egyptian escapades are most welcome news because they seem to eliminate his most dangerous and resourceful competitor. The crucial scene of reconciliation that follows immediately is quite different from Plutarch in the way it combines pragmatic politics, Roman solidarity and an impressive reminder of Egypt's magic attraction. No sooner is the political and fraternal alliance between Antony and Octavius concluded than we are presented with the most fascinating evocation of Cleopatra's enchanting powers so far. It is a brilliant poetical transformation of Plutarch's dispassionate and sober account from the mouth of a down-to-earth soldier and it is placed in such a way as to cast grave doubts on the idea of a lasting reconciliation. What is called in question is not so much Antony's sincerity as his true freedom and his ability to stay away from Cleopatra once and for all. Enobarbus who, even in conversation with Antony himself, appears as a very critical and clear-sighted observer in other parts of the play, here takes his side, at least to a certain point, by acknowledging the exceptional nature of Cleopatra, which cannot possibly be described by any traditional cliché, be it in terms of conventional love poetry or of moral evaluation:

> Age cannot wither her, nor custom stale
> Her infinite variety. Other women cloy
> The appetites they feed, but she makes hungry
> Where most she satisfies; for vilest things
> Become themselves in her, that the holy priests
> Bless her when she is riggish.   (II.2.240–5)

This glowing description can hardly be interpreted as either a celebration or a condemnation of Antony's love. It merely attempts to give an idea of her more than unusual qualities, her 'infinite variety'. For the Roman, Cleopatra represents the experience of exotic strangeness, but at the same time she combines in her person elements far beyond all the conventional female charms. Although the food metaphors, used in other places as well (cf. 'his Egyptian dish' (II.6.124)), suggest sexual indulgence and a purely sensual appeal, Enobarbus also singles out Cleopatra's amazing ability to confer majestic dignity on what in others would be common and trivial. Her inexhaustible capacities for change, surprise and adaptation invest Antony's infatuation with the reality of a deep and complex human relationship. Plutarch is the first to note the fascinating vitality and the unconventional exuberance of their union, their original forms of dissipation, Epicurean excesses and inventive pranks.[39] Such unorthodox resourcefulness and enchanting unpredictability is quite different from Shakespeare's other love tragedies. Neither Juliet nor Desdemona are fascinating partners in this sense. Neither of them is credited with 'infinite variety' as a particular virtue. It is not enough to contrast this 'worldly love' with the conventional ideals of 'courtly love' as one critic has done.[40] For Antony, Cleopatra means the possibility of a complete partnership, even though it seems only for the purpose of unlimited pleasure, a partnership not necessarily founded on the reliable harmony of mutual agreement but on the continual fascination of unexpectedness and contradictory personalities. In addition, the whole play implies that the two lovers are above their surroundings by virtue of their exceptional intensity, vitality and unorthodox courage and are thus, in a way, predestined for each other.

The play, however, underlines the dangerous and destructive aspects of this love as much as its potential happiness and its exemplary character. Thus, the most emphatic assertions of the glorious union usually come from one of the two lovers when he or she is separated from the partner and only one of them is on stage. Apart from the scene of Antony's death there are practically no love scenes in the conventional sense, nothing like the balcony scene in *Romeo and Juliet* or the first meeting of Othello and Desdemona in Cyprus. In nearly every case the encounters between the two protagonists are marred by irritation, scorn, distrust, or coquetry. Those who want to read the play as a glorification of unconditional love can only point to its ending, and even there the dramatist has put in some jarring notes.

On the other hand, Shakespeare rather plays down the unprincipled brutality of Antony's disloyalty towards Octavius and his sister whom he has accepted as his wife, whereas Plutarch makes much more of the pathos of her situation. Though Antony gives his consent to the politic marriage arrangement proposed by Octavius, his acquiescence, if it is sincere, lasts only a very short time. In the very next scene he remembers the powerful attractions of Egypt and already seems to have changed his mind:

> I will to Egypt;
> And though I make this marriage for my peace,
> I'th'East my pleasure lies. (II.3.39–41)

'My pleasure' can hardly be interpreted as an expression of disinterested love or even pure loyalty to the beloved. But Antony is neither presented as one tormented by a tragic dilemma or a conflict of irreconcilable loyalties nor as a deliberate hypocrite and cheat, even though his actual behavior strongly suggests insincerity.[41] His evident betrayal of Octavia and of Caesar is only shown as a fact, not as a gradual mental process or a conscious decision. His marriage to Octavia is hardly felt to be a real union in the play whereas Plutarch tells us that there were two daughters. The rapid change of scenes and points of view often seems to leave out the very moments when decisions are being made and moral issues debated: the vows of fidelity are followed, almost without transition, by the news of Antony's defection (III.6). Since the dramatist does not engage our sympathies on Octavia's behalf with any particular emphasis nor go out of his way to convince us of the absolute sincerity of those working towards a reconciliation, Antony's return to Cleopatra does not strike the audience as a sudden shameful relapse, but rather as the inevitable and predictable consequence of an irrepressible passion and the expression of an all-powerful affection. At this point, Shakespeare's departure from Plutarch's account is particularly important because there he found a second reconciliation, brought about by Octavia's pathetic entreaties and spoilt again by Antony's newly awakened infatuation, an episode Shakespeare chose to leave out althogether. This, of course, makes Antony's behavior much more blameworthy, and Plutarch leaves us in no doubt about his verdict:

Then beganne this pestilent plague and mischiefe of Cleopatraes love (which had slept a longe tyme, and seemed to have bene utterlie forgotten, and that Antonius had geven place to better counsell) againe to kindle, and to be in force, so soone as Antonius came neere unto Syria.   (Bullough,v,283)

Compared to this, Shakespeare's dramatic version makes quite clear that he was not interested in unambiguous condemnation or approval and that his picture of Antony's love is completely different, as is his presentation of time. Thus, the audience's impression of Antony's defection is very much influenced by the fact that we first learn about it from Octavius' hostile point of view (III.6). Octavia who is desperately trying to preserve the peace, is received by her brother as the shamefully forsaken wife of an enemy. Unlike Plutarch's authoritative disapproval, Caesar's anger has political motives as well as moral ones and, in the context of the play, can be for us no more than a personal and biased opinion, not the poet's own verdict, even though the dislike felt by many critics for Octavius often seems to have gone beyond what the text actually says.[42] Caesar is the representative of efficient and emotionless power politics, favored by fortune and destined to be finally victorious. Antony's sensual nature and unpredictable geniality are completely foreign to Caesar's stern character, but Shakespeare has left his outlines rather vague and he is evidently not meant to arouse violent emotions. There is no clear suggestion that he practises deception or acts from personal animosity against Antony. The sincerity of his love for the sister is also taken over unchanged from Plutarch. What is much more important for the dramatist than blame or praise is the irreconcilable contrast between the two antagonists. Caesar appears as the embodiment of all those Roman qualities Antony throws to the winds when he is in Egypt, even though he lacks Brutus' heroic patriotism and it is possible that for an Elizabethan audience he had something of the calculating and self-righteous Puritan in him.

These contrasts are brilliantly dramatized in the riotous scene of fraternization and carousing aboard Pompey's galley (II.7). The increasingly inebriate generals and soldiers, indulging in jokes and memories of exotic campaigns, more and more forgetful of their reputation and of their own interests, are sharply contrasted with Octavius, who has stayed sober all the time, rather nauseated by the drunken orgy and completely excluded from this noisy fellowship. In Shakespeare's comedies, such inability to forget oneself for a time in general festivity is often seen as a deficiency, a lack of true freedom and humanity. It is the mark of outsiders, like Malvolio. On the other hand, the drunken carelessness of these potential rulers of the world is rather different from the festive spirit of comedy because the global political background remains present throughout all the trivial entertainment and Octavius' most formidable competitors throw away their claim without being aware of it. Pompey's acquiescence is seen by his friend Menas as disastrous weakness ('Pompey doth this day laugh away his fortune' (11.6.104)), and in the course of the feasting he tries for the last time to exploit the unusual situation for political gain, if only by a most desperate and criminal scheme. Like the Fiend in the temptation of Christ, he offers the whole world to his comrade in arms:

> Wilt thou be lord of all the world? (11.7.61)

> I am the man
> Will give thee all the world. (11.7.64–5)

When Pompey, insisting on his honor, rejects the suggestion, Menas decides to leave him because he rightly foresees his fall.

Lepidus too, the third member of the triumvirate, finally proves his inferiority and drops out of the race. Enobarbus' witty comment when Lepidus is carried off senseless again illuminates the close relation between world history and the drunken orgy:

> 'A bears the third part of the world, man; (11.7.89)

Antony, the other third, remains as Octavius' only serious rival, but even before the feast Enobarbus has predicted his eventual return to Egypt because Octavia, 'of a holy, cold, and still conversation' (11.6.120–1), is unable to make him forget Cleopatra's attractions. Thus, Antony, like the others taking part in the carousal, becomes a victim of careless indulgence, while Octavius who is incapable of such self-forgetful relaxation, steps into their inheritance. No other scene combines in such concentrated form the various themes of the play and the contradictory nature of Rome's claim to world domination.

In contrast to *Julius Caesar*, disinterested service to the liberty, dignity and order of the community seem to play a very minor part in determining the actions of the chief characters. Even for Octavius, the controversy with Antony does not seem to be a patriotic conflict so much as a struggle for personal power, even though Shakespeare does not take up Plutarch's hint to the effect that he was looking for an opportunity to make war against Antony.[43] The world of politics remains more in the background so that Antony's betrayal of it does not make him as clearly a political criminal as would have been the case in the history plays or as Plutarch presents it. Antony's gravest strategic error and his most undignified action during the battle of Actium are most damaging to himself and do not seem to be directed against Rome. The decision to fight at sea as well as his sudden flight are the disastrous consequences of his blind infatuation which, at this point in the play, is branded in no less uncertain terms than in Shakespeare's source. The comments of the experienced soldiers are no hostile slander, but describe the reaction of most spectators as well:

> So our leader's led,
> And we are women's men.   (III.7.69-70)

and a little later:

> We have kissed away
> Kingdoms and provinces.   (III.10.7-8)

Like Pompey, Antony has thrown away a world empire and has betrayed all the heroic values which, in spite of all the criticism of Rome in this play, are not seriously questioned by the dramatist:

> I never saw an action of such shame.
> Experience, manhood, honour, ne'er before
> Did violate so itself.   (III.10.21-3)

The difference between this and Plutarch's account lies most of all in the way Antony's complete dependence on Cleopatra is presented by the historian as a long drawn-out state of mind to which he keeps referring. He speaks of 'shamefull deedes' (Bullough,v,283), of 'the sweete poyson of her love' (p.284), of Antony's 'effeminate mind' (p.289), and he calls him 'subject to a womans will' (p.296). Shakespeare, in contrast, reduces this long development to a crisis of some few dramatic moments, so as to create the impression of a tragic fall, not a character corrupted from the start. It is only now that Antony really becomes aware of the full extent of his perversion by Cleopatra's influence. The conflict between his Roman reputation and Egypt's fascination, which had hardly been seriously reflected upon by him, is fully experienced only when it is too late. Whereas at first, the play had presented Antony mainly from the outside, either from the Roman or from the Egyptian perspective, his fall now manifests itself most poignantly in his own recognition that he has been untrue to his own nature and betrayed those Roman virtues which, for all his scorn of Octavius Caesar's narrow ambition and for all his flamboyant rhetoric, had so far been undisputed norms of behavior. It is not so much his responsibility for the community he feels he has sinned against, as his honor and his reputation. He appears much less concerned with making his actions conform with a general, self-imposed ideal or with the promptings of his own conscience, like Hamlet and Macbeth, than with his fame and the world's opinion. His open humiliation by Octavius, 'the young man' (III.II.62), is for him the most tormenting aspect of his defeat. 'Shame' and 'reputation', like 'nobility', are for him, above all, public qualities and his desperate attempts to regain what is lost by hysterical professions of love to Cleopatra or unrealistic heroic offers to Octavius only confirm his fall and make it all the more evident. His undignified treatment of Caesar's ambassador (III.13) reminds us of Cleopatra's behavior towards a messenger in an earlier scene (II.5) and underlines his loss of heroic self-control. Like Othello, when tortured by jealousy, he loses all his former stature and commanding dignity. The dramatist, however, makes Antony's outburst somewhat more plausible by the brief appearance of the triumphant Octavius who mercilessly exploits the situation and is already counting on Cleopatra's opportunism (III.12). Thidias is instructed, 'From Antony win Cleopatra' (III.12.27) and to 'Try thy cunning' (III.12.31); yet the whipping of the loyal emissary and the rather childish challenge to Octavius are the futile actions of a despairing man. They demonstrate Antony's unwillingness to face reality and are rightly deplored by Enobarbus as lack of judgement:

> Caesar, thou hast subdued
> His judgement too. (III.13.36–7)

For the realistic soldier, Antony's behavior is only a sure sign of his complete collapse.

The whole scene presents Antony largely from Enobarbus' point of view. He has been one of his most faithful followers and does not, by any means, represent the hostile Roman attitudes, but at this point he can only register the disastrous finality of Antony's fall. Even before Antony enters the stage, Enobarbus insists to Cleopatra's face that Antony alone is guilty and responsible for the catastrophe because he 'would make his will/Lord of his reason' (III.13.3–4), and later in the scene he begins to ask himself whether loyalty to a fool is not mere folly (42–3). Time and again he comments on Antony's behavior, but not as a detached observer, like the biographer Plutarch, but as one who is deeply affected by it and who is confronted with the agonizing question whether he should, like all the others, foresake his fallen lord or be faithful to him even in his defeat and destruction. This moral conflict is very closely linked with Antony's own tragedy, and it is Enobarbus himself who points out the connection:

> Yet he that can endure
> To follow with allegiance a fallen lord
> Does conquer him that did his master conquer
> And earns a place i'th'story. (III.13.43–6)

The fact that Enobarbus is finally crushed by this dilemma underscores the tragedy of Antony's fall, as he himself realizes when he learns of Enobarbus' defection:

> O, my fortunes have
> Corrupted honest men! (IV.5.16-7)

That the most loyal supporters are leaving him ('Thy dearest quit thee' (III.13.65)) is an expression of his singular tragic collapse, but this inclusion of Enobarbus also prevents us from detached moral condemnation because we see that Antony, for all his fatal and destructive weakness, is respected and loved almost to the end. Enobarbus has the last word in this scence and his brief soliloquy once more describes Antony's decline which can no longer be idealized as a case of heroic passion, but is seen as the perversion of a great personality:

> Now he'll outstare the lightning ...
> I see still
> A diminution in our captain's brain
> Restores his heart. When valour preys on reason,
> It eats the sword it fights with. I will seek
> Some way to leave him. (III.13.194,196–200)

It is compassion, not hatred or contempt that informs Enobarbus' comment. Antony's fall does not make him an object of moral disapproval, rather we see him as the victim of a tragic development from which Enobarbus wants to dissociate himself, without success, as it turns out. Cleopatra's rather ambiguous behavior as well as Octavius' tactical superiority are presented by the dramatist with far less emotional intensity and they only serve to underline the hopelessness of Antony's situation. The dramatic technique confirms to a large extent Enobarbus' view of Antony as the most guilty in the sense that Cleopatra is seen almost exclusively in relation to him; it is her influence on the Roman general that is the main theme of the tragedy, not her own complex personality by itself. Her fascination and her caprices are of interest mainly for the effect they have on Antony. Thus, her double-tongued dealings with Thidias are bound to irritate Antony into white fury because (like Enobarbus) he begins to doubt her loyalty and even her protestations of love, teasing him into renewed hysterical euphoria, hardly convince us of the sincerity of her affection even though they may make Antony's infatuation more understandable. Their decision to indulge in a last orgy, 'one other gaudy night' (III.13.182), forgetful of themselves before their final ruin, can hardly be interpreted as a regaining of lost nobility or as a manifestation of exemplary love, but seems little more than a blind refusal to admit defeat. The conventional simile of death as love-act is reminiscent of *Romeo and Juliet*, though here it is an expression of desperate defiance rather than of dedicated love, ready to meet death:

> The next time I do fight,
> I'll make death love me, for I will contend
> Even with his pestilent scythe. (III.13.191–3)

As in Plutarch, Antony's impulsive and unpredictable nature is continually contrasted with the respect and admiration he commands from friends and subordinates. Even where, almost like Shakespeare's Richard II, he makes a ceremony of his downfall (especially in IV. 2) the reaction is pity and grief, not accusing anger or scorn. The strong emphasis on Antony's deep fall makes the memory of his former greatness all the more vivid and underlines the role of fate. Destiny has decided to turn against the Roman general, an idea Shakespeare might have found in Plutarch who, commenting on Antony's weakness, states clearly: 'for it was predestined that the government of all the world should fall into Octavius Caesars handes'. (Bullough, v, 292); he also mentions reports that during the night before the final battle sounds of supernatural music were heard which, according to the most reasonable observers, signified that Antony's own god, Hercules, was leaving him. Shakespeare took over these and other prophetic hints (see IV.3, and the role of the soothsayer), not to make Antony appear as the innocent victim of fore-ordained fate, but to avoid the impression of individual misfortune or an edifying balance of guilt and punishment.

It is important to note that even Plutarch is not satisfied with passing moral verdicts on the chief actors, but comes to the conclusion that Antony's fall was caused by a combination of admirable and deplorable qualities, and he insists, when comparing Antonius with Demestrius, that 'Antonius by his incontinencie, did no hurte but to him selfe' (Bullough, v, 320). The last part of Shakespeare's tragedy juxtaposes in a series of quickly changing and almost fragmentary character sketches the pitiful and the irritating, the undignified and the heroic, fusing all these impressions into a complex picture while at the same time lifting whole episodes and speeches almost literally from his source. The effective concentration of the action on some brief and crucial moments and the intensifying of the spoken word by memorable poetry and rhetoric are Shakespeare's unique contribution, while the action itself has hardly undergone significant changes. There is no indication that Shakespeare deliberately set out to alter Plutarch's evaluation of the characters, especially when we consider that he probably had to rely on his memory for large stretches of the story since he would hardly consult the heavy folio volume of about a thousand pages for every detail.[44]

It is the painful consciousness of having thrown away the most valuable possession and of having forfeited by his own error everything that makes life meaningful to him, that links Antony with Shakespeare's other tragic heroes.[45] More abruptly, however, than in *Hamlet* or *Othello*, stoic defiance, violent self-reproaches, anger, despair, and the desire to be revenged follow one another; experiences the spectator can share are often succeeded by others that are clearly based on misconception and therefore viewed by the audience with more detachment, such as Cleopatra's supposed treachery and, above all, her reported death. Like Romeo, Antony takes his own life because he cannot bear the thought of surviving his love; but by her deception Cleopatra is at least partly guilty of his death and Antony's suicide is not simply a confirmation of his Roman nobleness but also a final triumph of her seductive power.[46] With her death everything that had motivated his disastrous actions is at an end. He can neither enjoy the reward of his passion nor is a return to his Roman dignity possible except by a 'Roman' death that saves him from public disgrace and unites him with Cleopatra. Antony dies with a renewed belief in Cleopatra's love. For him, the false report of her death acts as an example demanding emulation, an instance of free courage that denies the enemy his last triumph. He is ashamed of lacking her nobility and determination:

> Since Cleopatra died,
> I have lived in such dishonour that the gods
> Detest my baseness. I, that with my sword
> Quartered the world, and o'er green Neptune's back
> With ships made cities, condemn myself to lack
> The courage of a woman; less noble mind
> Than she which by her death our Caesar tells
> 'I am conqueror of myself.' (IV.14.55–62)

The loss of his soldierly honor and the humiliation by Cleopatra's suicide play a more prominent part in this scene than grief at being separated from the beloved. The idea of a reunion after death is, however, stated with more emphasis than in Shakespeare's other tragedies of love or in Plutarch:

> – I come, my queen – ... Stay for me.
> Where souls do couch on flowers, we'll hand in hand,
> And with our sprightly port make the ghosts gaze:
> Dido and her Aeneas shall want troops,
> And all the haunt be ours. (IV.14.50–4)

Antony tries to create a myth of himself and Cleopatra, meant to exceed and to replace the fame of the classical lovers; but even in his suicide, the heroic stance is not as unqualified and wholly admirable as it is in the case of Brutus because Antony does not succeed in killing himself at once and feels he has made bad work of his last great effort. He is explicitly criticized for it by Plutarch. Antony, he says, 'slue him selfe, (to confesse a troth) cowardly, and miserably, to his great paine and griefe: and yet was it before his bodie came into his enemies hands'. (Bullough, v, 321). This, of course, is to judge his end by Roman rather than by Christian standards and Shakespeare's play does not explicitly endorse this criticism. Antony's lingering death does, however, make possible one last meeting with Cleopatra, a scene also described in detail by Plutarch and taken over by the neoclassical tragedies of Garnier and Daniel.

Shakespeare has deliberately extended this part of the action because the lovers' union in death is not only, as in *Romeo and Juliet*, the woeful end and, at the same time, the final triumph of their love, but a last attempt to recapture a glorious harmony that from the start was threatened by the nature of the partners themselves, not only from outside. It is not alone the conflict between Rome and Egypt that prevents us from ever really believing in the permanence of the union. Antony's divided character and Cleopatra's capricious unpredictability, her 'infinite variety', also make these lovers very different from Romeo and Juliet, or Othello and Desdemona. In contrast to these earlier tragedies, love is not presented as an ennobling relationship, but rather as a potential threat to one's own personality, as a tormenting succession of affection and disappointment, dream and disillusion. Critics as early as Bradley have drawn attention to Shakespeare's sonnets, where we find a very similar extension and exploration of conventional concepts of love. The poet experiences love not as worship of an ideal or longing for perfection, but as a terrifying sense of bondage and humiliating dependence. He is familiar enough with all the clichés of the spotless lady and her unmatched virtues, and yet he is in love with a woman whom he knows to be a liar:

> When my love swears that she is made of truth,
> I do believe her though I know she lies,   (Sonnet 138)

The irrational attraction and the corrupting power of love are described even more explicitly in the famous sonnet 129, of which the German critic Ernst Josef Wolff wrote in 1905 that it contained the whole tragedy in a nutshell:[47]

> Th' expense of spirit in a waste of shame
> Is lust in action, and till action lust
> Is perjured, murd'rous, bloody, full of blame,
> Savage, extreme, rude, cruel, not to trust,
> Enjoyed no sooner but despisèd straight,
> Past reason hunted, and no sooner had,

> Past reason hated as a swallowed bait,
> On purpose laid to make the taker mad;
> Mad in pursuit, and in possession so,
> Had, having, and in quest to have, extreme,
> A bliss in proof, and proved, a very woe,
> Before, a joy proposed, behind, a dream.
>   All this the world well knows, yet none knows well
>   To shun the heav'n that leads men to this hell.

There is little point in trying to interpret this autobiographically and to indulge in speculations on Shakespeare's mistress. Yet a closer look at these sonnets may well help to understand the way love is presented in *Antony and Cleopatra*. It is clearly distinguished from Petrarchan idealization, religious moralizing, or cynical levity by its disillusioned honesty and the variety of emotions produced by it. Antony does not deceive himself by a false picture of the beloved, as Troilus does. For him, she is neither 'merely' his wife nor just his mistress in any conventional sense. She is much more than simply an evil influence, like Lady Macbeth; yet the play does not finally refute Rome's conviction that she has ruined his life.[48]

The spectacle of Antony's death combines, more than it does in the source, tragic pathos and almost comic inappropriateness. Plutarch describes the scene of the dying Roman, hoisted up by three women to the window of the monument by chains and ropes, as a most touching climax: 'They that were present to behold it, said they never saw so pitiefull a sight' (Bullough, v, 309). Shakespeare's version is rather more ambiguous because Cleopatra's comment provokingly reminds the audience of the less heroic aspects of the situation:

> Here's sport indeed! How heavy weighs my lord!
> Our strength is all gone into heaviness,
> That makes the weight.   (IV.15.32–4)

The rhetorical wordplay does not necessarily undermine the tragic pathos. Elizabethan dramatists are often much freer in this respect than later readers have always been able to recognize. Yet the theatrical apparatus brings out the puzzling ambivalence of Antony's death. Since he has been clearly and deliberately deceived by Cleopatra, it is difficult to justify his suicide as a case of 'Liebestod' and his dying speech hardly makes any more mention of his union with the beloved. He tries to comfort her and he is concerned about her future, but he does not reaffirm his love with any particular emphasis and he views his own death above all as a means of restoring his Roman honor and reputation. Like Othello, he wants to leave a memory that preserves his greatness before his tragic fall. Not as a lover, but as an unvanquished Roman, as 'the greatest prince o'th'world,/The noblest' (IV.15.54–5) does he want to be remembered. Cleopatra's last words to him are an acknowledgement of this image of himself, 'Noblest of men' (IV.15.59) and of his claim to have been the greatest of soldiers:

> O, withered is the garland of the war,
> The soldier's pole is fall'n; young boys and girls
> Are level now with men. The odds is gone,
> And there is nothing left remarkable
> Beneath the visiting moon.   (IV.15.64–8)

Her praise of the dead implies that she does not contradict the public opinion which sees Antony's love as an unnatural aberration from his true self. His death restores, though not without qualification, his heroic dignity and stature whose loss was deplored in the very first scene of the tragedy, but it is not celebrated as a final affirmation of his love, as are the deaths of Romeo and Othello who both die with a kiss.[49]

This form of love-death is, in Shakespeare's last love tragedy, reserved for Cleopatra whose suicide is the centre of the final act and makes use of a number of traditional motifs absent from Antony's death. The separation of the two death scenes was already a feature of Shakespeare's source as well as of previous dramatic versions. It enabled him to present side by side the Roman's heroic suicide and the romantic pathos of the lovers in death. Antony's tragedy as the triumvir who throws away a whole empire, and the complaint of the bereaved lover, a favorite literary theme in the English Renaissance,[50] are the subject of two separate acts, and this may well be one of the reasons for the play's complex effect.

Cleopatra's lament for Antony is a powerful expression of her determination to become worthy of his Roman greatness. Whereas, near the beginning of the play, she referred rather slightingly to his 'Roman thought' (1.2.84), she now explicitly adopts his own values and strives to emulate him:

> We'll bury him; and then, what's brave, what's noble,
> Let's do't after the high Roman fashion,
> And make death proud to take us.   (IV.15.85–7)

In her death, at least, she wants to prove that her love is compatible with Roman nobleness.

The last act of the tragedy is mainly concerned with the working out of this heroic endeavor and with the battle of wits between Cleopatra and Octavius. They are the two survivors and representatives of the two worlds between whom Antony was finally crushed. During the whole of this last part, his spirit is as present as was the spirit of Caesar in the second half of *Julius Caesar* and though there is no doubt of his political defeat, it is his reputation and his memory that are at stake and they are closely linked with the fate of Cleopatra. Her death is meant to demonstrate to all the world that Antony's love which cost him his share in the domination of the world, was not, as it was presented in Rome, a shameful infatuation and dotage, 'To cool a gypsy's lust' (I.I.I0), but the mutual union of two exceptional individuals who cannot live without each other. Cleopatra's public humiliation by a triumph through the streets of Rome would also destroy Antony's reputation. Only by her deliberately 'Roman' death is she able to make Caesar acknowledge the lovers' greatness and indeed Cleopatra's equal rank as a worthy lover by a monument in their honor. As lovers they will be remembered and form part of Rome's history, but the funeral, with all military rites and honors, also pays tribute to Antony's greatness as statesman and general. Though victorious, Octavius Caesar concedes equal greatness to those whose ruin he brought about:

> No grave upon the earth shall clip in it
> A pair so famous. High events as these
> Strike those that make them; and their story is
> No less in pity than his glory which
> Brought them to be lamented. (V.2.357–61)

Antony's death is thus invested with a dignity it at first seemed to lack, and this undoubtedly contributes to the impression, shared by many spectators and critics, that Cleopatra's death is a kind of triumph rather than a tragic loss. This seems to me possible only because from the very beginning Cleopatra's fate is so closely linked to the personality of Antony that, as an independent dramatic character, she plays only a minor part and is not a tragic protagonist in the same sense as he is. There is no scene, before the pathetic last act, that shows her in a moral dilemma or any serious internal conflict. Her infinite variety, which has become something of a critical cliché, manifests itself chiefly in her changeable effect on Antony and does not mean that the dramatist wants to interest the spectator in the mind of a particularly complex character, as in the case of Hamlet or Macbeth. Nor is the fact that Antony's death inspires her to heroic greatness presented as a problem of character, an inner development to be explained in terms of human pyschology, but rather as a confirmation of Antony's exceptional stature and of the permanence of their union. If there is a certain abruptness in Cleopatra's transformation from fatal seductress to dedicated loving wife it is quite compatible with the dramatic structure and does not need any realistic justification. In any case, a good production will make us forget that there are possible inconsistencies in the text. Like many other 'character problems' in Shakespeare, Cleopatra's many-sided utterances and actions are suggestions for the actor and producer, and they cease to puzzle once they are creatively interpreted by the performing artist.[51]

The significance of Cleopatra's death for Antony's glorious memory is surely more important than the outwitting of Octavius achieved at the same time. The reaction of some critics to her suicide seems to me to be dictated by intense dislike for Octavius and satisfaction at his defeat more than the text warrants. Bradley is surprisingly explicit on this point and, as in many other cases, his interpretation is silently accepted by many later critics. He talks of the reader's 'exultation at the thought that she has foiled Octavius', and he repeats the same idea in a different study: 'And when Cleopatra by her death cheats the conqueror of his prize, we feel unmixed delight'.[52] This somewhat superficial sentiment may be taken as proof that Cleopatra's personal fate does not affect the reader very deeply, but I do not think that it is an adequate reaction to the last act of the tragedy. Unqualified admiration for Cleopatra's theatrical suicide and contemptuous antipathy for Octavius are rather too shallow and simple responses to this brilliant finale.

Thus the dramatist deliberately leaves the ultimate reasons for Cleopatra's decisive step rather vague. It is clear that she wants to prove worthy of Antony, but her diplomatic bartering with Octavius does not quite remove our suspicion that under different conditions she might have lived on and that it is only her clear conviction of Octavius' own treacherous intentions which makes her take the final step. There is an element of tactical cunning as well as the determination to 'Be noble to myself' (v.2.192) in her behavior, a dignity that inspires respect combined with theatrical rhetoric not quite justified by the actual events, as in the idealizing portrait of Antony she presents to Dolabella (v.2.76–100). It hardly agrees with the Antony the play has shown and strikes the spectator as a bravura act of self-justification, but also as the triumphant vindication of a love that is no more dependent on physical communion.[53] Love, as the dying Cleopatra understands it, is equality of nobleness and courage, not sensual infatuation or bondage:

>   – methinks I hear
> Antony call. I see him rouse himself
> To praise my noble act. I hear him mock
> The luck of Caesar, which the gods give men
> To excuse their after wrath. Husband, I come.
> Now to that name my courage prove my title!   (v.2.282–7)

By joining her husband in death, she vouches for the reality and truth of what at first seemed a purely rhetorical gesture:

> The nobleness of life
> Is to do thus – when such a mutual pair
> And such a twain can do't, ...   (1.1.36–8)

In this sense, one can certainly agree with Kenneth Muir's summary of the plays' impact: 'All Cleopatra's speeches in this final scene suggest to most members of most audiences that she is becoming worthy of her lover'.[54] The cautious wording, however, puts the emphasis rightly on the affective aspect of the scene and the essentially emotional effect of the rhetoric.

All this does not mean that the play simply endorses the protagonists' view and makes us forget the more problematic side of their love. Cleopatra's scorn for 'The luck of Caesar' and the calculated pragmatism of the victor who seems to be completely unsusceptible to her charms, have had the effect that in some interpretations it is he who emerges as the real loser. But an impressive death does not necessarily sanction every weakness and folly of the lovers in retrospect. To interpret Antony's defeat as a deliberately chosen alternative to a glorious military career, a considered decision in favor of love as the higher value, would be mistaken anachronism. The play does not suggest that a happy fulfilment of this love, a conventional marriage and a political settlement to accommodate the lovers, would have been a possibility, as it certainly is in *Romeo and Juliet* and even in *Othello*. Nor is Antony's love, like Romeo's, seen as an element of reconciliation and peace in the midst of a loveless society.

The difficulties of interpretation are partly due to the common tendency to confuse poetic intensity and moral approval.[55] L. C. Knights has tried to stress this distinction, although he seems to me to put rather more emphasis on the negative aspects of Antony's love than the text does:

It is, of course, one of the signs of a great writer that he can afford to evoke sympathy or even admiration for what, in his final judgement, is discarded or condemned. In *Antony and Cleopatra* the sense of potentiality in life's untutored energies is pushed to its limit, and Shakespeare gives the maximum weight to an experience that is finally 'placed'.[56]

Ernst Schanzer's comment on this passage illustrates how easily such kind of arguing can turn into subjetive impressionism:

So definite, so unequivocal a response does not seem to me to emerge. Shakespeare does not prevent those who wish to do so from applying to this play the subtitle of Dryden's adaptation, 'The World Well Lost'.[57]

Here, it seems, one is merely arguing about individual reactions, and the history of the play's reception shows that Shakespeare has indeed not prevented such a reading. I am still convinced, however, that it is against the intention of the text which decidedly does not adopt the lovers' point of view without serious qualification, nor is Dryden's title even an approximate description of Shakespeare's tragedy. There is also no real justification for treating Octavius Caesar who is favored by fortune and by his historical mission, as loser or as an inconsiderable personality as Bradley and many critics after him have done.[58] On the whole, Shakespeare has made him a more positive figure than he is in Plutarch even though he is, in keeping with the play's subject, presented with less dramatic intensity than the lovers. Octavius' lament for Antony, though it is partly a conventional tribute to the dead, confirms that the conflict was not so much a matter of personal enmity as of historical necessity. There is no triumphant satisfaction at the death of a political opponent or a hated rival, but only sorrow over the tragic inevitability of their clash and generous acknowledgement of the adversary's greatness:

> let me lament
> With tears as sovereign as the blood of hearts
> That thou, my brother, my competitor
> In top of all design, my mate in empire,
> Friend and companion in the front of war,
> The arm of mine own body, and the heart
> Where mine his thoughts did kindle – that our stars,
> Unreconciliable, should divide
> Our equalness to this. (v.1.40–8)

Many members of Shakespeare's audience would also have known that Octavius' victory marked the beginnings of a peaceful reign that to later generations seemed a golden age. In this sense, Caesar's announcement, 'The time of universal peace is near' (iv.6.5) has a clearly prophetic ring, hinting at the 'Augustan' age, a time that was also traditionally associated with the birth of Christ.[59] Politically, there is, at any rate, much more ground for hopeful optimism at the end of this tragedy than there is at the conclusion of *Hamlet, King Lear,* or *Julius Caesar,* much more even than at the end of *Henry V,* for all its patriotic enthusiasm and cheer. There is no other tragedy by Shakespeare in which the last word is given to a ruler who is so universally known to have started on a peaceful and prosperous reign. *Macbeth* is, perhaps, most like *Antony and Cleopatra* in this respect.

The historical context qualifies to a certain extent our impression of Cleopatra's heroic death and casts doubt on any interpretation in terms of 'The World Well Lost'. Even to the last, Cleopatra's greatness is seen above all in her seductive charms. The comic dialogue with the 'Clown' who provides the poisonous 'worm of Nilus' (v.2.) reminds the audience in no uncertain terms of the traditional analogy between death and sexual satisfaction, and Caesar's description of her dead body also refers to her chief role as temptress and snare:

> she looks like sleep,
> As she would catch another Antony
> In her strong toil of grace.   (v.2.344–6)

The play ends neither with a moral quintessence nor with an apotheosis of unbounded love and in this sense one can only agree with Ernst Schanzer who insists on the open ending of the tragedy.[60] But this does not make it a problem play because there is no deliberate confusion of moral standards or a juxtaposition of equally valid moral positions. The dramatist simply does not choose to present this, the most famous of all political love stories as a moral exemplum or to make the final evaluation of the characters his chief interest. The colorful circumstances and the emotional intensity of their love is, for him, more fascinating than the awarding of praise and blame, even though the history of the play's reception suggests that it was this very absence of authorial evaluation that has provoked many readers and spectators to take sides. This can, however, easily detract from the poetical vitality of the characterization and the surprising diversity of love experience presented here which makes the play so different from Shakespeare's other love tragedies. In *Romeo and Juliet* as well as in *Othello*, love and marriage are more clearly and predictably defined, whereas in *Troilus and Cressida* there is a noticeable absence of that mutual affection which is necessary for love's fulfilment. It is only in *Antony and Cleopatra* that the ennobling and the destructive potentialities of love are so inextricably linked; Cleopatra combines the characteristic qualities of Juliet and Cressida, of the ideal beloved and the humiliating seductress. This is also reflected in her particularly rich and suggestive language which is as far removed from Plutarch's measured prose as it is from the stylized blank verse of the neoclassical Cleopatra-tragedies or the comparatively monotonous rhythms of Dryden's adaptation. Its title alone is a revealing indication of its much simpler presentation of love, and the concluding couplet makes its distance from Shakespeare's infinitely more challenging version clear enough:

> Sleep, blest pair,
> Secure from human chance, long ages out,
> While all the storms of fate fly o'er your tomb;
> And fame to late posterity shall tell,
> No lovers lived so great, or died so well.[61]

Most spectators would probably agree that their final impression of *Antony and Cleopatra* could hardly be couched in such neat terms.

By reason of its unusual structure and its ambivalent effect, *Antony and Cleopatra* is not easily compared with Shakespeare's other tragedies although there are, of course, a number of important parallels. The play's first half contains rather fewer hints of the final catastrophe and less genuinely tragic conflict than most of his other tragedies. Antony's moral and political dilemma is more implied in the dramatic structure than realized in the intensity of characterization, and the end is tragic chiefly in a formal sense: by the death of the protagonists, not so much by the experience of heroic defeat, irreparable loss or tormenting disillusionment. Neither the dynamic nature of evil nor the destructive power of uncontrolled passion are central themes of this tragedy, and this is only partly due to the story material, which combines in a particularly provocative manner love romance with a context of historic dimensions without reducing them to an individual dilemma and a clear-cut moral decision. The conflicting loyalties are too unequal to sustain the impression of a tragic impasse and the comic or satiric perspective that suggests itself with regard to the love-plot is emphasized by Shakespeare rather than suppressed. The nagging question whether this love is really worth the existential price paid for it, remains open right to the end. Antony's heroic stature is asserted by the play in distinctly less unequivocal terms even than that of Macbeth. Nor is the lovers' freely chosen death presented simply as the last and final proof of mutual affection, as in the case of *Romeo and Juliet,* or a pathetic, exemplary 'fall', as in many other Elizabethan tragedies, but leaves an ambiguous effect, even though it may satisfy the audience's desire for poetic justice. Critics have repeatedly made use of the term 'reconciliation' in this context.[62] What they mean is that each of the main actors finally accepts the role they have chosen for themselves and its accompanying fate. No other ending seems possible as a convincing or even desirable alternative. No serious crime has to be expiated; murder, intrigue and deceit, which for many Elizabethan playwrights seem to have been the indispensable hallmarks of tragedy, play a comparatively insignificant part here, less prominent, for instance, than in' *Romeo and Juliet.* This also argues against a particularly significant thematic relationship between *Antony and Cleopatra* and Shakespeare's romances, such as has occasionally been suggested, because in those later plays, the nature of evil and human corruptibility is examined with far greater intensity.

The play's unusual structure and its ambivalent ending do not, however, seriously affect its place among Shakespeare's tragedies, which probably none of his contemporaries would have questioned, but they make any too narrow definition of what we consider to be the essence of Shakespearian tragedy rather problematic. There were, to be sure, a number of traditional criteria of form and content, such as the protagonist's death, a vaguely historical or mythical background, and social rank of the chief characters, as well as some loosely defined sub-types, like revenge tragedy or tragedy of love. Apart from that, Shakespeare evidently felt free to make a tragedy out of any episode from chronicle, historical biography, or novella-collection that appealed to him, without feeling obliged to adapt it pedantically to any fixed formula. *Antony and Cleopatra* gives an astonishingly faithful impression of the fascinating variety and the forceful realism of Plutarch's account, enriched by exuberant poetry and complexity of characterization; yet there is no consistent effort to make these anecdotic scenes conform to any strict rules of tragedy. Plutarch obviously was particularly interested in the inextricable tangle of historical crises and unpredictable personalities, and these intriguing contrasts are brought out even more sharply in Shakespeare's dramatization, whereas they get largely lost in those neoclassical tragedies that attempt to remodel Antony and Cleopatra according to the precepts of conventional tragic practice. No other more orthodox or more definitely tragical adaptation has succeeded in giving to this famous pair the same memorable vitality and radiance, while at the same time sticking so closely to Plutarch's historical narrative.

CORIOLANUS

Coriolanus is the third of Shakespeare's tragedies based on one of Plutarch's biographies, and again the dramatist has kept quite close to the outline of the story as he found it in his source. In contrast to Brutus, Caesar, Cleopatra and Antony, Coriolanus had, as far as we know, never been the subject of a tragedy before, and his career was generally much less widely familiar than that of other prominent Romans, so that Shakespeare was not at all bound to take any traditional images of his protagonist and the other chief actors into account and was able to adapt his material as freely as he wished, without any constricting precedent. The way he translated Plutarch's very consistent and at the same time complex character study into the scenic form of a tragedy is a particularly impressive instance of creative adaptation and dramaturgic virtuosity. This applies to his departures from the source, but no less to those many passages where he follows Plutarch with astonishing fidelity. These parallels, often practically literal quotations, suggest that he must have had an open volume of the biographies in front of him while composing his tragedy.[63]

There are several places where the action is tightened up and events which are far apart in Plutarch's narrative are brought into a causal connection, as, for example, the people's uprising, the siege and conquest of Corioles, the election of Caius Martius as consul, and his banishment. The parts of some characters who in Plutarch make only one or two isolated appearances, are extended to give them coherent roles as commentators or contrasting figures, such as Menenius, Volumnia and Aufidius, whose function in the play is much more important than in the source. Thus, the hero is placed in a context of human relationships and different perspectives that is crucial for the audience's impression of him, whereas the details of the political situation, Roman constitution and the tactical maneuvers between rivalling factions are pushed into the background.

Coriolanus is a legendary figure from the early beginnings of the Roman republic (about the beginning of the fifth century BC), and Plutarch dwells with evident interest on the technicalities of ballots and voting, the constitutional role of the tribunes of the people, and the tug of war between patricians and plebeians. Shakespeare reduces the political issue to the basic constrast between the people in need of responsible leadership and the class traditionally used to leading them, a contrast that also plays a major part in the source. Moreover, he places Coriolanus much more firmly in the centre of the action. His attitude towards the community he lives in, and his final defeat are the real subject of the tragedy.

Yet Rome is far more than merely a historical backdrop. It seems to have been the dramatist's intention, even more consistently than in *Julius Caesar* or *Antony and Cleopatra*, to reproduce the world of ancient Rome as the Elizabethans saw it, with its remote and unfamiliar yet impressive value standards, as faithfully as possible, and it has often been noticed that of all the tragedies based on Plutarch this is the most distinctly 'Roman', without, however, any of Ben Jonson's antiquarian and bookish patina[64] and without disguising possible associations with problems of the present. Coriolanus was written at a time (between 1605 and 1610) when the claims of the Commons for a greater share of political influence and power were becoming more articulate and had to be taken more seriously than in the time of Queen Elizabeth. It is possible that the 'Elizabethan compromise' has sometimes been idealized after the event, but at least it seems to have produced a situation of comparable stability and social equilibrium. It soon came to an end, however, after the accession of James I (1603), and there were unmistakable signs of social unrest, heralding later troubles.[65] There is no doubt that these developments gave a certain topicality to Shakespeare's tragedy which one should not, however, take too literally or make the chief basis of an interpretation, because it hardly affects the characterization of the main actors and seems of rather minor importance for the central conflict between the hero and his political environment, though it is very difficult for us today to assess the influence such topical allusions may have had on the reaction of a contemporary audience.

The close thematic affinity between *Coriolanus* and the tragedies written at about the same time, *Antony and Cleopatra* and *Timon of Athens,* has often been commented on. All three heroes fail to establish a workable relationship with the society they could so greatly benefit by their exceptional gifts, but whose demands, requiring some measure of compromise, adaptation and self-restraint, they refuse to accept. Their defeat and eventual destruction is not a consequence of criminal actions or the fatal perversion of potentially noble characters, as in the case of Othello and Macbeth, but rather the inevitable result of a particular constellation of incompatible principles and tempers. Coriolanus' personality, like that of Antony and Timon, is modelled by the dramatist in such a way that any lasting reconciliation with the expectations of society appears to be impossible; yet neither side is entirely at fault. This also affects the dramatic balance of the play. On the one hand, Coriolanus holds the centre of the stage more exclusively than earlier protagonists; there is no subplot and no other prominent character to deflect our attention from the hero. On the other hand, there is a significant change of perspective to the effect that the world of the play is only partly presented from Coriolanus' point of view. Of all Shakespeare's tragic protagonists he is characterized in the least straightforward manner. Dramatic suspense is created by controversial views about him and by his exceptional presence, not by any direct insight into his personal reactions or a sense of spiritual dilemma. There is hardly a soliloquy to give us any unfiltered self-revelation, and the audience has to direct its sympathies according to the contradictory opinions of observers, friends and enemies, and the unpredictable behavior of Coriolanus himself, as well as his powerful impact on the fate of the community. Nor are there any patently reliable 'choric' figures in whose judgement we can trust.

The play's exposition is in many ways reminiscent of *Antony and Cleopatra,* because it is from rather peripheral characters that we receive our first impression of the hero, and a most unflattering one at that, before he himself makes his appearance. In this instance, however, the introductory part of the scene is much longer and Coriolanus' entry less impressive, so that this first negative view is not at once corrected.

The very first lines establish the sharp and fundamental contrast between the hero and the citizens of Rome. The plebeians are presented as men with far more political insight and genuine willingness to cooperate with the powers that be than the undisciplined and emotional mob in *Julius Caesar,* and this makes their resentment against Coriolanus as 'chief enemy to the people' (1.1.6–7) more poignant. As in Plutarch, the people's rebellion is not an anarchic resistance against any form of hierarchical order, but rather a desperate act of protest against flagrant misuse of power. Shakespeare has compressed a long and complicated conflict into one dramatic scene and he has concentrated the citizens' wrath on the unjust distribution of corn supplies, whereas Plutarch mentions a number of other grievances, like the war and the effects of usury. Plutarch's citizens arrange a peaceful exodus from the city and it is only the eloquence of Menenius, sent after them by the patricians, that can persuade them to return to Rome. He concludes his speech with the fable of the belly (cf. Bullough, v, 510).

Shakespeare's Roman citizens have been judged very differently by critics, depending on whether the play was felt to be basically anti-democratic or more critical of the patricians. The fact that the dramatist turned the ordered departure from the city into a street demonstration and threats of murder, can be explained by dramatic reasons. He evidently wanted to introduce the antagonism between Coriolanus and the common people as early as possible, whereas in Plutarch it becomes apparent much later. In Shakespeare's play too, the citizens are by no means intent on blind destruction; what they demand is the stopping of particular abuses. In comparison with earlier crowd scenes in Shake-speare, their tone is remarkably moderate and reasonable. Even though their intention to do away with Coriolanus does not exactly show a great deal of political wisdom, it seems at least clear that they do not wish to act from envy or desire for revenge. Nobody denies that the people are famished and that this is a genuine grievance. The way they are willing to give Menenius a hearing also contributes to the rational and argumenta-tive character of the scene. It is not, so far, a disorderly revolt against the whole state.[66]

The portrait of Coriolanus evoked by these indirect means is from the very first ambivalent. The citizens' hatred makes fairly clear where he stands in the confrontation of the different political factions, and the debate about his services to the country adds some contours to his personality which are crucial for our attitude towards him throughout the play. Nobody denies that he has done much for Rome's glory, but the general suspicion that he only wants to feed his pride and to please his mother draws attention to the close connection between the welfare of the state and the personal disposition of those responsible for it. Coriolanus is not accused of any petty faults (like 'covetousness'), but of a fundamental disregard for the common good in favor of his own ambitious nature, which casts doubt on all his achievements. It is a one-sided picture, yet the basic agreement between the two citizens argues for a certain objectivity, even though, as often in Shakespeare's plays, the observers can only describe outward symptoms and have no real sense of the stature and complexity of an exceptional character. The audience expects an explanation for these controversial views from Coriolanus' personal appearance, yet when he enters the stage after about 160 lines, he does not really provide any satisfactory clues and only makes the clash more evident. In contrast to Menenius and the citizens, he is not even prepared to enter into any reasoned dialogue with the people, but breaks out into a vituperative tirade that, at this point in the play, is not justified by anything that has gone before and reveals an implacable hostility and high-handed contempt which seems directed not only against the plebeians themselves, but against the Senate and anyone who is prepared to listen to the grievances or to make concessions. The well-founded complaints of the people are for him only proof of their unreasonableness, although, even in his scathing account, they do not sound entirely senseless and negligible:

> They are dissolv'd. Hang 'em!
> They said they were an-hungry, sigh'd forth proverbs –
> That hunger broke stone walls; that dogs must eat;
> That meat was made for mouths; that the gods sent not
> Corn for the rich men only. (I.I.203–7)

Even considering the contemporary background of threatening popular unrest, one can hardly describe this as an expression of political wisdom or nobility of character, but only as evidence of a complete incapacity for rational discourse and lack of prudent self-restraint. His radical opposition to the institution of tribunes of the people – in Plutarch it is the considered opinion of a whole group of senators – is a distinctly anti-popular move, and his grim satisfaction at the news of the Volscian attack is, in this situation, another sign of personal ambition and spite. Foreign war is a welcome means of enlarging his personal reputation and of suppressing popular unrest. That the actual defence of the community against an enemy invader is not a major concern for him becomes clear enough from his cynical remarks about the role of the common people in the war:

> I am glad on't; then we shall ha' means to vent
> Our musty superfluity. (I.I.224–5)

There is the same nasty cruelty in his scornful comparison of the people with rats who are to feed on the enemy's corn stores:

> The Volsces have much corn: take these rats thither,
> To gnaw their garners. (I.I.248–9)

Like Othello, Caius Martius is called in by the leaders of the state as the chief support against a frightening enemy, and thus, for the time being, saved from a personal predicament. Yet, in contrast to Othello, his standing as a military hero is flawed from the start by his antagonizing arrogance, and the respect paid to him by his fellow-citizens is largely confined to his practical usefulness. There is also in Coriolanus' Rome an even closer identity of personal and collective fate than there is in the Venice of *Othello*. Anything like a truly private life seems to be out of the question for a public character like Caius Martius.

After his first appearance, the audience will hardly feel that the two tribunes' analysis of the situation is particularly malicious, even though we are by no means convinced that it is disinterested care for the people that makes them so clear-sighted. The structure of the scene gives emphasis to their position as Coriolanus' most dangerous opponents. They remain alone on stage when the hero and the people have left, to comment on the action. They put into words what the citizens seem to have known instinctively from the beginning of the scene. It is nothing but private ambition and an exaggerated sense of his own worth that directs his actions, not genuine patriotism, and this applies to all his political maneuverings against any plebeian influence in the government of Rome. The impression of personal egotism and petty rivalry is underlined in the play by the early introduction of Aufidius (1.2) who is mentioned by Plutarch at a much later stage. He too appears to be convinced of his superior worth and he recognizes in Caius Martius the chief threat to his own glory.

Shakespeare follows Plutarch's conception of his hero quite closely during the exposition of his tragedy. Plutarch begins his biography with a most poignant character sketch in which he lists a number of traits the dramatist has taken up and enlarged on. It is easy to see that here is the raw material for some of the play's most characteristic effects:

For this Martius naturall wit and great harte dyd marvelously sturre up his corage, to doe and attempt noble actes. But on the other side for lacke of education, he was so chollericke and impacient, that he would yeld to no living creature: which made him churlishe, uncivill, and althogether unfit for any mans conversation.

(Bullough, v, 506)

This inability to communicate and to form civilized human relationships is seen by Plutarch as the result of inadequate education and the all-powerful influence of the mother, and Shakespeare has clearly followed his lead.

Another aspect introduced by Plutarch is the Roman idea of virtue. He explains that in ancient Rome, virtue and military prowess were considered to be the same thing, and this historical footnote may well have influenced Shakespeare's portrait of his hero for whom military exploits seem to be the chief goal of his ambition:

Now in those dayes, valliantnes was honoured in Rome above all other vertues: which they called *Virtus*, by the name of vertue selfe, as including in that generall name, all other speciall vertues besides. So that *Virtus* in the Latin, was asmuche as valliantnes.
(Bullough,v,506)

This partly explains Coriolanus' high reputation and also his marked contempt for the people who, as he claims not without some reason, lack this very virtue. The charge of cowardice traditionally brought against the plebeians, marks, in the context of Roman ethics, one of the chief differences between the common citizen and the patricians. The contrast is even emphasized by Shakespeare who certainly does not balance the hero's repulsive arrogance by any idealization of the people.[67]

The famous fable of the belly told by Menenius might, at a first glance, be read as an authorial description of an ideally ordered common-wealth. The context of the scene, however, makes quite obvious that it is at the same time a piece of skilful political manipulation. The analogy between the rebellious members of the body and the hungry people holds good only on a very superficial level. Shakespeare has altered the circumstances in such a way that the citizens are really confronted with famine so that the cynicism of Menenius' soothing talk becomes all the more apparent. The people who think of him as of a friend, are actually cheated and their leader is, by a neat rhetorical trick, exposed to their laughter. Their real grievances are barely discussed, and the ideal picture of a community, where all the parts work peacefully for each other and for the common good, is descredited by the speaker himself and later by the whole Senate. Menenius' answer to Caius Martius reveals his attitude towards the plebeians and towards his own pacifying mission clearly enough:

> Nay, these are almost thoroughly persuaded;
> For though abundantly they lack discretion,
> Yet are they passing cowardly. (1.1.200–2)

Thus, the whole of the first scene provides an instance of a body politic where it is precisely this natural cooperation of all the different members that is lacking, and each group only has an eye to its own advantage. The war against the Volscians can momentarily detract from these domestic troubles and bring about a short-lived unity,[68] but the subdued exit of the citizens (*Citizens steal away* (1.1.250)), and Coriolanus' mockery ('Worshipful mutiners,/Your valour puts well forth' (1.1.249–50)) illustrate the distance between the idealizing fable and reality.

184

The first section of the play describes Caius Martius' rise as a popular war hero whose name of honor is meant to immortalize his daring exploit.[69] The one-sided glorification of personal valor and military achievement is made more prominent in the play than in Plutarch's narrative; the dramatist has deliberately intensified Coriolanus' reckless bravado, his contempt of the cowardly plebeians, and the lonely courage that sets him apart from the rest of the community.

The family scene (1.3) does not really advance the plot and has no precedent in the source. It is probably based on Plutarch's statement that Coriolanus married in accordance with his mother's wish, but never left her house. His extraordinary dependence on her is not presented by a scene of actual bullying, but made plausible as a formative influence and revealed in its rather narrow and limiting effect. The striking affinity of what claims to be a mother's natural love for her son with a kind of possessive and greedy ambition on his behalf, and the reduction of manly virtue to the qualities of a butcher add some more contours to our impression of the absent hero and hardly place him in a more favorable light. There is, perhaps, no other Shakespearian tragedy in which the hero remains a comparatively shadowy figure for so long and is characterized in such an oblique way. The whole family scene is almost exclusively concerned with him. The enthusiastic reports of his mother and of Valeria are contrasted with the quiet anxiety of his wife, whose natural aversion against blood and her husband's absence is decried as weak-minded denial of Roman virtues, but at the same time shows up their questionable and inhuman quality. The euphoric description of the little son, venting his anger on a butterfly and presented as the hopeful image of his father, once more underlines the impression of naive hero-worship and most superficial heroic ideals.

The actual battle scenes, too, show more of a childish display of muscle and a primitive eagerness to outdo the opponent than a genuine desire to serve the common cause. The first we hear from Coriolanus is violent abuse of his less warlike troops, followed by his rash single entry into the beleaguered city: it turns out to become his greatest personal triumph, but still exhibits rather more reckless daring and senseless bravado than military discretion. The soldiers watching him are at first little impressed and do not mean to be drawn into any dangerous adventure:

FIRST SOL. Foolhardiness! not I.
SECOND SOL. Nor I.
FIRST SOL. See, they have shut him in.
ALL. To th'pot, I warrant him.   (1.4.46–7)

The dramatist does not suggest, however, that Coriolanus is merely play-acting. In the end, he not only wins the soldiers' admiration, which is of doubtful value, but also appears much superior to all those for whom the whole campaign is only an opportunity for looting because he is not in the least interested in personal gain. His somewhat ostentatious aversion against any public recognition of his achievements reveals very clearly that it is not petty vanity that drives him on, and that he knows the difference between flattery and sincere praise. Of course, this kind of declamatory modesty is also an aspect of his pride; it is not that he wants to slip quietly out of the limelight, but he resents rhetorical eulogies that add very little to his personal triumph and let others participate in it. He is not prepared to share even the smallest part of his glory with anybody else. At the same time it must be remembered that Coriolanus' excessive prowess is only an extreme form of that Roman *virtus* which, Plutarch tells us, was identified with valor. In a way, then, Coriolanus personifies an ideal of Roman ethics which, as the sequel will show, can become a genuine threat to the state if it is not tempered with prudence and consideration of others. Comenius, the Roman general, is full of admiration for Coriolanus, yet his own strategy is more cautious:

> Breathe you, my friends; well fought; we are come off
> Like Romans, neither foolish in our stands
> Nor cowardly in retire. (1.6.1–3)

As far as outward success is concerned, however, Coriolanus' reckless impetuosity has paid off; again and again, his outstanding courage is praised, inspiring others, yet at the same time lonely and strange:

> he is himself alone,
> To answer all the city. (1.4.51–2)[70]

The contrasting figure of Aufidius, who is introduced by Plutarch only after Coriolanus' banishment, here obviously serves as a foil to show up the hero's superiority. They are united by their mutual hatred, by the inconclusive duel and self-centred rivalry, but Aufidius' reaction to the Roman triumph makes him appear as the weaker of the two, inferior in moral integrity and heroic stature. In future he will not scruple to use any means of destroying the enemy whom he cannot overcome by honest fighting (1.10). Again, Coriolanus, though absent, is really the centre of the whole scene, and in this instance it is to him that our sympathies are directed.

The long scene that follows (11.1) is another example of the predominance of indirect characterization; more than half of it is over before Coriolanus enters the stage, and he soon leaves it again so that the last third, too, consists almost entirely of various comments about the absent hero. His impact on the community is presented with more dramatic intensity and variety than the character itself.

In the first part of the scene, there is a rather striking relaxation of tone and a surprising element of comedy. Menenius appears in the role of a humorous old man, enjoying the freedom of a clown and telling the tribunes to their faces how much he dislikes them, without being able to refute their charges against Coriolanus. The prose dialogue contrasts effectively with the lively battle scenes and the pompous rhetoric of the military leaders. The noisy activity of the war is followed by petty argument at home, the sign of a deeply divided community. Menenius takes Coriolanus' part, of course, but his defence is hardly convincing enough to revise all the less favorable impressions on the part of the reader and spectator. The conversation between Menenius and the two ladies, Volumnia and Virgilia, also remains on the level of good-humored banter, which makes the cheerful listing of Coriolanus' wounds appear in a somewhat ambiguous light and also casts some doubt on his heroic achievements. A reputation that is measured by the number of gashes received is not an unqualified value, even in the Roman context of this play, and the glaring one-sidedness of Volumnia's pride in her son is presented even more critically here than in the first family scene. For her, he is still 'my boy' and 'my good soldier' (II.1.99,170). Again, Virgilia provides mainly a kind of mute commentary: her horror at Coriolanus' wounds and her tears for his absence introduce an element of simple human emotion in the midst of public and rather impersonal hero-worship, such as it appears with particular clarity in the hostile account of the tribunes and the messenger's report (II.1.203–66).

The brief appearance of the celebrated hero himself does not contribute much to a more detailed characterization, but confirms the impression that the play is more concerned with his fame and with the fact of his astonishing career than with his personality as such. Volumnia feels herself and her family honored in him, while the tribunes only discuss him as a political factor and a threat to their own position. Their role as antagonists and intriguers is made once more very obvious by the way they conclude the big scene, as they concluded the first scene of the tragedy. They are not, however, as Menenius suggests, merely self-satisfied and envious spectators, unable to join in the general enthusiasm. They foresee, with an apprehension not entirely unjustified, that the concessions to the people might be retracted and even their own office come to an end. The text does not really support their claim that it is only the welfare of the people they have in mind, but it would be just as wrong to see them as the real villains of the tragedy who are jealous of the hero's greatness and destroy him by their intrigues. Their unemotional, calculating tactics, relying on Coriolanus' specific weaknesses, illustrate the more unattractive aspects of the political game; yet their assessment of the situation is confirmed by the following events and their fight for their own interests is no more unscrupulous than that of the patricians.[71] What makes them so unsympathetic to many readers and spectators is their inability to recognize and to respect Coriolanus' heroic stature. The hero's exceptional courage and its inspiring impact on a society still very much occupied with finding its own identity and its political status, is time and again confronted with the realistic demands of political manipulation and material success. The initial situation is thus as ambivalent as it is in *Antony and Cleopatra*: the bold individualism of the protagonist makes the coldly political maneuvering of his opponents in comparison appear uninspired and somewhat inhuman, yet it is also clear that he only strives to realize his own personality and has very little sense of public responsibility. The conflicting views are juxtaposed, if anything, even more harshly than in *Antony and Cleopatra*, and they are, in human terms, even less attractive. There is nothing that corresponds to the glamor of Egypt, to Cleopatra's infinite variety, or to Octavius Caesar's world empire. Politics and power struggle, not passion and inspiring heroism, are the play's chief concern.

The scene of Coriolanus' proclamation as consul again begins with a dialogue between two detached observers who weigh his achievements against his pride and his egotism (II.2). The dispute ends without any agreement, but it reaffirms our impression of a hero who combines, as in Plutarch, Roman virtue with an antisocial contempt for the people. The same gifts that make him stand out from the average patricians and generals also make him quite incapable of becoming a loyal member of the community and of adapting himself to the demands of the common cause. The dramatist's manipulation of our sympathies effectively prevents us from taking sides for or against the hero with any confident assurance. Even where he is praised with the greatest rhetorical gusto, as in Comenius' elaborate public *laudatio* (II.2.82–122), doubts remain, and they concern his own humanity as well as the Roman ideal of valor in general. The eloquent glorification of the heroic warrior has rightly been placed in the tradition of classical hero-worship, with the splendor of Hercules and Achilles, and there is no doubt that Shakespeare could count on an audience much more receptive to this ideal of military prowess than most audiences today,[72] but the whole speech as well as its context direct our attention to the extreme one-sidedness of this martial demonstration. Coriolanus' path is marked by death and blood, and even the extravagant praise puts the emphasis on the terror he inspires rather than on more admirable qualities:

> his sword, death's stamp,
> Where it did mark, it took; from face to foot

> He was a thing of blood, whose every motion
> Was tim'd with dying cries: alone he enter'd
> The mortal gate of th'city, which he painted
> With shunless destiny, ...   (II.2.107–12)

Such rhetorical excess hardly allows an uncritical identification with the enthusiasm of the speaker. Even patriotic solidarity cannot go so far as to find this manifestation of Roman *virtus* wholly admirable and great. Nor does Coriolanus' contempt for any of the spoils of war in Comenius' emphatic report sound like the disinterested idealism of a true hero, but rather suggests arrogant self-satisfaction: to him, any share in the common gains would be a humiliating act of fraternization with his inferiors:

> Our spoils he kick'd at,
> And look'd upon things precious as they were
> The common muck of the world.   (II.2.124–6)

The squabbles about his election as consul end in the expected clash. Shakespeare has departed from his source at this point and has made the episode follow immediately after the military triumph, which makes Coriolanus' behavior more consistent and more understandable. The heroic virtues that have brought about his spectacular military success by no means qualify him for a political office that, according to the Roman constitution, demands a good deal of diplomatic flexibility and some peaceful arrangement with the people. By trying to evade this and even planning to abolish the office of the tribunes altogether, Coriolanus dissociates himself from the democratic tradition of the Roman republic, opposing it with an idea of personal autonomy that can only lead to conflict. He regards the kind of canvassing expected of him as shameful and theatrical bowing to the mob, as a symbolic abdication of his complete independence in office, and he is, of course, partly right. Yet the tribunes of the people, who again conclude the scene, commenting on the situation and planning their next move, recognize that his reaction betrays some fundamental contempt of the plebeians whose voice Coriolanus was only able to win by deceit and play-acting.

Rarely has Shakespeare translated incompatible convictions and temperaments into stage action with more brilliant effect than in this section of the play. Coriolanus finds himself urged into a way of behaving repugnant to his nature. The citizens are finally not prepared to accept his merely formal compliance with the traditional requirements; they realize that his show of humility is nothing but a tactical move. Plutarch gives a rather more simple account of the whole incident: Coriolanus conforms to the tradition without any particular reluctance and wins the plebeian vote, which he only loses again when he celebrates his triumph in a demonstrative manner. Shakespeare makes Coriolanus' discomfort as evident as his provocative role-playing. The citizens are not in principle disinclined to promise him their voices, but they expect some sign of yielding or at least graciousness on his part as well. Their behavior hardly justifies his insulting arrogance; it is not that they ask for any humiliating submission, but, as one of them explains, 'The price is, to ask it kindly' (11.3.75). This, in fact, puts the finger on one of the key concepts of the play, the idea of a natural, a 'kind' society in which each member has his or her useful function. The citizens do not ask for anything like equality; they freely accept Coriolanus' higher rank, but a republican community, even an oligarchy, cannot function without civilized discourse and mutual respect, which is exactly what Coriolanus does not admit. For him, the citizens are only 'voices' for which he has to beg as if they were alms.

When the tribunes impress this situation on the citizens, who find that they have been taken unawares, it is not so much their personal motives the dramatist tries to elucidate, but the general atmosphere of political manipulation which is in such sharp contrast to Coriolanus' own quite apolitical behavior. Nor is the plebeians' quick change of allegiance presented merely as the instance of the mob's irrational fickleness, as in *Julius Caesar*, but as the result of skilful persuasion. Again, however, the dialogue leaves the audience in some doubt whether it is really just the people's rights the tribunes have in mind, because they, too, appear to treat them like children without independent judgement who can be manipulated as pawns in the power-game. They do not, on the other hand, deliberately incite them to destructive mutiny, and their opposition is, after all, not directed against a statesman from whom domestic peace and responsible leadership can be expected. Yet the calculating way in which they count on Coriolanus' uncontrollable temper to expose him in public also makes him appear as the victim of a malicious stratagem, and the dramatist seems intent on directing some of our sympathy back to him, though he lets himself be provoked into a most imprudent outburst of anger which amply confirms all the plebeians' apprehensions and reveals his implacable hatred of any democratic restrictions of the patrician regime. Once again, it is impossible to draw a line between personal temper and political action. Coriolanus' irritation at the insinuations of the tribunes may be quite justified, but politically he clearly puts himself in the wrong. He reacts to civil unrest as if he were on the battle-field and thus manifestly steps outside the constitutional order of the community. Menenius and the tribunes between them manage to prevent the chaos of a civil war, which Coriolanus in his fury would not have scrupled to unleash. This gesture of heroic wrath links the protagonist with some of the classical demigods and characterizes him as a man who brings misery and defeat upon himself because he is unable to come to any sensible arrangement with the community he is part of. The whole scene is constructed in such a way that a clear evaluation of the characters according to right and wrong would be a gross simplification. Each party acts under a certain compulsion, moved by political interest and individual temper. The patrician's comment, when Coriolanus has left the stage after the first fray, is neither maliciously pleased nor contemptuous:

> This man has marr'd his fortune. (III.I.252)

Whereas Menenius' explanation is rather less unbiased:

> His nature is too noble for the world: (III.I.253)

This raises with particular intensity the question, dramatized also in George Chapman's tragedy *Bussy D'Ambois* (1604), of whether heroic greatness justifies a sovereign contempt for all rules and conventions of civilized society, of whether the exceptional personality has a right to put himself outside the pale of generally accepted moral behavior. But Shakespeare does not seem to be particularly interested in the concept of the 'complete man' in Chapman's sense, but rather in a heroic form of self-respect which is as nearly related to admirable integrity as it is to immoderate pride.[73]

The sense of a genuine moral dilemma is, without any precedent in the source, dramatically heightened by Shakespeare because Coriolanus finds himself beset by conflicting loyalties. The situation does more than just reveal his unyielding arrogance; it touches on some fundamental human and political themes of the play. The hero suddenly discovers that his uncompromising attitude is criticized where he least expected it, namely by his mother who brought him up in a spirit of proud independence and unbounded valor and is now trying to persuade him to make some concessions to the incensed plebeians. Yet the stubbornness of his inflexible pride has already removed him so far from the normal standards of the community that he sees this as a threat not only to his reputation but to his very life. The pleadings of his friends and his mother appear to the spectator only as a most sensible and well-meaning piece of advice, to defuse the precarious situation by some show of flexibility and conciliation, not to throw away every chance of political influence by stubbornly clinging to an all too narrow idea of honor. Yet the whole scene is once more typical of the provoking indefiniteness of the dramatist's manipulation of our sympathies in this tragedy. What at first glance appears to be childish defiance is by the hero himself felt to be the only possible attitude to preserve his moral integrity and self-respect. The dramatic impact of the conflict is not softened by any authorial verdict. Coriolanus' conviction that this is really a matter of moral principles and that the slightest concession would be a shameful betrayal of his own nature, is not shared by his friends or his mother. They only see that it is his political and even his physical survival which is at stake, and all they expect is a minimum of tactical deception and flexibility without which no political career is, in their view, possible. Each of the two incompatible points of view is proposed with full conviction, and there are good reasons on both sides, but, as the tragic event shows, no compromise is possible. Shakespeare presents the conflict in such a way that the spectator can neither write Coriolanus off as an impossibly self-centred individualist nor admire him as a bravely independent idealist, but finds himself divided between respect and incredulous bewilderment. Coriolanus' character seems incompatible with even the most basic form of self-interest.

Volumnia finally succeeds in persuading her son, not by any rational arguments but by using all her personal power over him; her last resource is a denial of kinship and a refusal to admit that valor and pride are the same thing:

> Do as thou list.
> Thy valiantness was mine, thou suck'st it from me,
> But owe thy pride thyself.   (III.2.128–30)

Yet Coriolanus' forced consent is from the start against his own deepest convictions and is never more than an outward gesture of submission. Volumnia has urged her son into a behavior he himself can only despise and in this sense it can indeed be said that she 'has destroyed his integrity'.[74] What could have been a victory of pragmatical sense thus becomes the unwilling suppression of an impulse, though not every spectator is likely to react as confidently as Kenneth Muir suggests: 'The hero's inability to be false to himself and his defiance of his enemies arouse the sympathy and admiration of the audience'.[75] This may be largely true, yet it simplifies Shakespeare's rather less unambiguous text; for not only the assumption that Coriolanus would be 'false to himself' if he reacted in a somewhat more conciliatory manner, but also the simple equation of the tribunes and the plebeians with 'enemies' are a matter of subjective interpretation and are by no means plainly confirmed by the whole play. As the contradictory accounts of the scene by various critics suggest, the audience's reaction is to a large extent dependent on individual temperament and political convictions, quite apart from the fact that the text leaves the actor a fair amount of freedom, and it is quite legitimate for a production to put the emphasis either on the immature stubbornness of the hero or his admirable firmness of character.[76]

The play's further development shows that Coriolanus has not really changed and is unable to keep up the role he has so reluctantly assumed. The rather cynical assessment of his character by the tribunes turns out to be quite correct and they succeed in provoking him to the kind of behavior that perfectly fits into their plans. Brutus lays down the tactics, building on Coriolanus' 'choleric' nature:

> Put him to choler straight; he hath been us'd
> Ever to conquer, and to have his worth
> Of contradiction. Being once chaf'd, he cannot
> Be rein'd again to temperance; then he speaks
> What's in his heart, and that is there which looks
> With us to break his neck.   (III.3.25–30)

The manipulation works according to plan, and the unscrupulous calculation of the tribunes makes Coriolanus appear as the victim of a cunning stratagem and thus deserving some sympathy. It is difficult to say whether one would respect him more if by superior and consistent deception he were to oppose the tactics of the tribunes. Again he allows himself to be provoked by one single word to such an excess of fury that he spoils his political career once and for all.[77] The tribunes find him hardly more difficult to manipulate than the plebeians so much despised by him for their lack of judgement. Here again, Shakespeare has altered Plutarch's sequence of events to produce an effect of sharp contrasts and a depressing sense of inevitable conflict.

The scene of his parting from mother, family and friends (IV.1) gives to Coriolanus a dignity which the play so far has rather denied him, even though the quiet composure with which he accepts his fate still shows something of his usual arrogance and pride. Loneliness, hope and defiance are combined in a suggestive image of solitary strength:

> I go alone,
> Like to a lonely dragon that his fen
> Makes fear'd and talk'd of more than seen ...   (IV.1.29–31)

It is fairly evident for the audience that Coriolanus will not, in the long run, put up with his banishment, but it is quite important for our reaction to what follows that the dramatist at this point seems more anxious than before to secure for him some of our sympathy; he has been unjustly treated and he is lamented by faithful friends.[78] During his absence from the stage, the audience is even more inclined to take his side or at least to preserve a favorable mental picture of him. The tribunes have little to set against the grief and anger of Volumnia (IV.2), and the brief encounter between the Roman defector and the Volscian spy confirms Coriolanus' prophecy that his absence will work in his favor (IV.3). The scene not only provides some important information, it also introduces the theme of betrayal and defection from one's native country.

When Coriolanus finally returns to the stage he is more than outwardly changed. His deeply hurt pride has moved him to do something that would have been completely incompatible with his former integrity. His banishment has made him even more self-reliant and unsociable, and it has not the effect of strengthening old loyalties, but seems to sever all previously sacred ties.[79] Coriolanus feels free to forget all his native obligations to Rome and to ally himself with her deadly enemy. This is where the real 'fall' of the protagonist begins, when he cuts himself off from all natural loyalties, from family, friends, and his native people, and wants to exist as a completely autonomous individual. The suspicion, nourished by the play all along, that he has always put personal ambition and glory before the welfare of Rome, is at last confirmed, and the fact that he seeks an agreement with his most implacable rival Aufidius of all people, underscores the impression of a blind and fixed desire for revenge, especially when we compare Shakespeare's play with its source, where at this point Aufidius is mentioned for the first time. Plutarch too, puts some emphasis on the hero's thorough change from impotent wrath to despicable hatred of his own country while Shakespeare's version leaves us in no doubt that personal spite has finally triumphed over human ties and any solidarity with the community in which he was brought up.

The hero's soliloquy before Aufidius' house in Antium – it is the only one in the whole play[80] – hardly gives us any insight into a genuine mental conflict; it merely confronts us with the new constellation, which he describes as an instance of the 'slippery turns' of the world (IV.4.12) but does not very deeply reflect on. He even seems to be aware himself of the inadequacy of his reasons; at least he is not trying to offer any convincing explanation for his course of action:

> O world, thy slippery turns! Friends now fast sworn,
> Whose double bosoms seems to wear one heart,
> Whose hours, whose bed, whose meal and exercise
> Are still together, who twin, as 'twere, in love
> Unseparable, shall within this hour,
> On a dissension of a doit, break out
> To bitterest enmity: so fellest foes,
> Whose passions and whose plots have broke their sleep
> To take the one the other, by some chance,
> Some trick not worth an egg, shall grow dear friends
> And interjoin their issues. So with me: (IV.4.12–22)

The superficiality of his justification – if it can be called that – suggests that it was not the dramatist's intention to present a tragic dilemma. He was evidently more interested in the particular situation created by Coriolanus' extraordinary switch of allegiance. His character is in some ways so predictable that we expect no complex process of moral decision; suspense is directed above all at the political and human results of Coriolanus' uncompromising defiance.

The reconciliation with the old adversary, as in Plutarch, follows with a suddenness that leaves very little room for psychological niceties. In a long and self-assured speech, Coriolanus offers his services to the old enemy, in order to have his revenge of Rome, and Aufidius, in his equally elaborate reply, declares his enthusiastic willingness to join forces with the hated rival. Thus, their mutual antagonism, introduced by Shakespeare very early in the play, turns out to be a kind of spiritual affinity which makes them fast allies, just as it had made them fierce competitors before.

Dramaturgically and as a means of characterization, the style of this scene is particularly effective and appropriate to the particular situation: the long and stylized speeches of the two antagonists are framed, as it were, by quite lengthy discussions among the servants, who at first greet the stranger with very little respect and later talk about the reconciliation at such length that the audience feels closer to the point of view of these unceremonious observers than to that of the two chief actors. The stature of Coriolanus, surpassing all those around him, is underlined by the comically disrespectful account of his reception by Aufidius:

Our general himself makes a mistress of him, sanctifies himself with's hand, and turns up the white o'th'eye to his discourse.   (IV.5.199–202)

The war against Rome is welcomed almost like a public fair. What for Coriolanus and Aufidius is an opportunity for revenge and glorious endeavor, is for their subordinates a time of refreshing activity. Their slighting references to idle peace throw a characteristic light on the political world of the play:

Peace is a very apoplexy, lethargy; mulled, deaf, sleepy, insensible; ... and it makes men hate one another. Reason: because they then less need one another.
                    (IV.5.230–1,236–8)

This is obviously the experience of those without power and influence and it also reflects on the play's concept of the heroic. At this stage in Roman history, as Shakespeare presents it, prowess in battle by no means implies the ability to keep a peaceful world in order. Coriolanus' most outstanding gifts need the proof of military action. In peacetime, he only becomes the helpless victim of calculating intrigue and of his own uncontrolled temper.

The inevitability of this development is brought out by many echoes and repetitions throughout the tragedy. Twice, Coriolanus humiliates himself in front of his opponents without being able to keep up the new role, and twice he is persuaded by his mother against his own conviction, which destroys his personality; twice the people are stirred up against him and he himself is provoked by a single pointed word to his own ruin. His disastrous inability to adapt himself to life within a community where a certain amount of conformity, adjustment and compromise is absolutely vital, is made particularly evident by these repetitions and correspondences.

On the whole, Plutarch's Coriolanus is much more politically motivated and reacts in a less emotional way. His fight against Rome is not informed by a blindly revengeful spirit against everybody, but has a rather more limited aim. He wants to stir up domestic mutiny and to inveigle the plebeians against the patricians. To this purpose, he deliberately spares the patricians' estates and only lays waste the plebeians' lands, thus successfully arousing their fury against the nobility, whereas Shakespeare turns this systematic and carefully limited campaign into an almost apocalyptic war of indiscriminate destruction, which is also at first described from the point of view of the terrified Romans and seems to consist more in hysterical visions than in actual fighting. Coriolanus is past pursuing any political ends and only wants to see Rome consumed by fire and sword. As he was, earlier in the play, convinced that he could only follow his mother's advice and make some conciliatory gestures towards the people by being untrue to himself, so he now again finds himself confronted by his mother, by Menenius and Comenius, his old associates, who all want him to lay down his pride and to change sides once more.

The two situations comment on each other by their similarity and also, perhaps, by their differences. During the earlier dispute, Coriolanus' firmness appears at first as a genuine reluctance against humiliating maneuvers and is, in human terms, by no means unsympathetic, even though it is rather shortsighted in the political context. In contrast, his revengeful campaign against Rome is a purely emotional gesture to vent his own spite, however justified his grievances against some of his former compatriots may be. This is why the great scene of persuasion in the Volscian camp before Rome (v.3) has a very different effect on the reader and spectator. It is the most famous scene of the tragedy, a scene that has inspired not only actors and critics, but great painters as well.[81] It is particularly interesting to see how closely Shakespeare has based it on

Plutarch's narrative, so closely, in fact, that there are long passages where he has only turned North's prose into blank verse;[82] yet, by small stylistic changes and, above all, by the dramatic structure and intensification of the contrasts between characters and moral issues, he achieves a tragic tension of unusual power and the impact of an agonizing dilemma, far more moving than anything in the first part of the tragedy. For one decisive moment, Coriolanus suppresses his impulsive desire to follow his own instincts. In doing so he does not even follow the dictates of political reason, let alone his own interest, but only the voice of nature which clearly places loyalty to one's own family and people above personal satisfaction and even one's own right. The fundamental quality of the issue is underlined by an important 'aside' of Coriolanus which, far more than his soliloquy in Antium (IV.4), gives the impression of an inner conflict and brings the hero closer to the audience than at any other time in the play. He is still firmly resolved to ignore all the laws of nature and to acknowledge nothing but the autonomous personality as standard for one's actions:

> But out, affection!
> All bond and privilege of nature break!
> Let it be virtuous to be obstinate.
> ... My mother bows,
> As if Olympus to a molehill should
> In supplication nod; and my young boy
> Hath an aspect of intercession which
> Great nature cries, 'Deny not'. Let the Volsces
> Plough Rome and harrow Italy; I'll never
> Be such a gosling to obey instinct, but stand
> As if a man were author of himself
> And knew no other kin.   (V.3.24–6,29–37)

Coriolanus has brought himself into a situation where he resembles some of the great villains of Elizabethan tragedy. For a moment, he seems to be in the position of Edmund or Macbeth, who deliberately shut their ears to the promptings of nature, and this is why his yielding is of such existential significance. It is clear that more is at stake even than the fate of Rome. The whole scene is also an instance of a particularly impressive use of rhetoric and gesture which mutually illuminate each other. Coriolanus' decisive change of heart is suggested by a mute gesture, felt by many commentators to be 'the most eloquent of all Shakespeare's stage directions':[83]

(Holds her by the hand silent.)   (V.3.182)

Coriolanus himself knows that his decision may cost him his life and he sees his mother's victory as a personal defeat from which only Rome will profit:

197

> O mother, mother!
> What have you done? Behold, the heavens do ope,
> The gods look down, and this unnatural scene
> They laugh at. O my mother, mother! O!
> You have won a happy victory to Rome;
> But for your son, believe it, O, believe it,
> Most dangerously you have with him prevail'd,
> If not most mortal to him. But let it come.   (V.3.182–9)

Shakespeare makes the personal encounter between mother and son the main issue and he thus leaves open whether Coriolanus is really obeying a natural impulse and humane considerations or whether he is just overwhelmed by his mother's eloquence and her powerful influence.[84] The momentary emotional effect of this great and dramatically brilliant scene, especially in a successful production, is possibly more impressive than is quite justified by Coriolanus' actual about-face, because the play does not reveal enough of the struggle within him. The whole confrontation is very important as a means of manipulating our sympathy, however, because for the first time we see the hero not only as the inflexible and rather predictable soldier, but as son, father and husband, who finally comes down on the side of family and community although it is the more difficult and also the less glorious course. Even his honor and his reputation are put in serious danger by it. Aufidius' brief comment draws our attention to this ominous aspect of the situation:

> [*Aside*] I am glad thou hast set thy mercy and thy honour
> At difference in thee. Out of that I'll work
> Myself a former fortune.   (V.3.200–2)

This sneaking satisfaction at the adversary's weakness shows at the same time how superior Coriolanus' own conception of honor and heroism is. Aufidius is like him in that he thinks of nothing but his own fame and advantage, but it is clear that he is prepared to stoop to means Coriolanus would not accept under any circumstances. The contrast makes Coriolanus appear as the incomparably greater man and even his glaring faults lose much of their seriousness when held against Aufidius' unprincipled cunning and dishonesty.

Plutarch denies real greatness to his hero's decision not to march against Rome because, as he says, Coriolanus acted neither from solidarity with his people nor in accordance with his new ally, but again followed only his own impulse. He also denies him any right to be incensed at the people's ingratitude and to want his revenge, because he himself had always been such an enemy to the people and had never thought of anything but his own ambition and pride (Bullough, v, 548).

For Shakespeare, this verdict is only one of several possible points of view, not a final authorial judgement. In the context of the whole tragedy, Coriolanus' behavior, his intransigence when Menenius speaks to him in the name of Rome, and his sudden collapse under the power of his mother's eloquence, is more than just an instance of extreme egotism because the dramatist concentrates on the personal conflict of the hero with himself as well as with the community more than Plutarch does, who is more interested in the political aspect of the dilemma. Bradley speaks of 'the conquest of passion by simple human feelings', and he concludes that *Coriolanus* is 'as much a drama of reconciliation as a tragedy'.[85] This seems to me a somewhat one-sided account of the scene, which, in Bradley's view, decides on the fate of Coriolanus' soul. It is probably true that no reader or spectator will hope for a different decision at this point; unlike Othello, Macbeth, and even Hamlet, the protagonist does not become guilty of any crime, but allows himself to be persuaded in favor of a humane course of action. By doing this, he does, on the other hand, violate the principle of political loyalty and offends not only his new ally, but shows clearly enough that his most momentous decision is made in solitary self-sufficiency, without any consideration of its effect on others.

The tragedy here is not in the experience of irreparable loss or the pain of disillusion, but in the fall of an exceptional popular hero, whose character makes him incapable of living within an ordinary society based on concession and compromise and finally destroys him, although there is no intriguing villain who actively promotes his downfall, and no wicked principle he has to stand up against. He lives in a world in which evil plays a much less spectacular part than in the 'great' tragedies and has none of the same poisoning omnipresence.

The differences between Shakespeare's later tragic heroes and the protagonists of the earlier tragedies have often been discussed. The question whether they are less flawed, less guilty, and less admirable, is not as relevant in this connection as the observation that the whole concept of the tragic appears to have changed. Much of what can be said about *Hamlet*, *Othello*, and *King Lear* does not apply to the later tragedies.[86] All of them deal with the fall of a larger-than-life individual in whom heroic greatness is combined with an absolute claim to self-determination and who therefore is quite unable to survive within an ordinary society. Brutus puts his finger on this crucial flaw when he tells Coriolanus,

> You speak o'th'people
> As if you were a god to punish, not
> A man of their infirmity.   (III.1.79–81)

The charge is well deserved and gives us an important clue to the hero's character, although the speaker is by no means unbiased.

The contrast between heroic gestures and the 'good ordinariness of a life lived among compromises'[87] is repeatedly underlined by brief scenes among simple plebeians, soldiers, servants, but also Coriolanus' friends. Menenius, in particular, represents a wise, humorous and good-natured, if a little senile, readiness to take things as they come and to show a cheerful face where others lose their temper. Even his impotent anger against the tribunes, whom he blames for Rome's predicament with almost something of a malicious satisfaction, is not particularly intimidating (IV.6). The repetition of his ironic accusation, 'You have made fair work', makes it sound amusing rather than aggressive, and his pathetic attempt to placate Coriolanus, surrounded by the comical disputes with his servants, underlines the emotional contrast. It is not, however, merely a question of weakness and strength being in opposition to each other, because the seemingly more than human hero proves to be most vulnerable in this world of pragmatic politics.

In the end, Aufidius makes use of the same tactics the tribunes had so successfully applied during the election for consul. Again, one word is enough to irritate Coriolanus into white fury and to put him exactly into a position where his opponents can at last destroy him. Mean and despicable as Aufidius' attack is, yet it is difficult to see Coriolanus' theatrical exhibition only as an admirable and just expression of heroic wrath. When, instead of justifying his extraordinary change of mind, he begins to boast about his spectacular feat at the siege of Corioles, he is not only committing a fatal and stupid blunder, but betrays a complete lack of insight into the sensibilities of the community on whose behalf he pretended to fight only a short while before. Nothing is more characteristic of his blind arrogance than his defiant retort:

> Alone I did it. Boy! (v.6.116)

It tells us more about his nature and about his tragedy than many other comments in the play (by him or about him). Coriolanus insists on his exceptional status, exempting him from the obligations of ordinary life, but the very values he claims to live by, such as glory, valor and respect for greatness, presuppose a sense of community and humane intercourse.

His death is swift and undignified. The hysterical cry of the murderers, 'Kill, kill, kill, kill, kill him!' (v.6.130), harks back to the first lines of the play and once more confirms the implacable nature of the conflict between the hero and the society he lives in. No other Shakespearian hero ends in such an unheroic manner, and even the conventional obituary has not the same authority as at the conclusion of other tragedies. The promise of a 'noble memory' (v.6.153) does not sound very convincing from the mouth of the murderer, and none of the survivors has the stature or the legitimate claim to be his worthy successor; Coriolanus dies far from Rome where, in the preceding scene, a triumphant reception is prepared for the three ladies (v.5) and the repeal of the banished hero is demanded. Plutarch does not forget to mention that the Volsces soon afterwards repented the murder of Coriolanus and were finally subjected by Rome, but Shakespeare's play gives no hint of the future. More than in his other tragedies we get the impression of an episode that has made no lasting impact on the community and leaves the survivors comparatively unmoved. All this contributes to the somewhat detached quality of the play. Most readers and spectators are probably not as firmly convinced as they are in the case of the other tragedies, that here they have experienced a fundamental clash of ultimate moral or political principles. Unlike Brutus and even Antony, Coriolanus does not sacrifice his life for an idea on which he has staked his whole existence because he deeply believed in its superior value, but seems the victim of an immature or insufficiently developed character and, as the source states, of an unnatural dependence on his mother. The tragic discrepancy between 'boy' and 'noble memory' remains unresolved to the last, and there is not the same generally felt contrast between the hero's greatness and the much more ordinary stature of the survivors as there is in most other Shakespearian tragedies, or only in a very superficial sense. Bradley's description of the ending seems to me to apply to *Hamlet* or *King Lear* much more that it does to *Coriolanus*:

life has suddenly shrunk and dwindled, and become a home for pygmies and not for him.[88]

Greatness is, at any rate, looked at much more critically in this tragedy than in many others.

The reception of the play in our century, especially in the theatre, seems to suggest a more political interpretation, which can be supported by a number of similarities with Shakespeare's history plays. The political theme is, of course, clearly implied in the story and can easily be brought out in performance more prominently than the text really asks for, but it is evident, I think, that Shakespeare has emphasized the human aspects of the tragic conflict more than its political implications. In spite of several topical allusions and a vague similarity with the domestic situation under James I, it is hardly possible to deduce from the text a detailed and pointed comment on the general function of the people within a complex social organism that goes beyond traditional commonplaces. It would be foolish, of course, to look for modern views on democracy in Shakespeare's play or to expect him to present the plebeians as equal partners in the government of the city; no less one-sided, however, are those interpretations that see the quintessence of the play expressed in Menenius' fable or suggest that Shakespeare's view of the people is the same as that of Coriolanus.[89] His tragedy, like *Antony and Cleopatra*, refuses to offer an authorial evaluation of the characters, and there is no comforting assurance that the tragic conflict is merely the result of one man's failing or that of a particular group. Perhaps it is this open and undecided quality of the play, which to some readers appears as a puzzling lack of orientation, together with the somewhat harsh and unpoetical style, that has made *Coriolanus* one of the least popular of Shakespeare's tragedies.[90] Even a number of interesting contemporary adaptations and some impressive productions have done very little to alter this general estimate.[91]

TIMON OF ATHENS

The text of this tragedy, preserved only in the First Folio of 1623, raises many questions, about the play's origin, its 'destination' and its genre, as well as its interpretation. It was obviously not from the first intended to be placed between *Romeo and Juliet* and *Julius Caesar* in this collection, but was hastily inserted when *Troilus and Cressida* was, for unknown reasons, retracted.[92] The text, as it has come down to us, shows clear marks of a rough draft, even if we assume that Shakespeare was experimenting with a new type of play, perhaps a kind of pageant for the company's new theatre, the Blackfriars, used by the King's Men from 1609, probably the first indoor playhouse available for regular performances by professional actors in England.[93] The play's structure is so different from that of the other tragedies that it is difficult to imagine Shakespeare ever having planned it as anything like *King Lear* or *Coriolanus*. Characterization is largely reduced to a few clear-cut, almost allegorically generalized attributes; and motivation, especially in the case of Alcibiades, is so fragmentary that there is much to be said for the theory that Shakespeare had done little more than sketch in some scenes, while others are so carefully worked out that they can compare with some of his most impressive passages. All this may explain why *Timon of Athens* has on the whole been rather neglected, by the theatre as well as by critics, apart from some occasional enthusiastic appreciations of its radical analysis of society and the extremes of tragic disillusionment.[94]

The dating of the play, without any reliable clues earlier than the Folio, is very difficult and depends largely on its place within a hypothetical development of the author's style. If we assume it to be an experiment with new forms of tragedy, then we might tentatively place it between *Coriolanus* and the romances, but critics who think of it as a sort of preparatory study for *King Lear*, opt for an earlier date. The tone in which society is portrayed as well as various thematic associations suggest a close relationship with early Jacobean drama; above all, the choice of subject argues for a date fairly close to *Antony and Cleopatra* and *Coriolanus*. This too, is no more than a hypothesis, however.

At any rate, Shakespeare could have found the rough outlines of the plot in Plutarch's biographies of Antonius and Alcibiades, and it seems likely enough that the three tragedies based on Plutarch were written roughly at the same time although in the case of *Timon*, the source provided much less coherent material and the scanty details of the hero's life to be found there hardly suggested any major tragic conflict. Timon is quoted by Plutarch as an extreme instance of a state of mind into which Antonius lapses for only a short time. For the fate of the man banished from his native city Shakespeare had a more extensive model in Plutarch's biography of Alcibiades, even more so in the dramatic account of Coriolanus on which he may have drawn for *Timon* as well as for *Coriolanus*.

Timon seems to have had the proverbial reputation of a determined misanthrope in the English Renaissance, but though his radical attitude was familiar enough, the details of his extreme isolation and the reasons for it were usually left vague.[95] Some interesting ideas are contained in a satirical dialogue by Lukian, where Timon's misanthropy is placed in a biographical and social context, and in an academic play about Timon preserved only in a manuscript version; this last raises its own dating problems, however, and can hardly be considered a source in any meaningful sense.[96] Whichever source the dramatist may have used, he had to rely on his own invention and original motivation to a much larger extent than in the case of *Antony and Cleopatra* or *Coriolanus* and the links with his other tragedies are as instructive as any source study.

The play's dramatic style is characterized by an almost morality-like simplicity and definiteness of the central scenes and, at the same time, by a deliberately artificial language, evoking unusual associations and suggesting a world in which simple communication is replaced by complex circumlocution and rhetorical masks.[97]

Thus the first two extended scenes of the play present a society of flatterers and parasites reminiscent of baroque courts, collecting around the spendthrift Timon, who himself is characterized as liberality and hospitality personified. The highly stylized dialogue suggests a wealth of themes, making the overall impression much more surprising and disquieting than the comparatively unsubtle characterization would lead one to expect.

The introductory conversation between the various spongers shows how all trades and crafts, but above all the arts, are eager to serve the generous patron and how integrity is sacrificed to opportunist obsequiousness. In this world, the border-line between art and nature becomes blurred and deceptive. The painter's picture is 'a pretty mocking of the life' (1.1.36); 'It tutors nature' (38). Art is misused by flatterers, but nature is hidden by masks and by the attributes of unnatural wealth. Muriel Bradbrook rightly links this beginning with allegorical representations of wasteful extravagance and liberality holding court, whose attraction makes this assembly a mirror of human society in general:

> See,
> Magic of bounty, all these spirits thy power
> Hath conjured to attend! (1.1.5–7)

To Timon himself the merchant ascribes 'untirable and continuate goodness' (1.1.11), but the stylistic context makes us distrust the word 'goodness' from the mouth of this speaker and does not really allow us a glimpse of Timon's real character. For the poet, too, Timon seems a symbolic figure rather than a real acquaintance, the man favored by Fortune; and the poetical work he claims to have in mind anticipates, in an allegorically generalized manner, the action of the tragedy. Timon seems to have become almost identical with his 'large fortune' (57), so much so that the man disappears behind the role; but it is 'fortune' that shapes his career. The traditional double sense of the word is brought out in the image of 'Fortune's hill' (see 1.1.66–91). Even before Timon himself enters the stage, at the very summit of his reckless liberality, his fall is anticipated in the poet's imagination and we are also prepared for the disillusioning experience that every one of his friends will forsake him as soon as his fortune begins to turn. It is a 'common' experience, made trivial by its universality, yet it is the duty of the artist to remind the fortunate of this moral commonplace. This didactic function applies to the visual arts even more than to poetry, and the painter's words may be taken as an affirmation of the theatre's claim to combine the two:

> 'Tis common.
> A thousand moral paintings I can show
> That shall demonstrate these quick blows of Fortune's
> More pregnantly than words. Yet you do well
> To show Lord Timon that mean eyes have seen
> The foot above the head. (1.1.92–7)

'More pregnantly than words' most aptly describes the dramatic style of this tragedy in which speech and spectacle work together in a most original way.[98]

Timon is introduced by a number of generous gestures that suggest imprudent bounty rather than ostentatious wastefulness; yet there is a strong impression of unworldly blindness and lack of real contact. The audience knows how unfounded Timon's trust in his 'friends' is and how unreliable Fortune's favors usually are, especially when they appear as exceptional as in this case. The whole scene strikes the beholder like the beginning of a conventional *de-casibus* tragedy because Timon is so obviously and demonstratively presented as a man at the very height of wealth and happiness, destined by tradition and experience to topple from this exalted position.[99] This expectation gives an ironic double meaning to almost every sentence. We are quite explicitly reminded of this when the Second Lord concludes the scene with the hopeful wish 'Long may he live in fortunes' (1.1.287). The warning note is intensified by the presence of Apemantus who already represents an extreme form of misanthropy at this early stage in the play, where it yet seems quite unfounded and casts him in the role of the fool, not taken seriously by anybody. His wholesale attacks on everything and everybody clearly connect him with the figure of the classical railer Thersites, a rather venomous version of the court fool with whom he shares his unlimited freedom of speech, his irresponsibility, and his disillusioned insight into hypocrisy and falsehood. He is the only one to see through the flatterers and to call Timon's blindness by its proper name, but it would be a grave mistake to accept his view as that of the dramatist or to see the whole play from his perspective. The virtues of friendship, hospitality, liberality and trustfulness, abused by Timon's guests and, in a way, by himself, are now even recognized by the mocking satirist, and his attitude of complete negation of all human intercourse is certainly not presented as an alternative to the opportunist sociability of the flatterers or Timon's imprudent generosity.

The second scene escalates this demonstration of boundless wealth to an emblematic tableau. The banquet, a traditional image of unity, peace and friendship, but also of affluence and wastefulness, is here employed in a complex manner. The detailed stage direction suggests that all available theatrical splendor was to be used. Timon's liberality is presented as a veritable passion of one-sided friendship: in the excessive security of his fortune, the hero even offers a challenge to his fate by expressing the hope for an opportunity to experience the mutuality of true friendship:

Why, I have often wished myself poorer that I might come nearer to you. We are born to do benefits. And what better or properer can we call our own than the riches of our friends? O, what a precious comfort 'tis to have so many like brothers commanding one another's fortunes! (1.2.97–103)

Even at this early stage of the action, it is unlikely that any spectator will miss the tragic irony of this exclamation, because there is little doubt that Timon's ideal of a friendship based on mutual dependence and generosity is, within the world of this play, an illusion without any actual foundation and that he is bound to be completely disillusioned as soon as this imagined friendship is put to the test. Apemantus' savage comments are ignored, just as the pregnant observations of Lear's Fool, but Timon feeds him, like the others, and tolerates his jibes with the same untroubled serenity as he accepts the flatteries of the parasites. Apemantus' 'grace', on the other side, underlines the attitude of universal distrust and comtempt for his fellow-men, believing itself to be absolutely independent of others and of corrupting wealth (1.2.61–70). The impression of unreflecting sensual enjoyment is further emphasized by the masque of the five senses and the dance which again symbolizes a deceptive unity that, for Apemantus, only veils the selfishness and hate underneath:

> I should fear those that dance before me now
> Would one day stamp upon me. 'T has been done.
> Men shut their doors against a setting sun. (1.2.140–2)

The continual presence of the railer casts doubt on all the trusting protestations of the hero and on all the fawning praise of his friends; it suggests a contrast between two incompatible attitudes, between a cynical contempt of humanity and unquestioning trust. In no other tragedy, except, perhaps, in *Troilus and Cressida*, is this contrast so sharply articulated and seems so irreconcilable from the very start. Apemantus plays the role of the traditional fool, but all the familiar devices of 'fooling', the witty puns, amusing invective and self-critical awareness, have turned into humorless insult and sour comment. Human falseness and social corruption are viewed with such implacable disgust and revulsion that they are not wittily exposed or ridiculed but brutally laid bare and generalized. Apemantus has excluded himself from humanity and he resembles the literal idea of the cynic who has more in common with dogs than with human beings. His name too, taken from Plutarch, suggests his affinity to an animal (ape). He is not by any means a 'choric' figure who utters the truth when no one else appears to see it; yet there is no doubt that he has a clearer vision of the possibility of human depravity than Timon and is much less likely to be disappointed. His futile attempt to warn him in time also places him in the tradition of the good counsellor whose wisdom is spurned, but sadly vindicated by the tragic course of the action. His final couplet at the end of the scene shows that he does not merely consider himself a vituperative spoilsport, but the spokesman of a moral awareness which Timon is totally lacking:

> O, that men's ears should be
> To counsel deaf, but not to flattery. (1.2.253–4)

The tone is that of a morality, directing the audience's attention to the paradigmatic character of the scene.

Like Apemantus, Timon's steward Flavius also represents the voice of clear-sighted reason; like Kent, he endeavors to protect his master from the consequences of his complete blindness as to his real situation, and his final couplet in a later scene once more formulates the same experience as that of Apemantus:

> That thought is bounty's foe –
> Being free itself, it thinks all others so. (II.2.238–9)

Unlike the 'churlish philosopher', as Apemantus is called in the Folio's list of actors, the steward does not see Timon's deafness as a sign of general human weakness, but as an aspect of his generosity. It is the unsuspicious and the truly liberal who is most in danger of misjudging the consequences of his actions and the possibilities of calculating deception, and thus of becoming a victim of his own goodness and innocence. Flavius' compassionate concern for his master prevents us from thinking him a foolish spendthrift, as Apemantus does. For him, it is precisely Timon's generous friendship that makes him forget all prudent considerations of thrifty housekeeping:

> Never mind
> Was to be so unwise, to be so kind. (II.2.5–6)

There is no doubt that, in the context of this play, 'to be so kind' is a higher and more human quality than wisdom. Timon himself justifies his behavior in similar terms, and it seems clear that this is an indication of the dramatist's own view:

> Unwisely, not ignobly, have I given. (II.2.179)

Lack of prudence and realistic distrust is, for him, not a flaw which casts doubt on his 'nobility'.[100] Similarly, Othello considers himself as one 'that loved not wisely, but too well' (v.2.340). Wisdom in this sense is only a very limited virtue. There is wisdom in the action of the Senator who foresees Timon's fall due to his unbounded generosity ('It cannot hold' (II.1.4 and 12)) and quickly wants to get the money back from him which he lent him in happier times. Here again, the play presents paradigmatically opposed principles of action, and Timon's history thus becomes an exemplum of an imprudent but unselfish waster. At the same time, contrasting attitudes towards money and wealth are set before the audience, as they are in *The Merchant of Venice*.[101] The senators stand for the principle of the usurer for whom money is only a means of personal enrichment: it is described in terms of fertility and natural growth (II.1.1–10). For Timon it is a possession to be given away without further thought in order to help others and to make friends. It is obvious, even without any specific topical allusions, that Shakespeare here touches on issues which do not only play a prominent part in the drama of the period, but must have been in many people's minds due to new developments in economy and trade.[102] The second half of the tragedy develops this theme further, with an intensity far beyond the earlier comedy and clearly reminiscent of contemporary satire, especially of Ben Jonson.

While the Senator (like Shylock) makes the debtor's innocence part of his calculation, Timon is not, like the merchant Antonio, hit by some capricious fate, but has caused the rapid dwindling of his fortune by his own reckless spending. Flavius' moving account of his master's wastefulness suggests not only generous hospitality, but uninhibited indulgence and drunken orgies, which partly justifies the creditors' anxiety about their money:

> So the gods bless me,
> When all our offices have been oppressed
> With riotous feeders, when our vaults have wept
> With drunken spilth of wine, when every room
> Hath blazed with lights and brayed with minstrelsy,
> I have retired me to a wasteful cock
> And set mine eyes at flow. (II.2.162–8)

This is very similar to the way courtly pleasure and decadent luxury are portrayed in many contemporary plays: drunkenness, blazing lights and 'minstrelsy' are recurring features, and it is more than likely that these dramatic accounts reflect what struck many as a new and repelling atmosphere at the court of James I.[103]

The sincere remonstrances of Timon's steward illuminate the precarious state of his affairs more clearly than Apemantus' indiscriminate railing, but they are, above all, an expression of personal loyalty and affection which make Timon an object of the reader's and spectator's compassionate sympathy and prevent us from assuming an attitude of moral censoriousness. It is only by such manipulation of the audience's sympathy that the dramatist succeeds in presenting the sudden turn of

Timon's fortune as a disaster appealing to our pity and sense of human solidarity rather than as a punishment gratifying our feeling of moral superiority and our expectation of a well-deserved lesson for the blind waster. The human warmth of the relationship between the steward and his master serves as a kind of balance against the largely schematic characterization due to ironic reversals and the exemplary simplicity of many scenes. Timon's unshakable confidence in his so-called friends, evidently not shared by Flavius, prepares for the moment of tragic recognition, but its effect is almost comic because of the clear discrepancy in the audience's awareness. Timon's innocence seems pathetic and ludicrous rather than tragic, being so obviously ill-founded and heading for a painful enlightenment.[104] At the climax of Timon's fatal blindness he re-enacts Lear's naive trust in the loyalty of his two elder daughters. Both tragic heroes are completely blind to the reality of human ingratitude and disloyalty, but Timon's error is presented more pointedly as an inescapable experience, common to all men. There is none of Lear's heroic stubbornness and majestic misjudgement in Timon's serene stupidity:

> And in some sort these wants of mine are crowned,
> That I account them blessings. For by these
> Shall I try friends. You shall perceive
> How you mistake my fortunes;
> I am wealthy in my friends.   (II.2.186–90)

The unmasking of the insincere flatterers, too, is dramatized with a simplicity of artistic means that is again reminiscent of a morality play. The expected refusal to lend money is repeated three times, varied only by the different reasons given by the false friends. The dramatic economy of these scenes and their unusual symmetry are quite typical of the schematic and comparatively simple structure of this tragedy.

The scene between Flaminius and Lucullus is partly comic by the lively prose and the ridiculously disappointed expectations on both sides as well as the slyly calculating treatment of Timon's confidant whose silent complicity Lucullus wants to insinuate:

> thou art wise, and thou knowest well enough, although
> thou comest to me, that this is no time to lend money,
> especially upon bare friendship without security. Here's
> three solidares for thee. Good boy, wink at me, and say
> thou sawest me not.   (III.1.40–4)

It is obvious that in the context of the play 'wise' is a rather negative quality: he is wise who ranks financial security above friendship and gratitude.[105] Timon's fatal lack of wisdom is thus, in retrospect, turned into a virtue and is made to seem decidedly attractive in comparison with the hypocritical close-fistedness of Lucullus.

The second refusal is framed by the comments of the three strangers who appear only in this scene and, as often in the plays of Shakespeare and his contemporaries, contribute an impartial assessment of the hero that is important as a guide to our own estimate, even though we need not entirely agree with it. Lucius' meanness is even more poignantly exposed when, before his own refusal, he expresses to the strangers his disapproval of Lucullus and protests that he himself would have answered Timon's request very differently. Here again, the exemplary significance of the episode is underlined by a comic reversal and the unmasking of the deceitful hypocrite. The disgusted reaction of strangers anticipates Timon's radical criticism of society and of human nature:

> Why, this is the world's soul,
> And just of the same piece
> Is every flatterer's spirit. Who can call him his friend
> That dips in the same dish? ...
>   O see the monstrousness of man
> When he looks out in an ungrateful shape –   (III.2.65–8,74–5)[106]

On the other hand, Timon's 'right noble mind' is emphatically affirmed (82) and the times are deplored in which such a man suffers disappointment. The diction of this dialogue again links *Timon of Athens* with a number of Jacobean tragedies, where the loss of traditional values is lamented in very similar terms:

> But, I perceive,
> Men must learn now with pity to dispense,
> For policy sits above conscience.   (III.2.87–9)

'Policy', in this context, is frequently used in the sense of an insincere, calculating and ruthless attitude, governed entirely by self-interest and opportunism; for the 'politic', pity and conscience are old-fashioned concepts which a man of the time can only ignore. This sense is also implied in the following scene, where Timon's servant talks about 'politic love' (III.3.35) after he has received Sempronius' offensive rebuff, and concludes that 'policy' must be the work of the devil:

The devil knew not what he did when he made man politic – he crossed himself by't.
      (III.3.28–30)

In this scene, too, it is clearly suggested that this has been a paradigmatic test of false friendship. In the words of Timon's servant,

> They have all been touched and found base metal,
> For they have all denied him.   (III.3.6–7)[107]

The friends' revealing denials, repeated three times, make Timon's experience a general demonstration of human ingratitude, with vague echoes of biblical parables, and this also makes his extreme reaction somewhat less surprising because it is presented on the same level of satirically distorted reality.[108]

Timon's actual disillusion is hardly shown in the play, because the tragedy is not really concerned with any psychological process, but with the sharp confrontation of the credulous innocent with a society based on self-interest and contempt for any altruistic values. When Timon reappears on stage in the scene following the third refusal, his trust in his friends' gratitude has already turned into an equally radical spirit of disappointment and isolation. It is emblematically generalized in a manner more akin to sixteenth-century morality plays or to contemporary satire than to Shakespeare's earlier tragedies:

> The place which I have feasted, does it now,
> Like all mankind, show me an iron heart? (III.4.83–4)

From here on, Timon, of whose 'discontent' Servilius speaks (71–2)[109] and who is considered a 'madman' by his importunate creditors (103), ceases to be a serious partner in any conversation. He is so full of his disillusioning experience and the idea of a hard-hearted society that he is no longer able to listen to any rational discourse. The creditors' messengers are to him as the blood-thirsty Shylock is to Antonio; the different context, however, gives a satiric precision to the image of flesh and blood as a means of payment. We are not confronted with the wickedness of a comedy villain but with the brutal rapacity of a money-oriented and inhuman society: 'Cut my heart in sums ... Tell out my blood' (III.4.93,95). This is not meant literally here, as in *The Merchant of Venice*, but the spirit behind the creditors' demands is more inhuman and at the same time more general than Shylock's private desire for revenge.

Timon's final reckoning up with his false friends is also presented in a manner that suggests the symmetry of a popular exemplum or a biblical parable. The former friends follow his new invitation with unashamed greed; the second banquet is a kind of parody of the first because Timon is no longer the naive host, but the enraged judge who confronts his guests with their blatant hypocrisy and chases them away, throwing stones after them.[110] The comedy of the moralistic episode seems more prominent than the tragedy of Timon's situation. The uncompromising thoroughness of his hate places a certain distance between him and the audience, just as earlier in the play, the boundless simplicity of his friendship and hospitality stood in the way of a confident identification with the hero:

> Burn house! Sink Athens! Henceforth hated be
> Of Timon man and all humanity.   (III.6.104–5)

Even Lear's shattering experience does not express itself in such sweeping condemnation and does not exclude him so totally from all human society. For Timon, his guests are nothing but dogs, and if he wishes them a long life he does it only because he wants mankind, of which he no longer feels a part, to suffer from the same vices he was hurt by for as long as possible. His disillusionment does not make him want to improve society, as even the most venomous satirist does, but leads to a complete break with society and mankind in general.

Timon has often been compared with Lear, usually to his disadvantage, because he does not appear to learn from his disappointment and suffering,[111] but this is to overlook the completely different nature of the two plays and their protagonists. It is partly due to the very different stories behind the plays. In the case of *Timon*, it is not so much the plot that impressed the classical authors as the proverbial figure of the misanthropist, and there is no hint in the sources that the man was made wiser by his experience or came to be reconciled with society. It has also become clear in the course of our discussion that *Timon of Athens* is indebted less to Shakespeare's earlier tragedies than to some more primitive as well as more modern forms of drama, to moral exempla, Jacobean satire, and emblematic spectacle.[112]

This also has a profound effect on the position and the character of the tragic hero. He is, more than anything, the spokesman of an extreme moral attitude, outside all familial and social relationships. In consequence, nearly every scene of the play demonstrates and comments on certain moral issues; at least, these are more central and prominent than any surprising turns of action or interesting confrontations of complex characters. Lear is characterized in a substantially different manner. His career and his psychological development are determined by a great number of various natural and political loyalties and by unpredictable, dynamic encounters that act as a challenge to his personality, changing, hardening, or disturbing it, as the case may be, in a way we do not find in *Timon*. Timon does not, for the most part, exercise any profound influence either on society or within his own domestic sphere, apart from the fact that his financial ruin also involves the end of his entire household. However, this too is seen primarily as a consequence of his predicted fall. The homeless servants make the collapse of the suddenly destitute hero all the more pathetic, and their undiminished loyalty is an important element in the dramatist's direction of our sympathy. But Timon's fall is not tragic in the traditional sense; it is not a consequence of a particular disposition or a moral dilemma. His unworldly innocence and wasteful liberality can hardly be compared with Lear's lack of self-knowledge or Macbeth's destructive ambition and even less with Othello's unwise love or Hamlet's 'melancholy'. What is revealed about the general state of human society is more important for the intention of the play than the mental state of the protaganist.

The servants lament the steep fall of their master which they have been made to share: 'So noble a master fallen' (IV.2.6), 'All broken implements of a ruined house' (16). Flavius, however, sees Timon as the victim of his own noble character and of a world in which riches and generosity lead to ruin. His sententious couplets attempt a simple moralization of this tragic experience, but they obviously trivialize the total impression made by Timon's radical disillusion on the audience:

> Who would not wish to be from wealth exempt,
> Since riches point to misery and contempt? (IV.2.31–2)

> Poor honest lord, brought low by his own heart,
> Undone by goodness! Strange, unusual blood,
> When man's worst sin is he does too much good.
> Who then dares to be half so kind again?
> For bounty, that makes gods, does still mar men. (IV.2.37–41)

More important, however, than the conventional denunciation of riches is the unconditional loyalty of the steward who, like Kent, would have good reasons to quit his master's service after all his well-meant warnings have been rejected, but, again like Kent, keeps faith even in his extreme humiliation and isolation. The play as a whole does not really endorse Flavius' view of Timon's character ('Undone by goodness!'), because his tragedy does not merely consist in his ruin by excessive generosity, yet his unquestioning, in no way calculating affection is a very important aspect of the play's total meaning and a telling comment on Timon's undifferentiated hatred of humanity. As in *As You Like It*, the morose account of the seven ages of man, ending in repulsive senility, is visibly refuted by the loyalty of old Adam,[113] and as Lear's despair at man's unnatural ingratitude is softened for the audience by the presence of the disguised Kent, so Timon's passionate diatribes against mankind are not left uncommented, but are qualified by the living evidence of a most humane and unselfish attitude which acts as a powerful corrective to Timon's wholesale misanthropy.

Flavius' soliloquy, in which he affirms his loyalty and his determination not to forsake his master in his misery, is inserted between Timon's two longest speeches, and their effect would be very different without this thematic counterpoint.[114] Timon's farewell to the society of men is a curse more radical and 'unnatural' even than Lear's repudiation of his daughters, because it is an unqualified rejection of everything that makes human life within a community possible, of all traditional values that are so central to Shakespearian drama and have often been discussed by critics as the very core of his social and moral world-view:

> Piety and fear,
> Religion to the gods, peace, justice, truth,
> Domestic awe, night-rest, and neighbourhood,
> Instruction, manners, mysteries, and trades,
> Degrees, observances, customs, and laws,
> Decline to your confounding contraries,
> And yet confusion live. (IV.I.15–21)

The impressive list makes clear that no time-honored values whatever are acknowledged any more. Timon's decision to retire into the wilderness, which is not suggested by Shakespeare's presumed sources, is an extreme and unromantic version of the banishment in the Forest of Arden:

> Timon will to the woods, where he shall find
> Th' unkindest beast more kinder than mankind. (IV.I.35–6)[115]

Such radical negation of everything human might strike us only as the perversion of an understandable disillusionment, or as purely destructive self-isolation,[116] if it were not accompanied by the unquestioning compassion of Flavius who does not look on Timon's failings any more, but sees only his misery, as an appeal to human solidarity and disinterested affection. It is clear that Timon's misanthropy comes from disappointed love, like Othello's jealousy and Hamlet's world-weariness, and even his most radical expressions of universal hatred are given some motivation by the context which prevents the spectator from watching his lonely struggle merely with detached and uncomprehending awe.

This also applies to the scene following on Flavius' soliloquy, the longest scene of the play (IV.3), in which Timon's misanthropy is presented in a series of contrasting encounters with increasing intensity, up to his final exit which is, at the same time, his exit from the world of the play.[117] The scene of the action is the wilderness outside the city, a visual contrast to the dangers to human integrity among the rich and powerful, as in some of Shakespeare's comedies, but the static nature of this section of the play shows that its chief purpose is the exhibition of Timon's notorious misanthropy in all its aspects, not any dramatic conflict or character development.

As in Lukian's dialogue, Timon, at this lowest point in his fortunes, suddenly finds gold enough to enable him to return to his former status, but his new wealth only shows up the greed and the false friendship of his former companions again and confirms him in his attitude of universal hatred and disillusion. Shakespeare's Timon is, by the sight of the all-powerful gold, inspired to a general reflection on the magic of money which Karl Marx and others after him have felt to be symptomatic of the new function of wealth in the period of rising capitalism, especially of the fateful interconnection between money and human integrity, so acutely felt by many Jacobean poets and dramatists.[118] Like other satirists of the time, Timon holds up the picture of a society in which gold has the power to corrupt everybody, to make any man betray his fellow and his own conscience:

> Thus much of this will make
> Black white, foul fair, wrong right,
> Base noble, old young, coward valiant.   (IV.3.28–30)

As in Jonson's *Volpone*, man is seen as one who can be bought, even in the sphere of the most sacred moral pieties and obligations, and this perversion by wealth is equated with the physical infection by prostitutes, as it is in *The Revenger's Tragedy*. The whores accompanying Alcibiades are only used as object-lessons by Timon, who sees them, like gold, as instruments of poisonous corruption and urges them on to further destructive activity. Here again, we are much closer to Jacobean satire or Jonsonian comedy than we are to Shakespeare's earlier tragedies. There is no genuine experience for Timon, because each new encounter only serves to confirm him in his radical denial of any human ties and loyalties, as well as in his implacable, yet pointed criticism of a degenerate society. This demonstration of a thorough-going negation of the whole community of mankind seems to me the true centre of the tragedy, and in this it is very different from *King Lear* or *Coriolanus*.

The individual encounters are variations on the theme of a corrupt society which is seen also within the context of a creation bent on mutual destruction and exploitation. The richly metaphoric language includes vegetation, animals and stars in the universal condemnation of human nature: wherever we look we find instances of rapacious aggression, infection and subjection, and Timon refuses to recognize any other principle than poisoning and destruction. Alcibiades and his whores are offered gold by him because they are the enemies of Athens, and in the same vein Timon tries to incite the two bandits, by gifts of gold and by the example of preying nature, to yet greater thieving activity, in which, however, he partly fails because even the bandits are repelled by his indiscriminate hatred of mankind. Flavius' honesty is acknowledged by Timon only with the important proviso that he is really the only honest creature on earth, a true exception within totally corrupted humanity, and the courtly flatterers, painter and poet, who have returned at the rumor of Timon's new wealth, are first exposed with satirical irony and then chased off (v.1.1–113).

It hardly seems possible to discover anything like a consistent development in this sequence of savage encounters. The variation of disgust is occasioned by the different visitors to Timon's cave. With none of them he accepts any form of community, neither with the enemies of the Athenian state nor with the bandits or even with the cynic Apemantus or with the official envoys of the city who ask his forgiveness and implore his help against the aggressors. His hatred is more implacable than that of Coriolanus because it is directed not just against his native city but against all mankind. Even his grave he wants to keep uncontaminated from any contact with society, by placing it beyond the seashore at low tide. Unlike all other Shakespearian tragic heroes, he does not die on stage, but walks off to his death.[119] No heroic gesture of suicide nor duel concludes his fall, but a retreat without any sign of reconciliation. It is almost like Shylock's and Malvolio's exit from the comedy world of *The Merchant of Venice* and *Twelfth Night*. This is why Timon's death can hardly be compared with the tragic ending of Antony or Coriolanus. He is not guilty of any capital crime which he has to expiate, nor is he the victim of any villainous intrigue or of a tragic dilemma. It is clear that the satirical theme has modified the dramatic structure significantly, and this applies most of all to the concept of the tragic protagonist.

Throughout the play, the hero is contrasted with two characters who act as a foil to his weakness as well as to his virtues. Apemantus, whose venomous cynicism superficially resembles Timon's misanthropy, has never believed in gratitude or loyalty, and he is from the start introduced as 'opposite to humanity' (1.1.277). His warnings have turned out to be more than justified, but this does by no means bring the two men together, because Timon emphatically dissociates himself from him whose hatred of humanity is rooted in his own nature and not in personal experience. The abusive dialogue between these two serves to define Timon's attitude by contrast to the traditional railer who is incapable of change or development and to whom the attitude of the detached and uncommitted satirist seems the most natural. When he accuses Timon of merely copying him because he cannot bear the reversal of his fortune, he voices a suspicion which the audience might well entertain likewise, at least during the first stage of Timon's disillusionment. Timon's universal hatred of mankind seems only the exact reverse to his boundless naive credulity – the same extreme pose, only in the opposite direction. As Apemantus tells him:

The middle of humanity thou never knewest, but the extremity of both ends.

(IV.3.302–3)

The truth of this verdict is qualified, however, by the speaker himself; for Apemantus hardly conforms to his own ideal of the 'middle of humanity' and Timon's tragic disillusion is quite beyond his comprehension. His indiscriminate distrust of everything and everybody is a form of 'wisdom' that Timon has never possessed. His misanthropy precisely does not mean that he considers himself to be on the same level as the animals, as Apemantus does, because for him, bestiality is a much lower form of life than his own misanthropy, as his satirical picture of the animal world shows (IV.3.329–47). Timon's hatred of humanity still implies the utopian vision of an ideal society, and he curses mankind only because it has betrayed these ideals. Apemantus has never had to go through Timon's trials because he has never been rich. His cynicism would never have let him become a generous waster, but even in the midst of wealth he would have become an animal, subject to its base instincts. Timon's dispute with the cynic makes particularly clear that his misanthropic fury comes out of a passionate commitment to humane values and that he has as little in common with Apemantus as with the false flatterers. The contrast is impressively brought home in the parody of an Apemantus blessed by the gifts of fortune:

> Thou art a slave whom Fortune's tender arm
> With favour never clasped. But, bred a dog,
> Hadst thou, like us from our first swath, proceeded
> The sweet degrees that this brief world affords
> To such as may the passive drudges of it
> Freely command, thou wouldst have plunged thyself
> In general riot, melted down thy youth
> In different beds of lust, and never learned
> The icy precepts of respect, but followed
> The sugared game before thee.   (IV.3.251–60)

It is the most eloquent apology for Timon's own use of his wealth because he himself did certainly not follow the 'sugared game', but thought of all his possessions as an opportunity to be generous to others. Nor does Apemantus know that Timon has already become rich again, that fortune has at least offered him the means of returning to his former state, an offer he has decided to reject. Thus, his insinuation that Timon would waste any new wealth again as he did his former (IV.3.242–3) is quite unfounded, as the spectator knows, and his scoffing description of a pitiless nature (222–32) misses its aim altogether because Apemantus does not understand the real grounds of Timon's misanthropy. The fact that the dialogue first turns into prose and then descends to the level of pure insult could be an indication of the play's unfinished state, but it also expresses the complete collapse of any rational discourse between the cynic and the man disillusioned by the vileness of mankind. After that, Apemantus has no further function in the play and does not reappear again.

More problematical is the figure of Alcibiades who is obviously conceived as a contrast to Timon. He is the centre of a subplot that in some ways resembles the Fortinbras episode in *Hamlet*. Like Timon (and Coriolanus), he turns his back on the native city and turns against it in revengeful hate.[120] But unlike Timon, he allows himself to be persuaded to a reconciliation and he concludes the play with an appeasing speech which is clearly reminiscent of Fortinbras' last words, but also of Octavius and Aufidius, the more or less successful antagonists who survive the fall of the hero and who are expected to shape the future of a shattered community.

Alcibiades' part in the play, however, seems only sketchily done, and it is difficult to imagine that this is Shakespeare's final version of it. There is much to be said for the assumption that his scenes are merely a first draft; this applies in particular to his rather abrupt and incompletely motivated introduction into the play, where we first hear him as the advocate of an unknown friend (III.5). We may never know whether this surprising scene was actually finished. It looks tentative and vague enough; yet it is not entirely inconsistent with the rest of the play, with its harsh contrasts, and it is thematically related to the surrounding scenes.[121] It is also worth noting that in performance the episode seems much less odd and puzzling than in the study.[122]

Comparison with Fortinbras and Aufidius may also help in coming to a more precise assessment of this figure, who is certainly not presented with the same dramatic and psychological intensity as the protagonist and can therefore hardly be understood as a positive alternative to his tragic failure. The injustice done to Alcibiades cannot really be compared with Timon's fundamental disillusionment, and his hatred is shown only in its practical results, not as a deep personal experience we are asked to share. The fact, related in Plutarch, that Alcibiades surrounds himself with prostitutes, is emphasized by Shakespeare in a manner scarcely appropriate for an exemplary character. Like Timon and Apemantus, Alcibiades is aware of the abuses in Athenian society and he mentions usury as a particularly grave offence against social justice (III.5.99–100), but he is quickly pacified by the rather pragmatic argument, 'All have not offended' (v.4.35), and quite prepared to make a distinction between those who are guilty and the rest of the people. Only the enemies of Timon and Alcibiades are to be punished. As at the end of other Shakespearian tragedies, a new and just order is promised, the impartial administering of reward and punishment. Yet Timon's experience of an ungrateful and hypocritical society cannot be simply wiped out by such summary justice. The restitution of outward stability and the military honors for the dead protagonist will not make us forget the impression of a poisoned and corrupt society that crushed him.

Even if we grant that the figure of Alcibiades is only a first rough draft, it is difficult to see his attitude as a kind of quintessence to the play and to agree with a statement like, 'He comes to terms with life ... he accepts man and his limitations; and in the light of his acceptance can exercise mercy'.[123] This, to me, seems rather too comfortable a view, passing over Timon's agonized revulsion too smoothly. Soellner's conviction that Shakespeare deliberately refuses to turn Alcibiades into a positive foil seems to me nearer to what the text says, which does not at all mean that the play necessarily becomes a demonstration of a thoroughly pessimistic world-view.[124]

From a more detached standpoint, however, Alcibiades conciliatory attitude can only be described as sensible and humane readiness for compromise. The senator's reply to his military action and his announcement of retribution also suggests an unheroic and moderate verdict on Athenian society:

> We were not all unkind, nor all deserve
> The common stroke of war. (V.4.21–2)

The senators plead effectively against the principle of collective guilt and for a distinction between those who have actually failed and those who have stood apart. But the whole play so far has hardly been concerned with this aspect of Athenian society; rather it has, in the generalizing manner of a morality, created the impression of universal hypocrisy and falsehood. Therefore, the suggestion to treat Timon's and Alcibiades' clash with society merely as a private conflict between individuals, without any general significance for the state of the whole community, sounds more like a piece of opportunist diplomacy than like an impartial description of what we have witnessed.[125] If one accepts the senators' view of things, as Alcibiades apparently does, Timon becomes an extreme individualist who, from private disappointment, draws the most sweeping conclusions as to the universal state of humanity, losing all sense of proportion for the ordinary distribution of good and evil. Such trivialization of his tragedy, however, falsifies the moral intensity and the aggressive satire of the whole play, even if it were in accordance with our own experience, just as the reduction of *Othello* to the tragedy of a credulous fool, incapable of true love, falsifies the obvious intention and effect of the text. Like Shakespeare's other tragedies, *Timon of Athens* presents a larger-than-life existential experience, whose validity and truth are not refuted by a rather less dramatic and more 'normal' reality, as often happens in comedy. Timon is no Shylock, Jaques, or Malvolio, who for a little while disturb the harmony of a basically sound and good-natured world. The critical questions pointed at society by his misanthropy are, at any rate, not finally answered by the conciliatory last words of the play. As in a number of other tragedies, the respectful memory of the dead, beyond the limits of the stage-play, is confidently predicted. Alcibiades' brief obituary is very similar to *Coriolanus*, where the hero is assured of a 'noble memory' by the chief survivor and beneficiary of his death:

> Dead
> Is noble Timon, of whose memory
> Hereafter more. (V.4.79–81)[126]

Thus Timon, too, is granted the heroic status of a tragic hero, whose suffering demands our compassion and respect, even though many readers will probably find the discrepancy between this apparent reconciliation and the depth of Timon's implacable hatred of mankind unsatisfactory or at least bewildering. The sudden bypassing of all the seemingly irreconcilable contrasts in a way anticipates the dramatic style of Shakespeare's romances or of some Jacobean tragicomedies, where we are often left wondering whether the diverging elements can ever be made to fit together, and the final harmony can easily seem superficial. In *Timon of Athens*, however, it is the satirical, the questioning, and the disturbing passages in particular that are the most impressive instances of Shakespeare's richly inventive dramatic art, and our final impression is one of an incomplete integration of the contrasting perspectives and dramatic methods. It is this impression that largely accounts for the conflicting assessments and interpretations of the play throughout the three hundred years of its critical reception.

TROILUS AND CRESSIDA

Troilus and Cressida is one of Shakespeare's most puzzling plays, not least so in respect of its unusual dramatic form. It refuses to be classed easily with any of the traditional types of drama, and the frequently applied, convenient label 'problem play' is not of much help in solving this difficulty.[127] For the editors of the First Folio, at any rate, the play belonged with the tragedies, primarily, we may assume, because the story material suggests a heroic rather than a romantic, a tragic rather than a comic treatment.[128] The love of Troilus and Cressida, to be sure, is a medieval addition to the classical Homeric myth of manly exploit and valiant fighting, but Shakespeare does not take it in isolation, as a romantic novella in the manner of *Romeo and Juliet*. He leaves us in no doubt that it is only an episode within the larger historic context of the siege of Troy.[129] More deliberately than in the two most famous earlier poetic treatments of the story, Boccaccio's *Il Filostrato* and Chaucer's *Troilus and Criseyde*, Troilus is presented in close relation to the other Trojan leaders, especially in the great debate about Helen's return (II.2), and the progress of the war is not a 'subplot' at all, but an equally important part of the play's total structure. Hector's death makes the final destruction of Troy imminent, and most Elizabethan spectators must have known that Troilus, too, was destined to die shortly at the hand of Achilles, as Chaucer, among others, tells us.[130]

Formally then, *Troilus and Cressida* belongs with the tragedies: it deals with matters of state and of historical as well as political significance, and it ends with the death of one of the heroes and the certain death of the other. There can be no doubt whatever, at the end of the play, as to which side will be the loser. More important, however, for the impact of the tragedy is the experience of Troilus, who finds himself cruelly disappointed in everything that has made life meaningful to him: women's love and the ideals of heroism. Betrayed by Cressida, he also collapses as an inspiring fighter, and it seems unlikely that he will be a very effective support for the Trojan cause. It is this close thematic interrelationship between the love story and the historical confrontation that makes *Troilus and Cressida* 'perhaps the most brilliant of all instances of the double plot'[131] and partly accounts for its unique structure. Moreover, the themes linking the two plots are discussed with an intensity very rare in the comedies, and the painful agony of the last scenes also puts the play in a category much closer to the tragedies than to any other dramatic genre. It is worth noting that Chaucer's poem, probably Shakespeare's chief source,[132] is explicitly called a tragedy by the author, although it contains more genuine comedy than Shakespeare's version of the story and has a rather more conciliatory ending.

Nevertheless, there are a number of elements – subversive comedy, multiple ironies, and satirical parody – that have made many readers hesitate to consider the play as a tragedy like other Shakespearian tragedies. It is probable that these elements have to be seen in relation to the play's early history and its original public.

We still do not know with any certainty whether *Troilus and Cressida* was first written with a more sophisticated and select audience in mind than that of the public theatres and afterwards adapted for performance at the Globe, or whether it was the other way round.[133] There is, at any rate, little doubt that the two surviving texts, the Quarto of 1609 and the

First Folio, represent two versions of the play which may well reflect two different occasions and audiences. There was, for instance, some disagreement, either genuine or for the sake of publicity, as to whether the play had ever been performed by Shakespeare's company at the Globe before its publication or not. The Epistle in the Quarto (in its second state), claiming that it had not – 'neuer stal'd with the Stage, neuer clapper-clawd with the palmes of the vulger' – also insists that it is a comedy, 'none more witty then this', and praises it as on a par with 'the best Commedy in *Terence* or *Plautus*'.[134] It is difficult to reconcile this with the genuine pathos, the heroic rhetoric, and the tragic ending, but the emphatic recommendation strongly suggests that *Troilus and Cressida* was expected to appeal to refined and intellectual tastes capable of appreciating the witty and original treatment of a familiar story more than Troilus' well-known tragedy. One might also point out that Shakespeare had already used some of the story's tragic potential in *Romeo and Juliet* and may well have felt that the figure of Troilus had already become too proverbially fixed to be convincingly presented as a tragic character.[135] Something of the sort had already, I am sure, happened in the case of Pyramus and Thisbe, another pitiful love story, suitable for burlesque parody within a comic structure like *A Midsummer Night's Dream*, but no longer thought to be capable of arousing tragic emotions. *Troilus and Cressida* is indeed so different from *Romeo and Juliet* that the basic similarities between the two plots are not often noticed. The play has been taken for a cynical parody of classical myths, for a satirical attack on war and false heroism, and it has been given as many labels as Polonius could have thought of. It is also worth noting that its popularity on the stage was never greater than in our own century, when the aggressive satire and the deflating comedy have generally been much more fully explored than the tragic pathos.[136]

Like *Timon of Athens* and the Roman tragedies, *Troilus and Cressida* is the dramatization of a story too well known, at least in general outline, to be radically altered, even though the familiar events might be given a new interpretation. Of course the play makes sense even to those who have never heard of Cressida and Pandarus before, but I have no doubt that the dramatist reckoned with an audience well aware of how it would all end and not entirely ignorant of Greek mythology. Many of the play's most interesting and provocative effects can only be appreciated by a reader or spectator who can recognize the deliberate discrepancy between traditional concepts of the story and Shakespeare's most original treatment of it, between familiar cliché and startling novelty.

When Robert Henryson, living about a century after Chaucer, wrote a kind of critical sequel to *Troilus and Criseyde*, he began with the provocative question, 'Quha wait gif all that Chauceir wrait was trew?'.[137] It is a question that Chaucer himself asked about several famous classical stories, and Shakespeare, too, looks at literary tradition with a sceptical eye, fully aware of its unpredictable and capricious nature. Troilus and Cressida themselves seem to be conscious of the fact that their respective roles in the story will be handed down by 'rhymes' and 'memory' and become stereotyped (III.2.171–94). Pandarus glibly summarizes their emphatic protestations and predicts the origin of a new literary cliché:

If ever you prove false one to another, since I have taken such pains to bring you together, let all pitiful goers-between be called to the world's end after my name: call them all Pandars: let all constant men be Troiluses, all false women Cressids, and all brokers-between Pandars. (III.2.197–202)

This, of course, is precisely what has happened, but it is much more than a case of simple dramatic irony. The whole play is an attempt to make us look at the characters' actions and motives afresh and wonder whether memory and rhyme have really done them justice.

It is often thought that Shakespeare has deliberately debased Chaucer's characters, as if he wanted to write a sort of *Shamela* to Chaucer's *Pamela*; but this view rests on a misunderstanding of Chaucer's poem as well as of Shakespeare's play.[138] Shakespeare is very far from presenting the love story simply through the eyes of Thersites. He places his characters in a context that makes it very difficult to condemn them out of hand. Pandarus may be a more simply comic figure than he is in Chaucer's poem, yet his actions, reduced to their bare outlines, are not very different, and the change in tone can be largely accounted for by the observation that Shakespeare did evidently not intend to make this a play about courtly love and friendship, but about war, heroic values, time and fame.

Cressida, like Pandarus, is at first introduced as a comic heroine, without any of Juliet's or Criseyde's innocence and unqualified loyalty, but again, Shakespeare has reduced her behavior to the unadorned essentials, and these are not as different from Chaucer's version as it is often assumed. Comedy has no time for elaborate verbal decorum or complex defences and, as Ann Thompson justly remarks, 'the events are the same'.[139] The difference lies above all in the dramatic pace and in the methods of characterization. Shakespeare's Cressida is allowed but one brief moment of happiness with Troilus, enjoyed only with some reservations, because she has no deep faith in happiness achieved and desire fulfilled. The brevity of their union – one hasty night, stage-managed by Pandarus – makes her betrayal a far less disturbing sin against love than Criseyde's swift collapse after more than a year of mutual trust and complete harmony. As in *Romeo and Juliet,* 'speed is the medium of fate',[140] and Shakespeare no more than Chaucer encourages righteous condemnation of his heroine, though he does not try to exonerate her, as Chaucer claims to do.[141]

In fact, Chaucer the author does no such thing. His whole poem turns on the disturbing contrast between the utter sincerity and the blissful happiness of this love, and the depth of Troilus' despair at Cressida's unbelievable faithlessness. Though the narrator is at great pains to think of excuses for his heroine and repeatedly protests that he is not at all interested in blaming her, yet her behavior is all the more shocking because it seems so out of character. Shakespeare is even less concerned with moral censure. His Cressida is not for a moment presented as an innocent object of male worship, as an ennobling influence on her lover, or as an unquestioningly dedicated mistress and wife, like Juliet and Desdemona. Nor does she have any of Cleopatra's majestic capriciousness and 'infinite variety'. She is simply what men make of her, a striking example of the relativity of most values or, in Hector's words, of the 'mad idolatry/To make the service greater than the god' (II.2.57–8). Again, this is not a question of personal blame or of an exceptionally wicked character, but an aspect of the general issue discussed with such insistence in this play:

> What's aught but as 'tis valued? (II.2.53)

Troilus' question is part of the great debate about the wisdom of keeping Helen. On the one side, there is Hector's pragmatic view:

> She is not worth what she doth cost the keeping. (II.2.52)

On the other, there is Troilus' conviction that this is not a question of intrinsic value, but of estimation and the power to influence men:

> Is she worth keeping? – Why, she is a pearl
> Whose price hath launch'd above a thousand ships,
> And turn'd crown'd kings to merchants. (II.2.82–4)

More important even is the heroic and ideal aspect of this kind of artificial value set on persons and things:

> She is a theme of honour and renown,
> A spur to valiant and magnanimous deeds,
> Whose present courage may beat down our foes,
> And fame in time to come canonize us; (II.2.200–3)

The same applies to Cressida, but in both cases the illusory foundation of such valuation will become evident. Love and heroism are equally vulnerable when they are based on such arbitrary values. The pearls may well be worthless as soon as there is no buyer to appreciate their particular qualities. Helen has become a myth, powerful enough to move armies and lead to the destruction of a whole city, while Cressida's value exists mainly in the mind of Troilus. Both women are frequently talked about as merchandize and goods with an exchange value, and it is certainly no accident that Cressida is given away by the Trojans in exchange for the man who will eventually betray the city,[142] just as Cressida will betray Troilus.

These fundamental issues were obviously more important to the dramatist than the analysis of individual characters, and this may partly explain why there is no real hero. Kenneth Palmer has demonstrated that the love plot occupies only about a third of the whole play, and though Troilus appears in other scenes of the play as well and in other capacities than as Cressida's lover, he is not the hero of the tragedy in the same sense as Romeo, Othello, or Antony.[143] There is no other Shakespearian tragedy in which two such different plots run parallel and yet are so separate, without any clearly dominating figure, as, for instance, in *King Lear*. The martial Prologue does not even mention the lovers, but appears to introduce a history play about the Trojan war, and indeed, the structure of *Troilus and Cressida* is more like that of some history plays than like that of Shakespeare's other tragedies. All this suggests that Shakespeare did not take the story of the lovers as seriously as Chaucer or Henryson did, and departed more freely from any conventional pattern of tragedy. He makes more extensive use of comic devices than in any other tragedy, except, perhaps, *Romeo and Juliet*, and the variations in tone and seriousness are particularly striking.

This lack of a clear focus begins with the Prologue which combines heroic pathos with a stylistic elaboration that repeatedly undercuts the high seriousness of its appeal to our attention. The speaker himself does not seem to be as confident of his task as, for instance, the Prologue to *Henry V*. He retreats behind 'the chance of war' (31) and does not even ask for the audience's approval, but defers to its judgement. Epic grandeur, deflating irony, and critical detachment are almost insepa-rately mixed in this passage and present a first challenge to our own comfortable expectations.[144] After this martial preparation, the actual beginning of the play is bound to come as a surprise. The very first words, spoken by the hero,[145] introduce us to the contrast between the spirit of war and the conventions of love poetry:

> Call here my varlet, I'll unarm again.
> Why should I war without the walls of Troy,
> That find such cruel battle here within?

> Each Trojan that is master of his heart
> Let him to field: Troilus, alas, hath none. (1.1.1–5)

Pandarus' dismissive reply, 'Will this gear ne'er be mended?', immediately undercuts what genuine romantic emotion there may have been aroused by these first lines, and throughout the scene, there is an uneasy clash of different levels of speech that will make many readers uncertain of their response. It is, however, basically a comedy scene, as is the second, in which the officious pander tries to interest Cressida in Troilus' qualities as a man and a lover, while all the time she sees through him and plays her own game. It is a battle of wits in the manner of Shakespeare's romantic comedies, with Cressida enjoying her command of quick repartee, as Portia, Beatrice and Rosalind do. Her final soliloquy expresses the typical pose of the young girl determined not to be caught by love because she does not trust in the traditional clichés and fears the loss of her liberty. Her sententiousness suggests that she is speaking from the book rather than from experience, as Beatrice does in *Much Ado About Nothing* before she falls in love with Benedick:

> Therefore this maxim out of love I teach:
> 'Achievement is command; ungain'd, beseech.'
> Then though my heart's content firm love doth bear,
> Nothing of that shall from mine eyes appear. (1.2.297–300)

Throughout the scene, Cressida has adapted herself to the frivolous tone of Pandarus, and it is only when she is alone that her style changes. I do not think that this is meant to make her a crafty hypocrite or to confirm, from the start, her proverbial reputation as a fickle woman![146] On the contrary, Shakespeare introduces his heroine as a spirited and independent maiden who is no more taken in by the cynical go-between than Chaucer's Criseyde and has decided that a non-committal attitude is, for the time being, her best defence against the clichés of romantic love as well as against the clumsy tactics of Pandarus. After our first impression of Troilus, we can hardly blame her for her caution.

Thus, Shakespeare has not really changed the initial situation, though he dispenses with many of Chaucer's courtly and rhetorical preliminaries and makes the contrast between sincere love and worldly knowingness much more poignant. This does not necessarily debase the characters, but it brings out the fundamental ironies and dangers of the situation more sharply. Cressida is anything but a fixed type; she is a character capable of unpredictable reactions and surprising development, though, of course, the scene can easily be played in such a way that the audience finds her exactly in keeping with her fame, or rather defame. The text, however, allows for a more sympathetic interpretation and for the possibility of complex emotions. It is suggestive rather than definite, and in no way censorious. It would certainly not be true to say that Shakespeare is simply reproducing the familiar characters or just a debased version of them. Without any radical changes of the action, he seems intent on opening the debate about the individuals and motives behind the well-known story all over again. He gives an exciting freshness to the events so often told before, and he places them in a context of themes and ideas that raises new questions and relates the play to the other tragedies.

The third scene, at last, seems to agree with what the Prologue has led us to expect. Its elaborate rhetoric suggests high seriousness, and while there is an uncomfortable discrepancy between the ideal concepts and the actual performance, it would be quite wrong to dismiss the Greek leaders as braggarts and hypocrites.[147] They appear to be in no doubt about the general justification of the war, but they are genuinely concerned about the deeper reasons for the lack of effective unity and purposeful enthusiasm. There is, of course, a disquieting contrast between the searching earnest of the argument and the shallow cunning of the outcome, but this does not make a farce of the whole debate, as is frequently assumed by critics and producers. The validity of the ideals under discussion is by no means undermined by the inadequacy of the speakers. It may be a little dangerous to take Ulysses' famous degree-speech (1.3.85–137) out of its context, as an authorial exposition of the Elizabethan 'world picture';[148] nevertheless, it is certainly not a parody and it shows clearly that Shakespeare is using the old story for a very serious discussion of fundamental issues, political and philosophical.

The same applies to the Trojan debate (II.2) where, as we have seen, the theme is extended to the even more general question of whether the whole war is worth the sacrifices involved. Not even in the Roman tragedies is there such an insistent examining of traditional values, again, not in a spirit of comedy, but with evident concern for the implications and consequences, although in the end, Hector's about-face and his announcement that he has already sent a challenge to the Greek camp illustrate once more the inconsistency of human idealism and the frustrating contrast between profession and action, high-sounding rhetoric and actual achievement.[149]

The seriousness of the debates is underlined rather than invalidated by the professional railer. Thersites is more offensive and more sweepingly cynical even than Apemantus in *Timon of Athens*, and the scenes in which he appears are often as uncomic and venomous as the blackest Jacobean satire. Yet he firmly belongs to the tradition of the licensed fool, and it is a mistake to take him too seriously, as if he were an authorial chorus to the play. He dismisses the whole Trojan enterprise in no uncertain terms:

All the argument is a whore and a cuckold: a good quarrel to draw emulous factions, and bleed to death upon. (II.3.74–6)

This is a way of looking at the events the dramatist does not ignore, but the whole play makes clear enough that it is not the only one and that the subject is rather more complex. In a way, it is the mentality of a Fortinbras that is under scrutiny here, and the play seems to ask, as Hamlet did, whether the actual price justifies the enormous effort, whether honor and reputation are worth bleeding for, and whether abstract moral and political ideals have any concrete meaning. The answer is not that Thersites is right and that all traditional values are nothing but deceptive words. The united endeavor to give them meaning and to translate them into positive action may be all too often vain and even ridiculous, but it is not despicable or useless. The high rhetoric of the debates throughout the play is not all hollow or insincere, even though it is not supported by inspiring achievement.

The love plot, after its swift introduction in the first two scenes, does not return for some time. Meanwhile, we see Troilus as a prominent speaker in the Trojan debate (II.2), where, for all his naive idealism, he appears to convince even Hector; but there is no mention of his infatuation, and when Cressida is next referred to, it is in the context of a decidedly frivolous domestic scene involving Paris, Helen and Pandarus. When the lovers themselves enter the stage again, their first night together has already been arranged by mutual consent, with Pandarus as the prurient stage-manager (III.2). Many readers and critics have had difficulties with this scene, and to compare it with the love scenes in *Romeo and Juliet* is to become aware of the difference between a more conventional wooing and the strikingly joyless coming together of these two lovers. They both seem to be afraid of imminent disappointment rather than happily expectant, and this is not just because Troilus' love is merely sexual appetite or because Cressida is a wanton.[150] Their vague apprehensions link the scene with the political debates in both camps, because they both have no real trust in the possibility of rewarding achievement and lasting happiness. The dramatist does not give us any deep insight into the true thoughts of the lovers: they seem to be performing their parts in a prepared script rather than acting out of a genuine impulse, and I think this deliberate withholding of reliable information and authorial verdict is an important part of the play's dramatic technique. The audience knows well enough that the fears expressed by Troilus and

Cressida are more than justified by the coming events: Cressida will have even more reason to be offended by her own company than she has now (III.2.142–8), and Troilus will all too soon be mocked by his achievements (IV.2.71). Yet the whole tone of the scene is not one of mischievous satire and cheap ridicule, but of detached knowingness. There is no youthful enthusiasm in this love scene nor the conviction that this moment is really the fulfilment of their deepest desires. This ambiguous tone, hovering uneasily between levity and sadness, is continued in the morning scene (IV.2), again so very different from the 'aubade' in *Romeo and Juliet* (III.5), a romantic version of the same traditional situation. What genuine affection and seriousness there is in the brief dialogue is quickly undercut by Cressida's suspicions and Pandarus' salacious mockery.[151]

In this case, too, however, the lovers can hardly be blamed for their subdued mood and their forebodings because they are overtaken by the swiftness of destiny at the very moment when they have finally come together. It seems to me most remarkable that Shakespeare has altered the time-scheme of his source in a way very similar to *Romeo and Juliet*. In Chaucer's *Troilus and Criseyde*, the lovers are allowed a period of complete happiness that lasts about a year at least, during which Criseyde is introduced to the full wealth of love experience and Troilus himself feels sorry for any man who is not in love.[152] Shakespeare telescopes the events in such a way that the exchange of Cressida for the traitor Antenor (demanded by the traitor Calchas) is arranged while she is lying with Troilus, just as Romeo's banishment is pronounced immediately before his wedding-night. This speeding up of the action has the important effect of not allowing the lovers any time to prove the sincerity of their love. They have had a moment of sensual satisfaction, but it was not, as in the case of Romeo and Juliet, meant as the final seal to their union, but a first favor granted by Cressida under some pressure and with misgivings. Her hysterical professions of everlasting faith cannot possibly be as deeply rooted as those of Chaucer's heroine because the play has not presented the lovers in complete harmony for more than odd moments (IV.2.102–8). This also, and it is perhaps the most important consequence, makes Cressida's opportunism and eventual betrayal of Troilus less damning or at least not so deeply moving as it is in Chaucer, because the love she abandons was so brief, superficial, and diffident. It is not that her faithlessness is condoned or made light of, but it does not come as an unexpected shock and it is not as deeply upsetting to all our assumptions about ideal love and the possibility of lasting happiness. The play has never encouraged such illusions and it has made abundantly clear that Troilus' expectations are founded on a rather limited view of reality. It is not only his false image of Cressida that will be shattered, but also his ideals of heroic fame and worthwile endeavor.

Shakespeare's treatment of these last stages of Cressida's career is very different from Chaucer's. After her departure from Troy she appears in two more scenes, both rather more comic than tragic, although her behavior is far from simple and Shakespeare does not condemn her out of hand any more than Chaucer does. Instead, he lightens the tone, makes Cressida a comparatively insignificant part of a much larger context, and introduces comedy where Chaucer presents a much more consistently tragic picture. Cressida's reception in the Greek camp is usually interpreted as if she has turned whore as soon as she is out of Troilus' sight. In fact, her reaction is not very different from that in her first encounter with Pandarus (1.2), and her witty replies only show that she attempts to meet the 'merry Greeks' (IV.4.55) on their own level. She has certainly lost none of her self-possession or her basic distrust of men. But the kissing 'in general' need not be seen as Ulysses sees it: he seems to compare her with Helen, as Patroclus does earlier in the scene (IV.5.28–9). The reminder of what the whole war is really about implicates the men as much as it does Cressida, because it is they who first put an exaggerated price on the woman and then abuse her when she does not live up to it. As Cressida had discovered much earlier, 'Men prize the thing ungain'd more than it is' (1.2.294). Ulysses' disgust is obviously not only occasioned by the scene just witnessed and should certainly not be taken as an authorial appraisal of Cressida; it expresses his angry impatience with a war fought in a ridiculous cause:

> O deadly gall, and theme of all our scorns!
> For which we lose our heads to gild his horns.   (IV.5.30–1)

Cressida is only another instance of the wrong value put by men on things, and the play is not concerned with her personality as much as with the false ideals she is expected to embody and with the discovery that she is not able to support this role. Such discovery can be tragic and comic at the same time, comic for those who have never believed in the original valuation and have been looking forward to the moment of enlightenment, but tragic for him who has put all his trust in an ideal partly of his own making and who suddenly finds himself cruelly deceived. It is the simultaneous presence of both points of view that gives the brilliant scene of double eavesdropping its comic and at the same time painful character (V.2). There is nothing quite like this scene in the whole canon.

On the whole, eavesdropping is a device used more often in comedy than in tragedy, especially when a character gives himself away to the very persons he wants to deceive.[153] There is usually a touch of *Cosi fan tutte* about it, especially when the betrayal is as swift and unlikely as it is here.[154] Whereas Chaucer goes out of his way to explain the tactics of Diomedes and Criseyde's hopeless dilemma, and refuses to tell us how long it took the seducer to overcome her resistance, Shakespeare has her yield to Diomedes as soon as she has arrived in Calchas' tent, and though some of the changes can be explained by the dramatic medium,[155] there was no need to make the speed of her fall so obvious. This again suggests that the dramatist was not particularly interested in Cressida's individual character. There is no exploration of her motives, no elaborate defence, as in Chaucer, and no deep moral concern, as in Henryson. The attention is all on Troilus and his tragic experience, but even this is not presented without some deflating commentary: Ulysses fails to understand Troilus' anguish, and Thersites only sees its absurd side:

> TROIL. Let it not be believ'd for womanhood.
>   Think, we had mothers; ...
> ULYSS. What hath she done, prince, that can soil our mothers?
> TROIL. Nothing at all, unless that this were she.
> THERS. Will a swagger himself out on 's own eyes?   (V.2.128–9,133–5)

The authority of an imagined ideal, of a value based only on personal estimation, is undermined by the authority of sensual perception. We, the audience, have actually witnessed Cressida's fall, and there is something pathetic as well as painful in Troilus' agonized attempt to understand what he has seen. The tortuous rhetoric, combining strained logic and overwhelming emotion, is very different from the other tragedies:

> This she? – No, this is Diomed's Cressida.
> If beauty have a soul, this is not she;
> If souls guide vows, if vows be sanctimonies,
> If sanctimony be the gods' delight,
> If there be rule in unity itself,
> This is not she. O madness of discourse,
> That cause sets up with and against itself!
> Bifold authority! where reason can revolt
> Without perdition, and loss assume all reason
> Without revolt. This is, and is not, Cressid.   (V.2.136–45)

This is quite unlike Hamlet's disillusioned world-weariness or Othello's heroic despair, though the experience is very similar, at least in the mind of the speaker. Critics have quoted Othello's 'when I love thee not,/ Chaos is come again' (III.3.91–2) in this connection, but the comparison seems to me somewhat misleading, because the context is so very different.[156] The whole play has shown that Troilus' idea of Cressida and of love's achievement was founded on an illusion, and the contrast between rhetoric and reality was at times so glaring as to be no longer tragic. Troilus' infatuation has not been presented to the audience with the full pathos and intensity of Romeo's passion or Othello's maturer love. It was never quite of the innocently pure and ennobling quality so much emphasized by Chaucer, and the lesson he learns is presented by dramatic devices that are as near to comedy as they are to tragedy. Cressida's fall, too, as we have seen, is far less seriously moving or morally disturbing than Criseyde's pitiful defeat by circumstances and her own weakness. It is chiefly because of all these contradictory impressions and emotions that the scene has been called 'the most complex scene in all Shakespeare's works'.[157] This is a rather large claim, but it is understandable because the scene makes such unusual demands on the audience's attention and sympathy. It is also closely linked with the earlier debates about value, reputation, and the workings of time, which gives added weight to Troilus' experience. The comedy of seduction enacted in Calchas' tent is an episode in a war fought in consequence of a very similar incident; Troilus is not the first to be so conspicuously betrayed.

Whether we find this conclusion more cynical and pessimistic than straightforward tragedy or satirical comedy is a matter of individual disposition, and a producer has to make the difficult decision where to put the emphasis; but it would certainly be an impoverishment to leave out any one of the conflicting elements altogether. The play would be much less disturbing if all the rhetoric were sincere, if Troilus' love had been all pure and idealistic, and if Cressida's betrayal were no more than what is to be expected of a whore. It is more helpful to recognize the unorthodox and experimental qualities of the play and to accept its refusal to conform to any of the traditional patterns. I do not, however, think that this kind of experiment would have been possible with a less well-known plot, and it seems obvious to me that it is addressed to an audience thoroughly familiar with the outline of the story and the reputation of all the chief actors. This general foreknowledge provides an important focus; without it, the unity of the play would be much harder to define.

The quick succession of brief scenes that concludes the play, hastily brings together the various strands of the action: it shows the total collapse of Trojan idealism and hope of survival as well as the temporary triumph of Grecian brutality and purpose. The battle is a hectic sequence of contrasting stances, of heroic noises, unchivalrous butchering and desperate resistance. Troilus' high ideals have given way to a despairing cynicism that, Aeneas fears, will 'discomfort all the host' (v.10.10). His repudiation of any 'vice of mercy' (v.3.37) frightens Hector, who calls him 'savage' (v.3.49), and his 'Mad and fantastic execution' (v.5.38) astonishes even Ulysses. They are obviously the result of his complete disillusionment with Cressida, whose letter is contemptuously dismissed as 'Words, words, mere words, no matter from the heart' (v.3.108).[158] It looks as if in the original version of the play, Pandarus was to be dismissed too at this point and the final scene was to end with the typical tragedy couplet:

> Strike a free march to Troy! With comfort go:
> Hope of revenge shall hide our inward woe.   (v.10.30–1)[159]

It is a feeble attempt to sound a note of confidence and hope, eventually doomed to failure, but it is very much in keeping with the conventional conclusion of a historical tragedy, whereas the alternative ending leaves the audience with a very different impression and clearly emphasizes the satirical aspects of the play. It certainly does not make it a comedy, but it brings out its particular qualities as a theatrical re-creation of familiar characters. The Pandarus who steps out of the world of the play to address the audience draws attention to his reputation and timeless role, and he makes fun not of the events of the play so much as of the whole occasion. It is also quite possible that the character of Pandarus and his 'conceited wooing', as announced by the Quarto's second title page, was so successful with the audience that the performance of *Troilus and Cressida* turned into a more comic event than the text would suggest. Pandarus' epilogue makes quite clear that it was all a theatrical entertainment, and he tries to establish some complicity between himself as the traditional pander and the men in the audience. This necessarily affects the tragic impact of the performance, but it does not completely alter the character of the play. It is certainly not a conventional tragedy, but it is easy to see why the editors of the First Folio would put it nowhere else but among the tragedies.[160]

Abbreviations

CL	*Comparative Literature*
EC	*Essays in Criticism*
JEGP	*Journal of English and Germanic Philology*
MLQ	*Modern Language Quarterly*
MLR	*Modern Language Review*
PMLA	*Publications of the Modern Language Association of America*
RenD	*Renaissance Drama*
RES	*Review of English Studies*
ShakS	*Shakespeare Studies*
ShS	*Shakespeare Survey*
SJW	*Deutsche Shakespeare-Gesellschaft West. Jahrbuch*
SP	*Studies in Philology*
SQ	*Shakespeare Quarterly*
UTQ	*University of Toronto Quarterly*
YES	*Yearbook of English Studies*

Notes

I   INTRODUCTION

1 *The Works of Geoffrey Chaucer*, ed. F. N. Robinson, 2nd edn (Oxford, 1957), p. 331 (Book II, Prose 2, 70–2).

2 Kenneth Muir, *Shakespeare's Tragic Sequence* (London, 1972), p. 12.

3 See also John Bayley, *Shakespeare and Tragedy* (London, 1981), p. 5, for comments on this diversity. Bayley's book is one of the most original and imaginative studies of the tragedies to have appeared recently.

4 See the classic study by Willard Farnham, *The Medieval Heritage of Elizabethan Tragedy* (Oxford, 1936), and the excellent edition of the *Mirror for Magistrates* by Lily B. Campbell (Cambridge, 1938; repr. New York, 1960; supplementary volume, Cambridge, 1946).

5 Quoted from the edition by Andrew Gurr, The New Cambridge Shakespeare (Cambridge, 1984).

6 The influence of Seneca on Elizabethan drama has often been studied. See the very useful survey by G. K. Hunter, 'Seneca and the Elizabethans: A Case-Study in "Influence"', *ShS*, 20 (1967), 17–26, repr. in Hunter's collection of essays, *Dramatic Identities and Cultural Tradition: Studies in Shakespeare and his Contemporaries* (Liverpool, 1978), pp. 159–73.

7 'Thus the tragic picture is incompatible with the Christian faith. It is equally incompatible with any form of religious belief that assumes the existence of a personal and kindly God', Clifford Leech, *Shakespeare's Tragedies and other Studies in Seventeenth Century Drama* (London, 1950), p. 18. Of course, Clifford Leech does not leave it at that. His whole discussion of the concept of tragedy (Chapters 1–4) is very helpful and stimulating.

8 Muir, *Shakespeare's Tragic Sequence*, pp. 140–1.

9 See the excellent brief excursus on Shakespearian tragedy in Ernest Schanzer, *The Problem Plays of Shakespeare. A Study of 'Julius Caesar', 'Measure for Measure', 'Antony and Cleopatra'* (London, 1963), pp. 57–63.

10 A. C. Bradley, *Shakespearean Tragedy. Lectures on 'Hamlet', 'Othello', 'King Lear', 'Macbeth'* (London, 1904); With a new introduction by J. R. Brown (London, 1985), pp. 28–9. On Bradley's critical premises and his impact on later criticism, see the valuable study by Katharine Cooke, *A. C. Bradley and his Influence in Twentieth-Century Shakespeare Criticism* (Oxford, 1972). Since the appearance of the book Bradley's contribution to our understanding of the tragedies has been appreciated even more fully than the author anticipated.

11 See Maynard Mack, *'King Lear' in Our Time* (Berkeley, 1965), p. 117, and Muir, *Shakespeare's Tragic Sequence*, p. 139.

12 See Ivor Morris, *Shakespeare's God. The Role of Religion in the Tragedies* (London, 1972), p. 308.

13 'a play or a poem says what cannot be said discursively', Norman Rabkin, *Shakespeare and the Common Understanding* (New York, 1967), p. 55.

14 See, for instance, Leonora L. Brodwin, *Elizabethan Love Tragedy 1587–1625* (New York, 1971).

2 THE EARLY TRAGEDIES

1 See the excellent study by Nicholas Brooke, *Shakespeare's Early Tragedies* (London, 1968). Nicholas Brooke includes *Richard II, Julius Caesar* and *Hamlet* among the early tragedies, which makes good sense in the context of his discussion. For my purpose, however, I have preferred a more conventional classification.

2 I quote from the excellent edition by Eugene M. Waith, The Oxford Shakespeare (Oxford, 1984).

3 Quoted from the edition by E. A. Horsman, The Revels Plays (London, 1960), Induction, 107–11.

4 On the play's early reception see the introductions by Eugene M. Waith, pp. 1–27, and J. C. Maxwell, in his still very useful edition, The Arden Shakespeare (London, 1953), pp. xi–xxx.

5 Quoted in Geoffrey Bullough, *Narrative and Dramatic Sources of Shakespeare*, vol. VI (London, 1966), pp. 4–5. On Ravencroft's adaptation, see also Waith's edition, pp. 45–6.

6 See the important older study by Howard Baker, *Induction to Tragedy. A Study in a Development of Form in 'Gorboduc', 'The Spanish Tragedy' and 'Titus Andronicus'* (Baton Rouge, Louisiana, 1939). The influence of Seneca is probably underestimated here, in opposition to earlier critics.

7 On Shakespeare's creative use of classical influences see the useful study by Grace Starry West, 'Going by the Book: Classical Allusions in Shakespeare's *Titus Andronicus*', *SP*, 79 (1982), 62–77, and, in a wider context, the chapter *'Titus Andronicus.* Rome and the Family' in Robert S. Miola, *Shakespeare's Rome* (Cambridge, 1983), pp. 42–75.

8 See the good discussion on the sources in Waith's edition, pp. 27–38, and the texts printed in Bullough's indispensable collection, *Narrative and Dramatic Sources*, VI, 34–79.

9 On the Vice Tradition see the seminal study by Bernard Spivack, *Shakespeare and the Allegory of Evil* (New York, 1958), and Robert Weimann, *Shakespeare and the Popular Tradition in the Theater: Studies in the Social Dimension of Dramatic Form and Function*, ed. Robert Schwartz (Baltimore, 1978), *passim*.

10 See the edition by Philip Edwards, The Revels Plays (London, 1959), and the excellent essay by G. K. Hunter, 'Ironies of Justice in *The Spanish Tragedy*', *RenD*, 8 (1965), 89–104, reprinted in G. K. Hunter, *Dramatic Identities and Cultural Tradition: Studies in Shakespeare and his Contemporaries* (Liverpool, 1978), pp. 214–29.

11 See Muriel C. Bradbrook, *Shakespeare and Elizabethan Poetry* (London, 1951), especially the chapter 'Moral Heraldry', pp. 96–111.

12 See Waith's note on the passage in his edition, p. 187, and J. W. Lever's edition of *The Rape of Lucrece*, New Penguin Shakespeare (Harmondsworth, 1971). The story of Lucrece is referred to twice in the play (II.1.109 and IV.1.62–3).

13 Most critics have commented on the influence of Ovid. See especially the studies by Baker and Brooke.

14 Philomela's story is already quoted by Aaron before the deed. See II.3.43 and Waith's note for further references. Further, Ann Thompson, 'Philomel in *Titus Andronicus* and *Cymbeline*', *ShS*, 31 (1978), 23–32.

15 See especially the passage printed from Arthur Golding's translation of the *Metamorphoses* (1597) by Bullough, *Narrative and Dramatic Sources*, VI, 54 (lines 705–15). On the staging problems and the play's artificial character, see Michael Hattaway, *Elizabethan Popular Theatre. Plays in Performance* (London, 1982), chapter 8: '*Titus Andronicus*: strange images of death', pp. 186–207. See also G. Harold Metz, 'Stage History of *Titus Andronicus*', *SQ*, 28 (1977), 154–69.

16 This is pointed out by Brooke. On the close relationship between theme and form see the important studies by Eugene M. Waith, 'The Metamorphosis of Violence in *Titus Andronicus*', *ShS*, 10 (1957), 39–49, and Alan Sommers, "Wilderness of Tigers": Structure and Symbolism in *Titus Andronicus*', *EC*, 10 (1960), 275–89. See also Richard T. Brucher, '"Tragedy, Laugh On": Comic Violence in *Titus Andronicus*', *RenD*, NS, 10 (1979), 71–91.

17 Brooke rightly praises the 'tremendous inventiveness and intelligence' manifested in this early tragedy (p. 16). See also A. R. Braunmuller, 'Early Shakespearian Tragedy and its Contemporary Context: Cause and Emotion in *Titus Andronicus*, *Richard III*, and *The Rape of Lucrece*', in Malcolm Bradbury and David Palmer, eds., *Shakespearian Tragedy*, Stratford-upon-Avon Studies, 20 (London, 1984), pp. 97–128.

18 I quote from the thorough edition by G. Blakemore Evans, The New Cambridge Shakespeare (Cambridge, 1984); see also the good editions by T. J. B. Spencer, New Penguin Shakespeare (Harmondsworth, 1967), and Brian Gibbons, The Arden Shakespeare (London, 1980), with an excellent introduction.

19 See especially Brooke, *Shakespeare's Early Tragedies*, and his earlier essay, 'The Tragic Spectacle in *Titus Andronicus* and *Romeo and Juliet*', in Clifford Leech, ed., *Shakespeare: The Tragedies. A Collection of Critical Essays* (Chicago, 1965), pp. 243–56.

20 The complete text of Brooke's poem is given in Bullough, *Narrative and Dramatic Sources*, I, 284–363; there are long excerpts in the editions by Gibbons and Evans. On earlier love tragedies see Leonora L. Brodwin, *Elizabethan Love Tragedy 1587–1625* (New York, 1971).

21 Bullough, *Narrative and Dramatic Sources*, I, 284–5.

22 See Gibbons' edition, pp. 36–7, and especially Ann Thompson, *Shakespeare's Chaucer. A Study in Literary Origins* (Liverpool, 1978), pp. 94–110, as well as her earlier, very perceptive essay, '*Troilus and Criseyde* and *Romeo and Juliet*', *YES*, 6 (1976), 26–37. See also Dieter Mehl, 'Chaucerian Comedy and Shakespearean Tragedy', *SJW* 1984, 111–27.

23 See particularly M. M. Mahood, *Shakespeare's Wordplay* (London, 1957), pp. 56–76, where the idea of the 'Liebestod' seems to me a little overstated.

24 See the discussion by Evans in his edition, pp. 8–11.

25 See the studies by Bradbrook and Mahood. Most critics comment on the play's lyrical qualities. For references to Elizabethan sonneteers see A. J. Earl, 'Romeo and Juliet and the Elizabethan Sonnets', English, 27 (1978), 99–119.

26 See the very interesting study by Susan Snyder, The Comic Matrix of Shakespeare's Tragedies. 'Romeo and Juliet', 'Hamlet', 'Othello' and 'King Lear' (Princeton, N.J., 1979), pp. 57–73.

27 See, for instance, Shakespeare's Much Ado About Nothing and The Winter's Tale, or Middleton's A Chaste Maid in Cheapside.

28 See the different views on the relative dating of the two plays in the editions by Gibbons (pp. 30–1) and Evans (pp. 5–6) as well as the editions of A Midsummer Night's Dream by Harold Brooks, The Arden Shakespeare (London, 1979), pp. xlii–xlv, and R. A. Foakes, The New Cambridge Shakespeare (Cambridge, 1984), p. 2.

29 Critics have greatly differed on this point. A rather extreme Christian reading which, I feel, does violence to the play, is proposed by Roy W. Battenhouse in Shakespearean Tragedy. Its Art and Its Christian Premises (Bloomington, Indiana, 1969), pp. 102–30. A little more cautious is Franklin M. Dickey, Not Wisely But Too Well. Shakespeare's Love Tragedies (San Marino, 1957), pp. 63–117; a very different interpretation is suggested by John Lawlor, 'Romeo and Juliet' in J. R. Brown and B. Harris, eds., Early Shakespeare, Stratford-upon-Avon Studies, 3 (London, 1961), pp. 122–43. My own view is much nearer to Lawlor than to Dickey or Battenhouse.

30 This is also a traditional motif in tragedy. See the very lucid introduction by Alfred Harbage to his useful anthology, Shakespeare. The Tragedies. A Collection of Critical Essays, Twentieth Century Views (Englewood Cliffs, N.J., 1964), pp. 1–9.

31 Quoted from the edition by Agnes Latham, The Arden Shakespeare (London, 1975).

32 The intensity and vulnerability of this love are stressed in several more recent interpretations. See, for instance, Norman Rabkin, Shakespeare and the Common Understanding (New York, 1967), pp. 162–84; Ruth Nevo, Tragic Form in Shakespeare (Princeton, 1972), pp. 31–58; Derick R. C. Marsh, Passion Lends Them Power. A study of Shakespeare's love tragedies (Manchester, 1976), pp. 46–88.

33 Brooke has some very acute remarks on the limitation of this love, rather more so in his essay of 1965 than in his book. (See above, note 19.)

34 See Bertrand Evans, 'The Brevity of Friar Laurence', PMLA, 65 (1950), 841–65, and, in some more detail, his Shakespeare's Tragic Practice (Oxford, 1979), pp. 22–51.

35 The relationship between the Nurse and Pandarus is even clearer in Brooke's poem. The nurse is rather more active and, like Pandarus, urges the lovers to consummate their love in very practical terms (Brooke in Bullough, Narrative and Dramatic Sources, I, 284–363, lines 890–900).

36 See Evans' notes on the passage, and the additional note on p. 202.

37 See the illustrated stage history in Evans' edition, pp. 28–48, with useful bibliographical references.

3 THE 'GREAT' TRAGEDIES

1 This is the title of the play in the two Quartos of 1603 and 1604. All quotations in this chapter are from the excellent and near-exhaustive edition by Harold Jenkins, The Arden Shakespeare (London, 1982). There is a briefer, but very helpful and rather more theatre-orientated edition by Philip Edwards for the New Cambridge Shakespeare (Cambridge, 1985), a good edition by T. J. B. Spencer, with an admirable introduction by Anne Barton, The New Penguin Shakespeare (Harmondsworth, 1980), and the classic New Variorum Edition in two volumes by H. H. Furness (Philadelphia, 1877, repr. 1963 by Dover Books), still indispensable for its generous sampling of older Hamlet criticism.

2 See the detailed and judicious account in Jenkins' edition, pp. 82–112; and Geoffrey Bullough, Narrative and Dramatic Sources of Shakespeare, vol. VII (London, 1983), pp. 3–189, where the most important texts are reprinted.

3 See the convincing estimate in Jenkins' edition, pp. 97–101.

4 On the history of Elizabethan revenge tragedy see F. T. Bowers, Elizabethan Revenge Tragedy 1587–1642, 2nd edn (Gloucester, Mass., 1959). For Hamlet see E. Prosser, Hamlet and Revenge (Stanford, 1967), and the excellent comments by Helen Gardner in her The Business of Criticism (London, 1959), pp. 35–51, reprinted in the useful anthology John Jump, ed., Shakespeare, 'Hamlet'. A Casebook (London, 1968), pp. 137–50.

5 Many critics have felt that there is a close thematic relationship between the first scene and the rest of the play. See, for instance, the influential essay by Maynard Mack, 'The World of Hamlet', Yale Review, 41 (1951–52), 502–23, reprinted several times, e.g. in Casebook, pp. 86–107, and Harry Levin, The Question of Hamlet (New York, 1959), pp. 20–1.

6 See, in particular, the important study by Anne Righter, Shakespeare and the Idea of the Play (London, 1962; Penguin Books, Harmondsworth, 1967), pp. 138–47.

7 This, too, is one of the unendingly discussed problems of Hamlet criticism. See John Dover Wilson's important discussion in What Happens in 'Hamlet' (Cambridge, 1935), pp. 51–86, and, with much additional material, Prosser's study Hamlet and Revenge, though her conclusions are very different from mine. See also, on the ambiguous role of the Ghost, E. A. J. Honigmann's very balanced interpretation in Shakespeare: Seven Tragedies. The dramatist's manipulation of response (London, 1976), pp. 54–76.

There are some very good comments in Jenkins' edition, pp. 154–7, and passim. For contemporary attitudes towards ghosts and their bearing on Hamlet see the interesting book by Roland Mushat Frye, The Renaissance Hamlet. Issues and Responses in 1600 (Princeton, 1984), pp. 11–29. The book will be found useful on many other problems of the play and their context.

8 A. C. Bradley, Shakespearean Tragedy. Lectures on 'Hamlet', 'Othello', 'King Lear', 'Macbeth' (London, 1985), pp. 103–4; apart from the discussion of such psychological pseudo-problems, Bradley's interpretation is still one of the most impressive attempts to understand the play.

9 See Anne Barton's introduction to the New Penguin edition, pp. 24–7.

10 See the note by Jenkins, pp. 462–3. The longer notes in his edition are invaluable for their good sense and the concise clarification of many traditional problems in Hamlet.

11 Quoted from Sir Philip Sidney, *Selected Poems*, ed. Katherine Duncan-Jones (Oxford, 1973), p. 139 (Sonnet 45).

12 See Righter, *Shakespeare and the Idea of the Play*, p. 145–6, and the passage in the anonymous play, *A Warning for Fair Women* (1599), quoted in Bullough, *Narrative and Dramatic Sources*, VII, 179–81.

13 Most interpretations of the play discuss the question of revenge and Hamlet's attitude to conventional views. On the older critics see the good survey by Clifford Leech, 'Studies in *Hamlet*, 1901–1955', *ShS*, 9 (1956), 1–15, reprinted, together with several other important articles, in Kenneth Muir and Stanley Wells, eds., *Aspects of 'Hamlet'. Articles Reprinted from* Shakespeare Survey (Cambridge, 1979), pp. 1–15.

14 On Shakespeare's use of the soliloquy, see the essay 'Shakespeare's Soliloquies', in Wolfgang Clemen, *Shakespeare's Dramatic Art. Collected Essays* (London, 1972), pp. 147–62.

15 On this famous soliloquy see the excellent discussion in Jenkins' edition, pp. 484–93; a different view is proposed by Edwards in his new edition, pp. 47–50, and notes on the text of the passage, pp. 146–7. Edwards' view is that Hamlet is definitely contemplating suicide. For some earlier comments see D. G. James, *The Dream of Learning* (Oxford, 1951), pp. 38–48, and L. C. Knights, *An Approach to 'Hamlet'* (London, 1960), pp. 71–80. See also the useful article by Catherine Belsey, 'The Case of Hamlet's Conscience', *SP*, 76 (1979), 127–48.

16 This is much more obvious in the chronicle sources, where Ophelia is put in Hamlet's way with a frankly sexual purpose. Shakespeare changed the motives, but some of the original baseness of the maneuver has no doubt survived in his version.

17 'The trite little couplet is recognizably Polonian', Barton's introduction to the New Penguin edition, pp. 25–6. Perhaps this is a little too definite, but the idea seems to me quite illuminating.

18 This is the much disputed theory by John Dover Wilson, often tried in the theatre; he has Hamlet enter as early as II.2.159, so that he overhears Polonius' first proposal. See Wilson's important edition, The New Shakespeare (Cambridge, 1934), pp. lvi–lix, and his editorial stage direction. The idea is firmly rejected by Jenkins, pp. 464 and 496–7.

19 See Levin L. Schücking, *The Meaning of 'Hamlet'*, transl. by Graham Rawson (London, 1937; repr. New York, 1966): 'His triumph in unmasking the King has led to no practical decision. The mountain has laboured and brought forth a mouse.... His principal task is forgotten' (pp. 135–6).

20 The literature on this scene is immense. For a summary see my *The Elizabethan Dumb Show. The History of a Dramatic Convention* (London, 1965), pp. 110–20; on the convention of the 'play within a play' see my 'Forms and Functions of the Play within a Play', *RenD*, 8 (1965), 41–61, with further bibliographical references. See also Lee Sheridan Cox, *Figurative Design in 'Hamlet'. The Significance of the Dumb Show* (Ohio, State University Press, 1973), who discusses the dumb show as part of the design of the whole play.

21 Spencer's note in his New Penguin edition, p. 281. John Dover Wilson's solution, occasionally adopted in the theatre, to have the King deeply engaged in conversation with the Queen during the dumb show, is quite unnecessary. See the

stage direction in his edition, III.2.133, and his note, pp. 200–1. Again Jenkins has a masterly long note on the subject, pp. 501–5.

22 A particularly gruesome example is Cyril Tourneur's *The Revenger's Tragedy* (1605–6), a play obviously indebted to *Hamlet*. See the edition by R. A. Foakes, The Revels Plays (London, 1966). See also R. A. Foakes, 'The Art of Cruelty: Hamlet and Vindice', *ShS*, 26 (1973), 21–31, and in Muir and Wells, *Aspects of 'Hamlet'*, pp. 28–38.

23 See the chapter 'Hamlet and Our Problems' in Michael Goldman's very original book *Shakespeare and the Energies of Drama* (Princeton, 1972), esp. pp. 79–86.

24 The idea of this scene again goes back to the chronicle source and it is interesting to watch Shakespeare transforming the original situation. There is some evidence that Shakespeare revised the last part of the scene. See Edward's edition pp. 14–19, and his notes on the text.

25 In John Barton's Stratford production of 1980 it was suggested that the Queen did, in fact, see the Ghost, but refused to admit it to herself or to Hamlet. It gave an interesting twist to the scene, though there is, of course, nothing in the text to support the idea.

26 Quoted from the edition by G. K. Hunter, Regents Renaissance Drama Series (University of Nebraska Press, 1965; London, 1966). On the relationship between the two plays see Hunter's introduction, pp. xviii–xxi.

27 In Belleforest, the mother explicitly joins forces with the revenger and insists on her innocence. There are clear traces of this version in the First Quarto of 1603. See the text of Q.1 in the New Variorum Edition, II, 72 (lines 1544–7).

28 Harold Jenkins' interpretation of the play (pp. 122–59) is particularly convincing on this point. His position is clear from his comment on T. S. Eliot: 'A critic who fails to perceive that *Hamlet* is a play about sons and fathers seems unlikely to have anything useful to say about it' (p. 134, no. 2).

29 See my 'Emblems in English Renaissance Drama', *RenD*, NS, 2 (1969), 39–57, esp. 52–4.

30 This is emphasized by the fact that Hamlet's age is now explicitly raised to 30. On the problem of Hamlet's age, see Jenkins' note, pp. 551–4. On the graveyard scene and the comic elements in *Hamlet* see the perceptive comments in Susan Snyder, *The Comic Matrix of Shakespeare's Tragedies* (Princeton, 1979), pp. 91–136.

31 See V.2.77–8. On the textual problems of the passage and their implications see Edwards' edition, pp. 17–19 and 56–8.

32 On this complex issue see Gardner's excellent interpretation. On Hamlet's 'development' see also Ruth Nevo, *Tragic Form in Shakespeare* (Princeton, 1972), pp. 128–75, and Bernard McElroy, *Shakespeare's Mature Tragedies* (Princeton, 1973), pp. 29–88.

33 See Kenneth Muir, *Shakespeare's Tragic Sequence* (London, 1972), pp. 90–2, and his more detailed interpretation, *Shakespeare: 'Hamlet'*, Studies in English Literature, 13 (London, 1963), pp. 53–61.

34 On the play's conclusion see Walter C. Foreman, Jr, *The Music of the Close. The Final Scenes in Shakespeare's Tragedies* (Lexington, 1978), pp. 73–112.

35 All quotations are from the excellent edition by Norman Sanders, The New Cambridge Shakespeare (Cambridge, 1984). See also the useful editions by

Kenneth Muir, New Penguin Shakespeare (Harmondsworth, 1968), and A. Walker and J. D. Wilson, The New Shakespeare (Cambridge, 1957); further material in the editions by M. R. Ridley, The Arden Shakespeare (London, 1958), and H. H. Furness, New Variorum Edition (Philadelphia, 1886).

36 See the edition by J. W. Lever, The Arden Shakespeare (London, 1965).

37 See Bullough, Narrative and Dramatic Sources, VII, 193–265, and, more briefly, Sanders' edition, pp. 2–10. For some additional observations see Maurianne S. Adams, '"Ocular Proof" in Othello and its Source', PMLA, 79 (1964), 234–41.

38 Bullough, Narrative and Dramatic Sources, VII, 251.

39 See Snyder, The Comic Matrix of Shakespeare's Tragedies, pp. 73–90; on the Italian tradition, see Leo Salingar, Shakespeare and the Traditions of Comedy (Cambridge, 1974), pp. 175–242. For some very interesting remarks on Shakespeare's Venice in Othello and The Merchant of Venice see A. D. Nuttall, A New Mimesis. Shakespeare and the Representation of Reality (London, 1983), pp. 120–43. See also, for some links between Othello and domestic tragedy, Peter L. Rudnytzky, 'A Woman Killed with Kindness as Subtext for Othello', RenD, NS, 14 (1983), 103–24.

40 Apart from the conventional comedy situation, the scene also reflects the traditional motif of the stranger who wins the love of a native girl; e.g. Jason and Medea or Aeneas and Dido.

41 See the chapter on Hamlet, above, p. 42.

42 The scene, only reported in the play, in which Othello tells of his adventure, has been the subject of pictorial representations; it may owe something to the famous scene in which Aeneas reports the destruction of Troy before Dido, which appears in Marlowe's Dido Queen of Carthage, II.1. and in Hamlet, II.2.446–514 ('Pyrrhus-speech').

43 This aspect is emphasized in the brilliant interpretation by Helen Gardner, 'The Noble Moor', British Academy Lecture 1956, reprinted in the useful anthology John Wain, ed., Shakespeare, 'Othello'. A Casebook (London, 1971), pp. 147–68. See also Reuben A. Brower, Hero and Saint. Shakespeare and the Graeco-Roman Heroic Tradition (Oxford, 1971), pp. 1–28; the chapter is entitled 'The Noble Moor'. For similar and very different views see the important survey of scholarship by Helen Gardner, 'Othello: A Retrospect, 1900–67', ShS, 21 (1968), 1–11, repr. in Kenneth Muir and Philip Edwards, eds., Aspects of 'Othello'. Articles Reprinted from Shakespeare Survey (Cambridge, 1977), pp. 1–11.

44 Bullough, Narrative and Dramatic Sources, VII, 242. See also his contemptuous reference to 'feathered Cupid' in 1.3.265. The contrast between this love and 'courtly love' is stressed in Leonora L. Brodwin, Elizabethan Love Tragedy (New York, 1971), pp. 197–221. I am not so convinced by her term 'Worldly Love'.

45 The much discussed question of Iago's motives seems to trouble critics less now than it once did. See the sensible summary in Muir, Shakespeare's Tragic Sequence, pp. 106–11, and the interesting discussion in Honigmann, Shakespeare: Seven Tragedies, pp. 77–100.

46 See particularly Spivack, Shakespeare and the Allegory of Evil, passim.

47 See Alvin Kernan's introduction to his Signet Classic edition of Othello (New York, 1963), reprinted in Alfred Harbage, ed., Shakespeare. The Tragedies. A Collection of Critical Essays (Englewood Cliffs, N.J., 1964), pp. 75–84.

48 This gives an unmistakable edge to Brabantio's threatening remark:
   For if such actions may have passage free,
   Bondslaves and pagans shall our statesmen be.   (1.2.98–9)
49 See the similar passage in *Romeo and Juliet* II.6.3–8.
50 Notably F. R. Leavis in his much-disputed essay, 'Diabolic Intellect and the Noble
   Hero: or The Sentimentalist's Othello', first in *Scrutiny*, 6 (1937–8), then in *The
   Common Pursuit* (London, 1952), repr. in Wain, *A Casebook*, pp. 123–46. His
   reading is vigorously repudiated by Helen Gardner in her two essays quoted
   above, n. 43, and it has generally been received with more scepticism than belief.
51 *Tom Jones*, ed. R. P. C. Mutter, Penguin English Library (Harmondsworth,
   1966), p. 81 (Book I, Chapter 11).
52 See Robert Weimann, *Shakespeare and the Popular Tradition in the Theater*
   (Baltimore, 1978), pp. 224–37 and *passim*.
53 On the religious dimension of the language see Brower's interpretation; a
   different view is expressed by Helen Gardner; see 'The Noble Moor' in Wain, *A
   Casebook*, pp. 149–50.
54 See especially, Gardner, '*Othello*: A Retrospect, 1900–67', for references.
55 See Leavis' interpretation. For an attempt to answer Leavis without agreeing with
   Bradley see Jane Adamson, '*Othello*' as tragedy: *some problems of judgement
   and feeling* (Cambridge, 1980), pp. 141–80. The whole book offers a thoughtful
   reading of the play in terms of characters and moral judgement.
56 See especially the older critics quoted in the New Variorum Edition.
57 Bradley, *Shakespearean Tragedy*, p. 158.
58 Wain, *A Casebook*, pp. 126, 123, 137.
59 Wain, *A Casebook*, p. 141, quoted approvingly by A. P. Rossiter in his
   challenging discussion, '*Othello*: A Moral Essay', in *Angel with Horns and
   Other Shakespeare Lectures*, ed. Graham Storey (London, 1961), pp. 189–208;
   see p. 203. The whole essay is, however, very critical of Leavis. See also Michael
   Neill, 'Changing Places in *Othello*', *ShS*, 37 (1984), 115–31.
60 This is the view of Brodwin, *Elizabethan Love Tragedy*, pp. 200–19. See also the
   chapter 'Self-charity and self-abnegation: the play's women in love' in Adamson,
   '*Othello*' as tragedy, pp. 214–63.
61 See the interpretations by Brower and Gardner.
62 See the comic treatment of jealousy in Shakespeare's *Merry Wives of Windsor*.
63 Edward Dowden comments perceptively on the different effects of 'jealousy' on
   Iago and Othello: 'Iago suspects his wife of every baseness, but the suspicion has
   no other effect than to intensify his malignity'; see *Shakspere: A Critical Study
   of His Mind and Art* (London, 1875), p. 243. The book is still worth reading for
   some very acute observations.
64 See Brodwin's interpretation.
65 See William Empson's brilliant essay 'Honest in *Othello*' in *The Structure of
   Complex Words* (London, 1951), reprinted in Wain, *A Casebook*, pp. 98–122.
66 It has often been noticed that there would have been hardly time for adultery in
   the rapid chain of events, so deliberately has Shakespeare condensed the play's
   action.
67 'from loss of love to loss of heroic self', Brower, *Hero and Saint*, p. 9.
68 On the language of the play see the seminal study of Wolfgang Clemen, *The
   Development of Shakespeare's Imagery*, 2nd edn (London, 1977), pp. 119–32.

Many critics have commented on the play's style. For a summary, see Gayle Greene, '"But Words are Words": Shakespeare's Sense of Language in *Othello*', *Études Anglaises*, 34 (1981), 270–81, and the interesting study by Catherine M. Shaw, '"Dangerous Conceits Are in Their Nature Poisons": The Language of *Othello*', *UTQ*, 49 (1980), 304–19, and Giorgio Melchiori, 'The Rhetoric of Character Construction: *Othello*', *ShS*, 34 (1981), 61–72.

69 Quoted from *Shakespeare's Sonnets*, ed. Stephen Booth (New Haven, 1977).

70 See the particularly successful translation of some of these effects to the opera stage in Verdi's *Otello*, and Winton Dean, 'Verdi's Otello: A Shakespearian Masterpiece', *ShS*, 21 (1968), 87–96.

71 See J. D. Wilson's introduction to his edition, pp. xlvii–lvi, where the traditional interpretation is vigorously affirmed.

72 Brutus in *Julius Caesar* is victim to a similar illusion:
    'Let us be sacrificers, but not butchers,' (II.1.167)

73 This painful tension between damnation and recognition has been described with different emphasis by several critics. See Bradley, *Shakespearean Tragedy*, p. 161, Gardner, 'The Noble Moor', pp. 160–4, and her note on p. 150 on the rather academic question whether Othello will be damned or redeemed. See also Gardner's '*Othello*: A Retrospect, 1900–67', p. 6, and John Bayley's stimulating essay, 'Love and Identity: *Othello*', in *The Characters of Love* (London, 1962), pp. 127–201, repr. in Wain, *A Casebook*, pp. 169–98 (excerpts).

74 Of course, with *Othello*, perhaps more so than with other tragedies, much depends on the production and the text leaves the actors much freedom, which is confirmed by the play's colorful stage history. See especially, Marvin Rosenberg, *The Masks of Othello* (Berkeley, 1961), for an exhaustive account, and the brief surveys in the editions by Wilson and Sanders.

75 Quoted from the edition by G. K. Hunter, New Penguin Shakespeare (Harmondsworth, 1972), p. 47; on the history of the play's reception, see pp. 45–52, and Maynard Mack, '*King Lear*' *in Our Time* (Berkeley, 1965), pp. 1–41; this excellent chapter ('Actors and Redactors') is also reprinted in the useful collection: Frank Kermode, ed., *Shakespeare, 'King Lear'. A Casebook*, (London, 1969), pp. 51–82; the anthology also contains Tate's preface. For Tate's adaptation see the edition by James Black, Regents Restoration Drama Series (University of Nebraska Press, 1975, London 1976).

76 German text:
    Mein Herz war in dem Augenblicke gleichsam zermalmt, ich wußte mich vor Schmerz kaum mehr zu fassen. Das hatte ich nicht geahnt, von einem Schauspiele war schon längst keine Rede mehr, das war die wirklichste Wirklichkeit vor mir. Der günstige Ausgang, welchen man den Aufführungen dieses Stückes in jener Zeit gab, um die fürchterlichen Gefühle, die diese Begebenheit erregt, zu mildern, tat auf mich keine Wirkung mehr, mein Herz sagte, daß das nicht möglich sei, und ich wußte beinahe nicht mehr, was vor mir und um mich vorging.
    from the edition of the Winkler Verlag (Munich, 1949), pp. 171–2. The actor was Heinrich Anschütz. See the admirable study by Marvin Rosenberg, *The Masks of King Lear* (Berkeley, 1972), p. 29, on his conception of Lear.

77 Bradley, *Shakespearean Tragedy*, p. 230.

78 The play is reprinted in Bullough, *Narrative and Dramatic Sources*, VII, 337–402,

along with a number of other important texts and a thorough discussion of the sources (VII, 269–420).

79 Bullough, *Narrative and Dramatic Sources*, VII, 407.

80 Most interpretations comment on the relationship between the two plots. On the convention of the multiple plot see the useful survey by Richard Levin, *The Multiple Plot in English Renaissance Drama* (Chicago, 1971). Shakespeare's plays are only mentioned in passing.

81 See the important study by William R. Elton, *'King Lear' and the Gods* (San Marino, 1968), with a wealth of contemporary material.

82 See Bullough, *Narrative and Dramatic Sources*, VII, 283–4. The most thorough exploration of thematic relations is Robert B. Heilman, *This Great Stage. Image and Structure in King Lear* (Baton Rouge, 1984; Washington, 1963). The book has influenced *Lear* criticism more than any other single study of the play.

83 This aspect is well brought out in Hunter's introduction to his New Penguin edition, pp. 7–27.

84 See the still indispensable collection J. W. Cunliffe, ed., *Early English Classical Tragedies* (Oxford, 1912) for the text of *Gorboduc*, and Irving Ribner, *The English History Play in the Age of Shakespeare*, 2nd edn (London, 1965), pp. 37–49, for an account of its qualities as a history play.

85 The barbarian image is reminiscent of Othello's 'I will chop her into messes' (IV.I.188).

86 See Hunter's edition, pp. 18–20, for the tradition of such paradoxes.

87 See Nicholas Brooke, *Shakespeare: 'King Lear'*, Studies in English Literature, 15 (London, 1963), pp. 27–8. Brooke provides a very stimulating running commentary on the play. Whether it is appropriate to exaggerate the noisy and destructive behavior of Lear's followers as some productions have done, is largely a question of interpretation as long as this does not appear to excuse the daughters' cruelty in any way.

88 On Armin's personality see M. C. Bradbrook, *Shakespeare the Craftsman*, The Clark Lectures 1968 (London, 1969), pp. 49–74; see also *As You Like It*, ed. Agnes Latham, The Arden Shakespeare (London, 1975), pp. li–lv.

89 Cf. also the use of familiar 'thou' by the fool.

90 On the wider implications see the thoughtful interpretation by L. C. Knights in *Some Shakespearean Themes* (London, 1959), quoted here from the Peregrine Books edition (Harmondsworth, 1966), pp. 80–97.

91 See the essay, 'Appearance and Reality in Shakespeare's Plays', in Wolfgang Clemen, *Shakespeare's Dramatic Art. Collected Essays* (London, 1972), pp. 163–88, *passim*.

92 See Hunter's note on this line: 'Presumably Cordelia is meant. We recognize this immediately; but it is not clear *why* we do so' (p. 218).

93 See Hunter's comment, p. 230; for a similar comment see the useful edition by Kenneth Muir, The Arden Shakespeare (London, 1952), p. 80.

94 See Goldman, *Shakespeare and the Energies of Drama*, pp. 96–7.

95 Mack, *'King Lear' in Our Time*, gives some negative examples. Aribert Reimann's opera *Lear*, first performed 1978 in Munich and available in a splendid recording, is a very interesting attempt to approach the play by way of music.

96 Bradley, *Shakespearean Tragedy*, p. 237. See also my note 'King Lear and the 'Poor Naked Wretches'', *SJW* 1975, 154–62, with further references. Bradley's

interpretation is defended by Kenneth Muir in his edition and in *Shakespeare's Tragic Sequence*, pp. 125–7.

97 See the influential chapter '*King Lear* and the Comedy of the Grotesque' in G. Wilson Knight's *The Wheel of Fire. Interpretations of Shakespearian Tragedy with Three New Essays* (London, 1930), pp. 160–76; it is also reprinted in Kermode, *A Casebook*, pp. 118–36. See also Snyder, *The Comic Matrix of Shakespeare's Tragedies*, pp. 137–79.

98 Hunter's edition, p. 258.

99 See Albany's comment:
>   This shows you are above,
>   You justicers, that these our nether crimes
>   So speedily can venge! (IV.2.78–80)

100 See the meeting of Launcelot Gobbo and his 'sand-blind' father in *The Merchant of Venice* II.2.

101 See Elton, '*King Lear' and the Gods*, *passim* on the contemporary background of many different forms of belief, superstition and scepticism.

102 This scene is the starting-point for John Bayley's very original interpretation in *Shakespeare and Tragedy*, pp. 7–48.

103 Cf. also Gloucester's 'I stumbled when I saw' (IV.1.19), often interpreted as an important statement of one of the major themes. See especially Heilman, *This Great Stage*, pp. 41–64.

104 The ending of the play has been interpreted in very different ways. See the careful reading by Foreman, Jr, *The Music of the Close*, pp. 113–58.

105 Bradley, *Shakespearean Tragedy*, p. 272.

106 Bradley, *Shakespearean Tragedy*, p. 274.

107 See Brooke, *Shakespeare: 'King Lear'*, pp. 51–60. He points out that the dramatist offers and rejects, as it were, several different endings.

108 See J. V. Cunningham, *Woe or Wonder: The Emotional Effect of Shakespearean Tragedy* (Denver, 1951), pp. 7–13, and the note in Muir's edition, p. 198.

109 Knights, *Some Shakespearean Themes*, p. 100.

110 Virgil K. Whitaker, *The Mirror up to Nature. The Technique of Shakespeare's Tragedies* (San Marino, 1965), p. 240. On the variety of different interpretations on this point see the useful brief survey by G. R. Hibbard, '*King Lear*: A Retrospect, 1939–79', *ShS*, 33 (1980), 1–12.

111 Bradley, *Shakespearean Tragedy*, p. 235. See also the careful readings by Nevo, *Tragic Form in Shakespeare*, pp. 258–305, Honigmann, *Shakespeare: Seven Tragedies*, pp. 101–25, and the undogmatic and challenging interpretation by S. L. Goldberg, *An Essay on 'King Lear'* (Cambridge, 1974).

112 Brooke, *Shakespeare: 'King Lear'*, p. 60; similar Mack, '*King Lear' in Our Time*, p. 116.

113 Mack, '*King Lear' in Our Time*, p. 117; Muir says almost exactly the same in *Shakespeare's Tragic Sequence*, p. 139 (without referring to Mack). See also Muir's balanced and helpful account of *Lear* criticism in Stanley Wells, ed., *Shakespeare. Select Bibliographical Guides* (London, 1973), pp. 171–88, with a good bibliography.

114 So Knights, *Some Shakespearean Themes*, p. 101. For a fresh and stimulating account of the play's indeterminate method see Stephen Booth, '*King Lear*', '*Macbeth*', *Indefinition*, and *Tragedy* (New Haven, 1983), pp. 5–57.

115 See the very helpful interpretation of the play's ending by Joseph H. Summers, '"Look there, look there!" The Ending of *King Lear*', in *English Renaissance Studies, Presented to Dame Helen Gardner In Honour of Her Seventieth Birthday* (Oxford, 1980), pp. 74–93, and in his collection of essays, *Dreams of Love and Power. On Shakespeare's Plays* (Oxford, 1984), pp. 95–114. Regarding the final tableau, Helen Gardner's own excellent interpretation aptly speaks of 'this secular Pieta'; see *King Lear*, The John Coffin Memorial Lecture (London, 1967), p. 28.

116 Throughout this chapter I have treated *King Lear* as a single play, not, as some recent critics would have it, a modern conflation of two different versions of Shakespeare's play or rather two stages of revision by the author. The debate is still going on, but it seems that the Oxford Shakespeare will issue two volumes of *King Lear* to make the issue clear. See Steven Urkovitz, *Shakespeare's Revision of 'King Lear'* (Princeton, 1980), and P. K. W. Stone, *The Textual History of 'King Lear'* (London, 1980).

117 Whitaker, *The Mirror up to Nature*, p. 260. All quotations in this chapter are from G. K. Hunter's edition, New Penguin Shakespeare (Harmondsworth, 1967); see also the useful edition by Kenneth Muir, The Arden Shakespeare (London, 1951).

118 See Honigmann, *Shakespeare: Seven Tragedies*, pp. 126–49 ('Macbeth: The Murderer as Victim') for some very perceptive comment on this point.

119 See Bullough, *Narrative and Dramatic Sources*, VII, 429–31 and 470–2. Bullough discusses all the historical background (pp. 423–69) and reprints the most important texts, especially the relevant passages from Holinshed's, *The Chronicles of England, Scotlande, and Irelande* (1587).

120 See Bullough, *Narrative and Dramatic Sources*, VII, 498.

121 This applies, with some reservations, to *King Lear* as well. See Bradley, *Shakespearean Tragedy*, where *Richard III* is several times referred to and Muir, *Shakespeare's Tragic Sequence*, pp. 26–30, where *Richard III* is discussed as prologue to the tragedies. The structural similarities between the histories and the tragedies are helpfully discussed in Emrys Jones, *Scenic Form in Shakespeare* (Oxford, 1971), pp. 195–224.

122 E. M. W. Tillyard, *Shakespeare's History Plays* (London, 1944; Peregrine Books, Harmondsworth, 1962), p. 315.

123 So Muir, *Shakespeare's Tragic Sequence*, p. 29. On *Richard III*, see the important interpretation by Wolfgang Clemen, *A Commentary on Shakespeare's Richard III* (London, 1968), pp. 218–24.

124 See Tillyard, *Shakespeare's History Plays*, p. 315.

125 Bradley, *Shakespearean Tragedy*, pp. 298, 299, 305.

126 See Weimann, *Shakespeare and the Popular Tradition in the Theater*, pp. 192–6, on 'Popular Myth and Dramatic Poetry'. *Macbeth* is only mentioned in passing, but the discussion is quite relevant here.

127 See Hunter's note on the passage, p. 143.

128 See the interpretation by Honigmann and by Bayley, *Shakespeare and Tragedy*, pp. 184–200. Bayley rightly speaks of 'the irrational feeling that we are closer to Macbeth than to any other character in Shakespeare' (p. 185). See also R. B. Heilman's excellent essay 'The Criminal as Tragic Hero: Dramatic Methods', *ShS*, 19 (1966), 12–24, reprinted in Kenneth Muir and Philip Edwards, eds.,

Aspects of 'Macbeth'. Articles Reprinted from Shakespeare Survey (Cambridge, 1977), pp. 26–38.

129 Bradley, *Shakespearean Tragedy*, pp. 294–301: 'an imagination on the one hand extremely sensitive to impressions of a certain kind, and, on the other, productive of violent disturbance both of mind and body. Through it he is kept in contact with supernatural impressions and is liable to supernatural fears' (p. 295).

130 Angelo in *Measure for Measure* has a very similar experience (cf.II.2.162-87).

131 Bradley, *Shakespearean Tragedy*, pp. 311–14.

132 See Muir, *Shakespeare's Tragic Sequence*, pp. 151–2, and his edition, pp. lxvi–lxx.

133 See Knights, *Some Shakespearean Themes*, p. 115; on the play's imagery see Kenneth Muir, 'Image and Symbol in *Macbeth*', *ShS*, 19 (1966), 45–54; there are some good observations in M. M. Mahood, *Shakespeare's Wordplay* (London, 1957), pp. 130–45.

134 For a very sensitive interpretation of this soliloquy, see Wolfgang Clemen, *Shakespeares Monologe. Ein Zugang zu seiner dramatischen Kunst* (München, 1985), pp. 159–66. An English translation of this book is in preparation.

135 See Hamlet's soliloquy immediately before the prayer scene (III.2.379–83), which seems much more conventional in comparison.

136 Bradley, *Shakespearean Tragedy*, p. 306.

137 Thomas De Quincey's famous essay, 'On the Knocking at the Gate in *Macbeth*', is reprinted in *Shakespeare Criticism. A Selection*, ed. D. Nichol Smith, The World's Classics (London, 1916).
    On the porter scene, see Muir's introduction to his edition, pp. xxv–xxxii, and John B. Harcourt, '"I Pray You, Remember the Porter"', *SQ*, 12 (1961), 393–402.

138 See Glynne Wickham, 'Hell-Castle and its Door-Keeper', *ShS*, 19 (1966), 68–74; reprinted in Muir and Edwards, *Aspects of 'Macbeth'*, pp. 39–52.

139 This is how the play appears in Jan Kott's influential book *Shakespeare Our Contemporary* (London, 1964), pp. 89–100.

140 See Muir's note, Arden edition, pp. 177–8, and Hunter's comment (Penguin edition, p. 159), with a reference to Iago's praise of Cassio in *Othello* (V.1.19–20).

141 See the thorough edition of *The Tragedy of Master Arden of Faversham*, ed. M. L. Wine, The Revels Plays (London, 1973).

142 On the various traditions of staging this scene, its emotional and symbolic dimensions, see Marvin Rosenberg's exhaustive study, *The Masks of Macbeth* (Berkeley, 1978), pp. 428–89. The book gives an invaluable account of how many great actors and producers have interpreted each scene of the play.

143 See Hunter's edition, pp. 21–3, and Muir's edition, pp. xxxiii–xxxvi.

144 See Terence Hawkes, *Shakespeare and the Reason. A Study of the Tragedies and the Problem Plays* (London, 1964), pp. 124–59; see also the good chapter on *Macbeth* in John Lawlor, *The Tragic Sense in Shakespeare* (London, 1960), pp. 107–46 ('Natural and Supernatural').

145 See IV.3.31, 100, 103–8, 164–73.

146 See the commentary in Hunter's edition, pp. 177 and 181.

147 See also 1.3.144–6, where it is said of Macbeth:
New honours come upon him
Like our strange garments, cleave not to their mould
But with the aid of use.

148 The passage is often singled out for its effect on our sympathy for the hero; it reminds us of the natural and ordinary sphere of life, from which Macbeth has excluded himself. See Bradley, *Shakespearean Tragedy*, pp. 305–6, Knights, *Some Shakespearean Themes*, p. 114, and Hunter's edition, pp. 26–7.

149 *Shakespearean Tragedy*, p. 305. It was De Quincey who first argued against a too narrow concept of 'sympathy'; see his essay referred to in n. 137 above.

150 Hunter very rightly speaks of 'the idea of a 'good' Macbeth, buried somewhere beneath the activites of a will dedicated to evil' (p. 26).

151 Cf. Bradley, *Shakespearean Tragedy*, p. 304; I quote from *The Poetical Works of John Milton*, ed. H.C. Beeching, Oxford Standard Authors (London, 1904).

152 See the excellent account of *Macbeth* criticism by R. A. Foakes in Wells, ed., *Shakespeare. Select Bibliographical Guides*, pp. 189–202, with a good bibliography, and G. K. Hunter, '*Macbeth* in the Twentieth Century', *ShS*, 19 (1966), 1–11, reprinted in Muir and Edwards, *Aspects of 'Macbeth'*, pp. 1–11. For a comparatively open-minded 'Christian' reading of *Macbeth* see Ivor Morris, *Shakespeare's God. The Role of Religion in the Tragedies* (London, 1972), pp. 310–22.

153 See also the very different interpretations of the play in Nevo, *Tragic Form in Shakespeare*, pp. 214–57, and McElroy, *Shakespeare's Mature Tragedies*, pp. 206–37.

154 This seems to me a very important point. See also Jones, *Scenic Form in Shakespeare*, p. 224: 'there is nothing of the jubilant mood of the conclusion of *Richard III*'.

155 Bradley, *Shakespearean Tragedy*, pp. 27–8.

156 Here again, the play's stage history can provide important clues to the interpretation and draw attention to problems the literary critic tends to overlook or to overestimate. Rosenberg's study, *The Masks of Macbeth* is invaluable in this respect. See also on various aspects of the play, especially in performance, John Russell Brown, ed., *Focus on 'Macbeth'* (London, 1982), a very stimulating collection of essays, including an interview with Peter Hall on his experience as a producer of *Macbeth*.

4 ROMANS AND GREEKS IN SHAKESPEARE'S TRAGEDIES

1 See the excellent essay by T. J. B. Spencer, 'Shakespeare and the Elizabethan Romans', *ShS*, 10 (1957), 27–38, and the useful survey of scholarship by John W. Velz, 'The Ancient World in Shakespeare: Authenticity or Anachronism? A Retrospect', *ShS*, 31 (1978), 1–12. There is also a very comprehensive and helpful annotated bibliography by John W. Velz, *Shakespeare and the Classical Tradition. A Critical Guide to Commentary 1660–1960* (Minneapolis, 1968).

2 Spencer draws attention to the fact that Shakespeare's contemporaries were usually more interested in Imperial Rome.

3 It appears that Ben Jonson's Roman tragedies were from the start much less successful than Shakespeare's.

4 See the good appendix, 'The Roman Plays as a Group' in Maurice Charney, *Shakespeare's Roman Plays. The Function of Imagery in the Drama* (Cambridge, Mass., 1961), pp. 207–18, and John Alvis, 'The Coherence of Shakespeare's Roman Plays', *MLQ*, 40 (1979), 115–34. See also J. L. Simmons, *Shakespeare's Pagan World. The Roman Tragedies* (Hassocks, Sussex, 1974) and Paul A. Cantor, *Shakespeare's Rome. Republic and Empire* (Ithaca, N.Y., 1976). Still very useful is M. W. MacCallum, *Shakespeare's Roman Plays and their Background* (London, 1910, with a Foreword by T. J. B. Spencer, 1967). There are perceptive interpretations of the plays in Derek Traversi, *Shakespeare: The Roman Plays* (London, 1963), especially on the language, and in Robert S. Miola, *Shakespeare's Rome* (Cambridge, 1983).

5 In 1972, for instance, the Roman Plays, including *Titus Andronicus*, were performed as a cycle. See Richard David, *Shakespeare in the Theatre* (Cambridge, 1978), pp. 139–63.

6 See the important essay by T. J. B. Spencer, '"Greeks" and "Merrygreeks": A Background to *Timon of Athens* and *Troilus and Cressida*' in Richard Hosley, ed., *Essays on Shakespeare and Elizabethan Drama in Honour of Hardin Craig* (Columbus, Missouri, 1962), pp. 223–33. In Nicholas Udall's comedy *Ralph Roister Doister* (about 1550) there is a comic character Matthew Merrygreek; see Spencer, pp. 227–8.

7 On the classic tradition of comedy and its impact on Shakespeare see the important study by Leo Salingar, *Shakespeare and the Traditions of Comedy* (Cambridge, 1974), pp. 76–174.

8 North's translation of Plutarch, at least the most relevant portions of it, is most conveniently studied in Geoffrey Bullough, *Narrative and Dramatic Sources of Shakespeare*, vol. v (London, 1964), under each Roman play, or in the useful edition by T. J. B. Spencer, *Shakespeare's Plutarch* (Harmondsworth, 1964), where the relevant passages from the plays are quoted as well. See also J. Barroll, 'Shakespeare and Roman History', *MLR*, 52 (1958), 327–43.

9 I quote from the excellent edition by Arthur Humphreys, The Oxford Shakespeare (Oxford, 1984); see also the very useful editions by Norman Sanders, New Penguin Shakespeare (Harmondsworth, 1967) and T. S. Dorsch, The Arden Shakespeare (London, 1955); the anthology Peter Ure, ed., *Shakespeare, 'Julius Caesar'. A Casebook* (London, 1969), provides a helpful introduction into some of the most important issues.

10 Spencer, 'Shakespeare and the Elizabethan Romans', 33. On the changing reputation of the two chief characters see the excellent chapter on the play in Ernest Schanzer, *The Problem Plays of Shakespeare. A Study of 'Julius Caesar', 'Measure for Measure', 'Antony and Cleopatra'* (London, 1963), pp. 10–70, Bullough's introduction, *Narrative and Dramatic Sources*, v, 3–57, and Virgil K. Whitaker, *Shakespeare's Use of Learning. An Inquiry in the Growth of his Mind and Art* (San Marino, 1953), pp. 224–50; excerpts from Schanzer and Whitaker are reprinted in Ure, *A Casebook*.

11 Velz speaks of 'illeism' in the play; see Velz, 'The Ancient World in Shakespeare', 9–10. On the dramatic technique of preparation, see Wolfgang Clemen, *Shakespeare's Dramatic Art* (London, 1972), pp. 49–59.

12 See Schanzer, *The Problem Plays*, pp. 38–40; on Cassius' soliloquy see Sanders' edition, p. 24 and commentary, p. 165.

13 In his commentary on 1.2.95–6 and 1.3.89–90, Sanders quotes relevant passages from Plutarch.

14 On Brutus as a tragic hero see, for instance, the chapter 'Marcus Brutus' in John Palmer, *Political and Comic Characters of Shakespeare* (London, 1962), and Moody E. Prior, 'The Search for a Hero in *Julius Caesar*', *RenD*, NS, 2 (1969), 81–101.

There is a good survey of scholarship, with a useful bibliography by T. J. B. Spencer in Stanley Wells, ed., *Shakespeare: Select Bibliographical Guides* (London, 1973), pp. 203–15.

15 Cf. 'there's the question' (II.1.13) with *Hamlet* III.1.56: 'that is the question'.

16 See Kenneth Muir, *Shakespeare's Tragic Sequence* (London, 1972), p. 47, and Schanzer, *The Problem Plays*, pp. 49–51, with reference to *Hamlet*.

17 See the chapter 'Brutus and Macbeth' in G. Wilson Knight, *The Wheel of Fire. Interpretations of Shakespearian Tragedy with Three New Essays* (London, 1930), pp. 120–39.

18 In *Othello*, too, sleep is an experience of a peaceful mind (see III. 3.331–4).

19 In the case of *King Lear*, however, the hero only discovers this in the course of tragic suffering.

20 See Anne Righter, *Shakespeare and the Idea of the Play* (London, 1962), p. 141; for an early poetic treatment of the vagaries of literary and historical transmission see Chaucer's *House of Fame*, and Piero Boitani, *Chaucer and the Imaginary World of Fame*, Chaucer Studies, 10 (Cambridge, 1984).

21 In *Macbeth*, too, the hero is referred to as 'butcher' (V.6.108).

22 In the anonymous tragedy *Locrine* (1591) Ate appears between the acts as a sinister prophet of coming disaster (Malone Society Reprints, 1908). The relationship between *Julius Caesar* and revenge tragedy is discussed in Norman Rabkin, *Shakespeare and the Common Understanding* (New York, 1967), pp. 105–19.

23 See Schanzer, *The Problem Plays*, pp. 47–9; similarly, Muir, *Shakespeare's Tragic Sequence*, pp. 52–3. Most interpretations of *Julius Caesar* comment on the two speeches. On the rhetoric of the play, see Gayle Greene, '"The Power of Speech/To Stir Men's Blood": The Language of Tragedy in Shakespeare's *Julius Caesar*', *RenD*, NS, 11 (1980), 67–93, and John W. Velz, 'Orator and Imperator in '*Julius Caesar*': Style and the Process of History', *ShakS*, 15 (1982), 55–75. On the play's language in general see the two chapters in G. Wilson Knight, *The Imperial Theme. Further Interpretations of Shakespeare's Tragedies including the Roman Plays* (London, 1931), pp. 32–95, Charney, *Shakespeare's Roman Plays*, pp. 41–78, and Traversi, *Shakespeare: The Roman Plays*, pp. 21–75.

24 See Schanzer, *The Problem Plays*, pp. 16–17, and *Hamlet*, ed. Philip Edwards, pp. 5–6.

25 See Schanzer, *The Problem Plays*, pp. 63–5; Muir is more critical of Brutus, pp. 51–3. It is in the controversial assessment of Brutus that interpretations of the play differ most markedly. See also the very balanced account of Adrien Bonjour, *The Structure of 'Julius Caesar'* (Liverpool, 1958), and the works referred to in n. 14 and 26 to this chapter.

26 See the good chapter on *Julius Caesar* in E. A. J. Honigmann, *Shakespeare: Seven Tragedies* (London, 1976), pp. 30–53, and the provocative study by J. I. M. Stewart, *Character and Motive in Shakespeare* (London, 1949), pp. 46–55. On the religious dimension of the play see David Kaula, '"Let Us Be Sacrificers": Religious Motifs in *Julius Caesar*', *ShakS*, 14 (1981), 197–214.

27 This is how Schanzer sees the play. I think he exaggerates the differences between *Julius Caesar* and the other tragedies, but his very perceptive interpretation is hardly dependent on the validity of his general thesis.

28 The play's stage history is also an important guide to its meaning and its reception. See the detailed account by John Ripley, *'Julius Caesar' on stage in England and America, 1599–1973* (Cambridge, 1980).

29 There is a good brief discussion of the play's critical fortunes in Schanzer, *The Problem Plays*, pp. 132–83, and *passim*. See also Michael Steppat, *The Critical Reception of Shakespeare's 'Antony and Cleopatra' from 1607 to 1905*, Bochumer Anglistische Studien, 9 (Amsterdam, 1980), for an exhaustive and systematic review of older criticism. All quotations from the edition by Emrys Jones, New Penguin Shakespeare (Harmondsworth, 1977).

30 So T. S. Eliot's famous dictum on *Hamlet*.

31 See Reuben A. Brower, *Hero and Saint. Shakespeare and the Graeco-Roman Heroic Tradition* (Oxford, 1971), pp. 350–3, and Miola, *Shakespeare's Rome*, pp. 122–7, with further references.

32 Most of the relevant texts are reprinted in Bullough, *Narrative and Dramatic Sources*, v, 254–449. See also Bullough's discussion of the sources, v, 215–53.

33 On the structure of the play, with particular reference to the theatre, see Harley Granville-Barker, *Prefaces to Shakespeare*, 2 vols. (London, 1958), I, 367–458. Excerpts from Granville-Barker are given in the useful anthology, John Russell Brown, ed., *Shakespeare, 'Antony and Cleopatra'. A Casebook* (London, 1968), pp. 88–112. See also the good chapter on the play in Emrys Jones, *Scenic Form in Shakespeare* (Oxford, 1971), pp. 225–65.

34 See Schanzer, *The Problem Plays*, pp. 162–7, where he compares the structure of the play with that of *Henry IV*.

35 Bullough, *Narrative and Dramatic Sources*, v, 273.

36 See 'Shakespeare's *Antony and Cleopatra*' in A. C. Bradley, *Oxford Lectures on Poetry* (London, 1909), pp. 279–308; quotation from p. 293; see Schanzer's comment on this passage in *The Problem Plays*, p. 147. Schanzer notes that the pendulum has swung the other way since Bradley. Today, critical opinion seems to be generally nearer to Bradley's view again. Bradley's excellent lecture is reprinted in Brown, *A Casebook*, pp. 63–87.

37 See the note on 1.3.102–4, in M. R. Ridley's edition, The Arden Shakespeare (London, 1954), with a reference to John Donne.

38 The comparison has often been made; see Schanzer, *The Problem Plays*, pp. 159–60, and n. 31, above.

39 See Bradley's perceptive comments on this aspect of Cleopatra. He calls her Antony's 'play-fellow, and yet a great queen' (*Oxford Lectures*, p. 296).

40 See Leonora L. Brodwin, *Elizabethan Love Tragedy* (New York, 1971), pp. 223–54.

41 See Bradley, *Oxford Lectures*, p. 285, and Schanzer, *The Problem Plays*, pp. 143–5.

42 See Bradley, *Oxford Lectures*, pp. 288–90, and Muir, *Shakespeare's Tragic Sequence*, p. 170.

43 See Bullough, *Narrative and Dramatic Sources*, v, 288: 'for that he might have an honest culler to make warre with Antonius ... '.

44 See Spencer, 'Shakespeare and the Elizabethan Romans', 33.

45 This aspect is well brought out by Schanzer, *The Problem Plays*, pp. 176–81.

46 As early as 1.3.11 she is warned, 'Tempt him not so too far'.

47 See Steppat, *The Critical Reception*, pp. 258 and 435–6. The sonnet is repeatedly quoted in this connection; see also the pointed interpretation in William Rosen, *Shakespeare and the Craft of Tragedy* (Cambridge, Mass., 1960), pp. 104–60, esp. pp. 148–52.

48 Plutarch mentions the children of the pair; Shakespeare is silent about them. The character of Cleopatra has been interpreted in most controversial terms. See the spirited discussion by Stewart, *Character and Motive in Shakespeare*, pp. 59–78, with his rather rude treatment of L. L. Schücking, whose important study tried to explain away the contradictions of Cleopatra's character by referring to dramatic conventions. See his *Character Problems in Shakespeare's Plays. A Guide to the better Understanding of the Dramatist* (Gloucester, Mass., 1959, repr. from the edition of 1922), pp. 119–41.

49 On Antony's death see Brower, *Hero and Saint*, pp. 236–7, and the literal correspondences in Plutarch: Bullough, *Narrative and Dramatic Sources*, v, 310.

50 See also Michael Shapiro, 'Boying her Greatness: Shakespeare's Use of Coterie Drama in *Antony and Cleopatra*', MLR, 77 (1982), 1–15.

51 On the stage history of the play see Margaret Lamb, '*Antony and Cleopatra*' on the English Stage (London and Toronto, 1980).

52 A. C. Bradley, *Shakespearean Tragedy. Lectures on 'Hamlet', 'Othello', 'King Lear', 'Macbeth'* (London, 1985), p.65, and *Oxford Lectures*, p. 289.

53 See L. C. Knights, *Some Shakespearean Themes* (Harmondsworth, 1966), pp. 126–7. In Plutarch, her motives are less complex; see Bullough, *Narrative and Dramatic Sources*, v, 313–14.

54 Muir, *Shakespeare's Tragic Sequence*, p. 167.

55 'there is the danger of confusing energy with moral stature and of so mistaking admiration for approval that Cleopatra's final moments are wrongly interpreted as a redemption and a transfiguration which makes all previous conduct of no account'; Rosen, *Shakespeare and the Craft of Tragedy*, p. 160. See also the careful intepretation in Honigmann, *Shakespeare: Seven Tragedies*, pp. 150–69.

56 Knights, *Some Shakespearean Themes*, p.127.

57 Schanzer, *The Problem Plays*, p. 149. On this crucial question see the diverging interpretations by John F. Danby, *Elizabethan and Jacobean Poets* (London, 1964; first edition as *Poets on Fortune's Hill*, 1952), pp. 128–51, Dorothea Krook, *Elements of Tragedy* (New Haven, 1969), pp. 184–229 (disagreeing with Danby), Franklin M. Dickey, *Not Wisely But Too Well. Shakespeare's Love Tragedies* (San Marino, 1957), pp.144–202, Derick R. C. Marsh, *Passion Lends Them Power. A study of Shakespeare's love tragedies* (Manchester, 1976), pp. 141–200, and Walter C. Foreman, *The Music of the Close. The Final Scenes of Shakespeare's Tragedies* (Lexington, 1978), pp.175–201.

58 See Bradley, *Oxford Lectures*, p. 302, and, more emphatically, Marsh, *Passion Lends Them Power*, p. 200.

59 See Andrew Fichter, '*Antony and Cleopatra*: "The Time of Universal Peace"', *ShS*, 33 (1980), 99–111.

60 See also Honigmann's and Foreman's interpretations, and Russell Jackson, 'The Triumphs of *Antony and Cleopatra*', *SJW* 1984, 128–48.

61 Quoted from John Dryden, *All for Love*, ed. David M. Vieth, Regents Restoration Drama Series (University of Nebraska Press, 1972; London, 1973), v. 514–18.

62 E.g. Bradley, *Oxford Lectures*, pp. 292 and 304 and Schanzer, *The Problem Plays*, p. 181. Muir (*Shakespeare's Tragic Sequence*, p. 167) agrees with the 'many critics' who have found that 'the ending of the play is not wholly tragic'.

63 See the discussion and the texts in Bullough, *Narrative and Dramatic Sources*, v, 453–563.

    All quotations are from the excellent edition by Philip Brockbank, The Arden Shakespeare (London, 1976); the New Penguin edition by G. R. Hibbard, too, is very helpful (Harmondsworth, 1967).

64 See Spencer, 'Shakespeare and the Elizabethan Romans', 35–7. See also Miola, *Shakespeare's Rome*, pp. 164–205, Gail Kern Paster, 'To Starve with Feeding: The City in *Coriolanus*', *ShakS*, 11 (1978), 123–44.

65 On the contemporary background see W. Gordon Zeeveld, '*Coriolanus* and Jacobean Politics', *MLR*, 57 (1962), 321–34, and Clifford Chalmers Huffman, '*Coriolanus' in Context* (Lewisburg, Pa., 1971); see also the useful review of scholarship by Maurice Charney in Wells, ed., *Shakespeare: Select Bibliographical Guides*, pp. 216–24, and W. Hutchings, 'Beast or god: the *Coriolanus* controversy', *Critical Quarterly*, 24 (1982), 35–50, repr. in C. B. Cox and D. J. Palmer, eds., *Shakespeare's wide and universal stage* (Manchester, 1984), pp. 218–33.

66 See Muir, *Shakespeare's Tragic Sequence*, pp. 172–5; he refers to the important study by Palmer, *Political and Comic Characters of Shakespeare*, pp. 250–310. (*The Political Characters of Shakespeare* first appeared separately in 1945).

67 See the very sensible interpretation by Brian Vickers, *Shakespeare: 'Coriolanus'*, Studies in English Literature, 58 (London, 1976): 'Shakespeare has downgraded both sides' (p. 18). This only applies to the first part of the play. On the indirect form of characterization, see Michael Goldman, 'Characterizing Coriolanus', *ShS*, 34 (1981), 73–84.

68 See the often quoted advice given to Prince Hal by his dying father:
    Be it thy course to busy giddy minds
    With foreign quarrels   (*Henry IV*, Part II, IV.5.213–14)
quoted from the edition by P. H. Davison, New Penguin Shakespeare (Harmondsworth, 1977).

69 On the act division, see Brockbank's edition, pp. 16–18; Vickers divides the play into three sections (p. 40).

70 See the emphasis on the word 'alone', from 1.6.76 to the climax in v.6.116.
    On the wider context, see Janette Dillon, '"Solitariness": Shakespeare and Plutarch', *JEGP*, 78 (1979), 325–44.

71 See above, no. 66.

72 See particularly Eugene M. Waith, *The Herculean Hero in Marlowe, Chapman, Shakespeare and Dryden* (London, 1962), pp. 121–43, and Brower, *Hero and Saint*, pp. 355–60.

73 For Chapman's *Bussy D'Ambois*, see the excellent edition by Nicholas Brooke, The Revels Plays (London, 1984).

74 Vickers, *Shakespeare: 'Coriolanus'*, p. 36.

75 Muir, *Shakespeare's Tragic Sequence*, p. 184.

76 See, for instance, Glynne Wickham, '*Coriolanus*: Shakespeare's Tragedy in Rehearsal and Performance' in J. R. Brown and B. Harris, eds., *Later Shakespeare*, Stratford-upon-Avon Studies, 8 (London, 1966), pp. 166–81; there is an interesting interview by G. Lloyd Evans with Ian Richardson on his acting of Coriolanus in 'Shakespeare and the Actors: Notes towards Interpretations', *ShS*, 21 (1969) 115–25.

77 In III.1 it was the word 'shall', here it is the word 'traitor' which lets him forget all prudent self-control.

78 See A. C. Bradley, '*Coriolanus*', in *Studies in Shakespeare. British Academy Lectures*, ed. Peter Alexander (London, 1964), p. 224. This lecture is full of stimulating observations (pp. 219–37).

79 On the role of banishment, see Hibbard's edition, pp. 42–3.

80 See, however, the important 'aside', in V.3.22–37.

81 See Brockbank's edition, p. 89.

82 See Brower, *Hero and Saint*, pp. 378–81, and some good observations in Hermann Heuer, 'From Plutarch to Shakespeare: A Study of Coriolanus', *ShS*, 10 (1957), 50–59.

83 See Hibbard's edition, p. 46. Most interpretations deal with this scene at some length.

84 Critics differ on this point. It is interesting to see that Plutarch is rather critical of Coriolanus here; see Bullough, *Narrative and Dramatic Sources*, V, 544–9. See also I. R. Browning, '*Coriolanus*: Boy of Tears', *EC*, 5 (1955), 18–31, and the chapter on *Coriolanus* in Rosen, *Shakespeare and the Craft of Tragedy*, pp. 161–207.

85 Bradley, '*Coriolanus*', p. 231–2.

86 See G. K. Hunter, 'The Last Tragic Heroes', *Later Shakespeare*, 11–28, and Willard Farnham, *Shakespeare's Tragic Frontier. The World of His Final Tragedies* (Berkeley, 1950), pp. 207–64. For a different view see H. J. Oliver, '*Coriolanus* As Tragic Hero', *SQ*, 10 (1959), 53–60; also the very perceptive interpretation in Honigmann, *Shakespeare: Seven Tragedies*, pp. 170–91.

87 Hunter, 'The Last Tragic Heroes', p. 25.

88 Bradley, '*Coriolanus*', pp. 232–3; Vickers speaks of a 'hollow and false epitaph' (p. 55).

89 See Brents Stirling, *The Populace in Shakespeare* (New York, 1965; first published 1949), and the older account in James Emerson Phillips, Jr, *The State in Shakespeare's Greek and Roman Plays* (New York, 1940); see also C. A. Patrides, '"The Beast with many heads": Renaissance Views on the Multitude', *SQ*, 16 (1965), 241–6, and David G. Hale, '*Coriolanus*: The Death of a Political Metaphor', *SQ*, 22 (1971), 197–202. Rossiter calls *Coriolanus* 'Shakespeare's only great political play', *Angel with Horns*, p.251; the whole chapter on *Coriolanus* is well worth reading (pp. 235–52).

90 On the play's style see Traversi, *Shakespeare: The Roman Plays*, pp. 205–88, and Charney, *Shakespeare's Roman Plays*, pp. 142–96.

91 There is a brief account of the stage history in Brockbank's edition, pp. 74–89.

On Bertolt Brecht's adaptation see Ladislaus Loeb and Laurence Lerner, 'Views of Roman History: *Coriolanus* and *Coriolan*', *CL*, 29 (1977), 35–53.

92 See the introductions to the editions by J. C. Maxwell, New Shakespeare (Cambridge, 1957), H. J. Oliver, The Arden Shakespeare (London, 1959), and G. R. Hibbard, New Penguin Shakespeare (Harmondsworth, 1970). All quotations are from Hibbard's edition. His introduction gives a particularly balanced and sympathetic interpretation of the play.

93 See the interesting chapter 'Blackfriars: The Pageant of *Timon of Athens*' in M. C. Bradbrook, *Shakespeare the Craftsman*, The Clark Lectures 1968 (London, 1969), pp. 144–67; for a different, but equally stimulating account of the play's unusual form see E. A. J. Honigmann, '*Timon of Athens*', *SQ*, 12 (1961), 3–20.

94 G. Wilson Knight's idealizing interpretation is provocative rather than convincing and has not generally been accepted. See the chapter 'The Pilgrimage of Hate: an Essay on *Timon of Athens*', in *The Wheel of Fire*, pp. 207–39. Wilson Knight himself has often played the title role. See his largely autobiographical account, *Shakespeare's Dramatic Challenge* (London, 1977). Maxwell's edition contains a brief stage history. See also Rolf Soellner, '*Timon of Athens*'. *Shakespeare's Pessimistic Tragedy*. With a stage history by Gary Jay Williams (Columbus, 1979), and, for the critical reception, Francelia Butler, *The Strange Critical Fortunes of Shakespeare's* Timon of Athens (Ames, Iowa, 1966). Maurice Charney gives a useful account of *Timon* criticism, with a good bibliography, in Wells, ed., *Shakespeare: Select Bibliographical Guides*, pp. 224–38.

95 See the discussion of the sources and relevant texts in Bullough, *Narrative and Dramatic Sources*, VI, 225–345.

96 For the text of the play, see Bullough, *Narrative and Dramatic Sources*, VI, 297–339. See also the additional material in James C. Bulman, Jr, 'Shakespeare's Use of the "Timon" Comedy', *ShS*, 29 (1976), 103–16.

97 This would also apply to a number of other Jacobean tragedies, especially the plays of Tourneur and Webster. On the language of *Timon* see also the useful article by W. H. Bizley, 'Language and Currency in *Timon of Athens*', *Theoria*, 44 (1975), 21–42.

98 See also William W. E. Slights, '*Genera Mixta* and *Timon of Athens*', *SP*, 74 (1977), 39–62. On the morality structure see Lewis Walker, '*Timon of Athens* and the Morality Tradition', *ShakS*, 12 (1979), 159–77.

99 See above, chapter 1, on traditional ideas of tragedy.

100 See Oliver's note on this passage: 'A finer judgment on Timon's situation than has been given by many commentators' (Arden edition, p. 48).

101 See John Russell Brown, *Shakespeare and his Comedies* (London, 1957), pp. 45–81.

102 On this background see the still most valuable study by L. C. Knights, *Drama and Society in the Age of Jonson* (London, 1937; Harmondsworth, 1962). For a more general survey see Christopher Hill, *Reformation to Industrial Revolution*, The Pelican Economic History of Britain, 3 (Harmondsworth, 1969).

103 See also the picture of corrupt court life in Tourneur's *The Revenger's Tragedy* and Webster's *The White Devil*. On the play's background see Robert S. Miola, 'Timon in Shakespeare's Athens', *SQ*, 31 (1980), 21–30.

104 See the chapter 'Innocents at Home: Timon (of Athens); Coriolanus (of Rome)',

in Bertrand Evans, *Shakespeare's Tragic Practice* (Oxford, 1979), pp. 281–324, and the brief remarks in Klaus Peter Jochum, *Discrepant Awareness: Studies in English Renaissance Drama*, Neue Studien zur Anglistik und Amerikanistik, 13 (Frankfurt, 1979), pp. 201–5.

105 See also *The Merchant of Venice* where Shylock describes the contrast between himself and Antonio in similar terms: 'in low simplicity/He lends out money gratis'; quoted from the New Penguin edition, ed. W. Moelwyn Merchant (Harmondsworth, 1967), 1.3.41–2.

106 See also the obvious reference to Judas Ischariot here and at 1.2.39–40.

107 Cf. Tourneur, *The Revenger's Tragedy*:
> I, sent from the duke's son,
> Tried you, and found you base metal,   (IV.4.30–1)
This is only one of several echoes or correspondences in theme and phrasing between the two plays.

108 This is anticipated by Flaminius' 'I feel my master's passion' (III.1.56) and, indeed, his whole soliloquy (51–63).

109 'Discontent' is another word that recurs, with a specific meaning, in Jacobean drama. See Tourneur, *The Revenger's Tragedy*:
> discontent and want
> Is the best clay to mould a villain of.   (IV.1.47–8)
Of his father, Vindice says:
> surely I think he died
> Of discontent, the nobleman's consumption.   (I.1.126–7)

110 Derek Traversi rightly claims that the banquet is the real centre of the action; see his *An Approach to Shakespeare*, 3rd edn (New York, 1969), II, 177.

111 See Maxwell's edition, pp. xxxvii–xxxviii, and Hibbard's edition, pp. 42–3.

112 See the interpretations by Bradbrook and Honigmann, quoted above, n. 93.

113 See *As You Like It* II.7.

114 See also Muir, *Shakespeare's Tragic Sequence*, p. 193.

115 See also the Duke Senior's speech in *As You Like It* II.1.1–17.

116 Cf. Traversi, *An Approach to Shakespeare*, II, 178–9.

117 As some editors note, there is no break between IV.3 and V.1. See the note in Hibbard's edition, p. 238, and Oliver's edition, p. 121.

118 See Hibbard's introduction, pp. 33–6, and Muir, *Shakespeare's Tragic Sequence*, pp. 189–90.

119 In *Macbeth* the hero is killed off-stage and his head brought back. In *Troilus and Cressida*, of course, the death of Troilus, a known fact to most readers and spectators, happens only after the play is finished.

120 Plutarch's careful comparison of Alcibiades and Coriolanus is instructive and may have suggested to Shakespeare some aspects of Timon; see Bullough, *Narrative and Dramatic Sources*, V, 544–9.

121 See the older opinion in Una Ellis-Fermor, '*Timon of Athens*: An Unfinished Play', *RES*, 18 (1942), 270–83, further Maxwell's edition, pp. xxxviii–xl, and Oliver's edition, pp. xlviii–xlix.

122 At least this was the impression I took away from Ron Daniels' impressive RSC production at 'The Other Place' in Stratford-upon-Avon, 1980.

123 David Cook, '*Timon of Athens*', *ShS*, 16 (1963), 83–94; quotation from p. 94.

124 See Soellner, '*Timon of Athens*'. *Shakespeare's Pessimistic Tragedy*, p. 62.

Soellner's interpretation is not as one-sided as the title might suggest, but covers many aspects of the play and gives a very well-considered account of it.

See also Lesley W. Brill, 'Truth and *Timon of Athens*', MLQ, 40 (1979), 17–36.

125 More impartial is the comment of the three Strangers in III.2.64–89. For them, Timon's experience is indeed symptomatic of the general state of society.

126 See Oliver's introduction, p. xlix, where he compares Alcibiades to Fortinbras, Octavius, and Aufidius. Cf. the last line of the play, 'Let our drums strike' (v.4.85), and 'Go, bid the soldiers shoot' (*Hamlet* v.2.408).

127 See, for instance, the influential discussion of the play in E. M. W. Tillyard, *Shakespeare's Problem Plays* (London, 1950; Peregrine Books, Harmondsworth, 1965), pp. 38–89. All quotations are from the excellent edition by Kenneth Palmer. The Arden Shakespeare (London, 1982); there is also a very useful edition by Kenneth Muir, The Oxford Shakespeare (Oxford, 1982).

128 See Brian Morris, 'The Tragic Structure of *Troilus and Cressida*', SQ, 10 (1959), 481–91, and Schanzer, *The Problem Plays of Shakespeare*, pp. 61–2 and 187–90.

129 On the play's sources see Bullough, *Narrative and Dramatic Sources*, VI, 83–221, and the useful sections in the introductions of Palmer and Muir. See also Robert Kimbrough, *Shakespeare's 'Troilus and Cressida' and its Setting* (Cambridge, Mass., 1964).

130 On Shakespeare's indebtedness to Chaucer see Ann Thompson, *Shakespeare's Chaucer. A Study in Literary Origins* (Liverpool, 1978), with further bibliographical references, and E. Talbot Donaldson, *The Swan at the Well. Shakespeare Reading Chaucer* (New Haven and London, 1985). Another very useful study is Gretchen Mieszkowski, *The Reputation of Criseyde 1155–1500*, Transactions of the Connecticut Academy of Arts and Sciences, 43 (1971), pp. 71–153.

131 See Rabkin, *Shakespeare and the Common Understanding*, p. 32; his whole discussion of the play is particularly stimulating, pp. 31–60.

132 Most critics nowadays agree that Chaucer's poem was Shakespeare's chief source; see the editions of Palmer (pp. 23–6) and Muir (pp. 12–5) for brief summaries, and Muriel C. Bradbrook, 'What Shakespeare Did to Chaucer's *Troilus and Criseyde*', SQ, 9 (1958), 311–19, reprinted in *The Artist and Society in Shakespeare's England: The Collected Papers of Muriel Bradbrook*, 1 (Brighton, 1982), 133–43.

133 See Palmer's edition, pp. 1–22, and Muir's edition, pp. 1–9, for details. For a very thorough reassessment of the evidence see the excellent study by Gary Taylor, '*Troilus and Cressida*: Bibliography, Performance, and Interpretation', ShakS, 15 (1982), 99–136.

134 See Palmer's edition, p. 95. Muir prints the letter in an appendix, pp. 193–4, with explanatory notes.

135 See my 'Chaucerian Comedy and Shakespearean Tragedy', SJW 1984, 111–27, for a discussion of the relationship between the two plays.

136 See the brief stage histories in the editions by Alice Walker, The New Shakespeare (Cambridge, 1957), pp. xlvii–lvi, and Muir, pp. 9–12, as well as the current reviews of contemporary performances in *Shakespeare Survey*, *Shakespeare Quarterly*, and *Shakespeare Jahrbuch*.

137 *The Testament of Cresseid*, 64; I quote from the excellent edition by Denton Fox, *The Poems of Robert Henryson* (Oxford, 1981).

138 See my 'Chaucerian Comedy and Shakespearean Tragedy', from which I have borrowed a few sentences.
   I find myself in agreement with much of Donaldson's brilliant reassessment of Shakespeare's indebtedness to Chaucer. See the chapters 'Criseyde Becoming Cressida: *Troilus and Criseyde* and *Troilus and Cressida*' and 'Lovers' Problems: *Troilus and Criseyde* and *Troilus and Cressida*', in Donaldson, *The Swan at the Well*, pp. 74–118.

139 Thompson, *Shakespeare's Chaucer*, p. 125.

140 See Gibbon's edition of *Romeo and Juliet*, p. 76.

141 For Chaucer's treatment of Criseyde in the context of her reputation, see Mieszkowski's fine study referred to above, n. 130, *passim*, and my *Geoffrey Chaucer: An Introduction to his Narrative Poetry* (Cambridge, 1986), chapter 6, pp. 65–97.

142 Chaucer makes this quite clear; see *Troilus and Criseyde*, IV. 202–5. There seems to me no doubt whatever that Shakespeare and most of his audience must have been aware of this irony, though many Shakespearian scholars and critics seem not to have noticed it. In view of this well-known background, it is rather comical to read: 'One character alone comes out of it without a scratch: Antenor'. See Rossiter, '*Troilus and Cressida*', in *Angel with Horns*, pp. 129–51, (p.151).

143 See Palmer's edition, pp. 38–9.

144 I would put it a little stronger than Palmer, who says, in a note to line 11: ' ... (despite the apparent mild irony of tone in parts of the Prologue), he meant the passage to sound heroic, according to the most obvious model' (The *Aeneid*).

145 No other Shakespearian tragic hero opens the play in this way.

146 Chaucer's Criseyde, too, sees through the go-between fairly quickly, and she has a long soliloquy in which she weighs the arguments for and against yielding (*Troilus and Criseyde*, II.687–812). On Shakespeare's characterization of Cressida see also R. A. Yoder, '"Sons and Daughters of the Game": an Essay on Shakespeare's *Troilus and Cressida*', *ShS*, 25 (1972), 11–25, and M. M. Burns, '*Troilus and Cressida*: The Worst of Both Worlds', *ShakS*, 13 (1980), 105–30.

147 See the interpretation of the scene in Palmer's edition, pp. 41–6; on the language of the debates, see Patricia Thompson, 'Rant and Cant in *Troilus and Cressida*', *Essays and Studies*, NS, 22 (1969), 33–56, and T. McAlindon, 'Language, Style, and Meaning in *Troilus and Cressida*', *PMLA*, 84 (1969), 29–43. Both critics take a more negative view of the Grecian rhetoric than I do.

148 See E. M. W. Tillyard's famous account, *The Elizabethan World Picture* (London, 1943; Harmondsworth, 1963), pp. 18–19 and 108–11. His own interpretation of the play is, however, very sensitive to its dramatic qualities: see above, n. 127.

149 On the Trojan debate, see Palmer's edition, pp. 46–9. On the general issues, see the valuable essay by W. M. T. Nowottny, 'Opinion and Value in *Troilus and Cressida*', *EC*, 5 (1954), 282–96. See also Muir's sensible summary in his edition, pp. 22–7.

150 See Muir's edition, pp. 31–2, for a brief assessment. See also Palmer's edition, pp. 49–53.

151 Chaucer's Pandarus is no less mocking on the morning after the lovers' first
    night together, though his prurient bawdiness is rather less unpleasant: see
    Troilus and Criseyde, III. 1555–82. The humorous complicity of his niece is very
    similar in both versions.

152 See *Troilus and Criseyde*, III. 1793–4:

> For, soth to seyne, he lost held every wyght,
> But if he were in Loves heigh servise, –

   We never see Shakespeare's Troilus in this elated mood, and his passion for
   Cressida is never presented as an instance of Love's glorious power.

153 See the comic eavesdropping scenes in *Much Ado About Nothing* and *Twelfth
    Night*. A rather more nasty example is the unmasking of Parolles in *All's Well
    That End's Well*.

154 Rossiter, too, mentions *Cosi fan tutte*, though in a slightly different context. See
    '*Troilus and Cressida*', p. 133.

155 The point is made by Palmer, p. 26, but I do not quite agree with his conclusion,
    'Cressida was bound to fall at once in the play'. Shakespeare could, of course,
    easily have thought of a less precipitous change of heart, even in a play.

156 See Bradbrook, 'What Shakespeare Did to Chaucer's *Troilus and Criseyde*', p.
    318, and Muir's edition, p. 33.

157 Muir's edition, p. 33. The scene and indeed the whole, unusually sympathetic
    presentation of Cressida made excellent sense in Howard Davies' wonderful
    production at Stratford in 1985. It was clear throughout the play that Cressida
    was the pitiful victim of male aggression and prejudice rather than a deceitful
    wanton. She gives in to Diomedes in desperation, after having almost been raped
    at her reception among the Greek generals. The production made clear that
    Cressida can be acted in a way very different from the usual cliché without the
    least violence to the text.

158 Chaucer gives Criseyde's letter in full (*Troilus and Criseyde*, v.1590–631) and
    makes very clear that it is 'no matter from the heart'. Troilus, however, is much
    slower to realize that 'al is lost that he hath ben aboute'. (v.1645).

159 See Palmer's edition, pp. 6 and 20–1, and Muir's edition, pp. 8–9. Taylor thinks
    that the present ending was cancelled when the play was adapted for perform-
    ance at the Globe: see his article referred to above, n. 133. On the mixture of
    genres see also the excellent article by R. A. Foakes, '*Troilus and Cressida*
    Reconsidered', *UTQ*, 32 (1963), 142–54, repr. in the Signet Classic edition of
    the play, ed. Daniel Seltzer (New York, 1963), pp. 265–81. It will have become
    clear that I am somewhat at variance with his conclusion: 'The play itself ...
    positively forbids a reading of the play as tragedy' (Signet edn, p. 266).

160 They seem to have made a genuine mistake, however, when they put *Cymbeline*
    among the tragedies, calling it 'The Tragedie of Cymbeline'. Again, the
    pseudo-historical subject matter might be an explanation. The happy ending,
    however, clearly relates the play to the romances.

   The most original treatment of traditional concepts and clichés in *Troilus and
   Cressida* has been further explored in a number of recent studies. See Jill L.
   Levenson, 'Shakespeare's *Troilus and Cressida* and the Monumental Tradition
   in Tapestries and Literature', *RenD*, NS, 7 (1976), 43–84; Douglas Cole, 'Myth
   and Anti-Myth: The Case of *Troilus and Cressida*', *SQ*, 31 (1980), 76–84; Juliet
   Dusinberre, '*Troilus and Cressida* and the Definition of Beauty', *ShS*, 36 (1983),
   85–95.

Select bibliography

Only books are listed. For articles, more specialized studies, and editions, the reader is referred to the notes.

REFERENCE BOOKS

Bullough, Geoffrey, ed. *Narrative and Dramatic Sources of Shakespeare.* 8 vols. London: Routledge & Kegan Paul, 1957-75
   (An indispensable collection of source material for all the plays, with very sensible introductions; there is no better anthology of texts Shakespeare knew well and made use of for the plots or the themes of his plays.)
Campbell, Oscar James and Quinn, Edward G., eds. *A Shakespeare Encyclopaedia.* London: Methuen, 1966; American edition under the title *The Reader's Encyclopedia of Shakespeare.* New York: Thomas Y. Crowell Company, 1966
   (A very full and reliable work of reference, written by many experts, with generous illustration and useful bibliographical references.)
Evans, Gareth Lloyd and Barbara. *Everyman's Companion to Shakespeare.* London: Dent, 1978
   (Less scholarly, but very informative on Shakespeare in his time, the plays in performance, with plot summaries and a list of *dramatis personae.*)
Halliday, F.E. *A Shakespeare Companion 1564–1964.* Harmondsworth: Penguin Books, 1964
   (A very helpful brief dictionary on various aspects of Shakespeare, his theatre, and his contemporaries.)
Muir, Kenneth and Schoenbaum, S., eds. *A New Companion to Shakespeare Studies.* Cambridge: Cambridge University Press, 1971
   (A useful collection of essays on some central aspects of Shakespeare's art and Shakespeare criticism.)
Schabert, Ina, ed. *Shakespeare-Handbuch. Die Zeit, der Mensch, das Werk, die Nachwelt.* Stuttgart: Alfred Kröner Verlag, 2nd edn 1978; 1st edn 1972
   (A most comprehensive work of reference on all aspects of Shakespeare's work and Shakespearian scholarship.)
Wells, Stanley, ed. *Shakespeare: Select Bibliographical Guides.* London: Oxford University Press, 1973
   (A valuable guide to scholarship on the plays up to 1973, with very useful bibliographies.)

Wells, Stanley, ed. *The Cambridge Companion to Shakespeare Studies*. Cambridge: Cambridge University Press, 1986
   (A collection of essays on the chief areas of Shakespeare criticism and reception.)

SOME GENERAL BOOKS ON TRAGEDY

Brereton, Geoffrey. *Principles of Tragedy. A Rational Examination of the Tragic Concept in Life and Literature*. London: Routledge & Kegan Paul, 1968
   (A survey of tragic theory and practice from Aristotle to Beckett.)
Heilman, Robert Bechtold. *Tragedy and Melodrama. Versions of Experience*. Seattle: University of Washington Press, 1968
   (A most stimulating discussion of the subject.)
Henn, T.R. *The Harvest of Tragedy*. London: Methuen, 1956
Kaufmann, Walter. *Tragedy and Philosophy*. New York: Doubleday & Co., 1968
   (Discusses ideas of the tragic in theory and practice from Plato to the modern drama.)
Krook, Dorothea. *Elements of Tragedy*. New Haven: Yale University Press, 1969
   (A stimulating discussion of individual examples, Shakespeare's *Antony and Cleopatra* among them.)
Leech, Clifford. *Tragedy*. The Critical Idiom, 1. London: Methuen, 1969
   (A good brief survey, with a bibliography.)
Mandel, Oscar. *A Definition of Tragedy*. New York: New York University Press, 1961
   (A useful systematic survey.)
Myers, Henry Alonzo. *Tragedy: A view of life*. Ithaca, N.Y.: Cornell University Press, 1956
   (A stimulating discussion of individual authors.)
Sewall, Richard B. *The Vision of Tragedy*. New Haven: Yale University Press, 1959
   (A particularly stimulating survey of great tragic writers.)
Steiner, George. *The Death of Tragedy*. London: Faber & Faber, 1961
   (A very influential book, but its main emphasis is philosophical and anthropological rather than literary.)

ELIZABETHAN AND JACOBEAN TRAGEDY

Baker, Howard. *Induction to Tragedy. A Study in a Development of Form in 'Gorbuduc', 'The Spanish Tragedy' and 'Titus Andronicus'*. Baton Rouge: Louisiana State University Press, 1939; 2nd edn 1965
   (Discusses the influence of Seneca and native traditions.)
Bradbrook, M. C. *Themes and Conventions of Elizabethan Tragedy*. Cambridge: Cambridge University Press, 1935
   (A seminal study of the major Elizabethan and Jacobean dramatists, often reprinted.)
Brodwin, Leonora Leet. *Elizabethan Love Tragedy 1587–1625*. New York: New York University Press, 1971; London: London University Press, 1972
   (A useful survey, though the classification is arguable.)

SELECT BIBLIOGRAPHY

Doran, Madeleine. *Endeavors of Art: A Study of Form in Elizabethan Drama.* Madison: University of Wisconsin Press, 1954
   (A most important and influential account of forms and conventions of English Renaissance drama.)

Farnham, Willard. *The Medieval Heritage of Elizabethan Tragedy.* Oxford: Basil Blackwell, 1936; several times reprinted
   (A very important study of medieval conventions.)

Felperin, Howard. *Shakespearean Representation. Mimesis and Modernity in Elizabethan Tragedy.* Princeton, N.J.: Princeton University Press, 1977

Herndl, George C. *The High Design. English Renaissance Tragedy and the Natural Law.* Lexington: University of Kentucky Press, 1970

Margeson, J. M. R. *The Origins of English Tragedy.* Oxford: Clarendon Press, 1967
   (A useful survey.)

Ornstein, Robert. *The Moral Vision of Jacobean Tragedy.* Madison: University of Wisconsin Press, 1960
   (A very original and stimulating study, more critical than historical.)

Spencer, Theodore. *Death and Elizabethan Tragedy. A Study of Convention and Opinion in the Elizabethan Drama.* Cambridge, Mass: Harvard University Press, 1936; 2nd edn New York, 1960
   (A stimulating study of the background of Elizabethan tragedy.)

Spivack, Bernard. *Shakespeare and the Allegory of Evil. The History of a Metaphor in Relation to his Major Villains.* New York: Columbia University Press, 1958
   (A very important and influential study of Iago's ancestry in the moralities and pre-Shakespearian drama.)

SHAKESPEARE'S TRAGEDIES

Battenhouse, Roy W. *Shakespearean Tragedy. Its Art and Its Christian Premises.* Bloomington: Indiana University Press, 1969
   (A very thorough though somewhat one-sided and dogmatic discussion of the tragedies.)

Bayley, John. *Shakespeare and Tragedy.* London: Routledge & Kegan Paul, 1981
   (A very original and suggestive reading of the tragedies.)

Bradley, A. C. *Shakespearean Tragedy. Lectures on 'Hamlet', 'Othello', 'King Lear', 'Macbeth'.* With a new introduction by J. R. Brown. London: Macmillan, 1985; 1st edn 1904
   (Still one of the most thoughtful and rewarding books on the major tragedies.)

Brooke, Nicholas. *Shakespeare's Early Tragedies.* London: Methuen, 1968
   (A very stimulating interpretation of the early tragedies, including *Hamlet.*)

Brower, Reuben A. *Hero and Saint. Shakespeare and the Graeco-Roman Heroic Tradition.* Oxford: Clarendon Press, 1971
   (A very good discussion of the classical background of Shakespearian tragedy.)

Campbell, Lily B. *Shakespeare's Tragic Heroes. Slaves of Passion.* Cambridge: Cambridge University Press, 1930
   (An influential study on some historical premises of the tragedies.)

Cantor, Paul A. *Shakespeare's Rome. Republic and Empire.* Ithaca: Cornell University Press, 1976
   (A thorough study of the political background of the Roman tragedies.)

263

Champion, Larry S. *Shakespeare's Tragic Perspective*. Athens, Georgia: University of Georgia Press, 1976
    (Useful on Shakespeare's 'tragic vision' and the way it is conveyed to the audience.)

Charney, Maurice. *Shakespeare's Roman Plays. The Function of Imagery in the Drama*. Cambridge, Mass.: Harvard University Press, 1961
    (Very good on the imagery in the Roman tragedies.)

Danson, Lawrence. *Tragic Alphabet. Shakespeare's Drama of Language*. New Haven: Yale University Press, 1974
    (Interesting discussion of the functions of language in the tragedies.)

Dickey, Franklin M. *Not Wisely But Too Well. Shakespeare's Love Tragedies*. San Marino: Huntington Library, 1957
    (Useful on Renaissance ideas on love, though perhaps a little too censorious.)

Evans, Bertrand. *Shakespeare's Tragic Practice*. Oxford: Clarendon Press, 1979
    (A discussion of 'discrepant awareness' in the tragedies.)

Foreman, Walter C., Jr. *The Music of the Close. The Final Scenes of Shakespeare's Tragedies*. Lexington: University of Kentucky Press, 1978
    (A thoughtful interpretation of the final scenes of the tragedies.)

Frye, Northrop. *Fools of Time. Studies in Shakespearean Tragedy*. The Alexander Lectures. Toronto: Toronto University Press, 1967
    (A very stimulating discussion of some general issues, especially archetypal elements.)

Harbage, Alfred, ed. *Shakespeare: The Tragedies. A Collection of Critical Essays*. Twentieth Century Views. Englewood Cliffs, N.J.: Prentice Hall, 1964
    (A very useful collection of critical essays on the tragedies.)

Holloway, John. *The Story of the Night. Studies in Shakespeare's Major Tragedies*. London: Routledge & Kegan Paul, 1961
    (Stimulating observations on the tragedies and our experience in reading them.)

Honigmann, E. A. J. *Shakespeare: Seven Tragedies. The dramatist's manipulation of response*. London: Macmillan, 1976
    (A particularly useful investigation in some dramatic techniques and the manipulation of sympathy.)

Knight, G. Wilson. *The Wheel of Fire. Interpretations of Shakespearian Tragedy with Three New Essays*. London: Methuen, 4th edn 1949; 1st edn Oxford University Press, 1930
    (A very influential study of the tragedies, with particular emphasis on images and themes.)

Knight, G. Wilson. *The Imperial Theme. Further Interpretations of Shakespeare's Tragedies including the Roman Plays*. London: Methuen, 3rd edn 1951; 1st edn Oxford University Press, 1931

Lawlor, John. *The Tragic Sense in Shakespeare*. London: Chatto & Windus, 1960
    (Stimulating discussion of some central issues.)

Leech, Clifford, ed. *Shakespeare: The Tragedies. A Collection of Critical Essays*. Chicago: University of Chicago Press, 1965
    (A very useful anthology of criticism from Dryden to N. Brooke, with an informative introduction.)

MacCallum, M. W. *Shakespeare's Roman Plays and Their Background*. Reissued

with a new foreword by T. J. B. Spencer. London: Macmillan, 1967; 1st edn 1910
  (Still very useful on many of the basic issues.)
McElroy, Bernard. *Shakespeare's Mature Tragedies*. Princeton, N.J.: Princeton University Press, 1973
  (A discussion of the world of the major tragedies, with particular emphasis on the tragic heroes.)
Marsh, Derick R. C. *Passion Lends Them Power. A study of Shakespeare's love tragedies*. Manchester: Manchester University Press, 1976
  (A very perceptive study of the love tragedies, including the romances.)
Miola, Robert S. *Shakespeare's Rome*. Cambridge: Cambridge University Press, 1983
  (A perceptive re-examination of Shakespeare's changing vision of Rome and some of his sources for the Roman plays.)
Morris, Ivor. *Shakespeare's God. The Role of Religion in the Tragedies*. London: George Allen & Unwin, 1972
  (A very thorough if a little one-sided examination of the subject.)
Muir, Kenneth. *Shakespeare's Tragic Sequence*. London: Hutchinson University Library, 1972
  (A very sensible and balanced survey.)
Nevo, Ruth. *Tragic Form in Shakespeare*. Princeton, N.J.: Princeton University Press, 1972
  (A very original interpretation of the tragedies, concentrating on their 'spatial' effect and our experience in seeing them.)
Proser, Matthew N. *The Heroic Image in Five Shakespearean Tragedies*. Princeton, N.J.: Princeton University Press, 1965
  (An interesting study of the discrepancy between the hero's self-conception and his full humanity as displayed in action.)
Ribner, Irving. *Patterns in Shakespearian Tragedy*. London: Methuen, 1960
  A stimulating discussion of some central issues, perhaps a little too affirmative.)
Rosen, William. *Shakespeare and the Craft of Tragedy*. Cambridge, Mass.: Harvard University Press, 1960
  (An interesting discussion of dramatic techniques, characterization, and audience response.)
Schanzer, Ernest. *The Problem Plays of Shakespeare. A Study of 'Julius Caesar', 'Measure for Measure', 'Antony and Cleopatra'*. London: Routledge & Kegan Paul, 1963
  (A very stimulating and sensitive study of the two tragedies as 'problem plays'.)
Siegel, Paul N. *Shakespearean Tragedy and the Elizabethan Compromise. A Marxist Study*. New York: University Press of America, 2nd edn 1983; 1st edn 1957
  (A very useful study of Shakespearian tragedy in its social, political and philosophical context.)
Simmons, J. L. *Shakespeare's Pagan World. The Roman Tragedies*. Hassocks, Sussex: Harvester Press, 1974
  (A study of Shakespeare's Rome and the implications of its paganism.)
Snyder, Susan. *The Comic Matrix of Shakespeare's Tragedies. 'Romeo and Juliet',*

'Hamlet', 'Othello', and 'King Lear'. Princeton, N.J.: Princeton University Press, 1979
 (A very original and perceptive study of the comic elements in the tragedies.)
Stirling, Brents. *Unity in Shakespearian Tragedy. The Interplay of Theme and Character*. New York: Columbia University Press, 1956
 (Mainly on the chief characters in the tragedies.)
Whitaker, Virgil K. *The Mirror up to Nature. The Technique of Shakespeare's Tragedies*. San Marino: Huntington Library, 1965
 (Good on Shakespeare and the drama of his time; Elizabethan views on tragedy.)
Wilson, Harold S. *On the Design of Shakespearian Tragedy*. Toronto: Toronto University Press, 1957
 (A rather too schematic classification of the tragedies, according to thesis, antithesis and synthesis.)

SOME IMPORTANT GENERAL STUDIES ON SHAKESPEARE

Clemen, Wolfgang. *Shakespeare's Dramatic Art. Collected Essays*. London: Methuen, 1972
 (A collection of very perceptive essays, some of them previously published, on various aspects of Shakespeare's art.)
Clemen, Wolfgang. *The Development of Shakespeare's Imagery*. London: Methuen, 2nd edn 1977; 1st edn 1951
 (A seminal study of Shakespeare's imagery and its dramatic functions.)
Goldman, Michael. *Shakespeare and the Energies of Drama*. Princeton, N.J.: Princeton University Press, 1972
 (A very stimulating study of the theatrical qualities of Shakespearian drama.)
Granville-Barker, Harley. *Prefaces to Shakespeare*. 2 vols. London: Batsford, 1958
 (Granville-Barker's influential prefaces, most of them first published in 1930, provide very sensitive and helpful interpretations from the theatre-goer's and the producer's point of view.)
Jones, Emrys. *Scenic Form in Shakespeare*. Oxford: Clarendon Press, 1971
 (A particularly interesting and useful study of structure in Shakespearian drama.)
Knights, L. C. *Some Shakespearean Themes*. London: Chatto & Windus, 1959; published together with *An Approach to 'Hamlet'*, as a Peregrine Book, Harmondsworth: Penguin Books, 1966
 (A series of particularly stimulating essays on several plays.)
Mahood, M. M. *Shakespeare's Wordplay*. London: Methuen, 1957
 (A valuable study of Shakespeare's verbal artifice and some implications.)
Nuttall, A. D. *A New Mimesis: Shakespeare and the Representation of Reality*. London: Methuen, 1983
 (A very original and stimulating study of 'realism' in Shakespearian drama.)
Rabkin, Norman. *Shakespeare and the Common Understanding*. New York: Free Press, 1967
 (A provocative and sensitive study on some fundamental issues of Shakespearian criticism; good discussions of particular plays.)

Righter, Anne. *Shakespeare and the Idea of the Play*. London: Chatto & Windus, 1962
    (A very original study of ideas of play and theatre in Shakespeare's drama.)

Rossiter, A. P. *Angel with Horns and other Shakespeare Lectures*, ed. Graham Storey. London: Longmans, 1961
    (A collection of very perceptive and stimulating lectures on a number of plays and themes.)

Styan, J. L. *Shakespeare's Stagecraft*. Cambridge: Cambridge University Press, 1967
    (A good discussion of dramaturgical and staging problems.)

Traversi, Derek A. *An Approach to Shakespeare*. 2 vols. New York: Doubleday & Co, 3rd edn 1969; 1st edn 1938
    (A close reading of all the plays, concentrating on language, imagery and themes.)

Weimann, Robert. *Shakespeare and the Popular Tradition in the Theater: Studies in the Social Dimension of Dramatic Form and Function*, ed. Robert Schwartz. Baltimore: Johns Hopkins Press, 1978
    (A revised translation of Weimann's very influential study of Shakespeare's vital connection with the popular theatre; first published in 1967.)

Index

Adams, M. S., 242
Adamson, J., 243
Aeschylus, *Oresteia*, 32
Alexander, P., 255
Alvis, J., 250
Anschütz, H., 244
Arden of Feversham, 121, 248
Aristotle, 7, 127
Armin, R., 87, 245

Baker, H., 236, 237
Barroll, J., 250
Barton, A., 239, 240
Barton, J., 241
Battenhouse, R. W., 238
Bayley, J., 235, 244, 246, 247
Beeching, H. C., 249
de Belleforest, F., *Histoires Tragiques*, 31, 241
Belsey, C., 240
Bizley, W. H., 256
Black, J., 244
Boccaccio, G.,
   De Casibus Virorum Illustrium, 3
   Decameron, 20, 57
   Il Filostrato, 221
Boethius, *Consolatio Philosophiae*, 2, 3
Boitani, P., 251
Bond, E., *Lear*, 5
Bonjour, A., 251
Booth, S., 244, 246
Bowers, F. T., 239
Bradbrook, M. C., 204, 236, 238, 245, 256, 257, 258, 260
Bradbury, M., 237
Bradley, A. C., 8, 9, 19, 38, 66, 73, 78,

93, 102, 103, 108, 111, 113–14,
118, 127, 129, 130, 154, 156–7,
169, 173, 175, 199, 201, 235, 239,
243, 244, 245–6, 247, 248, 249,
252, 253, 254, 255
Braunmuller, A. R., 237
Brecht, B., *Coriolan*, 256
Brill, L. W., 258
Brockbank, P., 254, 255
Brodwin, L. L., 236, 237, 242, 243, 252
Brook, P., 11
Brooke, A., *Romeus and Juliet*, 20–2, 25, 237, 238
Brooke, N., 103, 236, 237, 238, 245, 246, 255
Brooks, H., 238
Brower, R. A., 242, 243, 252, 253, 254, 255
Brown, J. R., 238, 249, 252, 255, 256
Browning, I. R., 255
Brucher, R. T., 237
Bullough, G., 158, 162, 164, 167, 169,
170, 181, 183, 184, 198, 236, 237,
238, 239, 240, 242, 244, 245, 247,
250, 252, 253, 254, 255, 256, 257,
258
Bulman, J. C., Jr, 256
Burns, M. M., 259
Butler, F., 256

Campbell, L. B., 235
Cantor, P. A., 250
Chapman, G., 254
   Bussy D'Ambois, 191, 255
Charney, M., 250, 251, 254, 255, 256